NIGHTMARE ALLEY

NIGHTMARE ALLEY

FILM NOIR AND THE AMERICAN DREAM

MARK OSTEEN

The Johns Hopkins University Press
Baltimore

© 2013 The Johns Hopkins University Press
All rights reserved. Published 2013
Printed in the United States of America on acid-free paper
9 8 7 6 5 4 3 2 1

The Johns Hopkins University Press
2715 North Charles Street
Baltimore, Maryland 21218-4363
www.press.jhu.edu

Library of Congress Cataloging-in-Publication Data
Osteen, Mark.
  Nightmare alley : film noir and the American dream / Mark Osteen.
     p. cm.
  Includes bibliographical references and index.
  ISBN 978-1-4214-0780-7 (hdbk. : alk. paper) — ISBN 978-1-4214-0832-3
(electronic) — ISBN 1-4214-0780-9 (hdbk. : alk. paper) —
ISBN 1-4214-0832-5 (electronic)
  1. Film noir—United States—History and criticism.   2. Motion
pictures—Social aspects—United States—History—20th
century.   3. American Dream in art.   4. National characteristics,
American, in motion pictures.   I. Title.
  PN1995.9.F54O88   2013
  791.43'6556—dc23   2012017652

A catalog record for this book is available from the British Library.

*Special discounts are available for bulk purchases of this book. For
more information, please contact Special Sales at 410-516-6936 or
specialsales@press.jhu.edu.*

The Johns Hopkins University Press uses environmentally friendly
book materials, including recycled text paper that is composed of at least
30 percent post-consumer waste, whenever possible.

CONTENTS

List of Illustrations   *vii*
Acknowledgments   *ix*

Introduction: Film Noir and the American Dream   1

1 "Someone Else's Nightmare": Exploring Noir Dreamscapes   19

2 Missing Persons: Self-Erasure and Reinvention   46

3 Vet Noir: Masculinity, Memory, and Trauma   77

4 Framed: Forging Noir Identities   106

5 Noir's Cars: Automobility and Amoral Space   132

6 Nocturnes in Black and Blue: Memory, Morality, and Jazz Melody   154

7 Femmes Vital: Film Noir and Women's Work   185

8 Left-Handed Endeavor: Crime, Capitalism, and the Hollywood Left   220

Conclusion: American Nightmares   249

Notes   *263*
Filmography   *293*
Works Cited   *297*
Index   *311*

ILLUSTRATIONS

The geek is a main attraction in *Nightmare Alley*'s carnival   7

The dream sequence in *Spellbound* features an array of
disembodied eyes   41

Ole Anderson (Burt Lancaster) and Kitty Collins (Ava Gardner) in
The Killers   52

Jane Greer as femme fatale Kathie Moffat in *Out of the Past*   57

In *Dark Passage* Vincent Parry (Humphrey Bogart) connects
with Irene Jansen (Lauren Bacall)   68

John Muller (Paul Henreid) prepares to cut his own face in *Hollow
Triumph*   72

Floyd Bowers (Steve Brodie) and Montgomery (Robert Ryan) in
Crossfire   85

In *Act of Violence* Frank Enley (Van Heflin) confesses to his wife,
Edith (Janet Leigh)   102

Detective McPherson (Dana Andrews) dreams of the eponymous
Laura (Gene Tierney)   111

Hardy Cathcart (Clifton Webb) tries to control his wife, Mari
(Cathy Downs), in *The Dark Corner*   114

Professor Wanley (Edward G. Robinson) is entranced by a portrait in
The Woman in the Window   117

In *They Live by Night*, Bowie (Farley Granger) and Keechie
(Cathy O'Donnell) fall in love   138

Bart (John Dall) and Annie (Peggy Cummins) at their convertible
in *Gun Crazy*   141

Emmett Myers (William Talman) abducts Bowen (Frank Lovejoy)
and Collins (Edmond O'Brien) in *The Hitch-Hiker*   146

Opening "The Great Whatsit" in *Kiss Me Deadly*   152

Lily (Ida Lupino) improvises with Pete (Cornel Wilde) in *Road House*   183

Rita Hayworth as Gilda ironically urges us to put the blame on Mame   196

Marie Allen (Eleanor Parker) is *Caged*   209

Dr. Quinada (James Mason) is dwarfed by Smith Ohlrig (Robert Ryan)
in *Caught*   213

The heist gang plans a "left-handed endeavor" in *The Asphalt Jungle*   242

In *The Prowler* Webb Garwood (Van Heflin) wants what he sees in
the Gilvray house   257

ACKNOWLEDGMENTS

This project has been long in the making, and many people have contributed to its completion. To thank everyone would require far too much space, but I would like to acknowledge and express my gratitude for the help of several people in particular.

I'm grateful to Professors Julie Grossman and Paul Saint-Amour for their support. My colleagues in the English Department at Loyola University Maryland have furnished a lively intellectual community where I could test the ideas found herein. I'm particularly grateful to my colleague Paul Lukacs for suggesting the Franklin and Emerson connections. My department's support also included encouraging me to teach courses in which my embryonic notions could grow; the students in those courses helped me develop those notions. To them I offer my hearty thanks.

Barbara Hall and the staff at the Special Collections Department of the Margaret Herrick Library deserve a special note of gratitude. The resources and staff at that institution—which for film scholars comes pretty close to heaven on earth—have deepened and enriched this project immeasurably.

I'm grateful to the anonymous reader for the Johns Hopkins University Press for perusing the manuscript so promptly and thoroughly; such alacrity is both laudable and rare.

As always, my greatest debt is to my wife, Leslie Gilden, for providing a patient ear as I rattled on about sometimes obscure films, for providing a second set of eyes as we viewed the movies together, and for voicing challenges that helped me to refine my ideas in our many and various discussions of these films.

An earlier version of chapter 4 was published in the *Journal of Film and Video;* an earlier version of chapter 5 was published in the *Journal of Popular Film and Television.*

All illustrations, except those in chapter 5, were purchased from the Kobal Collection. The rest come from Jerry Ohlinger's Movie Material Store. I thank these vendors for their assistance.

NIGHTMARE ALLEY

Introduction
Film Noir and the American Dream

"Is a guy born that way?"

Stan Carlisle (Tyrone Power), the protagonist of Edmund Goulding's *Nightmare Alley,* asks this question about the geek, an abject figure on the lowest rung of the carnival hierarchy, whose chief task is to bite off the heads of chickens. One of the darkest films in the noir canon, *Nightmare Alley* traces Carlisle's rise from carny assistant to slick mentalist performing in chic hotels, followed by a fall into destitution, which ends as Stan, now a groveling alcoholic, is hired as a carnival geek. The answer to his question is ambiguous: Stan's cynicism, arrogance, and greed motivate the bad choices he makes, as does his relationship with the scheming psychologist Lilith Ritter. Yet the film's circular structure and motif of tarot cards imply that Stan was indeed "born that way"—that he always has been a geek.

Carlisle's quest for fame is a quintessentially American tale that depicts the pursuit of happiness through individual striving, but it is an anti–Horatio Alger fable of the perils of ambition, a warning that transforming the self may also empty it of meaning. More broadly, the geek figure offers an opportunity to assess critically the American ideals of self-creation, individualism, free choice, and upward mobility. Though the geek's pursuit of happiness is drastically attenuated—he will do anything for a drink—it nonetheless resembles those of many film noir protagonists, obsessed with a desirable goal or object—a falcon sculpture, a seductive woman, a big score—or fleeing, like Stan, from a traumatic event. Indeed, Stan Carlisle's life evokes questions that have troubled Americans since before the nation even existed: what is the relation between personal history and present character? Is it possible to escape from one's past? Is identity inborn or a set of masks or performances? *Nightmare Alley* provides one answer to the question that lies at the heart of this book: what does film noir tell us about the American Dream?

In his study of that overused but little-understood phrase, Jim Cullen lists four dreams: those of upward mobility, equality, home ownership, and the West as a symbol of undying hope, best epitomized by Hollywood (8–9). I would add to his tally the ideals of free enterprise and personal liberty. Beneath each of these values lies an enduring faith in what the Declaration of Independence calls "the pursuit of happiness," a phrase that, Cullen proposes, "defines the American Dream, treating happiness as a concrete and realizable objective" (38). Underpinning even that goal is the ideology of individualism—the belief that personal effort enables one to determine one's own destiny and character; throw off the fetters of history; overcome class, gender, and racial barriers; and gain wealth and prestige. The crime films made in Hollywood between 1944 and 1959 challenge these beliefs by portraying characters whose defeat or death seems fated; by dramatizing the obstacles to class mobility and racial or gender equality; by asking whether anyone—whether detective, war veteran, or homeless woman—can truly reinvent him- or herself; by questioning whether new consumer products and technologies such as fast cars really liberate us; and by raising a skeptical eyebrow at the midcentury faith in psychoanalysis and the therapeutic ethos that supports it.

Stan Carlisle's question has been answered in two conflicting ways throughout American cultural history. One answer, perhaps best represented by Benjamin Franklin's *Autobiography*, portrays identity as an endless process of entrepreneurial invention. Thus young Ben leaves his childhood home in Boston to make his way to Philadelphia where, in part 2, he deliberately sculpts a new self through the sedulous application of reason and industry (see 79–86). For the rest of his life he constantly remakes himself: first a printer and publisher, he becomes at different periods a musician, an inventor, a scientist, an ambassador, a military leader, and a legislator. Franklin also inserts into his life story a letter from a friend, Benjamin Vaughan, who writes that Franklin proves "how little necessary all origin is to happiness, virtue, or greatness" (72). In this archetypal American success story, one's past is irrelevant to one's present and future: an American can be anything he or she wishes, so long as he or she maintains resilience and curiosity. Franklin's story is the Protestant conversion narrative—a narrative of being born again—shorn of supernatural trappings. Whatever a Franklinesque American becomes, he or she is never merely "born that way."

Set against this model of infinite reinvention is the philosophy presented by Ralph Waldo Emerson in his influential essay "Self-Reliance." For Emerson, a person cannot reinvent him- or herself; instead, one must discover and refine his or her true nature by looking within. Emerson holds that "a man should learn to detect and watch that gleam of light which flashes across his mind from within, more than the lustre of the firmament of bards and sages" (29). The self must be free of fetters—on this Franklin and Emerson agree—but unlike Franklin, Emerson argues that "no man can violate his nature" (35). Self-reliance thus presumes the existence of an authentic self to be relied upon. That "aboriginal Self" cannot be escaped, for it underlies "every former state of life and circumstances, as it does underlie my present" (38, 41). Nor does mobility make a difference. Emerson writes, "I pack my trunk, . . . embark on the sea, and at last wake up in Naples, and there beside me is the stern fact, the sad self, unrelenting, identical, that I fled from" (48). The precept that no one escapes his or her nature is indeed the lesson of the "missing person" noirs I discuss in chapter 2.

But self-reliance requires an aversion to conformity; it is individualist through and through. Despite their differences, then, and putting aside the nuances overlooked in this admittedly simplified distillation of the two figures' philosophies, it is clear that the Franklinesque and Emersonian models of identity share a foundational belief in individual choice. And this *agency,* according to Cullen, is the "bedrock premise" that "lies at the very core of the American Dream" (10). Without self-determination there can be no dream. But this premise also creates a problem: how to create a cohesive community composed of self-interested individuals. Cullen finds in the Puritans a balance between individualism and community that "straddles . . . the tension between one and many" (32); this is a balance that few noir protagonists achieve. Instead, in pursuing happiness they find themselves alienated, cast out, defeated; worse, their end seems fated, as if they have played only a minor role in engineering their own lives. As Ken Hillis comments, noir protagonists come to recognize "the difficulty—if not impossibility—of achieving modernity's implicitly cosmopolitan promise that an individual, by dint of hard work, education, and reason, can develop a politically robust subjectivity" (4). To put it another way, film noir often paints the pursuit of happiness as a chimera and shows self-creation constrained by forces beyond individuals' control. If, as John Orr proposes, the noir protagonist initially believes that "America is the dreamland of opportunity, where all possibilities can be considered," his or her story ends with an awakening into a chastening reality (160). The obstacles aren't merely character flaws; they are features of society. Thus, as Hillis notes, when noir protagonists do reach the top, they discover that life there is "as rotten as it is at the bottom" (7). In short, social mobility is seldom possible in noir and irrelevant when it does occur. Considering these patterns,

John Belton suggests that noir registers a "postwar crisis of national identity" related to the "dissolution of the myth of Jeffersonian democracy" (qtd. in Chopra-Gant 152). Noir, that is, posits an inversion of equality whereby almost everyone is equally trapped. Made during a period marked by social and political upheaval, films noir test and critique both the principles of the American Dream—individualism and self-determination, liberty, equality, upward mobility, capitalist enterprise—and their practice.

Made for It

Among the many forces that converged to create the phenomenon we call noir (I outline others below) were 1930s gangster films. Movies such as *Little Caesar, The Public Enemy,* and *Scarface* are fables of American entrepreneurship camouflaged as exposés or action thrillers. As Jack Shadoian notes, the 1930s gangster is "a paradigm of the American dream": an immigrant who, by ruthless force of will and relentless energy, rises to the top of his "industry" but is eventually punished for the very qualities that have fueled his elevation (3). Shadoian astutely observes that gangster films expose a fundamental contradiction in the American psyche: "It's fine to get ahead, but it's wrong to get ahead. It's good to be an individual, but then you're set apart from others." Such films, he continues, are often "disguised parables of social mobility as a punishable deviation from one's assigned place" (6). In them the Franklinesque and the Emersonian visions of identity collide head-on.

Shadoian's summary of this conflict also fits a substantial segment of noir, but the postwar milieu alters the prewar archetypes. World War II fed anxieties about identity: whether spent fighting or at home, the war years sliced a gap in citizens' lives, and the question of authenticity became, in the postwar years, a dominant American concern. Should we forget and discard the values and personae that bind us to our former selves and start over? Or is such forgetting impossible and, when attempted, merely invites the return of the repressed? And is our country the same? Faced with such troubling questions, many citizens yearned, as Jackson Lears writes, for "a solid sense of truth beneath a tissue of misleading appearances" (*Fables* 346). The issue of authenticity dwells at the center of many films noir—especially those, as I show in chapter 4, that explicitly concern forgery and portraiture—and manifests itself in noir's notoriously frequent doppelgängers, double-crosses, and duplicitous dames. Adding to this crisis of identity was what Lears describes as the "heightened expectations of authenticity" that characterize modernity: the "conviction that everyone would experience 'something thrilling and vivid' in the normal course of events, that a failure to do so meant that one had not 'really lived'" (356). This quest for authenticity as an essential component of the pursuit of happiness propels noir figures as diverse as former detective Jeff Markham in *Out of the Past,* bored bachelor Harry Quincy in *The Strange Affair of Uncle Harry,* and *Gun Crazy*'s sociopath Annie Laurie Starr.

Such pursuits were, in the postwar period, increasingly linked to the material aspects of the American Dream—wealth and prosperity. As Lary May argues, the war reoriented "democratic dreams and values from the public to the private realm of consumption" (157). A character in Don DeLillo's first novel, *Americana,* puts it pithily: "to consume in America is not to buy; it is to dream" (270). What Lears calls "packaged intensity" (*Fables* 357) was increasingly available in the form of consumer goods (whether they were cars, appliances, or sessions with psychiatrists), which advertisers promoted as emblems of upward mobility, freedom of choice, and individual distinction. Religion or pseudoreligion contributed to this "therapeutic ethos," as consumer items and psychoanalytic therapy were understood as comparable modes of self-improvement (Lears, "Salvation" 11). The creation of a new self became, as Mary McAleer Balkun remarks, equivalent to "the creation of an object" (12).

The identification with consumer goods and the chance to remake identity into "a shiny commodity without a past" (Hillis 9) actuates numerous noir protagonists. Thus, for example, Maud Eames's finishing school in *Caught* transmutes her into a marriageable property; *Kiss Me Deadly*'s Mike Hammer sculpts a hardened, cool persona by way of sports car, answering machine, and disposable women; *Body and Soul*'s boxer Charlie Davis is reduced to a "money machine" for promoter Roberts. At the same time, however, certain consumer products were associated with an idealized past, particularly with the faded folk communities memorialized in products such as Quaker Oats and Uncle Ben's rice. These advertisements' rhetorical strategies "dissolved the tension between past and present in the soothing syrup of pseudotraditionalism" (Lears, *Fables* 383). Paradoxically, these commodities were marketed as symbols of a realm outside of commodities. As such, they cemented a fraudulent sense of "continuous, coherent group identity" (384).

But the result was often the opposite. Fredric Jameson has analyzed a condition he calls "seriality": a sense that "the uniqueness of my own experience is undermined by a secret statistical quality. Somehow I feel I am no longer central, that I am merely doing just what everybody else is doing." Yet *"everybody else* feels exactly the same way" (76; emphasis in original). Hence, while the burgeoning consumer economy offered fungible goods as the means to happiness, it also induced further fragmentation, because those satisfactions remained private and required constant renewal. Noir diagnoses this fragmentation, demonstrating the fraudulence and ineffectuality of the therapeutic ethos as a remedy for anxiety and alienation. The pursuit of wealth, like the pursuit of mental health, is portrayed as a means of exploiting the disenfranchised or dissatisfied, of gulling the naive or impulsive with fantasies of achievement or perfection. The therapeutic ethos, as it links psychiatry to consumerism, ties both practices to American ideals of self-reinvention, class mobility, free enterprise, and the pursuit of happiness. These beliefs and associations are all displayed in *Nightmare Alley,* where Carlisle's enactment of the dream of upward mobility fuses what Cullen calls "earthly goals and heavenly means" (97).

Though Stan admits to the carnival's owner that he is fascinated by the geek ("you're not the only one," the owner replies; "why do you think we've got him in the show?"), he doesn't understand how anyone can "get so low."[1] Yet he loves the carnival life—the sense that carnies are "in the know" and audiences are "on the outside looking in." "I was made for it," he crows to Zeena (Joan Blondell), the star of a mind-reading act. The carnival worker indeed exemplifies the mobile self: one day freakish or superhuman—geek, strong man, or "electric girl" (the role played by Molly [Coleen Gray], Stan's soon-to-be lover)—the next day, or the next hour, a fire-eater, mentalist, or retail clerk. Never part of the masses, the carny exploits them, gives them what they want, then moves on to the next town. Yet, as Tony Williams points out, many carnies are "one step away" from "poverty and destitution" ("Naturalist" 133). In other words, these traveling entertainers are always, in some sense, geeks. And so, *Nightmare Alley* implies, are their audiences, hungry for the shows' packaged intensity to light a spark in their drab lives. Simultaneously titillated, disdainful, awestruck, and credulous, the crowds see in the carnies what they both wish and fear to be. Thus, as Zeena performs—answering questions written on cards that she never reads—the camera sits amid the crowd, shooting upward at her and Stan, who seem larger than life. But when we go backstage, we learn that Zeena's telepathy is a trick: the cards are given to her husband, Pete (Ian Keith), who sits below the stage and feeds her their contents as she gazes into her crystal ball.

If Stan feels contempt for his audiences, Zeena resembles them: she, too, believes in cards—tarot cards. She and Stan scheme to dump Pete and start a romance and a new act using a code system (a set of verbal clues to the contents of

The geek is a main attraction in *Nightmare Alley*'s carnival. *Kobal Collection / Art Resource, NY.*

the cards), but when the tarot predicts failure (the death card is found face down on the floor), Zeena backs out: "I can't go against the cards." Stan scoffs at her belief in "boob-catchers," but he is not immune from the allure of the inexplicable. That night Pete, now a beaten alcoholic, nostalgically recalls when he was "big-time," launches into his old act, and gives a "psychic" reading of Stan's early life. "I see . . . a boy running barefoot through the hills. . . . A dog is with him." "Yes," Stan responds. "His name was Gyp." Pete breaks the spell: "stock reading. . . . Every boy has a dog!" The shadowy mise-en-scène encourages us to recognize the fine lines between mind reader and geek, duper and duped. Stan, who had earlier bought a bottle of moonshine, takes pity on the old trouper and gives it to him. But when Pete is found dead the next morning, having drunk a bottle of wood alcohol that Zeena uses in her act, Stan blames himself for giving Pete the wrong bottle, and this (possibly unconsciously deliberate) mistake, along with the geek's howls, haunts him for the rest of the film.

Pete's death opens the door for Stan to become Zeena's assistant, but his big break comes when a sheriff tries to close down the carnival. Exuding a sincerity spiced with folksy references to his "Scotch blood" and blending biblical quotations and platitudes (many taken directly from William Lindsay Gresham's searing source novel: 596–99), Stan senses that the sheriff feels unappreciated and exploits his religious beliefs to save the show.[2] In the novel Zeena remarks, "Not much different, being a fortuneteller and a preacher"—or an alcoholic: later in the novel, Stan exults, "They drink promises. They drink hope. And I've got it to hand them" (556, 599). In the film Stan recalls learning to fake religiosity in reform school.[3] He seems to have no religious feeling himself. But he wishes he *could* believe in something to help him conquer the feelings of meaninglessness and helplessness that trouble him—the recognition that humans merely stumble "down a dark alley toward their deaths" (579)—and that motivate the recurring dream of enclosure alluded to in the title (587).

In both versions Stan's success prompts him to leave the carnival and, with Molly, begin a new, classier act as The Great Stanton, a nightclub "mentalist." At one show a woman sends him a card asking if her mother will recover; Stan discerns that her mother is actually dead, then exchanges gazes with the woman— Lilith Ritter (Helen Walker)—to acknowledge their kinship. And indeed, Lilith, a "consulting psychologist," performs a function similar to Stan's, delving into her patients' darkest fears, doling out reassurance or advice, but most of all making them feel important. In their early scenes together Stan and Lilith are presented as two of a kind, placed at the same level of the frame in matched singles or two-shots. The power differential begins to change, however, after a visit from Zeena brings back Stan's memories of Pete's death; tortured by guilt and haunted by the geek's howls, he goes to Lilith for advice. In earlier scenes Lilith had worn masculine suits and hats, a composite figure combining the parents Stan lost.[4] In this scene, however, she wears her hair down, dons a flowing robe, and, like a forgiving mother, reassures Stan of his normality by telling him he is "selfish and ruthless when you want something; generous and kind when you've got it," just like everyone else (Williams, "Naturalist" 135–36). He feels guilty, she says, only because he profited from Pete's death. Because of her advice, Stan pledges to proceed into the "spook racket," holding séances in which bereaved survivors contact their deceased loved ones. This is his ticket to the big time: "I was made for it," he declares.

Through Lilith and a wealthy client, Mrs. Peabody, Stan meets Ezra Grindle, a rich industrialist who carries a burden of regret over the death of Dorrie, a girl he loved and lost. Lilith and Stan engineer a swindle whereby Stan will receive $150,000 to "recall" Dorrie and permit Grindle to speak to her again. To do so, however, Stan must persuade the reluctant Molly to perform as the dead girl.[5] Although Stan exhorts her to help him save Grindle's soul, Molly demurs: mentalist acts are one thing, but this is "goin' against God." They might be struck dead for blasphemy! Stan assures her that his séances are "just another angle of show business." When Molly threatens to walk out, he resorts to his final ploy: phony sincerity. Admitting that he's a hustler but professing undying love for her, he persuades her to play Dorrie, complete with turn-of-the-century garb and parasol, in a scene staged for Grindle. (Goulding and his director of photography, Lee Garmes, employ deep focus and fog to make the bower resemble a late nineteenth-century postcard.) But the trick fails when Molly, moved by Grindle's pleas, breaks the illusion: "I can't, not even for you!" she cries, then flees (in the novel Grindle tries to grope Molly). Exposed as a "dirty sacrilegious thief," Stan—or at least his plan—is ruined.

No matter: he already has the 150 grand, which he retrieves from Lilith, who has been holding it for him. But Lilith turns out to be a bigger con artist than he, having replaced the roll of high denominations with one-dollar bills. When Stan tries to get the money back, she retreats into her psychologist persona and insists that he suffers from delusions. "You must regard it all as a nightmare," she informs him. Having learned from her research that Pete's death was "self-administered," she coldly tells Stan that his guilt is merely a "homicidal hallucination" and that he has made a "strange transference" to her. Just in case he doesn't get the picture, she also reminds him that she has recorded his sessions and can, if necessary, implicate him in fraud. Confused and desperate, Stan sends Molly away: along with his money he has lost the only person who loves him; perhaps worse, he has lost the swagger that enabled his success.

His fall is as precipitous as his rise: he begins drinking heavily, moving from one seedy, dark hotel room to another, hearing the geek's howls wherever he goes.[6] Before long he has become a hobo giving stock readings to other derelicts in exchange for a slug of cheap liquor. Echoing Pete's earlier words, he scoffs at his credulous listeners: "Every boy has a beautiful old, gray-haired mother. Everybody except maybe me." At last he seeks work as a carnival palm reader but is told that they don't hire boozers. On second thought, there may be a job for him—a temporary one, just until they can get "a real geek." Stan accepts the gig: "Mister, I was made for it." This is where the novel ends, but the film adds a semiredemptive epilogue (probably the work of producer Darryl F. Zanuck) in which Stan—shot amid deep shadows on the barred carnival set—goes berserk, then rushes into the arms of Molly, who happens to work in the same carnival. The film gestures toward the salvation narrative that the novel deliberately eschews. We are even given a moral, as one man, echoing Stan's question at the film's opening, asks "How can a guy get so low?" Answer: "He reached too high." This pat wrap-up does little to soften the disturbing tale we have witnessed and warns audiences that pursuing the American Dream may lead one down a nightmare alley. But Stan's fault isn't that he reaches too high; it is that he doesn't believe in his own greatness. Like many a performer, he is actually solitary and fearful, and the alienation that permits him to rise above the masses eventually pulls him down. He wants to feel superior to others yet dreads being different, thus exemplifying the gangster's paradox that Shadoian outlines. Indeed, the film suggests that Stan lives out his destiny, that he has always been and always will be a geek. His "geekness" lies partly in the willingness, shared by many noir protagonists, to do anything to get what he wants. Unfortunately, however, Stan doesn't know what he wants—or, rather, he wants conflicting things: both admiration and pity. We do as well: watching him, we at once relish our moral superiority and identify with him, suspecting that we, too, are secretly geeks.

Carlisle is just one of the film's objects of criticism, as it places him among gullible audiences who line up to be cheated and wealthy citizens duped by the elaborate con games called religion and psychoanalysis. Pursuing happiness through amusements or therapy, these citizens hope to fashion new identities out of consumer purchases, but their commodified selves are as bogus as the ghosts in his séances. Yet Carlisle's fate forcibly exposes the underside of the American Dream of upward mobility, singular achievement and fungible identity: his mobility isn't freedom; it is merely restless appetite. Nor does he ever have a home—the carnival being the antithesis of home—and his constant changes only bring him back where he started, to the no-place of the geek. This nonidentity, a sub-human persona that lacks even a name, is the accursed share of the pursuit of happiness. *Nightmare Alley* suggests, then, that Carlisle's decisions only push him to a destiny already ordained. His commodified identity as The Great Stanton is exposed as a hollow shell, inside of which dwells the geek. Individualism personified—caring for no one else; severed from community, lovers, and friends—Carlisle is a failed Franklin brought down by the Emersonian truth that no matter where he goes, he will meet himself—someone who is, at the core, nobody at all.

Why Noir?

Nightmare Alley is a particularly potent challenge to the dream of upward mobility, but it is not an anomaly in film noir. But how did such pessimistic and politically provocative themes come to appear in these crime films? An answer often given is that film noir was created in part by European (mostly German Jewish) émigré directors who brought their psychologically probing, highly mannered expressionist visual style and doom-laden worldview to American cinema as war broke out.[7] Other critics trace noir's origins and themes to American hard-boiled fiction writers—Hammett, Chandler, Cain, and Woolrich—though many fail to note the wide disparities in style, politics, and sensibility even among the four authors named.[8] These studies are valuable for unveiling noir's links to particular literary and cinematic traditions. My aim, however, is to locate noir within its more immediate social, cultural, and political context: the United States in the wake of World War II.

The war and its aftermath were by far the most significant cultural influence on noir. Frank Krutnik has suggested that noir's obsession with criminality and violence was a means of "displacing a critique of the 'social murder' legitimized through the war" (*Lonely* 54). But its effects are even more broad and profound. As I demonstrate in the chapters that follow, the war's echoes and effects are everywhere in noir: in the numerous traumatized veterans that populate the films; in their many missing or displaced persons; in the tensions noir records regarding women's role in the workplace and the domestic arena; in the postwar anticommunist backlash. Moreover, noir's seemingly obsessive focus on psychic disorder—which helps to explain the frequent appearance of psychiatrists in the films—may suggest what Krutnik calls a national "breakdown of confidence in the defining and sustaining cultural regimentation of identity and authority" (*Lonely* 55). As Philip Kemp and Warren Susman have argued, noir represents the reemergence of a "suppressed element of American culture" (Kemp 270; Susman is quoted in Neve, *Film and Politics* 152). Its role as a cultural barometer is one reason why noir has come to be recognized as a watershed in American cinema and why the wealth of recent scholarship has assumed such a wide array of approaches.[9]

There can be little doubt that noir is a product of a period of enormous upheaval. Massive population shifts occurred as veterans of both sexes returned home, producing dissonances in gender dynamics and definitions of domesticity. Increased racial agitation and organizing (CORE, for example, was formed in this period) occurred as African American citizens protested inequality and police brutality, and as black veterans discovered that Jim Crow practices lingered on the home front. The most popular music of the period was jazz, a hybrid, black-originated style that encouraged emotional liberation. A burgeoning consumer culture fueled the desire for self-improvement and social mobility while limiting its scope; and the postwar economic boom was accompanied by massive layoffs, renewed labor unrest, and heightened concerns about the stability of money and the plight of the worker. Strikes and antifascist political activism prompted a crackdown by reactionary governmental and nongovernmental forces.[10] Meanwhile, fears of communism and news of the Soviet Union's A-bomb tests terrified citizens and triggered an atmosphere of paranoia and prying. Noir both reflects this postwar hangover (residual anxieties about identity, gender, disability, and labor) and registers new fears about race, representation, capitalism, technology, privacy, and security. Amid this turmoil, films noir ask whether the American Dream of liberty and democracy is still viable and, if so, how it may be altered or fulfilled.

The above paragraph provides a version of what is dubbed (usually with pejorative connotations) the "Zeitgeist" theory: the idea that film noir (itself subject to varying definitions) reflected and shaped a peculiarly downbeat or anxious postwar mood and, as Kemp declares, exposes "the symptoms of a deformed society" (268–69; see also F. Hirsch 21). Recently this theory has come under attack. Richard Maltby, for example, observes that the Zeitgeist theory is "notoriously difficult to substantiate," since it depends "on the selective presentation of its evidence"; it may even be circular, as angst-ridden narratives are used as evidence of social problems that allegedly generated the angst-ridden narratives (41). Will Straw remarks that noir criticism is plagued by a contradiction, having come "to be understood, conveniently, as both a conscious, programmatic intervention by politically engaged filmmakers . . . and a cluster of symptoms through which collective or individual psyches betrayed themselves" (132).[11] This apparent contradiction has led Steve Neale, perhaps the Zeitgeist theory's most voluble critic, to announce that the entire category called film noir is hopelessly incoherent (174). But Straw's observation actually exposes complexity, not contradiction: noir was *in some cases* the product of conscious interventions by politically engaged filmmakers *and,* at other times, a phenomenon betraying a set of subterranean anxieties. A substantial number of crime films were made by radical leftist writers, directors, actors, and producers who, I suggest in chapter 8, deliberately set out to critique certain cherished American beliefs and values in order to awaken audiences from their slumbers. But the anxieties, hypocrisies, and frauds illuminated by these filmmakers were part of a larger set of fears and dissatisfactions that simmered beneath the surface of the culture and exerted pressure on the daily activities of ordinary people.

Influenced by Neale's argument, Mike Chopra-Gant argues that noir has been overrated as a sign of postwar America's mood. Noirs, he points out, were not among the most popular films of the era, and we should instead look to the period's hit movies to discern the real mood of the times. In contrast to noir's disturbing, downbeat stories, he proposes, Hollywood's mainstream films "represent an effort to reinvigorate" American myths and to "reinstate the cornerstones of American identity" (25). But if mainstream films sought to "reinvigorate" and "reinstate" American myths, that itself suggests that those myths were perceived to be imperiled. Chopra-Gant also acknowledges the difficulties in determining how many movies were seen by how many people (see 183–88). In any case, just because a lot of people see a film does not mean that it lingers in their minds, reflects their mood, or affects their behavior. In fact, one of the most influential Hollywood films—influential, that is, for the industry and other filmmakers—was Billy Wilder's *Double Indemnity,* a film firmly ensconced in the noir canon. I would also point out that two of the top-grossing films of 1946 (see Chopra-Gant 13) were *The Best Years of Our Lives,* a provocative, realistic story about veterans' readjustment that contains strong noir undertones, and *Notorious,* a romance-thriller with an atomic-bomb plot. These popular films *do* deal with anxieties that troubled the postwar world. Nicholas Spencer, quoting historian William Graebner, stakes out a middle ground by observing that American culture in the 1940s was swept by two broad, conflicting trends: "On the one hand, culture was characterized by nostalgia, sentimentalism, a belief in scientific progress, and a pervasive yearning for . . . a 'culture of the whole.' . . . On the other hand, it was a time when irony, historical contingency, a feeling of historical exhaustion and cultural fragmentation, and an attraction to existentialism borne [*sic*] of a sense of meaninglessness were evident" (Spencer 118–19). Noir reflects that latter strain.

Attempts to define *film noir* have generally failed to capture its complex, even contradictory, themes and manifestations. Of course, *film noir* is a retrospective critical construction; as Neale points out, most of the movies we call noir were at the time referred to simply as melodramas (180). Beyond genre concerns, the conditions of production also helped to create the cross-generic phenomenon we call noir. The bulk of the films, as James Naremore reminds us, were not Poverty Row creations but midlevel products of major Hollywood studios. In the wake of the *Loews v. Paramount* decision of 1948, a substantial number of noirs were made by independent companies such as Enterprise, Horizon, and Diana Productions, which offered greater creative freedom for their artists. In short, *noir* is the name we apply to a certain oppositional sensibility that was cultivated both within and at the margins of the industrial Hollywood system. Adopting and expanding genres that included the women's picture, the gangster movie, the hard-boiled detective story, the neorealist pseudodocumentary, the romance-thriller, the psychological study, and the social-problem picture, among others, filmmakers produced a counternarrative to the story of "reinvigoration," one that challenged not just the current practices but also the philosophical foundations of American culture. In his influential book *More Than Night*, Naremore defines film noir as a nebulous signifier of a "liminal space" lying "between Europe and America, between high modernism and 'blood melodrama,' and between low-budget crime movies and art cinema" (220). I endorse the spirit of this definition but would add that the best way to define noir is to examine specific films in detail and then use these explorations to generate prevailing patterns, themes, and tendencies. That is what I have sought to do in this book. The result, I hope, proves that *film noir* remains a useful term with which to designate a peculiarly interrogative, deeply moral, visually adventurous and politically aware sensibility that characterized American cinema between 1944 and 1959.

With their often darkly expressionist mise-en-scènes, their complex narrative structures, their violent, sexual stories, their sense of doom, and their skeptical treatment of American ideals and identities, noirs provide an ideal opportunity, as Maltby notes, for an "interpretation of American culture through its shared daydreams" (42). This recognition seems to call for a psychoanalytic approach akin to that of Kelly Oliver and Benigno Trigo, who see in noir evidence of "condensations and displacements between various concrete anxieties over race, sex, maternity, and national identity" (xv). Yet Oliver and Trigo offer virtually no historical context for their assertions. My approach is less psychoanalytic than cultural—an effort to chart noir's political unconscious. I argue, therefore, that noir's alienated characters act out antisocial urges shared by their audiences, being sanctioned to enact what others keep hidden. These characters—amnesiacs, ephebes, cynical men on the make, convicts; feckless adventurers, gullible youngsters, detectives enticed by mysterious women; gangsters and thieves, traumatized veterans, female professors, boxers—become sites where anxieties about identity, class, agency, individualism, technology, consumerism, race, gender, and trauma are played out, thereby reflecting and shaping the consciousness of a culture. Film noir, in short, was an underground theater where Americans staged the most urgent concerns of a society in transition.

I have argued that the film *Nightmare Alley* dramatizes a conflict in American conceptions of identity, mobility, and success. I concentrate in chapters 1 through 4 on similar themes to elucidate noir's critique of individualism and its ethos of self-making. It is odd that, despite the frequent description of noirs as "dream-like," no critic has thoroughly analyzed the films' dream sequences. The first chapter, "Someone Else's Nightmare," does just that, drawing from psycho-analytic theory to explore oneiric scenarios in films such as *The Chase, The Dark Past, Spellbound, Strange Illusion,* and *Uncle Harry.* Noir dreams, I find, expose pathologies that represent not just individual maladies but widely shared anxiet-ies about self, sexuality, and, most of all, about the relations between past and present: virtually all noir dream sequences concern a character's crippling at-tachment to the past. Only by severing oneself from history, these films suggest, can individuals restore an integrated identity; those who do not are doomed to remain trapped, like Stan Carlisle, in a vortex of repetition. The noir dream films, like the works treated in chapters 2 and 3, dramatize a collective neurosis: the conflict between remembering and forgetting.

The second chapter, "Missing Persons," investigates noirs involving amnesia and switched identities *(Street of Chance, The Killers, Out of the Past, No Man of Her Own, Dark Passage,* and *Hollow Triumph),* discovering in them an even more pessimistic outlook on self-fashioning. In these films, characters change their names or faces—like many real Americans who started over after the war—to escape the consequences of past actions. But unlike those in the dream films, these characters' reformations seldom succeed, and some of them experience to-tal self-erasure. Staging, then subverting, the Protestant conversion narrative and the immigrant success story, these films challenge an essential American myth, as noir's missing persons become synecdoches for a society of mobile indi-viduals anxiously suspended between a traumatic past and an uncertain future.

Casual viewers associate film noir with the stereotypical hard-boiled macho detective, but noir actually depicts a diverse array of masculine types. Films fea-turing cognitively disabled veterans *(Act of Violence, The Blue Dahlia, Cornered, High Wall, Somewhere in the Night),* for example, use disability to explore shift-ing attitudes about masculinity, achievement, and power. These films, analyzed in chapter 3, "Vet Noir," expose seams in the ethos of self-determination through their haunted ex-soldiers' attempts to heal their fractured psyches by paradoxically reenacting the traumas that have shattered them. Though the films show that self-recreation is possible, they also demonstrate that discarding the past may require amputation of key parts of the individual and national consciousness.

Chapter 4, "Framed," focuses on art forgery and portraiture films (such as *Crack-Up, The Dark Corner, I Wake Up Screaming,* and *Scarlet Street*) that ask vexing questions about representation, identity, and replication. Like the counterfeiting films I have analyzed elsewhere, the forgery films simultaneously celebrate and interrogate cinema as a medium of representation.[12] By blurring the lines between originality and forgery, subjectivity and objectivity, the real and its representations, these films imply that all identities are to some degree forged and that human character is too malleable and complex to be captured by any medium, including cinema. They thus train a skeptical eye on the American dream of self-reinvention, disclosing a suspicion that such operations are often a pretext for exploitation or a pathway to madness.

The next four chapters expand the focus to explore a spectrum of social phenomena depicted in noir, each chapter targeting a cultural formation in crisis and addressing one source of the social, political, or cultural anxiety described above. "Noir's Cars" examines how automobiles, in films such as *They Live by Night, Gun Crazy,* and *Kiss Me Deadly,* function as amoral spaces. While driving their cars, disenfranchised characters express antisocial urges and pursue fantasies of social mobility through automobility. Fittingly, the most common auto in film noir is the convertible, which perfectly symbolizes the American belief in mobile identities: convertibles, that is, represent the promise of self-convertibility. Yet the films analyzed in chapter 5 portray this vision of freedom as a trap sprung by fearful or hypocritical citizens who envy the liberation that cars allow; as a cynical ruse to entice gullible people; or as a Trojan horse used to introduce more deadly technologies that will increase mechanization and conformity and threaten American citizens.

Chapter 6, "Nocturnes in Black and Blue," proposes that jazz in noir signifies shifts in racial attitudes and notions of masculinity. In *Black Angel, Nocturne, Detour,* and *Nightmare,* jazz melodies provide clues to forgotten events—often a musician/protagonist's own violent act. Although African Americans seldom appear in the films, white musicians are "noired" through jazz's affiliation with blackness, decadence, psychic disturbance, illicit sexuality, and interracial contact. *Sweet Smell of Success* alters this pattern, portraying jazz as an island of integrity set against a continent of corruption; and two films featuring female jazz singers *(The Man I Love* and *Road House)* present improvisation as the basis for a creative selfhood. Contravening Hollywood's general demonizing of jazz, these latter films reveal the potential for emotional and sexual liberation through a music that exemplifies America's own hybrid, improvised nature.

Whereas the femme fatale embodies a dubious brand of empowerment, another set of films—very much like the two I've just described—that I am calling *femme noirs* offer more nuanced portrayals of women caught between two forms of labor: motherhood and nondomestic work. These pictures, most of them written, produced, or directed by women, are significant both for that reason and for their provocative content. Yet they have never before been studied as a group. Chapter 7, "Femmes Vital," rectifies this neglect by analyzing how women filmmakers both challenged and reflected cultural contradictions in their work. Like chapter 3, this chapter sounds out postwar gender dissonances and probes the fissures that these social changes exposed. These femme noirs offer critiques of marriage *(Caught, The Bigamist)*, dissect gender politics *(Gilda, The Damned Don't Cry)*, and condemn patriarchal institutions *(Caged, Possessed)*, while also mirroring a divided society in their ambivalent portraits of working women in films such as *Mildred Pierce* and *The Accused*. The multivalent efforts of producer-director-actress Ida Lupino, whose jazz singers provide a positive example of the mobile self, also best represent the ideal of the femme vital, through her revolutionary approach to women's creative labor and pioneering contributions to cinematic authorship.

The final chapter, "Left-Handed Endeavor," and the conclusion, "American Nightmares," analyze an important group of noirs made by committed leftists such as Joseph Losey, Abraham Polonsky, Cyril Endfield, Jules Dassin, Robert Rossen, and Dalton Trumbo *(Body and Soul, Force of Evil, The Prowler, Try and Get Me!)*, demonstrating how they portray class barriers, unfettered capitalism, and hypocritical institutions as obstacles to equality and democracy. In these so-called "films gris" (Andersen, "Red" 257), which I have renamed *red noirs*, crime is portrayed as what a character in *The Asphalt Jungle* calls a "left-handed form of human endeavor." For these films' lower-class characters, indeed, crime seems the only pathway to success in a society in thrall to conformism and corporatism. Expanding the analogy between crime and capitalism advanced in 1930s gangster movies, these pictures dramatize how the pursuit of happiness enshrined in the American Dream camouflages the rapacious pursuit of power. Though these artists were blacklisted, their challenges to the status quo stand as one of noir's most enduring achievements and remain trenchant today—a period similarly marked by war, economic and social upheaval, rampant greed, and ubiquitous uncertainty.

These crime melodramas diagnosed a spectrum of social ills and fears, promulgating troubling messages about American values and institutions in an era that prized conformity, celebrated capitalism, and championed law and order. Film noir, in short, challenged Americans to live up to the ideals they professed to endorse.

"Someone Else's Nightmare"
Exploring Noir Dreamscapes

A ghostly man walks through an eerie, indeterminate space as driving rain falls upon him. Suddenly he is standing beneath an umbrella, but the umbrella has a hole in it, and though he frantically tries to plug the hole, water continues to drip through. The umbrella grows bars and becomes a cage. He is overwhelmed by guilt and dread, and he can't get out!

This recurring nightmare constitutes the central enigma in Rudolph Maté's film *The Dark Past*. As analyzed by Dr. Andrew Collins (Lee J. Cobb), the dream holds the key to understanding the dreamer, Al Walker (William Holden), a psychopath who has just escaped from prison and taken Collins and his family and friends hostage in Collins's rural cabin. Collins explains Walker's nightmare according to Freudian orthodoxy: it was "caused by something that happened when [he was] a child," and everything in it "is a substitute for something else." He eventually unearths its origins in Walker's relations with his parents. But what is most strange about this dream—stranger even than its appearance as negative footage—is that Walker does not relate it himself.[1] Instead, the dream is described by Walker's girlfriend, Betty (Nina Foch), who asks Collins to interpret it and quell Walker's mania for killing. In other words, this dream is presented as someone else's nightmare. In fact, it is twice-removed from its dreamer, since Collins recounts these events later to prove that psychoanalysis can cure social problems.

It is a critical commonplace that films noir—with their bizarre circumstances, disorienting settings, and obsession with darkness—are "like bad dreams."[2] Foster Hirsch further observes that noir directors, by maintaining a neutral, even clinical, stance toward their characters' pathologies, treat the stories as if they were "*someone else's* nightmare" (115; emphasis his). *The Dark Past*, as we've seen, records Walker's dream in just that way—secondhand. But Hirsch's phrase resonates in other directions and offers not only a means to understand noir dreams but a blueprint for a key aspect of noir's role in American culture. Noir nightmares are "someone else's" in several senses. According to the Freudian theory that underpins them, dreams emerge from the unconscious. Their latent content or motivating wish is condensed or displaced into a disguised manifest content, so that the dream-work goes on, as it were, behind the dreamer's back. Denied access to his or her own motives, the dreamer is at once him- or herself and someone else. Second, once the dream is recounted or written down, it becomes a text, not an experience—and thus no longer belongs to the dreamer. Third, noir's tormented dreamers act as surrogates for audience members' own struggles with renewal, reinvention, or return. But because the characters' past identities are often abhorrent or irretrievable, they are severed from the self who dreams and from the audience as well: they become as much objects of scrutiny as of sympathy. Hence, noir dreams stage ruptures in identity and integration that are not just individual but collective.

I thus propose that noir dream sequences dramatize key questions about identity in the World War II and postwar period. Noir's nightmares first of all register Americans' ambivalence about the rapidly changing postwar world, which suddenly seemed to carry as much peril as possibility. The war had cut a gap in lives and minds (as rendered explicitly in the disabled-veteran noirs discussed in chapter 3) that required survivors either to fashion new selves or seek to integrate past and present selves. Because the war years were filled with violent trauma, a nostalgia remained for the prewar period, which now seemed more innocent, less fraught. Not surprisingly, virtually all noir dream sequences concern a character's crippling attachment to the past: to a traumatic experience, a lover, a parent, or a violent episode. Discovering the meaning of the dream— whether through psychoanalysis or reenactment—is believed to free the character from that past. Only by severing oneself from one's history, the films suggest, can one either start over or craft an integrated identity; those who do not become, like Stan Carlisle, enslaved to that history.

The noir dream films, like the switched identity films and veteran films I treat in later chapters, stage a collective neurosis that emerges from an unsolvable conflict between the need to remember and the need to forget. Conversion narratives that invoke Protestant redemption tales and allude in some instances to the biographies of their émigré directors, noir dream sequences dramatize and test the American mythos of mobile identity and self-renewal, as these characters encounter an obstacle frequently faced in actual nightmares—the inability to act. As I suggested in my introduction, the question of agency lies at the heart of noir's analysis of the American Dream: in depicting characters whose demise seems fated, or who are trapped by circumstances, the dream films expose the limits of personal liberty and self-determination.

These films' analyses also target their own medium; that is, they both affirm their status as reliable representations of identity and consciousness and question that status by showing how easily images can be misread. Although dream sequences interrupt their realist narratives and direct us to read them as psychoanalysts, this reading can be accomplished only in retrospect, because many of the films disguise the fact that they are dreams. Moreover, some of noir's dreams— like real-life dreams—incorporate the tropes and devices of other films, as if to remind us that they are "only" movies; meanwhile, the characters, unaware of their fictionality, wander in partial blindness through their dreamscapes. Audiences' visual decoding compensates for the characters' lack of sight. The dream films' frequent motifs of blindness and vision thus invite us to scrutinize the cinematic medium itself.

The Stuff Dreams Are Made Of

The parallel between cinema and dreams is almost as old as film itself. Early surrealist filmmakers, for example, saw the mental production of dream images as analogous to the cutting necessary for film editing (Gabbard and Gabbard xxi).[3] But movie dreams are not solitary: as C. J. Pennethorne Hughes observed back in 1930, cinema is "the transmuted and regulated dream life of the people" (qtd. in Lebeau 4). And if films are dreams, so dreams are often films: Jean-Louis Baudry reminds us how often a dreamer will wake and say, "It was like in a movie" (qtd. in Lebeau 32). Hollywood is not called "the dream factory" for nothing. Not only do movies influence American dreams in a metaphorical sense, by furnishing stories that shape audiences' ideas about success, self-transformation, love and a host of other themes; they also provide images and situations for actual dreams, which may resemble thrillers, horror movies, detective stories, or romances. Indeed, some of the cinematic dreams I examine below generate a kind of mise en abyme: a dream within a movie that alludes to other movie dreams. Thus, as Vicky Lebeau notes, because dreams inevitably partake of the culture at large, dream theory supports a "psychoanalytic study of culture" (23).

Films noir serve this function better than most movie genres, for they are full of bad dreams; indeed, the picture many describe as the first film noir, Boris Ingster's 1940 *Stranger on the Third Floor,* features a lengthy dream sequence that fosters the protagonist's change of heart and forecasts his incarceration. More generally, Nicholas Christopher remarks that the noir cycle constitutes the "complex mosaic of a single, thirteen-year urban dreamscape" (43). Given this fascination with the oneiric, it makes sense that noir is heavily populated by psychiatrists and psychoanalysts—both good and bad—along with its psychopaths and psychics.[4] Ordinary citizens were increasingly exposed to psychiatry through its role in treating traumatized World War II veterans, and a large number of Hollywood personnel underwent psychoanalysis in the 1940s (see Thomas 72). Yet American cinema has seldom offered a realistic portrayal of psychoanalysis—perhaps not surprisingly, since, as Alain de Mijolla notes, real psychotherapy is far from cinematic (197). In most Hollywood films (then and now) the psychiatrist is depicted as a detective who solves problems that are immediately "forgotten once a culprit has been identified" (Gabbard and Gabbard 58–59).[5] Presenting a homology between psychoanalysis and detective work (Freedman 91) permitted Hollywood filmmakers to appropriate the analytic situation into conventional narrative patterns of repetition, delay, and recuperation (Doane, *Desire* 47). As a result, Hollywood cinema overrepresented the talking cure, often illustrating the method through tropes of vision and insight (Gabbard and Gabbard 28; Doane *Desire* 47).[6]

Along with an identifiable set of stereotypical characters, one plot convention in psychiatry pictures encompasses all genres: the cathartic cure (Gabbard and Gabbard 28). Most positive portrayals of psychoanalysis involve the "derepression of a traumatic memory," often through dream analysis (Gabbard and Gabbard 28). Classic psychoanalysis laid itself open to such simplifications by arguing that pathology usually stems from the repression of "disturbing impulses, memories, thoughts or feelings" (Ringel 169). In Freudian theory a dream consists of a manifest content (the particular images or situations within a dream) that camouflages latent content (the motivating emotions or memories). The dream-work transforms that latent content through condensation and displacement, the former permitting a single image to represent several ideas or emotions, the latter enabling a motivating emotion or image to be replaced by related ones (Freud, *Interpretation* 312–44). Both processes (which, as Bert States observes, are forms of metonymy and synecdoche: 100) contribute to "overdetermination"—the recognition that "for any given manifest content, there can be more than one latent content, or [that] any one dream can express several quite separate wishes" (Wollheim 80; cf. Freud, *Interpretation* 342–43). Even so, for Freud all dreams are wish-fulfillments whose meaning may be discovered by interpretation. Freudian dream-interpretation is, in short, a theory of reading, in which the analyst extracts hidden emotions and traumas through thoughtful, attentive explication of the manifest content. Recent dream theory deemphasizes symbolic hermeneutics, instead stressing dreams' emotional contexts and contents, but midcentury Hollywood's dreams were Freudian through and through.[7] Yet the films generally reduce Freud's methods to a one-to-one mapping in which a symbol (say, an umbrella) is determined "really" to be, say, a table, or rain a memory of blood. Hollywood overlooks overdetermination in pursuit of melodrama, with the psychiatrist serving as stage manager or dramaturg. Traveling the royal road to the collective unconscious, films noir focus mostly on the destination, which is usually a traumatic memory or familial conflict for which the dream functions as a rebus.

Freud understands the dreaming psyche as a site of conflict where the dreamer's mind is torn between "wish and defense, wish and censorship, wish and repression" (Lebeau 40). The dreamer, he insists, is blocked from understanding his or her own dream—a contention that many theorists now dispute (Rieff 52; Lebeau 76).[8] For Freud, the dreamer is a divided entity trying, as Peter Gay puts it, "to dispose of unfinished business" (146) but unable to do so because "the desire to recall is countered by the desire to forget" (Gay 128). In this respect the psychoanalytical subject mirrors the noir subject—a creature obsessed with the past, unable either to let go of it or to embrace it. As Richard Wollheim remarks, there are "two separate people amalgamated in the dreamer, one of whom has the wish whereas the other rejects it, and it is only the former who is satisfied" (78). In Freudian theory, then, *every dream is someone else's.* Noir films capture this condition by placing viewers in conflicting subject positions, first bombarding us with disorienting, disturbing images, then requesting that we scrutinize them dispassionately. We are asked to serve as both dreamer and analyst, while gaining a vantage point superior to both: only we both have the dream and understand it.

Midcentury Hollywood, with its plethora of psychiatrists onscreen and off, helped to engender the "therapeutic ethos" I outlined in my introduction, which "replaced religious or moral sanctions with considerations of mental hygiene, psychic balance, and above all personal 'growth'" (Freedman 79). Psychiatry, along with self-help books and all manner of commodities, promised to make people into better versions of themselves, almost by magic. Hollywood eagerly purveyed conversion narratives in which antisocial values belonged to "characters' earlier rejected selves" (May 151). But film noir gave audiences a chance to have things both ways—to undergo a "cure" or whitewash of their former selves while also experiencing pathology as package intensity. Noir psychoanalysis thus betrays a deep ambivalence: as Krutnik explains, it is represented as a science that successfully treats disorder and deviance, while also exposing and exploiting a fascination with a "destabilizing undercurrent of excessive and disordered desires" (*Lonely* 53). Noir dreams—whether nocturnal or diurnal—thereby open "the royal road to the cultural unconscious" (Freud, *Interpretation* 647; Lebeau 6).

The Eternal Triangle

The most typical dreams, according to Freud, involve the Oedipus complex (*Interpretation* 294–300), in which the son faces a paradox: "be like your father (be a man, love a woman) but also do not be like your father (you may not have all that your father has; you may not wish for your mother)" (Lebeau 80). The Oedipus myth underlies many noir dreams, including Al Walker's in *The Dark Past*. Let us revisit the scene: police psychiatrist Andrew Collins, his family, and friends have been taken hostage by the twitchy, hyperaggressive Walker, who is also afflicted with paralyzed fingers on his right hand. Noticing that Walker is fascinated with a book he finds on his shelf—*Sociological Aspects of Insanity*—Collins draws him a rudimentary diagram of the mind, explaining that the conscious and unconscious minds are divided by a "sensor band." Criminality and insanity result when the unconscious crosses the barrier. The idea seems to be that neurosis—that is, the repression of impulses—is necessary for civilization (as Freud argued in *Civilization and Its Discontents* 110). Unable to repress his, Walker is tortured by guilt compounded by violent hatred. Collins's job is to expose the source of his emotions and actions and thereby dispel them. And so, after hearing Betty describe Walker's dream, Collins gradually induces his reluctant patient to discuss his childhood. We learn that Walker's father was an abusive hustler who abandoned his family and, when he returned, monopolized his mother's attention. Therefore, Al hated his father. Using word association, Collins helps him recall the origin of his nightmare in a traumatic incident. As Walker finally tells his own story, the ghostly negative footage used in Betty's account is replaced by point-of-view shots showing the child Al leading police to a saloon where his father was hiding. While the boy cowered under a table, the cops shot his father, who staggered to the table and collapsed upon it. Al picked up his father's gun as dad's blood dripped down onto the boy's hands.

The dream's bars were policemen's legs, the umbrella a table. The rain? Paternal blood. Everything in the dream—once converted via metonymy and synecdoche, or condensation and displacement—is now explained, and Walker's history of violence traced to this single incident.⁹ The cause of his pathology—and of his paralyzed hand—is oedipal guilt: whenever Walker kills someone, he is shooting his father again, both to eliminate him and to gain some of his (phallic) power. Voila: once Walker's nightmare is unraveled (he'll never have the dream again, Collins assures him), his paralyzed fingers loosen. Unfortunately for his criminal career, he is also unable to kill: when he takes aim at a police officer, the man's face dissolves into that of Walker Senior, and Al can't pull the trigger. His cathartic cure thus results in his capture. Curiously, the presentation of the originating incident—seedy saloon, card players, guns—mixes artifacts from 1930s gangster films with the trappings of a western: it is less a dream than a Hollywood pastiche. If this dream testifies to Walker's rather impoverished stock of mental props, it also implies that both his memory and his criminal persona have been borrowed from movies, just as his hostage-taking plan seems to have been pilfered from such films as *The Petrified Forest*.

The Dark Past offers the most positive treatment of psychoanalysis in all of noir, while epitomizing the conventions of movie psychiatry: the tracing of pathology to a single event (often involving an oedipal complex); the linkage of specific manifest images to particular latent sources; the shrink's role as detective (Collins is, after all, a police psychiatrist); and the magical cure. The film presents Walker's dream as someone else's nightmare, not only because of Betty's and Collins's interposition between dream and viewer but also because it places us in the positions of both analyst and dreamer: we are both Walker and Collins and neither of them. Once Walker is cured, the nightmare is permanently out of reach, for it belongs to the man he will never be again.

The film also has a social agenda: Collins's flashback is meant to prove that criminals can be cured by psychoanalysis. Mental illness, he tells his listener, is a "festering" disease, and Walker's pathology is no different from that of another young man whom Collins picks out (before the flashback) as curable. If treated early enough, he confidently declares, such delinquents will never become Al Walkers. Psychoanalysis is thus represented as a form of social engineering that, applied broadly, would ameliorate crime. These naive liberal sentiments reveal how noir uses individual dreamers to represent larger segments of society whose problems stem from a debilitating attachment to the past.

Few noirs share this confidence, but oedipal dreams are far from rare. A prime example occurs in one of the earliest noirs, Edgar G. Ulmer's 1942 *Strange Illusion*. A pastiche of *Hamlet* written by Adele Comandini, the film traces the predicament of young Paul Cartwright (James Lydon), whose father, Albert, a judge and former lieutenant governor, was killed two years earlier in a mysterious train accident.[10] Like Shakespeare's protagonist, Paul believes that his father was murdered and is troubled by strange dreams. In the dream sequence that opens the film, Paul's mother (Sally Eilers) tells him his father has returned in the form of her new lover, but Paul shouts, "You're not my father," and asks for help from his sister, Dorothy (Jayne Hazard), to whom her mother's lover has given a bracelet. A hurtling train crashes, after which the usurper intones, "Just what I've been waiting for." A Schumann piano concerto—Albert's favorite piece—begins to play, and Paul's protests go unheeded until he wakes up.

The dream's oedipal elements are obvious enough. Unlike Al Walker's dream, however, Paul's blends his recollection of trauma with current events and forecasts of the future. But like Walker, Paul is tormented by guilt. He must both emulate his father and "kill" his influence, while also eliminating his rival, Brett Curtis (Warren William), the man with designs on his mother's fortune. In the process he must also confront two patriarchal doctors: his friend, Doc Vincent (Regis Toomey), and Curtis's co-conspirator, the psychiatrist Muhlbach (Charles Arnt). If Muhlbach and Curtis are sinister, Doc Vincent is sympathetic but skeptical: after Paul recounts his dream and reminds Vincent that, after the wreck, the train engineer saw a sign for the Acme Trucking Company, Doc dismisses him with "you've been working too hard at school."

Instead of appearing to his son as a ghost, the elder Cartwright speaks to Paul in more mundane ways. He has left a letter urging the youth to guard his mother from "unscrupulous impostors," and when Paul first meets Curtis, the two men stand with Paul's mother, Virginia, before a large portrait of Judge Cartwright, who looms behind them like an apparition urging Paul to "list." Though Paul rejects his mother's claim that Curtis "looks like father," his own duty is to "look like" his father—to judge the scheming Curtis and finish the criminology textbook his father was writing when he died. Like Hamlet's, Paul's determination is tested as his dreams begin to come true: Curtis gives Dorothy the "traitorous gift" (*Hamlet* 1.5.42) of a bracelet, and the young man collapses upon hearing the Schumann concerto. Soon Paul finds in his father's papers accounts of one Claude Barrington, accused but never convicted of attacks on young girls. A long slow pan left begins as Paul learns that Barrington was involved with a widow who drowned; as he finishes reading, the camera tilts upward and comes to rest on his father's portrait. The judge has given him his orders: stop Curtis (i.e., Barrington) from marrying (and probably killing) his mother.

After Curtis and Muhlbach consult about Paul (that "persistent little devil"), Muhlbach decides that the young man "sounds like a subject for mental analysis." So their plan takes shape: admit Paul to Muhlbach's sanitarium, Restview Manor, to get him out of the way and, after Curtis marries Virginia, kill him off. Paul provides the ideal pretext for the first step when he faints after hearing Curtis proclaim that this opportunity is "just what I've been waiting for." The dream is coming true! Muhlbach informs Paul that when "filial devotion to a mother goes beyond the borderline of normality," it can produce hallucinations. He concludes that "it is your emotional aversion to your mother's remarriage which produces these neurotic symptoms." In short, Paul suffers from an oedipal complex.

The film's vision motif emerges after Paul is admitted to his room at Restview, where Muhlbach spies on him through a two-way mirror (this scene rhymes with the earlier scene in which Judge Cartwright's portrait seemed to gaze down at him). As patriarchal authority is transferred to the psychiatrist, Paul's goal shifts from completing his father's unfinished business to throwing off all the paternal influences symbolized by these phallic, panoptic gazes. To do so, he must enhance his own vision. So when Muhlbach brings him to the roof of the clinic, Paul borrows his binoculars and spots an abandoned farm building not far away, while Muhlbach looks on with evil intent. Muhlbach (implausibly) then allows Paul to take a drive with Doc Vincent; though he watches them from the roof, he cannot penetrate the inside of the building, where the two discover the remains of a car, along with a mutilated sign for the ACME TRUCKING COMPANY. The sign—ME RUC OMP—is a rebus signifying the truth: Muhlbach and Curtis conspired to kill the judge by engineering the train crash.[11] After Vincent enlists the district attorney's help, Paul confronts Muhlbach, who again locks the young man in his room. The moment arrives for Paul to assert himself: smashing through the mirror, he enters the room beyond, shattering Muhlbach's visual control. Indeed, in breaking through the looking glass to enter the realm beyond the dream, Paul has thrown off not just Muhlbach's and Curtis's dominance but his father's as well.

After Muhlbach is arrested, Paul and his friends race to the family cabin, where Curtis threatens to molest Dorothy. Wrestling with Curtis before the latter is shot and captured, Paul is knocked unconscious and experiences the dream that ends the film. In it he is walking with his mother. "Look, mother," he declares, "we can see ahead." They're joined by Doc Vincent, who advises her, "Don't look back. It's all over." The father is nowhere to be seen, and Paul walks out of the frame—and out of his nightmare alley—with his girlfriend, Lydia

(Mary McLeod). He has convinced one father surrogate, Doc Vincent, that he's not crazy, and he has overcome the sexual and scientific machinations of two other older males. He has made himself a man by appropriating these men's attributes: his father's sense of justice, the doctors' analytic powers, Curtis's sexual confidence.[12] And he has defeated the phallic gaze of his patriarchs by borrowing their binoculars. Crafting a new identity by uniting the shards of the past and then discarding them, young Cartwright executes a feat that neither Hamlet nor many noir protagonists achieve: liberating himself from the perturbed spirits of the past.

Another young protagonist also faces Horatio's question about revenge undertaken in the name of the father:

> What if it tempt you toward the flood, my lord,
> Or to the dreadful summit of the cliff?
> . . . assume some other horrible form,
> Which might deprive your sovereignty of reason
> And draw you into madness? (*Hamlet* 1.4.75–80)

In Joseph Losey's *The Big Night* George La Main (John Barrymore Jr.) watches as his father, Andy (Preston Foster), is beaten and humiliated, then seeks revenge on the man who perpetrated the beating, influential sportswriter Al Judge (Howard St. John). The film unfolds in a single night, enacting a waking oedipal dream in which a son aims to prove he is stronger than his father and in which the primal scene of a father's beating, along with its blatant symbols (his father's gun, Judge's phallic cane), seems to issue from his unconscious.[13] Its concise nocturnal story—set on the evening of George's sixteenth birthday—traces a rite of passage on a *Walpurgisnacht* during which George evolves from child to adult by realizing the limitations of violence and testing the varieties of masculine identity.[14] As in a fable, each scene stages a temptation or test.

Early in the film "Georgie" is visually diminished: after some other boys rough him up, a long shot uses forced perspective to make him look tiny. He is further diminished during the beating sequence. As his father and the patrons of Handy Andy's Bar and Grill celebrate George's birthday, Al Judge enters with his entourage and begins issuing commands: "Take off your shirt, La Main; I want to see some skin!" Forcing Andy to his hands and knees, Judge flogs him with his cane. Shockingly, Andy silently submits to this humiliation. Indeed, the dialogue and blocking suggest that he is not only stripping but being made to perform fellatio.

Meanwhile, Flanagan (Howland Chamberlain), Andy's live-in partner of sixteen years, holds Georgie down and crushes the boy's glasses. These queer signifiers (which also exist in the novel) both advance the vision motif and invoke the film's explicit themes: masculinity, love, and justice. George vows to kill Judge, both to "overcome his own insecure sense of masculinity," writes Tony Williams, and to "disavow the shameful spectacle of his . . . father's symbolic castration" (*"Big Night"* 101). Like Paul Cartwright, George becomes his father's surrogate, borrowing his gun and donning his much-too-large suit to undergo tests of manhood that his father, he believes, has failed.[15]

Instead, George repeatedly proves his immaturity. Thus, for example, on the way to a boxing match (the two tickets were gifts from Andy), George tends a friend's baby, while playing with his father's loaded pistol. Oblivious to his risky behavior, the child's mother praises George as a "real father." Entering the arena, he is accosted by a man named Peckinpaugh (another "punitive father figure," according to Williams: 102), then sits next to Dr. Lloyd Cooper (Philip Bourneuf), from whom he borrows binoculars (George doesn't watch the fight; he's spying on Judge). Cooper's interest at first seems paternal, but mostly he uses George as an excuse to get drunk, while occasionally manhandling him.[16] Later George follows Judge to a club where a black chanteuse sings with her band; from George's point of view we watch the drummer's hands become Judge's hands flogging Andy, and as George remembers his birthday cake, the singer asks "Am I Too Young?"[17] An intoxicated George then makes his way to Cooper's apartment, where he passes out, to be awakened by Marion (Joan Lorring), the sister of Cooper's girlfriend. He and Marion exchange a chaste kiss, and he tells of his father's humiliation, concluding that he's not "a real man," that he "turns out just to be a fake." Yet he naively believes he can tell with one look that Cooper is "all right."

At last George finds Judge in the apartment of Frances, his father's fiancée, where Judge reveals that Frances was his sister and explains why he beat up Andy: Frances committed suicide after Andy refused to marry her. George spares Judge, but when the tables turn, with George taking Judge's cane, Judge grabs George's gun and threatens to kill him. A struggle ensues in which Judge is shot, apparently to death, and the panicked George appeals to Cooper for aid. His naive vision of the man is proven wrong when Cooper—his new, "all right" father—kicks him out. A truer form of loyalty is depicted next in a beautiful, wordless scene shot through a window, in which we watch Andy remove his son's clothes, put him to bed, then don the jacket and meet the police. Andy is prepared to sacrifice his life for his son. Andy—not Cooper, and not Judge, who had abjectly begged for his life when George threatened him—is the real man, the person willing to accept blame for another. Yet Andy's protective instincts also prevent his son from taking responsibility for himself. So as Andy is being led away, George leaps up and confesses, only to discover that Judge was only superficially wounded. In the aftermath George asks his father, "What's the use of my living? There's nothing matters to me anymore, and nobody I matter to." Andy replies, "You matter to me," and divulges his big secret: George's mother is not dead, as he has told his son; she left Andy for another man. Because Andy is still married to her, he couldn't marry Frances. "That's how it is with some men," he concludes. "There's only one woman in the whole world for them." He believes he merited Judge's punishment, but George will likely receive a light sentence.[18]

Over the course of the film Judge and George become identified. Not only do their names sound alike, but both are, like Paul Cartwright and his father, judges: Al metes out rough justice for his sister's death, and George presumes to judge both his father and Judge. In their final confrontation, however, George proves himself the better judge by mustering the empathy that Judge cannot. Andy and Al Judge are also counterparts: each is haunted by, and perversely attached to, a lost woman, and these allegiances trap them in an age-old ritual of punishment and revenge. George, however, is now free to forge a new identity, not by incorporating the attributes of these father figures but by sloughing off their worn-out cane and jacket. Perhaps he will see better without his glasses. In any case he has awakened from his dream of macho revenge.

Even so, the film's definition of masculinity remains troubling. One might argue that, like his father, George wants to be punished, because in so doing he can serve as scapegoat for his father's perceived crime and for his own violation of family roles, and because scapegoating fits the retributive justice in which he still believes. The film also leaves several vexing questions unanswered. Is Andy a long-suffering, righteous man or a pathetic fool carrying the torch for a woman who doesn't love him? In protecting his son, is he preventing him from seeing evil or precluding him from understanding genuine goodness? Is a "real" man one who suffers for others or one who permits others to accept and exercise their own agency? And can any young man ever be free of patriarchs who stage such powerful sadomasochistic rites of protection and domination? With these questions lingering, it seems less likely that George will fashion a new dream, a new self.

See No Evil

Down-and-out veteran Chuck Scott (Robert Cummings) finds a wallet filled with cash and returns it to its owner, wealthy Miami businessman Edward Roman (Steve Cochran). Roman is a little Caesar—a tyrant who abuses his wife and servants and kills a man who refuses to do business with him (he sics his enormous dog on the unfortunate fellow). Roman reserves his affection for his "adviser," Gino (Peter Lorre). Why did Chuck return the wallet? asks Roman. "I guess I'm just a sucker," he replies. Roman approves of his answer, and hires Chuck—whom he gives the doglike nickname of "Scottie"—as his new chauffeur. Adapted from Cornell Woolrich's *The Black Path of Fear*, *The Chase* features a typically passive Woolrich protagonist. Though no ephebe like Paul or George, Chuck too desires to build a new self, and this lucky break offers a chance. Unfortunately, his self-description seems apt: unwilling or unable to see the evil around him, Chuck frequently plays the sucker. His partial blindness is also illustrated by the film's dark, brooding mise-en-scène (courtesy of director Arthur Ripley and cinematographer Franz Planer) and by its repeated images of portholes, keyholes, and small windows.

But Roman's desire for a driver is odd, for—in a blatant metaphor for his domineering personality—he has rigged his car so that he can operate the accelerator and brakes from the rear while the driver steers. The world's most annoying backseat driver, Roman uses the contraption to test Chuck's obedience by racing a train to a crossing, only to slam on the brakes at the last second. It seems, then, that Chuck has just traded his navy uniform for the suit of a trained monkey serving a sinister master. But Roman also allows him to chauffeur his aptly named wife, Lorna (Michele Morgan), to the beach, where she gazes forlornly at the crashing waves and contemplates sailing to Cuba. She even offers Chuck a thousand dollars to take her there and away from the husband she loathes. Foolishly, Chuck agrees to do it.

After he enjoys a quick rest in his apartment, we see him through a porthole playing the piano for a rapturous Lorna; then he closes the porthole: lovers need privacy. But they remain the subjects of spying: in Havana they are abandoned by their driver, and, as they listen to romantic music in a club ("Havana, like the stars in a dream song / . . . you're a promise of love"), their photo is taken. Suddenly Lorna falls dead, and the hapless Chuck pulls a knife from her body.

During the police interrogation Chuck's memory is hazy, but he does recall purchasing a knife the previous night—but not the one the detective holds, its jade handle displaying a monkey covering his eyes. Chuck insists that he bought a different knife—"hear no evil," not "see no evil." But the saleslady fingers him as having bought the murder weapon. In any case both monkeys represent Chuck, so blinded by love and deafened by heartstrings that he neither saw nor heard the plot enveloping him. He pretends to confess, then escapes. What follows is decidedly weird: Chuck is hidden by a weeping, cigar-smoking woman, then finds the club photographer dead (because he had photographed the real murderer). Creeping around in the dark, he overhears Gino with the knife lady and learns that he and Roman are framing him for Lorna's murder. When the saleslady refuses to cooperate further, Gino shoots her and then, spotting a light behind the curtains where Chuck is hiding, bursts through. Out of the frame we hear gunshots and then see Gino dragging Chuck's body through the door. Is our hero dead?

No. A phone rings, and the camera dollies back from the receiver to show the living Chuck lying on his bed: he has dreamed the entire Cuban sequence. No wonder it seemed so illogical, its darkness so oppressive, its symbols so bizarre. Yet something is still amiss, for Chuck staggers around, swallows a handful of pills, gazes at himself confusedly in the mirror, then calls Commander Davidson, a psychiatrist, at the Naval Hospital: "It's happened again," he says. Davidson (Jack Holt) informs Chuck that he's a "shock" case with an "anxiety neurosis," or, as we would call it today, posttraumatic stress disorder. Like the traumatized vets we meet in chapter 3, Chuck experiences recurring nightmares coupled with amnesia and remembers neither how he got his new uniform nor the Cuban escape. Ripley crosscuts between Chuck and Davidson at the nightclub and Lorna at home, where she realizes that she has been "bought and paid for" by Roman. Both she and Chuck are trapped—she by her husband, he by his mental condition. But after Roman and Gino enter the club (a nicely executed crane shot reveals their proximity to Chuck), Chuck feels the ship tickets in his pocket, remembers the plan, and runs off to rescue Lorna. Discovering that Chuck and Lorna are headed for Cuba, Roman and Gino drive after them—or rather, Gino steers while Roman floors the gas pedal. But this time they don't beat the train to the crossing, and both men die in the smash-up. In Havana for real, the lovers are chauffeured by the same cabbie and repeat the same words of love they uttered in Chuck's dream. "Tell me again," she implores him. "I love you," he answers. "I want you to keep telling me that as long as we're together." "That'll be forever."

Chuck's dream, unlike those of most noir vets, is not a memory of war but the forecast of a future that he ultimately avoids. Yet he does little to alter his destiny and instead is saved by a deus ex machina in the form of a train. Though his dream lacks the condensed metonymies of Al Walker's nightmare, its monkey symbolism blatantly evinces Chuck's fear that he is fated to remain a flunky, as if his PTSD keeps him chained to his traumatized old self. A conventional reading of the conclusion would suggest that Lorna's love enables him to pass through his oedipal stage by engineering the death of the dominant father figure, and then to enter an adult heterosexual relationship. But the dream's details tell a different story and lay bare a different side of Chuck—his "Scottie" side, perhaps. This story acts out Chuck's hatred not of Edward but of Lorna; indeed, given her death in the dream, one might argue that the person Chuck really desires is not Roman's wife but Roman himself. The affair with Lorna may be a displacement of Chuck's desire to possess her husband. After all, in his dream he confesses to killing her, maybe because doing so will end the love triangle and permit him to resume the homosocial relationships familiar to him from the navy. And though he is technically innocent, the dream exposes his guilt feelings, as if he believes he should die at Gino's hands because he and Gino are rivals for Roman's affections. And at the end of the dream, having acted out Roman and Gino's murderous misogyny, Chuck must be sacrificed (by Roman's apparent lover) for doing so. The dream thus dramatizes Chuck's dreadful, desirable homoerotic urges, his masochism and self-hatred, while still blocking him from hearing and seeing these parts of himself. Hence, his dream is someone else's nightmare. Though the film seeks to drown out these undertones with its heterosexual love story, the dream sequence that takes up a third of the film makes them impossible to ignore. Curiously, Chuck's American dream can be fulfilled only elsewhere—in the dreamscape of Cuba—just as his self-hatred and sexual ambivalence must remain hidden behind a porthole cover. Because Chuck can't remember his dream, he may be doomed to reenact it and forever chase himself.

The filmmakers present the dream as "reality," only to pull the rug out from under us. The Cuban scenes fool us because their heavy romantic music and brooding atmosphere only slightly exaggerate the tone of the rest of the film, as if the dream and waking worlds permeate each other. Indeed, although the ending—with its gushy dialogue and sweeping score—aims to wash away the film's unsettling residues, it seems as unreal as the dream sequence. It is no accident that the lovers speak virtually the same lines, visit the same places, and meet the same characters in the dream and in "reality," for their dream of eternal love is just as false—or true—as Chuck's nightmare. Moreover, the dream sequence alludes to expressionist cinema: not only does it feature the strange characters and impenetrable darkness displayed in those films (some of them the work of Planer); it even gives us Peter Lorre (famous for his role as a child-murderer in Lang's *M*) as a serial killer! The filmmakers suggest, in other words, that Chuck's paranoid dream has been influenced by motion pictures. If a movie can contain a dream, why can't a dream contain a movie? The ending permits the filmmakers to have things both ways: to assert the reality of what we see in Florida, while acknowledging the artificiality of its Hollywood ending. A movie, *The Chase* suggests, is always a dream, a pursuit of chimeras by viewers whose perceptions are being controlled by a Roman (or a German) in the backseat.

The Strange Affair of Uncle Harry, produced by Joan Harrison and directed by Robert Siodmak, uses a similar ploy: a dream that becomes known as such only after the fact. Again a protagonist must decide whether to remain harnessed to the past or start over with a new self (and partner). Harry Quincy (George Sanders) lives in a large house in the small New England village of Corinth with his two sisters, Hester (Moyna MacGill) and Lettie (Geraldine Fitzgerald), the latter a valetudinarian who manipulates her siblings and tortures her sister with catty remarks. Harry seems resigned to this prison until he meets attractive young New Yorker Deborah Brown (Ella Raines) at the textile mill where he works as a designer. He takes her out, but not to the George Washington House (representing the town's stodgy past) recommended by the sisters; instead, they attend a women's softball game. The sporting event typifies Deborah, with her athletic build, mannish suits, and forward manner. Although she spends much of the game with a man named John, afterward she accompanies Harry to his carriage house to gaze through his telescope at Saturn and Venus. The carriage house, open at the top, is Harry's sole domestic retreat in the stifling manse. Shown his paintings, Deborah urges him to "slash it on," to do something stronger than drawing prim rosebuds at the mill. She also offers Harry a revitalized sexual life—an opportunity to investigate the terrain of Venus—though her assertiveness unnerves him.

And not only him: while Hester welcomes this new blood, Lettie feels threatened and tries to drive Deborah away by informing her that Harry "has never grown up" and is easily imposed upon. As if in response, Deborah manipulates Harry into proposing to her by implying that she might accompany John to Europe. But Lettie, who would be displaced from her home by this coupling, is not to be defeated and prolongs the house-hunting process to the point that Deborah is ready to call off the engagement: "Lettie has no intention of giving you up. Not as long as she lives." At last Lettie asks Deborah to postpone the marriage. She refuses, advising Lettie to realize that "Harry is like other men." Lettie answers,

"You may not like the new Harry he becomes. . . . You'll spoil it." Harry, in short, is already married—to Lettie. As the two women argue—Lettie wearing a black-and-white outfit and hat that makes her resemble a stylish nun, Deborah in sleek pants and satin blouse—they are surrounded by drawings of female fashions, suggesting the array of female types from which Harry might choose. Each woman is also vying to create the Harry who might fit her self-image: a mobile, assertive man or a static, celibate mannequin.

When Lettie collapses the day that Harry and Deborah have planned to move to New York, he must choose between the women. Unwilling to leave his ailing sister, he lets Deborah depart (soon afterward, he hears that she has married John). The sisters quarrel bitterly, as Harry, alone in his upstairs room, finds a vial of poison, which Lettie allegedly used as pesticide, and then repairs to his all-male club, where the boys sing and clap each other on the back like super-annuated high-school kids. Although Harry gains some relief here, the scene proves Lettie's point that he has never grown up; indeed, its dull bonhomie seems as imprisoning as his home. At the club the local pharmacist tells Harry that Lettie actually bought the pesticide to kill Weary, their aged dog. Later, back in his observatory, Harry thoughtfully holds the vial, then calls Lettie up to the room. As she approaches in her filmy white gown, she resembles nothing so much as a bride, and what follows amplifies these creepy erotic undertones, as brother and sister reenact the scene between Harry and Deborah. Harry muses, "We are mere drops of nothing compared to a sun which is a hundred million miles from our backyard. So why do we torture ourselves, trying to discover what's good and what's evil, what's right and what's wrong? It's so unimportant." The lines provide a nice rationale for his plan: drop poison into Lettie's hot chocolate.

A tense scene ensues in which Harry and the audience wait for Lettie to drink the poison. She carries two cups—one of them contaminated—upstairs to Hester, then returns. "You need a change," she tells Harry. "We've all been cooped up here too much. . . . Three women in one house. It would strain any man's nerves." It's as if she has suddenly become Deborah. But the sisters are the ones who have changed places, which we grasp when we hear Hester fall to the floor dead, having drunk the poisoned cocoa. Nona, the housekeeper, angrily accuses Lettie of the crime. "You said you wanted to get rid of her and you did." Turning to Harry, Lettie says, "Nona seems to have gone out of her mind." Harry coldly replies, "I wonder if the jury will think so. . . . I'm sorry, Lettie, but that's the way things are."

After Lettie's conviction (thanks to Nona's damning testimony about the sisters' fights), a guilt-ridden Harry confesses to the unbelieving judge. But when Harry asks Lettie to corroborate his story, she serenely refuses. "I wanted to be free, that's all, free," he protests. "Then it's turned out beautifully," she responds, and predicts Harry's horrible future: racked by guilt, he'll be unable to think, sleep, eat, or drink. With a cruel smile on her face, she quotes his own words: "I'm sorry, Harry. But you see, that's the way things are." Surrounded by barred shadows, she walks down the hall to her death. But then a dissolve occurs (Harry, asleep in his chair, is momentarily superimposed over Lettie's deathward walk) and a revelation: the incidents with Lettie in the carriage house, the murder, and the aftermath were all just Harry's dream. Relieved, he disposes of the poison and welcomes back Deborah, who didn't go through with her marriage to John. Hester is also alive, and Harry asks her to deliver this message to Lettie. "Tell her I'm sorry, but that's the way things are."

A caveat appears after the ending: "In order that your friends may enjoy this picture, please do not disclose the ending." The warning makes it seem that the conclusion was planned all along, but in fact, as Alain Silver explains, the picture was previewed in Los Angeles with five different endings "aimed at appeasing the Hays Office." When the dream ending was selected, producer Joan Harrison "quit Universal" ("*Uncle*" 297) in protest. As with Fritz Lang's *Woman in the Window* (discussed in chapter 4), it is hard not to feel cheated by the gimmick, since there is little previous indication that the murder is a dream.[19] Indeed, the ploy seems like a nasty joke on the audience: "see, we can make you believe anything!" But the dream also opens the royal road to Harry's unconscious: it begs us to psychoanalyze him, and what we find is not pretty. As Silver argues, the "most disturbed psyche" is not Lettie's but Harry's, as his dreamed "recourse to an elaborate murder scheme rather than a direct, adult confrontation reinforce[s] the likelihood that his reverie is a manifestation not just of his deep-rooted psychological dependency on his sister but also of profound guilt over his sexual attraction to her" (297–98). Indeed, Harry's dream, like Chuck Scott's, bears out Freud's contention that all dreams are wish-fulfillments by acknowledging his incestuous feelings and implying that he'd rather stay with Lettie than become Deborah's husband. In his dream he gets rid of Deborah and has Lettie kill his other sister so he can have Lettie to himself. Yet his guilt over these wishes compels him to have Lettie executed and then punish himself, less perhaps for the murder than for his failure to live up to socially acceptable standards of masculinity. After all, Harry is much more like Lettie—a hothouse flower, a man who spends his days drawing rosebuds—than like the young, assertive Deborah, whom he fears. Hence, Harry's dream is also someone else's: though it permits him to enact his incestuous and murderous impulses, it prevents him from acknowledging them.

Harry's dream also invokes the question that underpins so many noir dreams: shall I remain tethered to the past or try to remake myself? Ostensibly, the film suggests that Harry must dream through his living death before he can bury his old self like the corpse of poor Weary. As created by German émigré Siodmak (and émigré producer Harrison), the film also hints at the plight of the immigrant who wishes both to retain his or her old culture and to engender a new American self. But does Harry even have a self? As Lettie points out to Deborah, Harry is easy to "impose upon." At the end, then, does he merely allow himself to be imposed upon by Deborah, a strong woman who resembles Lettie? Has he really made a choice, or has he just let someone else choose for him? Like that of *The Chase*, this film's saccharine ending fails to banish a sour aftertaste. It, too, draws attention to its own artifice, asking us to question the dream contrivance, to wonder whether we can ever trust what we see; it reminds us that we, like Harry, prefer dark undertones to sugary main themes.

Double Doors

"That Freud stuff is a lot of hooey!" declares JB (Gregory Peck), an amnesiac in Alfred Hitchcock's *Spellbound*.[20] The rest of the film seems to contradict him. Indeed, the second of its two epigraphs lauds psychoanalysis as, if not a cure for society's ills, at least a reliable means of ensuring civility: "The analyst seeks only to induce the patient to talk about his hidden problems, to open the locked doors of his mind. Once the complexes that have been disturbing the patient are uncovered and interpreted, the illness and confusion disappear . . . and the devils of unreason are driven from the human soul." It's difficult for twenty-first-century viewers not to roll their eyes at this testimony to the wondrous powers of psychoanalysis and at the religious language ("devils of unreason") that presents it as exorcism or conversion (Morris 148).[21] However, the film itself presents psychiatry more ambiguously, as a profession riddled with political infighting and tainted by human foibles. As Freedman notes, *Spellbound* both enhances the patina of psychiatry and pokes fun at it (85).[22] Moreover, its ultimate concern is not so much with opening the mental doors of Peck's tortured amnesiac as with opening the emotional doors of Dr. Constance Petersen (Ingrid Bergman). Far from needing to drive devils of unreason from her soul, the film suggests, she needs to welcome warm emotions into her frozen heart. For while Dr. Petersen acts as psychiatrist/detective for much of the film, she is also partly constituted, observes Mary Ann Doane, as the film's analysand (*Desire* 46)—the character who achieves a fuller selfhood through the therapeutic process.[23]

Early in the film she is contrasted with patient Mary Carmichael (Rhonda Fleming), a sexually aggressive woman who hates Constance, whom she calls "Miss Frozen Puss." Those sentiments are echoed by her leering colleague, Dr. Fleurot (John Emery); indeed, the entire Green Manors medical staff act like fraternity brothers, constantly gossiping about their only female colleague and vying for dominance. This situation is supposed to change now that Constance's mentor, Dr. Murchison (Leo G. Carroll), is being replaced by Dr. Edwardes, acclaimed author of *Labyrinth of the Guilt Complex*. However, when Edwardes (Peck) shows up, his initial contribution is instead to light a spark in Constance. But something is wrong: when she traces lines on a tablecloth with her fork (Constance is constantly associated with sharp objects, as if psychoanalysis were a form of cutting), Edwardes becomes agitated and disoriented.

That evening, after the two have shared a picnic lunch, she can't sleep. Walking upstairs (she is also associated with upward movements throughout the film), she takes his book from the library and enters his office. Hitchcock organizes the following sequence around a series of doorframe shots. First Constance stands in the threshold and then sees Edwardes nodding in his chair. From behind him we watch her hesitantly ask to discuss his book, then sheepishly admit that this is only a "subterfuge." Approaching her, but framed in the doorway from her point of view, Edwardes declares that "something has happened to us . . . like lightning striking," and crosses the threshold. A series of close-ups focuses on the two characters' eyes to imply that his vision pierces and thaws her. As the music swells, a shot of Constance's eyes dissolves to four doors successively opening onto bright light. The scene ends with the two passionately kissing. Clearly these are Petersen's doors opening, not Edwardes's: their vaginal associations are not exactly subtle. Yet what she thinks she sees—Dr. Edwardes—is false, and, almost until the moment of the climactic kiss, Peck remains framed in the doorway, as if coffined—appropriately, since the real Dr. Edwardes is dead. As we soon learn, this man is an impostor who hides a debilitating guilt complex of his own.

The blissful moment ends when "Edwardes" recoils at the sight of Constance's striped robe; then he experiences a breakdown at the operating table ("Doors. Unlock 'em. You can't keep people in cells! . . . He did it, he told me! He killed his father!"). When he signs his name, Constance sees that his signature does not match that of the real Edwardes (who had signed her book). These lines scratched on paper, indicating his true self, rhyme with the vertical lines that prompt his flashbacks: a mental line connects them. Soon the fake Edwardes admits to killing the real Edwardes and adds, "I'm someone else. I don't know who. . . . I have no memory. It's like looking into a mirror and seeing nothing but the mirror." The vision that seemed so penetrating when gazing at Constance becomes opaque when it comes to seeing himself. Murchison verifies that the man is an impostor by examining a photograph of the real Edwardes: vision may ratify truth or be manipulated by unconscious wishes or master technicians like psychiatrists or directors.

"Edwardes" (who recalls only that his actual initials are "JB") leaves for New York to find himself; Constance follows, aided by a hotel detective who assumes she is a librarian or schoolteacher looking for her husband. (A bit later, JB also compares her to a "smug, know-it-all schoolteacher.") The detective boasts that he knows such things because he's a "psychologist . . . you gotta be, in my line." If a detective has gotta be a psychologist, the rest of the film demonstrates that a psychologist has gotta be a detective too: Constance locates JB by examining his handwriting in the hotel register (he signed his name "John Brown"). "Brown" admits, "I'm haunted, but I can't see by what." JB, that is, can't forget what he is unable to remember. When she advises him that a "guilt complex" "speaks for" him, he responds that she is crazier than he is, having "run off with a pair of initials": she has fallen for an outline, a person whose identity is both hidden and disclosed by lines scratched on a surface.

Hoping to learn more, the lovers travel to the home of Constance's mentor, Dr. Brulov (charmingly portrayed by Michael Chekhov), posing as honeymooners. On the journey JB again grows angry when she presses him about his guilt fantasy, railing against her "double-talk." But it's really JB, the man who impersonated Edwardes, who signed his name "John Brown," and, when he gazes into a mirror, sees only the mirror, who is composed of double-talk. He is a double inside a mirror locked behind a door. Earlier he had described amnesia as the placing of whatever horrible thing you don't want to remember "behind a closed door." Constance remarks, "We have to open that door." In so doing, she also opens doors to aspects of herself—teacher, detective, mother, lover, newlywed—that have been shut: her identity is far from constant. Both characters, in short, pass through a succession of identities, a series of doors, on the road to self-discovery or self-creation.

That evening JB proves his doubleness by becoming disoriented and agitated at the sight of a chair and bathtub, and especially by the vertical lines on Constance's chenille bedspread. Zombielike, he walks downstairs with his razor (JB is associated with downward movements throughout the film), but Dr. Brulov soothes him with twin bromides—a sedative paired with platitudes about milk-drinking (Pomerance 89). The next morning, Brulov warns Constance that her lover is dangerous—"a schizophrenic, and not a valentine"—but she insists that "the heart can see deeper sometimes" than the brain, that vision may penetrate the surface only if it is not merely scientific scrutiny. She is indeed emulating JB, who had earlier intimated that he could see her heart (romance here becomes a kind of countertransference). Despite JB's resistance ("That Freud stuff's a lot of hooey!"), Brulov becomes JB's "father image," encouraging transference to jog his memory and discover the source of his trauma. The secrets to JB's nature, he explains, are "buried in your brain." The key to unlocking this buried treasure? Dreams, which "tell you what you are trying to hide. But they tell it to you all mixed up, like pieces of a puzzle that don't fit. The problem of the analyst is to examine this puzzle, and put the pieces together in the right place, and find out what the devil you are trying to say to yourself."

What follows is one of the most famous dream sequences in Hollywood cinema. Though JB narrates the dream himself, it is, again, presented as someone else's—first filtered through his narration, then illustrated by Hitchcock, with the help of Salvador Dalí. In Freudian terms the dream registers the conflict of rival selves—the narrating JB set against that ghostwriter, his own unconscious. And because JB doesn't know his real identity, the dream is doubly removed even from his narrative presence, for the experience motivating the dream happened to the person he used to be, known now only as a "pair of initials." Further, once Brulov and Petersen interpret the dream material, it is abstracted, dissected, and held out for the audience's speculation: it becomes not his but *our* nightmare.

Fittingly, the dream begins with an array of disembodied, peering eyes—on the draperies, says JB, of a gambling house. A man with a large pair of scissors cuts through the draperies (an apparent allusion to the early Dalí/Bunuel film *Un chien andalou*), and then a scantily clad woman (who looks "very much like Constance" and is played by Rhonda Fleming, who earlier performed as Mary Carmichael) walks around kissing everyone. The narrator is found playing cards (most of them blank) with a bearded man, and when he overturns a seven of clubs, the man says "that makes twenty-one. I win." Enter the angry proprietor, his face masked, to accuse them of cheating. The next portion is a different but related dream. The bearded man falls from the roof of a tall building. To the rear, the masked proprietor hides behind a chimney, holding a small, malformed wheel,

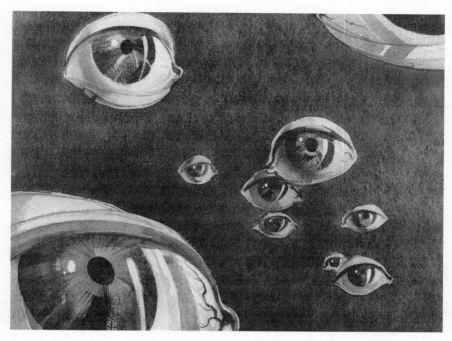

The dream sequence in *Spellbound* features an array of disembodied eyes. *Kobal Collection / Art Resource, NY.*

which he then drops. It ends with the dreamer being chased down a hill by a "great pair of wings."[24]

The first portion of the dream goes unanalyzed until the end of the film. But the second portion immediately leads somewhere, as Constance maps this nightmare alley, miraculously connecting the sled marks on the street outdoors to the vertical lines that have bothered the amnesiac. They must be a memory of ski tracks, she deduces, and by word association the three determine that the dream refers to Gabriel Valley ski resort (wings = angel = Gabriel). Amazingly skilled rhetoricians, these doctors sense that JB's dream images operate by metonymy and synecdoche—one of the two "main dream processes," according to Bert States (94)—which enable the dreamer to replace the source events with associated images. For some reason they decide that only reenactment can "break the spell" of JB's childhood trauma (and may solve the mystery of the ski marks as well). So Constance and JB travel to the resort and go skiing. Just as they are about to swoosh off the cliff, JB remembers: "I killed my brother!" Cut to the face of a grimacing boy, mutely warning another child to be careful; we then inhabit JB's point of view as he slides down a railing, sweeping his brother onto the prongs of an iron fence. The truth emerges: "I didn't kill my brother. It was an accident!" It's hard to say how he knows it was an accident since the memory says nothing about his motives. Nevertheless, he is liberated by the recollection.

The past comes flooding back: his name is John Ballantine; he ran into Edwardes at the resort while recovering from "nerve shock" due to his war experiences and saw Edwardes die in a skiing accident. Constance explains that he took on Edwardes's identity to prove to himself that the doctor wasn't dead and hence that he couldn't have killed him. Swift, accurate dream reading, cathartic cure: it's all too pat.[25] As Jerrold Brandell observes, the film permits only one correct interpretation, which explains not only the "distal causes and pathogenesis" of Ballantine's disorder but also the particular form it takes ("Eighty" 66). Yet the dream also invokes a theme that reverberates throughout Hitchcock's oeuvre and the noir canon: a "wounded past envies the present and prevents its rejuvenation" (Brill 240).[26] It also exemplifies the pattern I have been investigating: like Al Walker, Paul Cartwright, and Andy La Main, Ballantine is debilitated by his attachment to a traumatic past event. In breaking the chain through dream interpretation, he may be free to reinvent himself.

Or maybe not. Hitchcock dissolves over the lovers' triumphant embrace a police report stating, "new evidence uncovered. Makes surveillance essential." The phrases hint that psychoanalytic surveillance has uncovered new evidence freeing JB and that he has exercised loving "surveillance" over Constance to unearth the warmth beneath her icy exterior. In terms of the plot, however, the lines mean that the police have found a bullet in Edwardes's body, which proves that he was murdered. A brisk montage covers Ballantine's arrest and jailing; those newly opened doors seem permanently closed once again. Constance's colleagues urge her to forget it all and bury herself in work. But she is not satisfied, and her suspicions are further aroused when Murchison offhandedly mentions that he "knew Edwardes." The words echo in her mind as she stands in a Green Manors doorway, for if Murchison knew him, why didn't he recognize Ballantine as an impostor? Again she walks upstairs to confront a colleague, but this time it's Murchison. When she asks him to analyze Ballantine's dream, Murchison's self-protective instincts collide with his scientific curiosity. The latter wins, as he unpacks the very dream images that incriminate him: the gambling house is Green Manors, and Murchison is himself the proprietor, angry at the bearded man (Edwardes) for taking his job. The dream exposes Green Manors as a hotbed of professional jealousy and sexual rivalry, a gambling club where practitioners employ a mix of gamesmanship and guesswork. The seven of clubs leads (through condensation, or metonymy) to the 21 Club in New York, where Murchison angrily confronted Edwardes. The wheel? A revolver (synecdoche)—which Murchison now points at Constance. We shift to Murchison's point of view behind the gun as Constance, softly talking, walks out the door. Then he turns the gun on himself and shoots—us.

In a sense Murchison has already turned the gun on himself by analyzing Ballantine's dream. Indeed, whereas in JB's dream the eyes are snipped, the rest of the film depicts the psychoanalytic eye as a cutting weapon capable equally of salvation or soul murder. Just as the old Ballantine and the phony Edwardes (not to mention John Brown) died because of psychiatric scrutiny, so Murchison kills himself by reading a dream through Ballantine's eyes. He is thus exposed as Ballantine's double—an impostor, both doctor and psychopath, an amnesiac who has "forgotten" a crime he committed. In this final turn psychoanalysis is at once glorified and debased, presented as a partial solution to its own murderous tendencies (Freedman 86). The final point-of-view shot also implicates the viewer in this analytic scrutiny. In the course of the film we have been both psychoanalyst and patient, experiencing Ballantine's dreams and participating in their analysis. Thus, in a sense we are as guilty (or innocent) as JB or Murchison—guilty of using our eyes to cut people up, guilty of blaming and of loving them. Someone else's nightmare is now our own. To be cured of our neurosis and our complicity in such murderous gazing, we too must be killed. Ultimately, then, the revolver—through the metonymy of dream logic—becomes the camera, a small wheel held by a man whose eye exposes our hidden desires.

This final turn further complicates the motif of self-creation, for the eye can save as well as shoot. Constance's eye imagined a new self for JB, one that, as Marlisa Santos explains, is neither the old Ballantine nor his blank double but a "'third self'—the product of the unity of his blank self and his phantom 'other'" (xxii). Perhaps it would be more accurate to call this a fourth or even a fifth self, one conjured out of the combination of Ballantine, Edwardes, and the selves exposed in his dream. Further, in reading Ballantine's dream, Constance reads herself, for Ballantine saw—and created—a different Constance. Brill thus concludes that at the end "Constance and John at once remember and learn who they are" (256). Or perhaps, as Thomas Hyde determines, she forges a new identity by "tapping a suppressed capacity within herself for feeling and committed action" (154).

The word *forge* points to conflicting possibilities, one of which is that, by assuming a series of roles, Constance learns that the life she has been living is an impersonation (see Morris 150). Like Ballantine and Murchison, she kills herself by using her eyes, and now she will be reborn as someone else: Mrs. Ballantine.[27] But if her emotions led her to believe in Ballantine, it was her intelligence that let her see through Murchison's lies and trap him into self-incrimination. Like JB, she ultimately becomes neither her original self nor her second (the lover) but a unique entity melding disparate elements.

Perchance to Dream

What dreams may come to noir characters? We have examined three major types: (1) trauma rendered into recurrent nightmares, as in *The Dark Past* and *Spellbound*. In them the dreamer is victimized by a double bind—desiring to forget what he can't quite remember; (2) a forecast or message from beyond, as in *Strange Illusion*, where the dream becomes the apparition of a dead patriarch, urging the son to act for and transcend his father. *The Big Night*, though its nightmare is implicit rather than explicit, also fits this category, as George becomes at once his father's agent and his rival; and (3) a warning coupled with a wish-fulfillment, as in *The Chase* and *The Strange Affair of Uncle Harry*, where dreams dramatize alternate futures in which a character's unconscious wishes come true—and, somewhat disturbingly, enable him to repress them again.

We may further distill these categories by analyzing the dreams' tropic arrangements and emotional content. According to the psychiatrist Ernest Hartmann, who has published extensively on dreams, the most significant element in any dream is not its specific imagery but its dominant emotion, which induces the dreamer to combine images and associations from various parts of the brain to create explanatory tropes (Hartmann 4, 119). In other words, what matters is less the vehicle of the metaphor than the tenor it aims to convey. With that in mind let us review the dominant emotions in these noir dreams:

The Dark Past: terror, hatred
Strange Illusion: fear, jealousy
The Big Night: hatred, envy
The Chase: self-hatred, illicit sexual desire
The Strange Affair of Uncle Harry: jealousy, illicit sexual desire
Spellbound: guilt

Guilt, in fact, motivates each of these dreams: it is the definitive noir dream tenor. And what is guilt but an attachment to a past action that prompts a need to relive it and make it right? Guilt leaves noir dreamers cowering under a table, trapped in a stifling house, steering a car that someone else is driving, or forever skiing down an endless slope. How to escape from these nightmare alleys? By re-enacting the event and then forgetting it. Yet if these noir dreams imply that the American Dream of self-reinvention is possible, they also leave a residue of doubt. For example, the surreal quality of *The Chase*'s conclusion raises questions about the durability of Chuck's new self; *Uncle Harry*'s ending fails to erase the disturbing aspects of the protagonist's psyche that his dream has unveiled. In reminding us of their own constructedness, these two films alert us to the artificiality of their happy conclusions. Similarly, *Spellbound*'s love story is acceptable only if we agree that women are better off as lovers than as doctors, and *The Big Night* furnishes a dubiously sacrificial, even masochistic, image of manhood. Only *Strange Illusion* and *The Dark Past* offer relatively straightforward endorsements of self-reinvention, and they suggest that looking backward is valuable insofar as doing so frees one from the past. The self, newly cleansed by psychotherapy or the power of love, may be infinitely renewable, but only if its eyes are at least half closed.

Missing Persons
Self-Erasure and Reinvention

Mr. Flitcraft of Tacoma is blessed with a wife, two children, a successful real estate business, and the "rest of the appurtenances of successful American living" (Hammett 442), including a golf game at four o'clock each afternoon. Then one day a beam falls from a high building, barely missing him; that day he leaves Tacoma without telling anyone, wanders for a few years, and ends up in Spokane. There, as Charles Pierce, he marries, has a child, owns a prosperous automobile business, and gets away for a four o'clock golf game almost every afternoon.

Private investigator Sam Spade tells this story to an unimpressed Brigid O'Shaughnessy in Dashiell Hammett's novel *The Maltese Falcon*. Neither Spade nor Hammett explains this curious, meditative digression in an otherwise fast-paced tale. Spade does, however, delve briefly into Flitcraft's motives. After the beam falls, Spade says, Flitcraft feels "like somebody had taken the lid off life and let him look at the works" (444). He had believed life to be a "clean orderly sane responsible affair," but the falling beam had shown him it was none of those things. This good citizen-husband-father could be wiped out between office and restaurant by a simple accident. Neither orderly nor sane, human life is but a collection of random occurrences governed—or not governed—by luck. He was out of step with the workings of the world; to bring himself in step, "he would change his life at random by simply going away" (444). But the most interesting part to me (and, I think, to Spade) is that Flitcraft reconstitutes the life he had left: "He adjusted himself to beams falling, and then no more of them fell, and he adjusted himself to them not falling" (445).

Although John Huston's film adaptation omits this vignette, it nonetheless introduces a major theme of film noir: that of an absurd cosmos ruled by unseen forces that limit human agency. You cope best by forgetting its absurdity, but you must remain alert, for a beam could fall on you at any moment. Foster Hirsch reads the episode as a coded defense of Spade's philosophy, linking it with the detective's later assertion that "when a man's partner is killed, he's supposed to do something about it" (581–82); Hirsch writes, "In the face of uncertainty and duplicity, Sam Spade retains his honor" (31). I wish to use a different reading of this story as the keynote for this chapter.

Everyone in Hammett's novel pretends to be someone else: Brigid first gives her name as Miss Wonderly, then fakes love for Sam, then plays both ends against the middle; Gutman swears that he loves Wilmer, his gunman, like his own son, but barely hesitates to set him up as the fall guy when their plan to take the falcon fails; even Spade feigns anger when he doesn't feel it. In *The Maltese Falcon* identity seems fluid, as fungible as the falcon, which inspires each character's dreams (it's "the stuff that dreams are made of," according to Spade's memorable final line in the film version). But near the end of the novel—just after the line that Hirsch quotes—Spade explains why Brigid must pay for murdering his partner, Miles Archer: "I'm a detective and expecting me to run criminals down and then let them go free is like asking a dog to catch a rabbit and let it go. It can be done, . . . but it's not the natural thing" (582). Similarly, Flitcraft starts a new life that ends up identical to the one he abandoned. The novel and vignette thus reiterate the Emersonian tenet that one cannot change his or her nature: I may travel to Spokane, but when I wake up, "there beside me is the stern fact, the sad self, unrelenting, identical, that I fled from" (Emerson 48). If you're a detective, you're one forever; if you're a businessman, changing your name, spouse, and job won't make you an adventurer.

As I pointed out in my introduction, this view contradicts the Franklinesque faith that self-invention is not only possible but desirable. If, as Cullen observes, the "cornerstone" of the American Dream is that "things . . . could be different" (15), those "things" begin with the self. Americans have always been a restless, mobile people, and the years after the war accelerated that movement. The 1950 census, for example, shows that more than 2.6 percent of the population had moved to another state in the previous year; if this rate was consistent for a decade, more than one-fourth of the American populace had moved between states in the 1940s (1950 census; Table 4B, 13; the rates are higher for men and women under thirty years old). Moving to another state means leaving behind jobs, loved ones, friends—most of the communal ties that define one's social self. It also means beginning anew—perhaps even becoming someone else.

We have seen how fantasies of self-reinvention pervade noir dreams. A second group of noirs, involving mistaken or switched identity, often accompanied by amnesia, also stage narratives of conversion that parallel the Protestant redemption story and invoke—only to challenge—the Franklinesque ethos of self-renewal.

The protagonists of *Street of Chance, My Name Is Julia Ross, No Man of Her Own, Dark Passage,* and *Hollow Triumph*—and those of the more celebrated films *The Killers* and *Out of the Past*—are faced with, or forced into, changing identities. In so doing they enact a prototypical American story: that of the immigrant or internal exile.[1] These mistaken-identity films present an alternate life—whether as service station owner Jeff Bailey, shady Danny Nearing, psychiatrist Victor Bartok, or a wealthy heiress named Patrice—as a chance to enact unconscious urges, discover hidden desires, cross class boundaries, or erase a mistake. Yet what often results (sometimes in spite of the narratives' manifest content) is the bad dream of American optimists: the persistence of the past or even the total loss of selfhood. These films thus expose flaws in the ideology of individualism, reminding us that an autonomous self is often an alienated self—perhaps so alienated that the self may be rendered unrecognizable. In other instances the story's outcome illuminates the theme of the Flitcraft episode: that the more one alters the trappings of identity, the more one's inner self is revealed and, paradoxically, the more inauthentic that original self seems. These movies offer a pointed critique of American values by suggesting that individualism, faith in the pursuit of happiness, and self-creation actually foster isolation. In these pictures the community that might mitigate this isolation exists only as a distant promise.

Like the noir dream films, the mistaken-identity movies question the cinematic medium. In one sense the geographically and socially mobile audiences watching these characters shift shapes may have felt they were seeing themselves as in a mirror. But those mirror images may also have raised as many questions as they answered. For if the dream films at once affirm and challenge movies' status as authentic representations of our inner and outer worlds, the switched-identity films are more radical, suggesting that there may be little or no correspondence between inside and outside, image and inner reality, or, conversely, that the outside is the *only* reality. They leave us with two extremes, each one untenable: that one's essence remains unchangeable, one's past sins inescapable, or that the self is but a series of performances, a process in constant flux with no center at all. If the latter is true, then identity is something that neither photos nor movies nor writing can ever capture.

We Move Anything

Walking past a sign with these words (the slogan of Empire House Wrecking) one day, a man (Burgess Meredith) is hit by a chunk of falling plaster. He is shaken but unhurt—except that he doesn't recall why he is on this street or where he has been. He does know that his name is Frank Thompson. So why do his hat and cigarette case bear the monogram "D. N."? When he goes home, he learns that his wife has moved away, although he believes he saw her that morning. And when he finds her living under her maiden name elsewhere, she tells him he disappeared over a year ago.

This echo of the Flitcraft episode opens Jack Hively's early noir, *Street of Chance*—the first of many noir adaptations of Cornell Woolrich novels—and serves as prelude for the missing-person noirs that follow it. "It doesn't make sense," Frank tells his wife. "It's like a bad dream." But once he returns to his office job with the excuse that he had a nervous breakdown, we may wonder which life is the bad dream. The enormous room behind his office window, presaging the hive-like, identical cubicles in Billy Wilder's *The Apartment,* similarly implies that Thompson is a worker bee. Perhaps he hated this humdrum life and longed to pursue happiness as someone else.

Not only does this missing year remain an abyss at the center of his memory; he is also being pursued by a mysterious man (Sheldon Leonard) and has no inkling why. Revisiting the streets around the accident site, Frank encounters Ruth Dillon (Claire Trevor). Though he doesn't remember meeting her, she knows him, insists his name is Danny Nearing, and chides him for disappearing, worrying that "all our plans, all our dreams, gone." He soon learns that Nearing is wanted for the murder of a wealthy man named Diedrich and that the man stalking him is police detective Joe Marucci. Although Ruth is noncommittal about whether Danny is guilty of the murder (Alma, the dead man's wife, and Bill, his brother and Alma's lover, seem more likely suspects), she vows to protect him. At one point during their discussion Frank/Danny stares at himself in the mirror, as if to acknowledge that he possesses two selves, straight businessman and shady character. Yet he avers to Ruth that "the me that's inside wouldn't let me kill anyone"—that his Emersonian "aboriginal" self is good. But since he doesn't know who Nearing is, what he has promised or done, how can he be sure?

To find out the truth, Frank/Danny returns to the Diedrich house, where he meets Grandma Diedrich (Adeline De Walt Reynolds), an invalid who can neither move nor speak. In a compelling scene, they devise a means for her to communicate through eye blinks (once for yes, twice for no). This curious encounter is a meeting of doubles: the woman who can't speak addresses the man who can't remember—missing body meets missing mind. As Marlisa Santos remarks, her "mute and paralyzed state" signifies "Thompson's inability to prove his innocence or identity" (90). It's as if Frank is attempting to gain access to his own absent memory through her. And her eyes—which compensate for Frank's/Danny's blindness to his own motives and emotions—are also a gateway to truth, since she witnessed the murder. The next day he induces Grandma to spell out words letter by letter, but she resists telling him about the murder because she is "a-f-r-a-i-d." That night he tries to learn more, and she quickly eliminates Bill and Alma. Who could it be, then? The answer enters the room: Ruth, whom Grandma saw stab Diedrich via a reflection in the bedroom mirror. This image is fitting, for Frank has become Grandma's mirror, itself an element in the looking-glass world where he is Danny Nearing.

Claiming she committed the murder "for us," Ruth begs him to flee with her. He refuses: "I don't love you. I've only known you two days. I'm not the man you think I am. . . . My name is Frank Thompson, and I'm married." As she prepares to shoot Frank, Marucci enters and guns her down; dying, she admits that "Danny" is innocent. But is he? Why did he drop out of his life as Frank Thompson to become a feckless character consorting with a murderous maid? Was he, as I speculated above, sick to death of his life as the staid Mr. Thompson? Or did he, like Flitcraft, somehow glimpse the randomness of existence and suddenly decide to live "in step" with its absurdity? We never find out. Although Frank asserts that the "me inside" isn't a killer, he already "killed" Frank Thompson once, just as he now puts Danny Nearing to rest: if not a murderer, he is at least a kind of suicide. Ironically, he reinhabits his old self only through the ministrations of Nearing, who is then sacrificed for his troubles. One set of past attachments is severed so that he can take up another set. Was his life as Nearing a "journey into his own unconscious, a dream-world" (98), as Santos suggests? Or is Nearing his aboriginal self, the identity he so yearned to occupy that he was willing to give up everything for it? Will he do so again? Even at the conclusion Frank Thompson remains a partial person, as disabled in his own way as Grandma Diedrich—and far less honest.

"I Did Something Wrong—Once"

As haltingly spoken by "The Swede," also known as Pete Lund (Burt Lancaster), these words reverberate throughout Robert Siodmak's brilliant *The Killers*. They are the Swede's only explanation for why he waits passively in his room for two thugs to execute him. He is not merely resigned to his fate; he believes he deserves it. Why? That question motivates Jim Reardon (Edmond O'Brien), an insurance investigator whose interviews with Lund's acquaintances compose most of the film. This narrative structure (borrowed, perhaps, from *Citizen Kane*) pushes the signature noir flashback device nearly to its limit, splintering the narration into eleven dramatized narrations by eight characters, each one supplying a different memory of the Swede, whose real name was Ole Anderson. A different character for each narrator—reliable gas station attendant, suicidal hotel guest, boxer and childhood buddy, mooning lover, intimate cellmate, double-crossing rat—Ole is at once mysterious and simple. Many flashbacks begin or end with lap dissolves from the narrator's present face to his or her face at the time of the action, indicating that each tale is less about Ole than about the teller's own fears and aspirations (and excuses for not helping him): Ole is a mirror. At other moments narrators' faces dissolve to Reardon's, implying that in listening he "becomes" each one—on his way to "becoming" the Swede.

Ole's haunting words testify that he can't outrun his original self or forgive his original sin. They also suggest, as Shadoian remarks, that he was already "dead while he was alive" (81). Indeed, as he lies waiting for the killers, Ole's face is engulfed in shadow: he is literally effaced, just as he has effaced himself by changing his name to hide from the gang of Jim Colfax (Albert Dekker), whom he betrayed after they robbed a hat factory of its payroll. His initial erasure is revealed in an early flashback by his childhood friend, police lieutenant Sam Lubinsky (Sam Levene), who recalls how, after the Swede broke his right hand in a boxing match, he became a worthless commodity to his trainer and manager. As Ole showers behind the pair, they discuss his replacement. Cinematographer Woody Bredell's use of deep focus is telling: the washed up Ole literally recedes into the background. Similar compositions characterize many shots in the flashbacks, as Swede is consistently crammed into the corner or overshadowed by others. Likewise, as the backlit Ole strides down an archway after refusing Sam's offer to become a cop, Siodmak implies that he is already enclosed by fate.

Indeed, Ole is rarely the primary agent in his own story, and when he is, he makes foolish decisions, such as pursuing Kitty Collins (Ava Gardner)—even going to jail for her—instead of staying with the stable Lily (Virginia Christine), and then becoming involved in the hat factory heist instead of emulating his mentor, Charleston (Vince Barnett), who finds the job too risky. The first time Ole sees Kitty, in fact, Siodmak renders his infatuation almost comically, by placing a brightly lit phallic bulb between him and the singing siren. Ole can't take his eyes off her, but another organ motivates him even more powerfully. The Swede isn't very bright; but more than that, as the structure implies, he is a secondary character in his own life.

In *The Killers*, Ole Anderson (Burt Lancaster) falls in love with Kitty Collins (Ava Gardner) at first sight. *Kobal Collection / Art Resource, NY.*

Charleston, his former cellmate, remembers him fondly. In fact, Charleston was in love with Ole and spent long evenings in prison teaching him about astronomy and advising him that women, whom he's "studied up on" when not in stir, aren't reliable. But Ole doesn't listen and continues to stroke the green, harp-covered handkerchief that Kitty gave him—the fetishized "symbol of [his] dreams" (Shadoian 84). This handkerchief becomes Reardon's fetish as well, as he carries it with him throughout the investigation. This totem raises the question of why Reardon becomes obsessed with the murder of a man he calls a "nobody." There's very little in it for the insurance company: the $2,500 death benefit Swede left to the hotel maid is not worth Reardon's time; the money from the heist will merely become part of next year's rate adjustment (while his boss relays this fact, Reardon plays with Kitty's handkerchief).

One answer is that Reardon is an investigator by nature. Like Sam Spade, he delights in the thrill of the hunt; he's a hound for truth and believes there is such a thing. But another, more complex, answer speaks to the theme of self-reinvention. We know nothing about Reardon before the pursuit begins: in contrast to Anderson, who exists only as a collection of others' memories, Reardon has "no past" (Shadoian 83). The more absorbed he becomes in Ole's life, the more like Ole and his underworld associates he grows: his first interviews are with law-abiding folk, but his later interviews are with Charleston, Blinky Franklin, Dum Dum (Jack Lambert), Colfax, and Kitty—criminals, every one. Indeed, partway through his investigation Reardon occupies the same room in Brentwood where Ole was killed—ostensibly to catch Dum Dum but also to reenact the death scene. The mise-en-scène here even repeats the shadowy atmosphere of that sequence, as Reardon, a novice at the detective game, waits for Dum Dum. But this time Reardon holds the gun: he has become "the killer." He even lets Dum Dum believe that he wants the money for himself. In short, just as the opening scene's killers parrot the tough-guy lingo of 1930s gangster movies (as in the Hemingway short story on which the film is loosely based), so Reardon now plays at being a movie thug. But not very successfully: Dum Dum easily takes the gun away and subdues him.

Reardon is clearly fascinated by these crooked characters and gets a thrill from associating with them; he "fills his emptiness with a vicarious dream" (Shadoian 84). This adventure gives him a chance to inhabit a much more exciting world than the bland offices where he spends his days as a functionary. In some respects he even resembles Anderson: if Ole is an unwitting victim of others' machinations, Reardon is subject to the cold realities of the actuarial tables. Like Ole, Reardon is a secondary character in his own life. Late in the film, at the conclusion of Reardon's chat with Colfax, the now-legit gangster's face dissolves to Reardon's: the point is that he wants to *be* Colfax, which becomes even clearer in the justly famous Green Cat sequence.[2] As Reardon and Kitty converse there, a candle rests between them, recalling the phallic bulb shining between Kitty and Swede at *their* first meeting; Reardon too is falling for her. "I'd like to have known the old Kitty Collins," he declares, even after she has just told him how she betrayed Swede! When she suggests returning to his hotel with him, his eyes light up at this apparent sexual come-on. But she does to him what she did to Ole—"takes a powder," as Reardon earlier put it. It's almost as though Reardon wants to be killed, or perhaps, like Ole, he feels dead, with only the prospect of violence capable of reviving him.

Though the convoluted story of how Ole was betrayed and disappeared—a skein of double crosses engineered by Colfax, using Kitty as bait—is finally explained, Ole's true nature is not. Just as he exists for us only as a set of fragments, so he was even for himself a puzzle with pieces missing, a collection of half-understood dreams and impulses organized around a handkerchief. At the end he remains, like Frank Thompson, broken into parts, as the coroner's early description of his demise implies: the slugs "near tore him in half." Perhaps Reardon believes he can be the glue holding Ole together. But what holds Reardon together? Clearly he and the Swede are doubles, or halves of a single self. Whereas Ole could never escape his past, Reardon acquires one by sifting through Anderson's. Their mirrored trajectories imply that self-integration, let alone self-renewal, can be for him only fleeting or imaginary. Hence, at the film's end Reardon is informed that the investigation that nearly cost him his life will merely generate a minuscule difference in next year's rates. He hasn't become a gangster, boxer, cop, or lover; come Monday, he'll be back to work as a cipher. Similarly, the film's structure draws the viewer's attention to its own artful construction, reminding us that "Ole" (like the other characters, but more so) exists only as a piecemeal concoction of "cuts": *we* put him together, living, like Reardon, vicariously but fleetingly through his exploits.

Jeff Markham (Robert Mitchum), the protagonist of Jacques Tourneur's justly celebrated *Out of the Past,* also tries to reinvent himself (in an odd coincidence that recurs several times in noir) as a gas station owner. He has changed his name to Bailey and started a new life in the small town of Bridgeport. Whereas once he engineered glamorous escapades in Acapulco and San Francisco with a beautiful, dangerous woman, he now seeks to satisfy himself as a modest businessman catering to the mobile lives of others. But his masquerade unravels when an old associate, Joe Stefanos (Paul Valentine), shows up in his convertible and undoes Jeff's conversion. Jeff, too, did something wrong once: not only did he fail to fetch Kathie Moffat (Jane Greer), the girlfriend of gambler Whit Sterling (Kirk Douglas), as he was paid to do; he ran off with her and then stood by as she murdered his partner, Jack Fisher (Steve Brodie). Lacking Sam Spade's rigorous ethics ("when a man's partner is killed, he's supposed to do something about it"), he has never paid for either error. From the beginning Markham is self-divided, and when he becomes Bailey, he brings his dual nature with him. Thus, although Jeff does a lot of moving in the film, his identity isn't really mobile: he can't reinvent himself because he doesn't really want to.[3]

To illustrate Jeff's cloven self, the film contains numerous symmetries and doublings. First and foremost are the settings: on the one hand is bucolic Bridgeport and environs, on the other the corrupt cities where shady business transpires. Tahoe, where Whit maintains a house, lies between the two, and provides the setting for many of Jeff's pivotal decisions. The early scenes in Bridgeport use horizontal lines, whereas the city scenes emphasize verticality. In bright, sunny Bridgeport everybody dresses casually (and the night scenes are shot day for night); the city scenes take place after dark (are shot night for night), and people dress more formally. Thus, when Stefanos first appears in Bridgeport, he looks ludicrously out of place in his dark suit and trench coat (and even more so later when he hunts Jeff in the woods, wearing the same getup). When Jeff obeys Whit's summons and drives to Tahoe (during which he reveals his past to his girlfriend, Ann), he dons his old trench coat and fedora. Ann (Virginia Huston) and Kathie reflect the same duality: the nice, trusting small-town girl versus one of noir's most dangerous, duplicitous, and bewitching dames. For each woman Jeff vies with another man: Jim (Richard Webb), a dull government employee, is in love with Ann (but she doesn't love him, being more intrigued by "the mysterious Jeff Bailey"); Whit, the corrupt gambler, loves Kathie. If Jim is the man Jeff is trying to become, Whit is closer to his aboriginal self. Indeed, Jeff and Whit are doubles, as both are in love with Kathie, and Jeff initially acts as Whit's proxy.[4]

Jeff's wishful identity is embodied by his protégé in Bridgeport, a young, un-named deaf boy (Dickie Moore) who works at his gas station (and who also drives a convertible, representing Jeff's hoped-for conversion). Having remained mute about his past, Jeff has rendered others deaf to his motives and actions: he never told Whit about running off with Kathie, and he never came clean about his com-plicity in the death of his partner. The motif of hearing permeates the film. For example, when Stefanos first arrives in Bridgeport and enters Marny's Cafe, she insinuates that Jeff and Ann are lovers: "I just see what I see." Jim replies, "Are you sure you don't see what you hear?" She later tells Stefanos, "Seems like everything people ought to know, they just don't want to hear." Later Whit asks Jeff, "Can you still listen?" Jeff answers, "I can hear." But he can't hear Whit's real motives—or his own. If Jeff first acts as Whit's surrogate, the deaf boy later acts as Jeff's, using his fishing rod to pull Stefanos from a cliff to his death, and at the end allowing Ann to believe that Jeff was in love with Kathie, so as to free her to marry Jim.[5]

Jeff does tell the truth—or what he believes to be the truth—to Ann during the drive to Tahoe: that he aims to square things with Whit, pay for doing some-thing wrong once, and dismiss Markham forever. But not only is Whit setting him up as a fall guy; Kathie is manipulating both men for her own ends. Indeed, she is Jeff's closest foil in the film: both are riven by conflicting emotions and allegiances, and their resemblance is suggested repeatedly through dialogue, blocking, and cinematography. The most significant moment in their relation-ship occurs after Jeff and Kathie return from their Mexican "dream" ("maybe we thought we'd wake up . . . in Niagara Falls") and, after parting, meet again in a secluded house. But Fisher has tracked her and demands the forty grand she insists she doesn't have. As the scene unfolds, Jeff is gradually engulfed in shadows; then, in a superb quasi-expressionist sequence, the two men fight while Kathie, clearly enjoying the spectacle, looks on. At the very moment Jeff appears to have knocked out his ex-partner, Kathie shoots and kills Fisher, then absconds. The scene's shadows convey Jeff's emotions—depression, guilt, and shame for being duped—and his recognition of his complicity (it is *his* flashback). During the fight sequence the two men's shadows are indistinguishable as they play over Kathie's face: she doesn't care who wins, so long as she gets the dough. Fortuitously, she leaves behind a bankbook revealing that she has indeed stolen Whit's $40,000. As Jeff stares at the evidence, his shadow, now larger than he, stands beside him: it is the second self his actions have created, an embodiment of the misdeeds that will eventually come calling. This scene, which culminates Jeff's flashback, is the moment when he first grasps Kathie's true nature: she is a liar and a cold-blooded killer. It's also the moment when Jeff understands his own role: he's the fish and Kathie the fisher. The shadows also presage his death, which will be the ultimate consequence of his entrapment in Miss Moffat's web. But when he buries Fisher, he is neither sorry nor sore: "I wasn't anything," he tells Ann. Precisely. Having vanished into Kathie's shadow, he became no one at all. In the aftermath he never truly comes to life as the humble Jeff Bailey, for he still loves Kathie and the Jeff she made.

When he next sees her, at Whit's, he insults her ("you're like a leaf that the wind blows from one gutter to another"), mostly to convince himself he doesn't still want her. To pay his debt to Whit, Jeff becomes enmeshed in his plot to avoid paying income tax, but he soon realizes that, as he tells the cabbie who drives him around, he is "in a frame"—that he'll be set up for the murder of the lawyer Eels, actually committed by Stefanos. Fittingly, during these city scenes, Markham is constantly framed by doorways, windows, or small rooms. More to the point, he is boxed in by his own self-division. Like Reardon, Jeff finds the underworld more exciting than Bridgeport, lethal Kathie more enticing than bland Ann. He thinks he *should* desire Bridgeport but has left his heart in San Francisco. Hence, when Kathie professes to love him, protesting that she "couldn't help" signing an affidavit framing him for Fisher's murder, he can't resist her allure.

Even after Kathie sends Stefanos to kill Jeff, and then murders Whit, Jeff—though he does take time to phone the police and set her up to be captured—admits that they "deserve each other." But he makes sure they are caught on the

In *Out of the Past,* shadows loom as Kathie Moffat (Jane Greer) watches Jeff Markham (Robert Mitchum) outmuscle his ex-partner. *Kobal Collection / Art Resource, NY.*

road, virtually assuring that he'll be killed either by them or, as actually happens, by her. He's not good enough for Ann but spares her the pain of loving him, while managing to take Kathie down with him. It is tempting to read his final gesture as a heroic sacrifice, which would imply that the good Jeff Bailey is his real nature, the Markham side (marked for death, perhaps?) merely a shadow brought to life by Kathie. But it's not Jeff who spares Ann; it's the deaf boy. Jeff remains split throughout the film, lying to Ann and to himself, veering wildly in his attitude to Kathie; although disgusted by the reflection of himself he reads in her, he can't bring himself to discard it. Ultimately, as James Maxfield summarizes, Kathie embodies "the evil that he now recognizes within himself" (64)—the evil that he also loves. Bailey/Markham never reinvents himself, never exchanges his dark dream for a bright one, not because fate or Whit or Kathie prevents him but because he remains his *own* double. Whereas Ole Anderson's identity switch fails because he has no self to change, Jeff's identity is frozen in its schizophrenic state, as he clings to the wrong he committed, unable to sever his attachment to a past that he loves more than anything else, even himself.

Mrs. X

Despite their visual and thematic riches, *The Killers* and *Out of the Past* both use their female characters primarily as plot devices or aspects of the male protagonists. But two other switched-identity noirs place women at the center, and their female-authored screenplays employ the missing person device to enable critical analyses of marriage. *My Name Is Julia Ross* (written by Muriel Roy Bolton) and *No Man of Her Own* (scripted by Catherine Turney and Sally Benson) use their Gothic plots to suggest that all married women undergo identity conversions. Though each film supplies a conventional Hollywood ending, complete with a happy couple, their critiques of marriage and gender roles linger beyond their perfunctory conclusions. Each film also scrutinizes the dream of social mobility, as their struggling lower-class protagonists are thrust into the upper class, surviving only through lies and violence. The films question the central institution of middle-class society and cast doubt on the American mythos of infinite class mobility.

Though American-made, *Julia Ross* takes place in England, but if its setting universalizes its dissection of marriage, it scarcely blunts it. Julia (Nina Foch), a newcomer in London who claims to be absolutely alone (though she has a new boyfriend, Dennis Bruce [Roland Varno], who has just broken off his engagement for her), visits an employment agency and finds a job as the secretary for a wealthy family, the Hugheses.[6] Upon taking the job, she is drugged, dressed up, and driven to a mansion in Cornwall, where she is told that she is really Marion Hughes, the wife of Ralph (George Macready), the lord of the manor who stabbed the real Marion to death. He and his mother (Dame May Whitty) aim to persuade Julia, along with the servants and townspeople, that "Marion" is mentally ill so that they can kill her and eliminate any lingering suspicions about Ralph (this scheme makes little sense, but never mind). When Julia first awakens in her room at their mansion, a quick survey reveals the monograms "HH" and "MH" on her bedclothes and toiletries; the large picture window opens onto a sharp drop to the ocean. Like *Spellbound*'s Ballantine, Julia is a pair of initials—but these are not her own. Unlike that of the male missing persons, Julia's "amnesia" is sustained only by those around her; she remains firm in her original identity, despite the nefarious machinations of the psychopathic Ralph and his blandly sinister mother.

These sensational Gothic trappings mask a more sober investigation of female identity and social roles. For example, in a scene not long after Julia arrives at the manor, the maid, Alice (Queenie Leonard), tells Julia that she has "a beautiful home, nice relations, pretty clothes—everything a woman would want"; she should be satisfied with these things instead of "letting [herself] be took up by illusions, letting it gnaw at [her]. . . . It's all in the mind." This canny working-class woman would abide a marriage to a man she doesn't love, so long as she had "everything" else.[7] According to Alice, "Marion" should just grit her teeth and get used to it— even if she really *is* Julia Ross. Later, while walking on the beach with Ralph, Julia pretends that she has accepted her new identity but can't remember her old one. He informs her that, like Julia, Marion had no family or loved ones. In other words the real Marion Hughes was just as trapped as Julia is and was killed because she hated the husband who had forced her to take his name. (He had also lied about his income but now lives on her legacy.) As Ralph confides that he loves the sea because it "never tells its secrets. But it has many, very many secrets," Julia peers over his shoulder, only the top half of her face visible. Santos writes that this moment indicates "the threat of her slow disappearance from the world as she fights to hang on to her reason, signified by her gaze." This claustrophobically close shot, she continues, is a disorienting moment for the viewer, who "experiences a kind of vertigo on the cliff with Julia" (152). More to the point, the shot transforms Julia into Ralph's appendage—just as Marion was. Julia's plight, in short, is that of any woman, alone in the world, who marries into a wealthy family: she is at their mercy. Her condition is a synecdoche for the legal vertigo of female self-erasure through marriage. Any woman who became Mrs. Hughes would become Mrs. X.[8] The switched identity plot, then, demonstrates how marriage can be a form of abduction.

Everything Julia does seems to reinforce her kidnappers' story. Defeated in her attempt to send a note outside, she tries to escape with a visiting vicar, but he returns her to Ralph, who, smugly believing that he has also intercepted Julia's letter to Dennis, drives her to town in his convertible and even lets her post the letter, unaware that she has fooled them with a decoy. Increasingly desperate and unsure that Dennis will get her message, Julia fakes a suicide attempt. But instead of a doctor, the Hugheses bring in a minion named Peters (Leonard Mudie), whom Julia tells about the letter and who is then sent to London to intercept it before it reaches Dennis. That night Ralph, pretending to be Dennis, tries to lure Julia down the dark stairs and kill her. Instead, she flees to her room; following her, he finds the window open and sees Julia, apparently dead, on the rocks below. "Well, she saved us a lot of trouble," he says with relief. To make sure, he descends to the beach and grabs a rock to brain her, but is shot dead by Dennis and a policeman (Peters was nabbed back in London; Dennis alerted the police). Julia had only faked suicide, throwing down her monogrammed robe (the symbol of her Marion Hughes identity) to fool Ralph.

At the conclusion, as Julia and Dennis take a drive in *his* convertible, he tells her he has a job for her: "a combination secretary, nurse, companion, housekeeper." "That sounds like a wife!" she interrupts, and quickly accepts. Despite her determined resistance to being Mrs. Hughes, she readily agrees to be converted into Mrs. Bruce. Her working life will be subsumed by a "job" in which he is the boss and which, judging by his description, will be a demanding one. Julia happily accepts "amnesia" about her former identity, because she has *chosen* Dennis. But the similarities between the two men's automobiles, and the brief description of the first Mrs. Hughes, send a more ambiguous message about marriage: that it may constitute an abduction and a conversion, if not an utter elision, of a woman's identity.[9] Although the film's class theme is less coherent and somewhat muffled by the English setting, it nonetheless addresses upward mobility by demonstrating how lower-middle-class women, when thrown among the grasping, amoral aristocracy, are deprived of their money and humanity. Julia is perhaps better off settling for the middle-class Mr. Bruce than trying to rise too high; maybe a job as his secretary/nurse/companion/housekeeper is really "everything a woman would want."[10]

Two young pregnant women—one newly wedded to a wealthy man, the other abandoned by her sleazy lover and left with only a railroad ticket and five dollars— share a train compartment. The carefree newlywed, Patrice (Phyllis Thaxter), generously allows the other woman, Helen (Barbara Stanwyck), to wear her wedding ring. As luck would have it (and just as Patrice declares, "I couldn't have bad luck"), the train crashes, killing Patrice, her husband, and their unborn child but sparing Helen, who gives birth to a son in the hospital. She remains unconscious, her wedding ring identifying her as Patrice Harkness. Having never seen her or even her photograph (their son, Hugh, married Patrice in Europe), her new in-laws will readily accept Helen as Patrice. Should she reveal her true identity or impersonate the heiress? This is the ingenious premise of *No Man of Her Own*, adapted from Cornell Woolrich's novel *I Married a Dead Man* by Benson and Turney.[11]

Touted in promotional ads as "the story of a woman who lived a magnificent lie" (Paramount press sheets), *No Man of Her Own* went through several title changes (it was called *The Lie* almost until its release) and numerous drafts. Benson's first draft opens with a long prelude describing Helen and her former lover, Steve Morley (Georgesson in the novel). Turney's versions, however, begin with a prologue set after the main action, with "Patrice" having already married Hugh's brother, Bill.[12] The bulk of the film is her flashback, and this structure more effectively highlights the story's central deception and its legal and moral implications. Those implications seem straightforward: impersonating Patrice is fraud. Yet we cannot help but sympathize with poor Helen, unwed and pregnant, with exactly seventeen cents to her name. Moreover, the identity switch happens without her knowledge, as rendered by director Mitchell Leisen via a bewildering blur of flashing lights, keening sirens, masked faces, and cryptic phrases. Upon learning of the error, Helen weakly protests, but a nurse reads her a note from her in-laws: "You are all we have now, you and the little fellow. . . . Hugh's legacy to us."[13] Like an heirloom or piece of property, she has been willed to the Harknesses. Would she have been placed in this lovely private room if the baby weren't their grandson? Helen asks. Hardly, answers the nurse: "We'd put you right into one of the wards." The class implications couldn't be clearer: heiresses and homeless, unwed mothers receive different medical treatment, and so do their children. Hence, although on the train ride to meet the family Helen tries to persuade herself that she can "still back out," one look at her son overrides her compunctions: "for you," she vows in voice-over, "for you" (these lines were Turney's additions). No longer merely a way to move through space, the train has become her vehicle for upward social mobility.

Helen assumes the identity of Patrice (a fitting name for a patrician family) to give her baby a better life than she has. It's a shortcut, but so what: isn't she living the American Dream? Yet she remains haunted by the disparity between her new self and the old Helen symbolized by those seventeen cents. When the nurse asks her, "Are you trying to tell me he isn't her grandson?" a dissolve over Helen's face shows her holding the seventeen cents. "Patrice's" counterfeit nature is even clearer in the novel, where Woolrich contrasts Helen's memory of the seventeen cents with the fifty dollars found in Patrice's handbag after the accident (837). As Helen considers whether to assume Patrice's identity, she fingers the coins. "An Indian-head penny. A Lincoln-head penny. A buffalo nickel. A Liberty-head dime": all of them signify American history and the national creed of honesty, enterprise, and freedom (842). These icons suggest, in other words, that she is simultaneously living out and betraying the American Dream. Is class mobility possible only as a kind of counterfeit money, which, as Marc Shell notes, is always a tale of false origins (160)? If (as I have shown in detail in an article about noir counterfeiting films) counterfeit and legitimate money depend on each other (each one ratifying the other's value), so Helen's impersonation relies on a faith in Patrice's genuineness—and vice versa.[14] Yet was Patrice, herself a woman with no family and no apparent wealth who married into money, any less a counterfeit than Helen? The coins raise the possibility that Helen and Patrice aren't opposites but rather mirror images (as also implied when they gaze in the mirror together in the train compartment) and together represent the common condition of the newly married woman.[15] Both novel and film thus ask whether class, like modern money, is merely a fiction based on expectation and belief. After all, if a nobody like Helen Ferguson can pass herself off as a member of the elite, then social class must be no more than a masquerade. Or is there some essence that members of the elite recognize in each other that an impostor can never duplicate? In other words, is a woman "born that way?"

Helen is immediately accepted by the Harknesses—a remarkably generous, loving, and trusting family—but she makes mistakes, briefly alluding to a childhood in San Francisco that the real Patrice didn't have and failing to recognize Hugh's favorite song ("Barcarolle" in the novel [856]; an Irish folk song in the film).[16] Yet most of "Patrice's" anxieties and awkward moments are identical to those any young bride might feel in the presence of wealthy in-laws: Am I saying the right thing? Do they love me for myself or only because I married their son and am the mother of their grandchild? Indeed, the real Patrice confessed just such fears to Helen on the train: "Do you think they'll like me? Suppose they don't? Suppose they have me built up in their expectations as someone entirely different?" (cf. Woolrich, *I Married* 822). Like *Julia Ross*, then, this film and novel propose that *all* women who marry undergo a kind of adoption, efface their former selves, and perform an impersonation.

Helen almost ruins it all while shopping with Bill (John Lund), who has taken a shine to her. Trying out a new pen, she unthinkingly writes "Helen F.," before stopping in horror. Bill looks at her peculiarly; later we learn that he has suspected all along she isn't really Patrice. As in *Spellbound,* writing certifies identity both legally and morally, a theme that becomes clearer when Helen/Patrice receives a telegram from Steve (Lyle Bettger), asking, "Who are you? Where did you come from? What are you doing there?" Writing also verifies the legality of marriage, which is essential to Steve's plot to blackmail "Patrice" by threatening to divulge her fraud unless she marries him. As her husband, when "Patrice" inherits three-fourths of the Harkness estate (Bill changed the will to ensure that), Steve would own that property. In the meantime he forces her to open a bank account and write a check to him to use as evidence if he ever needs it. Then he drives her to a justice of the peace in a different town. Helen/Patrice resists, but when Steve phones her mother-in-law (Jane Cowl), she yields. The ironies thicken during the ceremony, when the ring—the real Patrice's wedding ring—is described as a token of "sincerity, affection, and fidelity" (in early script drafts, the film was titled *With This Ring*). But Steve has already assured her that "I don't want you; I want what's coming to you." Their marriage will be a sham undertaken for legal and financial purposes only—like Helen/Patrice's marriage to Hugh. Again marriage is depicted as abduction or blackmail, at best a mercenary arrangement by which men acquire female property worth considerably more than seventeen cents.

Seeing no other way out, "Patrice" pilfers the family revolver, finds Steve in his shabby room, and shoots at him, only to discover that he is already dead. Bill, who had followed her after his mother told him about the aborted phone call, helps her dispose of the marriage license and the body in a tense, night-for-night scene. Where do they dump Steve's remains? On a railroad car. Initially the vehicle for the film's social mobility metaphor, the train now sardonically comments on Helen's American dream: yes, you can move into the upper class but only by leaving a trail of bodies behind you. Throughout the film, indeed, the impending arrival of Steve or any other threat to Helen's impersonation is signaled by a train whistle. It is a reminder that one can never leave behind one's lower-class identity, a call from the conscience that screams, "I did something wrong once." The whistle continues to speak to the lovers even after Bill confesses that he knew all along that she wasn't really Patrice. "I don't care who you were or what you've done," he professes. "I love you, not a name. . . . As far as I'm concerned, you were born the day I met you."[17] Helen knows better: "No matter how much you love me," she tells him, the things they've done "will always be there, like . . . a sword hanging over us ready to drop. We'll never forget."

She's right. As I noted earlier, the beginning of the film takes place three months after the major events. Helen (as Patrice) and Bill have married, but their guilty secret drives a wedge between them and prevents them from enjoying their comfortable upper-class life. At the film's opening, "Patrice" tells us in voice-over that the summer nights in Caulfield, where they live, are pleasant, "but not for us." Their fulfillment of the American Dream is tainted by the crimes and compromises committed to obtain it; their beautiful street is really a nightmare alley. The novel and film both depict this situation but differ in their denoue-ments, and the various script drafts show the writers struggling to come up with a conclusion that would both salvage plausibility and satisfy the censors. In both novel and finished film a deathbed letter from Mother Harkness is uncovered in which she confesses to killing Steve after finding out about the forced wedding. In the novel she writes a second letter retracting the first, but in neither version is she prosecuted, for her first letter is a lie. In the novel she offers the retraction as her "wedding gift" to "make your happiness even more complete" (970); it's not clear if she is being sardonic. In Benson's first draft Mother Harkness's letter ad-mits that she knew about Helen's impersonation; we never learn for sure who kills Steve Morley, but we infer that Bill's mother did it.[18] In Turney's draft of May 5, 1949, the letter includes a line saying, "I committed it in anguish and despera-tion, against everything I ever believed was morally right." These lines were probably added to placate the Breen Office, which had requested a rewrite that would include a condemnation of murder. Ironically, the lines are deleted from the final "censorship dialogue" script of December 16, 1949.[19] These gestures do little to mitigate the ending's implausibilities, but they do demonstrate the slip-pery moral question at issue: sweet Mother Harkness, symbol of loyalty and de-votion, is either a liar or a murderer, or both, and her "help" would contaminate her son's marriage and grandson's future life. The problem, however, is not with her but with the institution of marriage, which, both novel and film suggest, is founded on deception.

In the finished film it is ultimately proven that Steve was killed by gamblers over a debt, which gets Mother Harkness off the hook. The real killer is never revealed in the novel, but Bill and "Patrice" allow the gamblers to take the rap anyway.[20] In other words the film erases the lovers' secret, which in the novel re-mains a permanent blot on their union. Woolrich's vision, then, is much darker, implying not only that this marriage is a lie but that marriage itself is a tissue of formalities, the American Dream a counterfeit. Even the film's unlikely coinci-dences and hastily wrapped-up happy ending leave intact its critical analysis of marriage and its warning about the dream of social mobility. Helen gets away with her subterfuge, but several people die. All versions thus imply that you may change your identity, but the price is steep: the loss of your moral and existential center and the sacrifice of anyone who knows who you are—including yourself.

New Faces

An escaped convict rolls off a truck in a barrel, buries his clothing, and is picked up by a man in a convertible, who asks probing questions about his background. The escapee knocks the driver out and steals his clothes. Suddenly he is approached by a beautiful young woman who knows who he is and wants to help him. A dark passage through a tunnel takes them to San Francisco and the promise of a new life, because the woman, Irene Jansen (Lauren Bacall), believes the escapee, Vincent Parry (Humphrey Bogart), to be innocent, perhaps because her own father was unjustly accused of a similar crime. What makes these opening scenes of *Dark Passage* (written and directed by Delmer Daves) so striking is that they are shot largely from Parry's vantage point, a device that continues for the first third of the film. We never see his face in these scenes; indeed, we don't see it for forty more minutes.

This technique places the viewer in an unusual position. Dana Polan argues that it intensifies the "aggressiveness of the camera *and* the aggressiveness of the outside world against that look," thus creating a "claustrophobia of sight," while also denying us (or at least deferring) the satisfaction of seeing Bogart's face (195). Usually a first-person shot is followed by a shot of the person looking outward, or vice versa; when viewers are denied that payoff, we feel trapped or unfulfilled. Hence, we experience our own dark passage upon entering the theater and occupying Parry's point of view: the first driver's insistent, close-quarters stares and persistent questions make us feel as though *we* are being interrogated. This film plays constant changes on motifs of recognition, sight, and surveillance, since Parry, as an escaped convict, must avoid being recognized. Ironically, although he has slipped the confines of the penitentiary, he remains imprisoned by the fear of being seen (Telotte, *Voices* 123): thus when Irene leaves her apartment, he remains locked inside. Constantly talking to himself (a habit he picked up in prison), Parry is another self-divided soul, existing both as a convicted murderer and as the innocent man he claims to be. Likewise, the viewer is split between the self seeing the world through Parry's eyes and the person outside the film's reality, squirming because he or she wishes to see more. J. P. Telotte further suggests

that the subjective camera not only "develops a crucial relationship between seeing and identity" but also renders Parry invisible, so that, despite our privileged
sharing of his perspective, he remains distanced from us (123, 122). Trapped in his
first-person point of view and barred from seeing Parry's face, viewers share
his imprisonment, and as Parry disappears, so do we. We can see, but only with *his*
eyes. The subjective-camera device, then, isolates and entraps not only Parry but
the viewer as well.

The technique also captures the city into which Parry passes—a domain filled
with isolates. Virtually everyone Parry meets professes to be lonely. Irene admits
that she was "born lonely," and Sam (Tom D'Andrea), the cabbie who refers Parry
to the physician who will perform plastic surgery on him, also complains of loneliness. Parry responds, "You see people," to which Sam replies, "They don't talk
to me." In fact, they *don't* see him—though he sees them and judges their characters by their faces. And although Sam does see and recognize Parry, he doesn't
find the possibility that he murdered his wife shocking, for his own sister and her
husband also fight constantly (but "she duck[s]"). When Parry tells the cabbie his
wife "hated [his] guts," the cabbie responds that theirs was a "nice, happy, normal
home." Others enact this worldview. Madge (Agnes Moorehead), Parry's dead
wife's friend (who also happens to know Irene), and her sometime boyfriend,
Bob, argue so frequently and vehemently that Irene remarks, "Causing her un-
happiness is the only thing that gives him happiness."[21] They hate each other but
can't be apart. In this world every husband is a potential murderer, every wife a
shrew, and marriage merely leavens loneliness with strife. Dr. Coley, the creepy
surgeon who performs Parry's operation, presents an even more chilling worldview. After playing with Parry's mind ("If a man like me didn't like a fella, he
could surely fix him up for life. Make him look like a bulldog or a monkey. Ha
ha. . . . I'll make you look as if you've lived"), he concludes, "We're all cowards.
There's no such thing as courage. There's only fear, the fear of getting hurt, and
the fear of dying. That's why human beings live so long." We cling together because the only thing we hate and fear more than each other is the dark, lonely
passage to death. Parry has merely moved from one prison to another: he has died
and been reborn in hell.

And now he dies again, as the surgery montage implies. Under anesthesia he
sees face after face—three mannequin faces cut in half, Irene, Madge, his friend
George, Sam, and, worst of all, the doctor in multiple superimpositions invoking
the bulldog and monkey, then laughing maniacally. Only Irene's face and voice
are reassuring. When Parry awakens, the doctor warns him not to speak or return.

"You're through with me and I'm through with you": even changing a man's face is merely a brief, impersonal encounter. The way Parry's face has been physically cut and altered, moreover, mirrors the way his visage is manipulated by the camera and editing. *Dark Passage,* that is, identifies doctor and director, each of whom "operates" by cutting on Bogart/Parry to change his identity. We see Parry's "real" face only in brief shots of newspaper photos, but these images are never connected to his voice. Thus, even before surgery, he is cut into pieces, his head figuratively amputated from his body. The doctor further manipulates our vision by altering Parry's face into Bogart's. The film's self-reflexive point-of-view shots draw viewers into this matrix as well, severing us from our comfortable viewing position and resculpting us into paranoid watchers. Once these operations are complete, we finally see Parry from the outside. Yet we are still denied satisfaction, because Bogie's face is covered with bandages. In short, we can believe only some of what we see—and we can't see everything. In reminding us that faces can be changed, and that what we see is not to be believed, the filmmakers enclose us within a paradox: what lies before us on film seems a genuine depiction of our world, but we know the camera can lie, because we have seen how it is subject to the ministrations of editors and directors and because we know that Parry is really Humphrey Bogart. The film thrusts us away even as we enter it, so we end up more alone and disoriented than ever.

Parry does have one true friend: George (Rory Mallinson), a forlorn trumpet player who claims that Vincent is "the only guy who ever liked me." He offers Parry a place to stay while he recovers, but after Parry wakes up, he finds George murdered. Afterward, confined to Irene's apartment, unable to speak, and forced to sleep with his hands tied, Parry has become more constricted than he was in prison. But then comes the moment we have been waiting for—the unveiling.[22] As Parry walks down the stairs wearing his new face, Irene's phonograph plays "Someone to Watch over Me"—whose title both captures the film's atmosphere of spying and conveys Irene's caregiving role. For the first time since the operation, Parry is able to speak, yet his transformation seems, according to the other side of Irene's record, "Too Marvelous for Words" (this tune also played during their first romantic encounter). What he tells her, however, isn't marvelous: he must leave her and acquire a new name, which she then gives him—Alan Linnell. Yet her power to make him over comes not from surgery but from love.

Alas, Parry's conversion fools no one. As soon as he leaves Irene's apartment, he is accosted by a policemen who wonders why he has the shakes and carries no identification ("Alan" claims he's hiding from his nasty wife). After eluding him,

In *Dark Passage* the face of Vincent Parry (Humphrey Bogart) is covered with bandages after his plastic surgery, and he is confined to the apartment of Irene Jansen (Lauren Bacall). *Kobal Collection / Art Resource, NY.*

Parry checks into a hotel under this "very unusual name" (according to the registrar), only to be found by Baker (Clifton Young), the man in the convertible. Aware of Irene's wealth, Baker shakes "Alan" down, reminding him that she, as an accessory to his crime, will go to prison if he is found. That should be worth sixty grand, decides Baker, who recognized Parry by his suit. Soon Parry learns that another car has been following him around: an orange convertible driven by Madge. Then, beneath the Golden Gate Bridge, the two men wrestle and Baker is knocked off a cliff to his death, freeing Parry to confront Madge at her apartment. Despite his new face, she also quickly recognizes him. She also admits that she, coveting Vincent's affections, killed his wife and George so that nobody else could have Parry. This twisted "love" starkly contrasts with the one shared by Parry and Irene: they part because they love each other, whereas Madge hates Parry but can't let him alone. Yet Madge refuses to confess to the police, and without her confession Parry has no proof. "In every paper in the country I'm a

killer," he growls, but "I never thought it possible to kill anybody until this minute." He vows that she'll "never get out of [his] sight." But as he draws near, Madge
falls from her window to her death.[23]

This implausible event does not even resolve the story: Parry can't clear
himself, since the proof of his innocence is dead. Though he manages to escape
from town, he remains a fugitive. And so, just as earlier we "filled in" Bogart's
face through his familiar voice and phrasing, we now fill in the conclusion we
desire, even though the film doesn't provide it. Parry may be technically innocent, but he was quite prepared to kill Madge, and because of him, two more
people have died. And though he has been given a new face and name, his essential nature—the "me inside him," that Emersonian "aboriginal self"—remains un-
altered. Hence he remains alone in a world populated by "isolates, prisoners, and
fugitives from imprisonment," writes Telotte (*Voices* 127), where "one is either
completely alone" or hounded by those one knows too well. "Solitude or community here are equally . . . disturbing conditions," concludes Polan (197). The cynical
philosophies of the cabbie and plastic surgeon, as well as the loneliness expressed
by every character, imply that the pursuit of happiness via self-interest produces
a world oppressed by fear and animosity.

Yet there is a condition between these two gloomy extremes, one hinted at
during Parry's wait at a bus station, where a man laments that nobody cares
about "the other fella" and recalls a time when "folks used to give each other a helping hand." He speaks these words to an overwhelmed mother herding two young
children. After she agrees with him, he adds, "We've got something in common—
being alone." Parry then plays "Too Marvelous for Words" on the station jukebox. Perhaps the lonely man and the harried mom will find solace together, as
Irene and Vincent do in the epilogue, after she walks into the Peruvian café where
he waits. This possibility of intimacy mitigates, to some degree, the film's bitter
picture of alienated urban individualism. Parry may be reborn: Irene gives him
new life by believing that he is lovable, which suggests that his aboriginal self is
not a murderer but a lover. Through the eyes of another person who sees beneath
the face, the film implies, one may pierce the darkness to reveal and redeem
one's buried self.

That possibility seems remote, however, in a film that rivals *Nightmare Alley*
as the bleakest of all noirs. *Hollow Triumph* (also known as *The Scar*) is *Dark
Passage* stripped of the possibility of love. Like Vincent Parry, John Muller (Paul
Henreid) has just left prison. But he is not an escapee; rather, he is released at the
film's opening, as the warden reads his biography (Muller attended medical

school, was arrested for practicing psychoanalysis without a license, is a "big spender"). Yet John Alton's moody cinematography renders Muller's freedom moot. Moreover, though Muller is given a decent job at a medical supply house, he immediately returns to crime by engineering the heist of a gambling den. His partners are dubious about the scheme—the casino is operated by a gangster named Stancyk, notorious for tracking down anyone who crosses him—but Muller assures them they'll be able to walk right in: "people, they'll never notice," he crows, "they're all wrapped up in themselves." The partners are right: Stancyk vows revenge and hounds Muller, who goes into hiding.

But Muller is also right, and his assertion is borne out repeatedly, as nearly every person in the film is too self-involved or smug even to notice when Muller takes on another man's identity. This man, a psychiatrist named Victor Bartok, looks exactly like Muller (Henreid plays both roles). Learning this fact from a dentist who works in Bartok's building, Muller visits the doctor's office and fools his secretary, Evelyn Hahn (Joan Bennett), who is carrying on an affair with Bartok. After they kiss, she realizes he's not Bartok, and Muller remarks that her "subconscious mind" exposed her as a "wild bundle rarin' to go." She asks, "What are you, anyway, an analyst or a patient?" He claims only to be a "bystander"—an apt term for most of the film's characters, who stand by while others commit crimes. Muller's other alter ego—his brother, Fred—warns him that Stancyk's boys are still looking for him. The frightened John darkens the room as his brother reminds him, "You were everything I wasn't, everything I wanted to be, everything we'd all like to be." John always took risks, was always on the lookout for a big score. But Fred knows that "sooner or later, it always catches up with us." John dismisses his brother, but "it" almost catches up with him that very evening, when he is again forced to flee from Stancyk's men. Fred's words describe a man who does reckless things for excitement but inspires envy in others. Perhaps that fact explains why the minor characters seem so unobservant: they actually enjoy watching others do what they themselves are afraid to do. It may also explain Muller/Bartok's ultimate downfall: even a Freudian psychiatrist isn't immune from *Schadenfreude*.

This was screenwriter Daniel Fuchs's view; we know it was because he left detailed notes for Henreid and director Steve Sekely, describing Muller as "the superman, the intelligent outlaw, the rebel against a lumpish, indifferent society" (1). The audience, he continues, will "identify with Muller's ambitions, will wish him well." He is "a hero—a Napoleon in modern clothes." But even if he represents "all the longings of the audience to rebel against their own dingy circumstances," his ultimate failure will make the audience "feel good," because it "confirms their resignation."[24]

Fuchs likely exaggerates the audience's sympathy for Muller, whom Henreid plays with a chilly arrogance. The film, indeed, upsets our intuitive desire to empathize with Muller by portraying him as a cold, self-absorbed character, thereby rendering us as alienated as the other people in the film. Thus, during Muller's first date with Evelyn, the two watch some ants at work—a metaphor for the straight life that Muller cannot tolerate. A cynic herself, Evelyn knows another when she sees one, and she sketches Muller's character astutely: "First comes you, second comes you, third comes you, and after that comes you. You're one of those egotistical smart alecks with big ideas. You think you've got a right to get away with murder." He replies, "No woman alive could possibly resist a man as attractive as all that." Muller's fear of Stancyk's men, we understand, is only one reason he decides to assume Bartok's identity. He also does it to assert his sense of superiority and for the sheer thrill. No one else in the world matters, so why not take on another man's identity for a change? Yet Muller does not stand out in a city (it's Los Angeles this time) where, as Evelyn states, everyone is trying to "take somebody." Of all the characters in the film, only Fred seems to care for someone else—and even he envies his selfish brother. The world of *Hollow Triumph* is indeed hollow, a realm of radical individualists and guilty bystanders, all alike in their alienation and selfishness.

Muller prepares to adopt the doctor's identity by reviewing psychology texts, listening to Bartok's clinical recordings, practicing his signature, taking up smoking, emulating the doctor's foreign accent.[25] Then he tells Evelyn he's leaving the country. Not to worry, he assures her; someday she'll pass him on the street and "won't even know who I am." Now comes the moment of transformation: using a photo of Bartok as his guide, Muller gazes into a mirror, surgical instruments arrayed before him. In one shot we see three versions of the same person: the man in the photo, the man in the mirror, and the man (seen only from behind) staring into the mirror. Muller, who has already made a career of assuming various roles—prisoner, phony psychiatrist, gang leader, and cab driver (his current cover)—will soon own three identities at once: Muller, Bartok, and a third persona created by the blend of the two. After Muller injects his face with anesthetic, the camera stays on his cigarette, which, over two dissolves, burns a "scar" into the desk. He holds a photo of Bartok as he draws a line on his own face. In the photo, as seen in its mirror reflection, the doctor's distinctive vertical scar marks what looks to be his left side (which is, in fact, his right side, since we and Muller see only its mirror image). Therefore Muller marks and cuts his right side (he does *not* mark his left side, as Pelizzon and West assert: 7).[26] Yet when he returns to the photo shop where the picture was developed to pick up the negative, the clerk doesn't have the time (or the courage) to inform the curt Muller that the photo was flopped: Bartok's scar is actually on the *left* side of his face. Muller has scarred himself on the right (that is, the wrong) side! The other clerk says it's no problem; he has flopped hundreds of negatives and "they never notice. . . . Instead of being on the left side of the face, the scar is on the right. Well, is that so terrible?" It's terrible for Muller, who now attempts to appropriate Bartok's identity while wearing a mirror image of the doctor's scar. His mistake is telling: although he has seen Bartok in person, he has nevertheless confused the doctor's mirror image with his real face. In short, Muller is as unobservant as everyone else. But his "mistake" may not really be a mistake; perhaps, as Santos suggests, it is a "Freudian slip" indicating that Muller wants to "assert his own identity" (33). Muller's handiwork is like that of a forger, whose success depends on its *not* being recognized as such. Perhaps this "egocentric smart aleck" wishes his work to be noticed; or perhaps he unconsciously wishes to be caught. In any case, the scene demonstrates that only by careful observation can we distinguish the dexter from the sinister—whether they appear in a mirror, in a photo, or in real life.

In any case, during the cutting sequence we never see Muller in full shot; we see only his face or head, with separate shots depicting his hands and torso. Muller's head and body are separated, as if he is amputating himself—as the editing does. Thus Pelizzon and West are correct that the scarring scene, like the surgery sequence in *Dark Passage*, "links the diegetic cutting of Muller's face with

In *Hollow Triumph*, John Muller (Paul Henreid) stares at the photo of Dr. Bartok in a mirror as he prepares to cut his own face. *Screen capture.*

the extra-diegetic cutting of the film strip" (par. 26). If "photographic technology is presented as the domain of mishaps and flaws" (par. 28), and the film we are watching reveals the photograph's error, Pelizzon and West continue, cinema is therefore presented as a "higher . . . authority" than photography. But the paradox is actually the same one found in the forgery noirs we encounter in chapter 4: the film *at once* asserts its superiority to photography and undermines that claim by revealing the unreliability of cinematography. Of course, the real flaw is not in the photographs but rather, as Pelizzon and West's and Muller's mistakes about the scar's placement reveal, in faulty human powers of observation. *Hollow Triumph* questions the veracity of the cinematic medium because, like photographs, it is only as reliable as human perception. And because we humans are "scarred"—fallible, inattentive—our communication and connection can never be perfect. Hence, like those "it was only a dream" films discussed in chapter 1, *Hollow Triumph* denies the viewer's belief in what he or she sees onscreen, even while immersing us in that alternate world.

With his scar in place Muller carries out his plan by getting Bartok alone in his cab and murdering him.[27] We don't witness the murder, which is rendered as a quasi-expressionist montage of faces and voices that concludes with a stop sign changing to "Go." As in the scarring scene, the director's and editor's cuts hide the physical violence, again reminding us that our perceptions are subject to manipulation. But Muller's observation is now direct, and as he examines the body, he discovers his mistake. Yet he has no choice but to proceed with the impersonation. It's an ironic moment when the dentist who had originally noted Muller's resemblance to Bartok fails to register the reversed scar, while boasting about his own superior powers of observation. Four out of five men, he asserts, wouldn't notice if "the next fella was breathing or dying." Most people are so caught up in their own "petty little . . . preoccupations," he declares, "all they can think about and talk about is themselves."

The next scene, a montage of Dr. Bartok "treating" his patients, proves him right. He chain-smokes meditatively but says nothing as they lament their lonely, unloved lives. Ironically, the man who had boasted of his lack of interest in others now must feign such interest to maintain his imposture: he must efface himself. The patients never notice that their doctor has been supplanted by a double, and perhaps don't care, for what they really need is someone to listen and make them feel important. The clinical setting permits them to make a connection, albeit fleeting, commodified, and one-sided, with another human. Thus, while *Hollow Triumph* depicts psychoanalysis as a con game, masquerade, and, as the next scenes imply (echoing *Spellbound*), a type of gambling, it also insinuates that it serves a necessary function in a modern urban society that lacks true intimacy. Still, the chief point is not so much, as Pelizzon and West propose, that "Bartok's" patients prefer him to the "real" doctor (par. 12), as that the two men are the same: just as Muller was already a psychoanalyst (as was revealed in his first scene with Evelyn), so Bartok is already a thief and gambler.

When, the next day, Evelyn tells the doctor he has been "strange," he accuses her of "seeing somebody" (she was "seeing" him as Muller, but doesn't "see" him as Bartok) and of bitterness. She answers, "It's a bitter little world full of sad surprises, and you don't go around letting people hurt you." She hasn't trusted anyone since she was nine years old. "You never can go back and start again, because the older you grow, the worse everything turns out." In other words your current self incorporates the past; your experiences may scar you, but they also make you wiser. "Bartok" isn't really listening, because her words forecast why his carefully planned masquerade will fail: in believing he can sever himself from his past, he only dooms himself to repeat his own mistakes. Like Markham, Thompson, and Parry, Muller "kills" himself to become someone else. At the end of his journey, however, he discovers the Emersonian truth that to become Bartok is only to become more himself. But first he must be subjected to further ironies. One occurs when Fred returns, looking for his brother, and passes along the news that Stancyk is about to be deported and is no longer pursuing John. Fred pleads with "Bartok": "You don't know him. He's smart, got big ideas, willing to take any kind of chance." Bartok puts him off, but Fred is right—John Muller doesn't know himself. As the barred shadows on the wall indicate, this escapee has moved from the state's prison to one of his own making and is now trapped in the identity he so hates and loves, in a world where no one cares for anyone else.

Evelyn has learned the truth about Bartok, and plans to leave the country on the next ship. During their last conversation Muller/Bartok reiterates his philosophy: "You take care of yourself and that's all!" She replies sarcastically, "Watch out for number one; always play it for yourself." Bartok: "That's right. . . . This is the way it is and you know it." He slaps her, but by the end of the argument he has agreed to leave with her: for once the characters have revealed some genuine emotion. Then, as Bartok makes his way out of the building, the film's most tender moment takes place. A cleaning lady stops him and hesitantly points out that his scar used to be on the other side. He smiles, touches her face, and gently squeezes her shoulder. This humble woman, who has seen him many times but whose existence he has never acknowledged, thinks he is important. Only she notices "Bartok's" scar because no one else really sees him; they see only their idea of him, their own needs and prejudices mirrored. Not one other soul gives a damn for Victor Bartok; in abandoning his own identity, Muller has sacrificed his ties to others.

Nor does he make it to the ship: on the way he is accosted by goons looking for Bartok, who owes Maxwell's casino $90,000 in gambling debts. These are Bartok's debts, not Muller's: the eminent psychiatrist also took too many chances.[28] Facing death, "Bartok" pleads that he's really Muller: see, the scar is on the wrong side! Ironically, when Muller tries to assert his "real" identity, nobody believes him. But why should they? The film has shown not only that he *is* Bartok but that he *always has been* Bartok. John Muller has succeeded too well—erased himself and been accepted as Victor Bartok—but it is a hollow triumph, for Bartok was a hollow man. As he lies dying on the pier, he gazes up at the people waving, but not one of them is waving to him. At this moment he is neither Bartok nor Muller; he is not even a geek, for at least those pathetic figures magnetize the eyes of others. He is nobody at all—just a dying animal, frightened and alone. After he expires, bustling crowds pass his body without a second look. Muller's exciting experiment has left him in nightmare alley with nothing, not even a name.[29]

Bartok was a lie that even Muller believed. But Muller can't escape himself, and he brings with him his own flaws—the same flaws Bartok possessed. Muller's hyperindividualist worldview is thus exposed as empty. Yet his repellent philosophy is also enacted by virtually every other character, all those people who never notice Bartok's reversed scar, the self-involved throngs who don't register a dead man lying at their feet. Even more thoroughly than *Dark Passage, Hollow Triumph* portrays an unredeemed world of isolates where the American Dream of liberty, self-determination, self-reinvention, and the pursuit of happiness has become a grotesque travesty. In short, the ending, as Fuchs's notes state, validates Muller's cynicism (59). Pure freedom is embodied by the ability to change your identity at will, but that freedom generates a world that has undergone fission. In such a world, freedom is indistinguishable from imprisonment.

Certain autobiographical elements resonate here as well. Muller/Bartok is played by émigré Paul Henreid, and the picture was directed by Steve Sekely, born István Székely, in Budapest. Both artists changed their names, abandoned their original tongues, and remade themselves as Americans. Henreid, who also produced *Hollow Triumph*, tailored the role for himself. Their biographies not only lend the film an additional poignancy (how could they not have realized that the tale mirrors their own life stories?) but add veracity: who is better equipped to comment on Americans' individualism and self-obsession, our blind pursuit of happiness and liberty at all costs, than immigrants? Of course, viewers know that Muller is fictional, being enacted by a person named (or rather, renamed) Paul Henreid. The film thus projects mirrors within mirrors, as we watch a European man pretend to be an American man impersonating a European man.

Hollow Triumph also asks us to trust our eyes, while reminding us that we can't trust our eyes—or rather, that we err when we don't look closely enough. By questioning the veracity of photography and cinema, the film challenges our reliance on surface truths, our intuitive faith that what we see is what is really there. Like all of the missing person films, it also suggests that America has become a nation of guilty bystanders, a people so alienated from each other that we cannot even recognize that others *are* ourselves. All these stories of mistaken identity and botched vision ask us to look more closely—or, indeed, *not* merely to look but to listen and to feel. They also gesture toward what is not there: active empathy, an antidote to the hyperbolic self-interest and pursuit of happiness that, *Hollow Triumph* and *Dark Passage* demonstrate particularly well, cannot occur without social connection. As Fuchs's notes state, his film presents a "charge to the audience," an "appeal . . . not to be brutish" (1–2). Likewise, the missing-person noirs reveal that Franklinesque self-reinvention is possible only insofar as the self is a product of others. You cannot truly change your nature because it is not really yours; rather, it is constantly molded by the other people who perpetually make and remake you.

Vet Noir
Masculinity, Memory, and Trauma

"You oughta see me open a bottle of beer": ex-sailor Homer Parrish, who has lost both hands in World War II, boasts of his hook dexterity to two other veterans in William Wyler's *The Best Years of Our Lives*.[1] War vets in films noir usually possess less obvious physical disabilities; more obvious ones are generally given to peripheral characters who function as counterparts to, or extensions of, nondisabled protagonists. Thus the deaf youth in *Out of the Past* serves as what David Mitchell and Sharon Snyder call a "narrative prosthesis": a crutch on which authors lean for "representational power, disruptive potentiality and social critique" (17). Such characters enact a protagonist's needs or other characters' traits. Thus, according to Michael Davidson, the deaf boy mirrors Jeff Bailey's "flawed yet stoical integrity, providing a silent riposte to the glamour of and tough-guy patter between the other males in the film" (57): he is a trustworthy alternative to the liars Whit and Kathie.

Elsewhere in film noir disabilities represent nondisabled protagonists' moral flaws (Davidson 73). For instance, in *Murder, My Sweet* Philip Marlowe's temporary blindness indicates his inability to recognize that B-girl Velma Valento has remade herself into wealthy matron Helen Grayle; the hearing impairments of gangsters Frank Hugo in *Ride the Pink Horse* and Joe McClure in *The Big Combo* symbolize the moral "deafness" of their films' protagonists, Lucky Gagin and Lt. Leonard Diamond, respectively, each of whom is obsessed with revenge on his darker counterpart.[2]

Cognitively disabled veterans in film noir, however, play more significant roles. First, they fit the typical noir narrative of an investigator's quest for truth and identity. Marlowe's pursuit of Velma, for example, is a pretext for his own search for selfhood through repeated encounters with alter egos such as Moose Malloy and Lindsay Marriott. In the amnesiac vet noirs, however, this quest for selfhood becomes literal, for these returning soldiers truly don't remember who they are. These characters lend sociopolitical weight to the noir theme of alienation and isolation by acting as synecdoches for a whole generation of displaced men and for American society in its postwar transitional phase.

The frequent presence of disabled returning veterans in film noir reveals broad cultural tensions and traumas. One such tension involved shifting definitions of masculinity, as veterans were forced to discard wartime rituals and roles. Thus noir's traumatized veterans are often hypermasculine, aggressive, impatient with women, and incapable or unwilling to alter their warrior mentality for the humdrum realities of civilian life (see Polan 248). Such veterans—in *The Blue Dahlia*, for example—define masculinity *against* disability: if masculinity equals strength and achievement, disability must signify weakness and inadequacy. Hence, the vets hide their cognitive or emotional dysfunctions, if they recognize them at all. Noir veterans also struggle to transfer their emotional bonds from all-male soldier "families" to heteronormative relationships and conventional domesticity, a pattern apparent not only in *The Blue Dahlia* but also in *Crossfire* and *Dead Reckoning*. As Frank Krutnik has observed, these films "offer a range of alternative or 'transgressive' representations of male desire and identity, together with a . . . skeptical framing of the network of male cultural authority" found in the military, law enforcement, and psychiatry. In so doing, they expose a "crisis of confidence" about male-dominated culture (*Lonely* 88, 91).

As Mike Chopra-Gant notes, these characters also embody anxieties about America's inability to "settle veterans into productive postwar roles" (151). Thus *Cornered*'s Lt. Gerard suffers from fugue-like attacks and pursues a vendetta against the Nazis who killed his wife; *The Blue Dahlia*'s Buzz has a brain injury that induces debilitating headaches and murderous rages; Lucky Gagin's war experiences have left him a cynical cipher. Unable to forget the war, these veterans try to relive it, both to rectify wrongful deaths and to regain the moral clarity they felt in combat. Their cognitive disabilities thus function as what Mitchell and Snyder call a "master metaphor for social ills" (24)—not just for gender role adjustments but also for shifting ideas about labor and productivity, and for emerging Cold War fears of invasion.

But perhaps most telling are those ex-GIs suffering from amnesia. Steven Kenet in *High Wall*, Eddie Ricks in *The Crooked Way*, and George Taylor in *Somewhere in the Night* have lost their memories because of war injuries, and their inability to retrieve their prewar identities dramatizes real-life veterans' adjustment difficulties. More metaphorically, former POW Frank Enley, in *Act of Violence*, has purchased bourgeois stability at the cost of "forgetting" his questionable acts during the war, only to be reminded of them by a revenge-seeking fellow prisoner. This pair encompasses both extremes: if Enley has willed amnesia, pursuer Joe Parkson cannot forget. Both still dwell in a mental and moral prison. All these characters, indeed, dramatize postwar America's dialectic of memory and forgetting, a dance or duel between the conflicting desires to forget and to remember the war: though citizens wished to honor their heroes, they realized that war memories might interfere with the construction of a postwar society.

These disabled veterans thus reflect a larger existential crisis in American society as it moved from postwar to Cold War moods and discourses. The vets' struggles to redefine masculinity and to recover or remodel their selves testify to America's own identity crisis, presenting a powerful challenge to the national ideology of self-reinvention, that essential component of the American Dream. The vet noirs' key question, posed directly in *Somewhere in the Night*, is this: does war change one's nature, or does it merely expose hidden aspects already present? More broadly, these films ask again the question underwriting the dream and missing-person pictures: is a guy born that way? Vet noir dramatized options for American society—a society of immigrants and hence one forged from willed amnesia—to redefine or remember itself.

Remembering

Some veterans don't lose their memories but have been stripped of their emotional resilience and their humanity. Yet they wish to reenact or recapture their warrior life—its camaraderie, its intensity, its clear sense of purpose—and return to the very incidents that traumatized them. In these reenactment scenes, which appear in almost all of the films discussed below, noir vets display the clinical symptoms of posttraumatic stress disorder, characterized by "persistent, intrusive reexperiencing of the traumatic event through flashbacks and recurrent dreams with persistent avoidance of stimuli associated with the trauma, numbing of general responsiveness and persistent symptoms of increased arousal" (Nadelson 90).[3] Despite their constant intrusions into the vets' minds, these experiences and their associated feelings remain largely "indigestible" (Nadelson 95): they can neither be forgotten nor integrated. Such traumatic episodes exemplify what Roger Luckhurst, paraphrasing Cathy Caruth, calls a "crisis of representation, of history and truth, and of narrative time" (Luckhurst 5; Caruth 7): that is, because the events are generally not consciously incorporated into the characters' experiences or psyches, they are not spoken or written about. In this regard that prototypical noir narrative device, the flashback, serves an essential function.[4] As Luckhurst points out, trauma "issues a challenge" to narrative. "In its shock impact trauma is anti-narrative, but it also generates the manic production of retrospective narratives that seek to explain the trauma" (79). Veterans' combat flashbacks invariably interrupt and arrest the films' narratives yet also contain crucial plot elements or unveil key motives. These reenactments disrupt the realistic surface of the films; even in films with conventional mise-en-scènes, filmmakers employ antirealist, expressionist techniques to depict them. Such scenes epitomize Michael Rothberg's definition of "traumatic realism," whereby "the claims of reference live on, but so does the traumatic extremity that disables Realist representation" (106): they remain unintegrated into the films' style, as if to reflect the vets' psychic disintegration.

Noir veterans undergo purgative rituals in which their old selves die and new ones are born. Some also play out the conventions of what Arthur Frank calls the "restitution narrative"—the "culturally preferred narrative" of institutional medicine—in which the agent is not the patient but a drug, a doctor, or, as in many vet noirs, a woman. This process requires that the disabled or diseased body (which includes the brain) be displayed, divided into parts, commodified, and/or disciplined before being fixed (Frank 83, 86, 88). These characters submit their identities to institutional remodeling: in short, most vet noirs are stories of "social control" (Frank 82).[5] These veterans' struggles expose a cultural yearning to punish and then redeem, in which hope for restitution collides with profound anxieties about disability and memory as threats to the stability of the society and the psyche. The films thus suggest that self-reinvention may be possible, but only after extreme trauma and a kind of self-amputation.

Readjustment

Cognitively disabled veterans weren't, of course, merely fictional. In 1943 the armed services began discharging so-called psychoneurotic veterans at the rate of ten thousand cases per month. The army alone had discharged 216,000 soldiers for psychiatric problems by 1944, and overall an estimated 30 percent of American war casualties were of this type (Waller 166). Physically disabled soldiers such as Homer Parrish were even more common, as the United States tallied more than 670,000 wounded during the war.[6] But even able-bodied vets had to cope with a variety of readjustment problems. In his 1944 book *The Veteran Comes Back* sociologist Willard Waller predicted that the returning veteran would soon be "America's gravest social problem" (13). His book provides a blueprint that the returning-veteran noirs follow point by point. He writes that veterans would return to families they scarcely knew and who had found other interests in their absence (83); that vets would need to adapt to a postwar world where combat values didn't fit (113); and that their lost years of employment would make it difficult to find work (92). Many veterans, he writes, feel like *"Immigrants in Their Native Land"* (180; Waller's italics). Waller even declares that "Every Veteran Is at least Mildly Shell-Shocked" (115)—each one forever changed by his or her experiences and troubled by the transition to peacetime. For these "Cinderellas" of the services, as another contemporary pundit named them, "the return to civilian life [was] the clang of midnight" (qtd. in Chopra-Gant 30).

The difficulties of three such Cinderellas are movingly dramatized in *The Best Years of Our Lives,* a hugely popular and critically acclaimed movie that provides a nonnoir touchstone for my discussion. Homer Parrish, trained to use his hooks, is proudly dexterous when showing off to his male friends but becomes clumsy when near his pitying family (Chopra-Gant 125). They "got me nervous," he tells his Uncle Butch (Hoagy Carmichael), by either staring at his hooks or "staring away from 'em." Fearing he'll be a burden, Homer resists proposing to his prewar sweetheart, Wilma (Cathy O'Donnell). His pivotal moment occurs when he asks her to watch him remove the harness holding the hooks; without his prostheses he can put on his pajamas but can't button them, nor can he open a door, read a book, or drink a glass of milk. "Dependent as a baby" without them, he confesses, he'll always need her help. She assures him that she'll never leave him, then maternally tucks him in.

"All I want is to be treated like everybody else," Homer protests. In fact he *is* treated much like the two able-bodied vets he meets on the plane home, middle-aged banker Al Stephenson (Fredric March), and soda-jerk-cum-bombardier Fred Derry (Dana Andrews), both of whom are alternately patronized and lionized by their families and friends. Early in the film Al's wife, Millie (Myrna Loy), indulges his desire to go out on the town with her and daughter Peggy (Teresa Wright), but he and Fred both end up passed out in the backseat of Al's car. Millie comments, "They make a lovely couple, don't they?" Peggy adds, "They'll be very happy together." Behaving more like soldiers on weekend leave than adult civilians, the men cleave to each other—and to wartime carousing rituals—rather than to their female loved ones; as Waller explains, they "Feel at Home Only with other Veterans" (177). The next morning, as a hungover Al sits in his bedroom, reflected simultaneously in two mirrors, we see that he is divided between his grand soldier identity and his ordinary civilian self. Gazing at a photo of himself wearing a business suit, he seems to wonder if he is the same person he used to be. At the end of the scene Al tosses his military boots out the window; this change from military to civilian garb (seen in many vet noirs: Chopra-Gant 102) signifies his resumption of his old identity (but of course his old clothes don't fit). His war experience earns him a promotion and raise, so he seems to refute the melancholy words of his favorite song, "Among My Souvenirs": "There's nothing left for me / Of days that used to be," although his alcoholism (exacerbated by the war) leaves lingering doubts.

Fred's transition is less smooth: of the three he is most like an immigrant in his own country.[7] He's also the only one clearly plagued by posttraumatic stress. Thus, on the night of the binge he awakens Peggy, asleep in the next room, with his cries. The film veers into noir territory as cinematographer Gregg Toland briefly abandons the solemn deep-focus photography employed in the rest of the film for quasi expressionism. We hear low rumbles of a plane's engines, and then, as dim light seeps through venetian blinds, Fred's anguished visage becomes the face of PTSD: "It's on fire!" he shouts. "Godorski, get outta that plane! . . . She's burning up! Get out! Get out!" Peggy soothes him back to sleep, but Fred's waking hours are also a bad dream. He has come to loathe Marie (Virginia Mayo), the shallow, materialistic woman he married just before enlisting and, upon resuming his job at the drugstore, endures multiple blows to his manhood: a boss who pointedly informs him that his war experience is irrelevant (a pattern Waller notes [92]), a supervisor who was once his underling, and an emasculating post at the ladies' perfume counter. Suspended between states, Fred cannot let go of the war, recapture his prewar identity, or remake himself. When at last he visits an airfield filled with derelict bombers, an overhead shot renders him tiny and alone, and as he enters the nose of a B-17 bomber called "Round Trip," he breaks into a sweat, then makes a round trip back to the war. But when he exits the plane, he is offered a job recycling plane parts for prefabricated houses. Like the plane, Fred is war surplus—a used part who will be refitted for the postwar world with a new job and a marriage to Peggy.

If *Best Years* displays a "blend of optimism and wariness" about veterans' ability to assimilate (Dixon 165), its vets' restitutions are nevertheless relatively complete, as each one is healed by the love of a good woman. The first vet noirs follow a similar trajectory, while shading the situation in darker hues. *The Blue Dahlia*, a "dystopian" version of *Best Years* (Chopra-Gant 169), depicts the postwar world as an "emotional minefield" (Dixon 175) where veterans are ill-equipped to sidestep explosions. The most vulnerable of this film's three navy vets, Buzz (William Bendix), wears a metal plate in his head, and in the opening scene he flies into a violent rage when another soldier plays loud jazz ("monkey music") on the juke. As Buzz loses his cool, we hear the low rumbling that signifies a combat flash-back. Buzz's friends, Johnny Morrison (Alan Ladd) and George Copeland (Hugh Beaumont), manage to placate him, but Morrison's disability is nearly as severe, as becomes apparent when he angrily confronts his cheating wife, Helen (Doris Dowling), and her lover, nightclub owner Eddie Harwood (Howard Da Silva), at a party. Helen dismisses her friends by announcing that her husband "probably wants to beat me up," and Ladd's grim demeanor hints at the truth in her quip. For Morrison, as for many vets, "mortal combat remains at his emotional center and his perceptions, and he continues to yearn for the focused arousal state he once found in war" (Nadelson 57).[8] Helen (who is soon murdered) diagnoses Morrison's condition more simply: he has "learned to like hurting people." Buzz, originally written to be the murderer until the navy forced the filmmakers to change the story, is Johnny's double, the man who could perpetrate the crime that Johnny "desired but was not able to commit" (Krutnik, *Lonely* 68).[9] Each vet is a casualty, a man who, when not at war, is simply at sea.

In the opening scene a sign behind the vets' heads reads, "Second Home." The problem is that they no longer have a *first* home. So these vets, like those in *Best Years,* cling to their all-male surrogate family, with Buzz serving as rebellious son, George as mother, and Johnny as hypermale father (see Krutnik, *Lonely* 69). Buzz's constant pawing of Johnny also implies homoerotic yearnings he cannot express. Buzz's disability renders him both uncontrollably masculine and dan-gerously dependent—"a sexual inscrutability otherwise unspeakable" that Da-vidson finds in many of noir's disabled characters (59). For men like Buzz and Johnny, writes Nadelson, "women are dangerous . . . [because] their loyalty is never that of comrades" (150).[10] A minor character named Leo states the fear more bluntly: all women are "poison."

Not quite all: at his words we dissolve to the face of Harwood's wife, Joyce (Veronica Lake), who picks up Morrison during a rainstorm and later protects him from both her husband and the police hunting him for Helen's murder. Al-though she empathizes with Morrison, he is unable to trust her and tells her his name is Jimmy Moore. Eventually, however, his relationship with Joyce unveils a pattern that subtends most vet noirs: a woman enables the veteran to release his rage and rediscover or remodel his identity. Women represent the civilian world where antisocial males must be punished, deflected into heterosexuality, or soothed by a maternal presence. Yet females remain dangerous. In this regard the film's title is significant. The Blue Dahlia is the name of Eddie Harwood's night club, and he uses the flowers as a calling card. But the same flowers remind Morrison of Helen's infidelity and of the lost domestic world that once included his son, killed when an inebriated Helen crashed their car. Dahlia petals were also found in the room where Helen was murdered; the sight of Joyce's plucking them later upsets Buzz and prompts him to recall the night in question. The dahlias are thus linked both to Buzz's cognitive disability and to a major source of Johnny's alienation: the unbridgeable gap between military and civilian domains and the alienation that breeds violence in this "second home." Once they are pulled from the flower, these petals, like the veterans' psyches, can't be reattached.

Though the murder mystery is eventually solved (a preposterous climax exposes Dad Newell [Will Wright], the detective at Helen's apartment complex, as Helen's killer), and Johnny ends up with Joyce, Buzz's amnesia and liability to violence are never fixed, and his readjustment remains very much in doubt.[11] The same is true in *Crossfire,* a film made by the trio of producer Adrian Scott, director Edward Dmytryk (both former Communists who were later indicted as members of the Hollywood Ten), and writer John Paxton. Though this film's primary target is anti-Semitism, the novel from which *Crossfire* was adapted, Richard Brooks's *The Brick Foxhole,* focuses on the problems of soldiers caught between war and peace.[12] The novel's title refers to the feelings of noncombatant soldiers immured in a "brick casket filled with living corpses" for whom "real war would [be] a gift" (Brooks 9, 73). Only hatred can "overcome their despair and loneliness" (81)—emotions palpable in the novel's protagonist, Jeff Mitchell, who entertains thoughts of killing his supposedly unfaithful wife. Like Fred Derry and Johnny Morrison, Mitchell is neither quite a soldier nor quite a civilian: he lies about having killed "Japs" (110) yet hates the uniform that tells "the world everything about him" (140).

Mitchell's sergeant, Monty Crawford (named Montgomery in the film), despises just about everyone and murders a gay man (who becomes a Jewish man named Samuels in the film). In contrast to the novel's all-too-obvious mouthpiece for fascist doctrine, the film's Monty voices many veterans' rage. Montgomery (played with frightening intensity by Robert Ryan) was doubtless a bigot before the war, but his military experience has hardened him into the picture of Waller's angry veteran who resents those who didn't fight (97) and for whom the civilian world is confusing and frightening (113). Indeed, as Capt. Finlay (Robert Young), the police detective who solves the murder, observes, "He was dead for a long time. He just didn't know it": Montgomery's humanity died in the war.[13] Samuels

(Sam Levene), the Jewish veteran who becomes Montgomery's victim, explains the problem to Mitchell (George Cooper) in a famous speech:

> For four years now we've been focusing our mind on . . . one little peanut. The win-the-war peanut. . . . All at once, no peanut. Now . . . we don't know what we're supposed to do. . . . We're too used to fightin', but we just don't know what to fight. You can feel the tension in the air. A whole lot of fight and hate that doesn't know where to go. A guy like you maybe starts hatin' himself. . . . One of these days maybe we'll all learn to shift gears. Maybe we'll stop hatin' and start likin' things again.

Whereas Montgomery's "peanut"—his PTSD—is manifest in violence, Mitchell's is passivity and hopelessness. A "sensitive, artist-type," Mitchell miserably wanders around Washington, DC, missing his wife and wearing a uniform that looks too large for him. As Robert Mitchum's big-brotherly Sgt. Keeley explains,

Single-source lighting casts eerie shadows on the faces of Floyd Bowers (Steve Brodie) and Montgomery (Robert Ryan) in *Crossfire*, just before Montgomery murders Floyd. *Kobal Collection / Art Resource, NY.*

"He's got snakes": Mitchell is depressed and paralyzed by a feeling of meaning-lessness. These vets' problems are illustrated in two striking cinematic moments. Just before Montgomery murders Samuels, the camera assumes Mitchell's point of view to show Montgomery's face blurring and splitting in two. This device at once captures Mitchell's drunken, alienated perceptions and the dissolution of Montgomery's psyche. In the second sequence a southern soldier named Leroy, at the behest of Finlay, baits Montgomery into hunting down Floyd Bowers, who had witnessed the murder of Samuels (and whom Montgomery has already killed; but Leroy suggests that Floyd is not dead). As Floyd and Montgomery stand at the sink shaving, Montgomery's face is shown in a small mirror hanging slightly above and to the left of Leroy's reflected face; Monty (already dead spiri-tually and soon to die bodily) is coffined by his hatred and prejudice. But Leroy, who once shared his bigotry, is free to move and to give up his war "peanut."[14] The two thus exemplify the choices for noir vets.

When Mitchell's wife, Mary (Jacqueline White), at last arrives and persuades him to give himself up, she is confronted by the bar girl, Ginny (Gloria Grahame), who can provide Mitchell's alibi. "Where were you when he needed you?" she asks Mary—as if the women abandoned the soldiers rather than the reverse. The war fractured marriages, but Mary and Ginny represent civilizing virtues—heterosexual domesticity, above all—that seem nearly as powerful as those espoused by Finlay ("our spokesman," according to Scott: Ceplair and Englund 453), who, with the Capitol building behind him, teaches Leroy a lesson in "real American history"—a tale of the dangers of prejudice and violence against minorities—designed to counteract Montgomery's bigotry. The House Un-American Activities Committee (HUAC) was less sanguine about these sentiments: the film drew the committee's attention and effectively ended Scott's career. But perhaps *Crossfire's* leftist ideals offended them less than its portrayal of American soldiers as inca-pacitated, murderous, and lost.

Restitution and Revenge

Montgomery's crime is motivated by a specific hatred but also by unfocused rage and a burning desire for a scapegoat. The same is true in *Cornered,* the previous film by the Scott/Dmytryk/Paxton trio, in which Lt. Lawrence Gerard (Dick Powell) pursues a vendetta against the Nazis whom he believes killed Celeste, his French war bride.[15] Sporting a long scar across his temple and subject to fugue-like attacks and blackouts, Gerard is every bit as cognitively disabled as Buzz or Fred Derry, and when Celeste's father (who chides Gerard for his obsession) lists the names of civilians who died alongside her, Gerard "hears" her name shouted amidst gunfire and nearly passes out. To find the collaborator responsible (a man named Jarnac), and to relieve his feelings of helplessness and guilt, Gerard is compelled to reenact the war and win it all over again. He angrily accuses Celeste's father of forgetting "too easily," but his own problem, like that of many noir vets, is that he can't stop remembering it.[16] Gerard explains: "War does something to your memory. Gets sharper. You forget the way people looked and remember the important things. That kind of remembering keeps you warm on cold nights." To keep the flame alive, he flies to Argentina to pursue the hiding Germans, then blunders and blusters about, nearly ruining the careful plans of the cadre of anti-fascists who have preceded him. "There's no place in our program for revenge or murderous hate," their leader declares. "We must have facts, . . . facts, facts!"

Gerard has little use for facts; he's a creature of emotion, an angry man who has gone "kill crazy." He fits Nadelson's description of a person "disabled in peace partly because he is not able to give up memories of war's wonder and of a contest survived," and whose repeated exercise of "control and dominance over terror becomes addictive" (78, 46). Gerard's insensitivity to others is displayed in a scene with Mme. Jarnac (Micheline Cheirel as a young French woman coerced into marrying the fascist). She speaks, but her words are drowned out by the noise of departing buses, and when the din induces another posttraumatic headache for Gerard, she comments, "You are sick with fear. You've been hurt so deeply you cannot trust anyone. . . . You're even more alone than I am." Jarnac himself taunts Gerard similarly near the end of the film, accusing him of being a "fanatic without real purpose"—with personal, rather than political, motives. Despite Gerard's nominal Canadian nationality, we may detect in him an implied criticism of American exceptionalism, that notorious unwillingness to negotiate or include others in our plans. Yet Gerard also enacts a more positive North American historical stereotype. Europeans dithered and appeased until North Americans took charge and triumphed over fascism, which the film depicts as a brand of hedonist decadence perpetuated by rich capitalists—in keeping with the filmmakers' Popular Front agenda (see Langdon-Teclaw 160).[17] At the end of the film Gerard's maverick methods are vindicated. And though his injury may have disabled him, those haunting memories have impelled him to reenact his wartime trauma and, perhaps, to prevent another war. The film's politics, then, are conflicted, at once criticizing Gerard's bullheadedness and celebrating his power. Like its protagonist, the film is suspended between past and future, both replaying the war and questioning the value of such reenactments.

Two later vet noirs present similar quests by ex-soldiers: each veteran seeks to repay or vindicate a friend's death and thereby release his own feelings of loss and betrayal. In *Dead Reckoning* Captain Rip Murdock (Humphrey Bogart), learning that his missing war buddy was an indicted murderer, tries to clear his name. Lucky Gagin (Robert Montgomery), in *Ride the Pink Horse,* seeks restitution from the mobster who killed his wartime friend, Shorty Thompson. Both vets struggle with PTSD, and both encounter women who serve as catalysts—in opposite ways—for their recovery. Like *Cornered,* these films dramatize how, as Nadelson writes, trauma victims "often desperately try to regain control by repeating and revisiting the event in dreams, fantasies, or re-enactments. . . . They repeat the experience to achieve mastery, *this time*" (88).

Dead Reckoning begins with ex-paratrooper Murdock recalling to a (uniformed) priest the last time he saw his friend, Sgt. Johnny Drake, just before he vanished during a train trip to Washington, where he was to receive the Medal of Honor. Rip had urged his friend to forget "that blonde" he couldn't stop thinking about. After Johnny disappears, Rip follows him to Gulf City, Florida, and there finds a message from "Mr. Geronimo" (named for the paratroopers' battle cry). Rip tells his confessor that "after what we'd been through, we could read each other's minds. He knew I'd want to help and trail him." The key clue is a Yale fraternity pin belonging to a Johnny Preston, the real name of Drake, who had joined the military to avoid imprisonment for killing a wealthy businessman. In other words Johnny gave himself "amnesia" to erase his prewar identity, then redeemed himself through combat heroism. In contrast, Rip can't forget either his friend or the wartime values of male friendship (and homosexual attraction), loyalty, and single-minded combat.

Before Rip can locate him, however, Johnny dies, burned beyond recognition in a car crash. Seeking a letter that Johnny had written to him, Murdock breaks into the office of the gangster Martinelli (future blacklistee Morris Carnovsky), who has tried to frame Rip for another murder in Gulf City.[18] Discovered in Martinelli's office, Murdock is blackjacked, after which he experiences a war flashback, replayed through those now-familiar expressionist techniques. "Just like going out the jump door, I was falling through space," he says in voice-over. A shot of a man jumping from a plane is followed by one of an opening parachute. Coming to, Rip sees Martinelli and his minion, Krause (Marvin Miller), who, Martinelli tells him, "suffered an injury to his brain once" and has been a psychopath ever since. The two criminals are Rip's and Johnny's dark doubles, figures of "sinister homosocial bonding" (Krutnik, *Lonely* 174) who also represent the fascist nations (Italy and Germany) against which Rip and Johnny fought. This posttraumatic episode unveils Rip's motives: he needs to relive the war not so much to redeem his lost buddy as to recreate the war's division of the world into obvious enemies and friends. And just as he wishes both to restore his former self and to create a new one, he also desires to remember *and* to forget.

His investigation becomes more complex after he meets and falls for the "Cinderella with a husky voice" whom Johnny loved—"that blonde," Coral Chandler (Lizabeth Scott), also the murdered man's widow. Just after they meet, she sings a tune that offers a stark choice: "Either it's love or it isn't. / You can't compromise." But loving Johnny's woman *would* compromise Rip's friendship with his buddy, and Rip's fear of women renders him incapable of intimacy. He tells Coral that "women ought to come capsule-sized, about four inches high. When a man goes out of an evening he just puts her in his pocket, . . . and that way he knows exactly where she is." And "when he wants her full-sized and beautiful, he just waves his hand and there she is, full-size." Understandably offended, Coral surprises Murdock by discerning the anxiety behind his words: "What you're saying is . . . a woman may drive you out of your mind, but you wouldn't trust her. And because you couldn't put her in your pocket, you get all mixed up." Rip's confusion about Coral is displayed in the names he gives her. First calling her "Dusty" (Johnny's nickname for her), he later dubs her "Mike": since only men are trustworthy, he must transform her into a male. Krutnik's analysis here is illuminating: her various names reveal a "chaotic circuit of conflicting allegiances, with Coral as: (i) Johnny's girl; (ii) Rip's rival in love for Johnny, and (iii) Rip's replacement for Johnny" (*Lonely* 176). Rip can love Johnny *through* her, love her instead of him, or hate her as a competitor. What he can't do is love her—or even see her—as herself. He needs her to be a fetish, a pinup or token that a soldier might carry for comfort during combat, not a woman.

It doesn't help that Coral gives mixed signals about her identity. After Rip accuses her of conspiring with Martinelli, she admits that she killed her husband and let Johnny take the rap, recalls her impoverished childhood in Texas, then picks up the phone to call the police so Rip can turn her in. Convinced by her story, Rip heartily kisses "Mike." This quasi-heteronormative relationship appears to have supplanted Rip's homosocial wartime love. But the film doesn't end there. During a climactic confrontation Martinelli informs Rip that Coral is actually *his* wife, her Texas childhood a fabrication, and that he himself shot Chandler. Unsure whom to believe, Murdock reverts to what he knows—war. He tosses two incendiary grenades ("How would you like yourself? Medium rare?")

and forces Martinelli to hand over Johnny's letter. As they flee the burning build-ing, Coral guns down Martinelli, and Rip realizes that she has set him up: he was supposed to be the first one out the door. After telling "Mike" that he's on to her game, he concludes, "You're going to fry, Dusty." The rest of the scene recalls the end of *The Maltese Falcon*. "When a guy's pal's killed," says Bogie's Rip, "he ought to do something about it." Coral: "Don't you love me?" Rip: "That's the tough part of it. But it'll pass. . . . Then there's one other thing: I loved him more." Instead of meekly returning to his pocket, however, she shoots him, and their car slams into a tree. The entire sequence thus replays the circumstances of Johnny's death—car, burned body, confused identities. But why does Rip call her "Mike" and then "Dusty"? Because Rip must now *become* Johnny, and to do so, he must turn Coral back into Dusty—Johnny's girl, the one who earlier betrayed him—both to justify his need to punish her and to punish himself for trusting her. In sacrificing Mike *and* Dusty, he also eliminates a rival for Johnny's affection—a full-sized woman he couldn't control.

After the crash, the shots from Rip's earlier PTSD awakening are repeated—except that this time it's Coral who sees the looming faces. Formerly Johnny's surrogate, she now becomes Rip's, taking his place as the sacrificial victim who reenacts and pays for Johnny's death. Rip comforts her: "It's like going out the jump door. . . . Don't fight it. Remember all the guys who've done it before you. . . . Geronimo, Mike." In dying for Johnny and Rip, Coral has reverted to Mike, a soldier who perishes so that others may live, just like Medal of Honor–winner Johnny. And though Rip first loved her *because* she was Johnny's girl, he can now bid her a safe, loving good-bye by placing her back within the framework of his wartime buddy relationship. Yet if her death clears Johnny's name, it hardly purges Rip's fear. Even with his lover(s) gone, Rip can't accept that the war is over (Krutnik, *Lonely* 181); like Gerard's, his purpose for living has vanished. "Mike's" death, then, fails to be truly sacrificial, because it doesn't give Rip a new life or new identity. He has recreated the war but not won it; lacking friend and lover, he remains an emotional amputee.

A similar sacrificial motif appears in *Ride the Pink Horse,* a noir set in the border town of San Pablo during La Fiesta (The Day of the Dead), which com-mences with the symbolic killing of a large effigy of Zozobra, the God of Gloom. Lucky Gagin, a "disillusioned patriot" and "haywire veteran," arrives in town armed with plans to kill his personal God of Gloom by extorting $30,000 from Frank Hugo (Fred Clark), a hearing-impaired gangster who murdered Gagin's friend Shorty Thompson.[19] Though lacking an obvious disability, Gagin is nonetheless a casualty of the war: unwilling to feel anything for anyone, he, like Gerard, can think only of revenge. Bill Retz (future blacklistee Art Smith), a federal agent also pursuing Hugo, diagnoses Gagin's disorder: "You're like the rest of the boys. All cussed up because you fought a war for three years and got nothing out of it but a dangle of ribbons. Why don't you let your Uncle Samuel take care of [Hugo]?" Gagin sneers, "Doesn't the government work for Hugo? It did all during the war." Gagin possesses a canceled check written by Hugo to a politician who was "making patriotic speeches" while Gagin was "getting a tan" in a "place called New Guinea." Hoping to blackmail Hugo with it, Gagin refuses Retz's demand to turn the check over to him: "Don't wave any flags at me. I've seen enough flags." Hugo's hearing impairment thus represents not only the evil of governmental collaboration with organized crime but, as I noted above, Gagin's moral deafness. Indeed, though repulsed by Hugo (whose identification with Zozobra is shown by lap dissolves from the figure to his face), Gagin is Hugo's effigy—a replica of his own bête noire. Poised on the border between humanity and inhumanity, Gagin can either become a miniature Zozobra or a force for good: he can die or be reborn.

Throughout the film Gagin is depicted as out of place: he orders whiskey in an all-Mexican bar that serves only tequila and is frequently shown in overhead shots walking against the grain of the festive crowd, the only person not smiling. Pancho (Thomas Gomez), an affable carousel operator, tells Gagin he's the "kind of man I like, the man with no place." Gagin's surly reply: "I'm nobody's friend." Over the course of the film he is humanized by Pancho and Pila (Wanda Hendrix), a young girl from a neighboring town who gives Gagin a good luck figurine to dispel his internal Zozobra. Indeed, the occasion of the festival is appropriate, according to Pila: "I saw his [Gagin's] face. Dead. His eyes were closed, the skin was white. He was dead." Like Montgomery, Johnny Preston, and other noir veterans, Gagin is a ghost in search of a new body. His desire for restitution thus involves conflicting urges: the need to kill his old self, purge his wartime trauma and become human vies with his wish to be inhumanly invulnerable.

Pila resurrects the good Gagin by eliciting his sympathy and showing him that he can't remain isolated. Thus, after Gagin is stabbed by Hugo's thugs, she reasons that they did it "because they are bad." "And I'm good, huh?" "Yes," she says, "I will take care of you." Gagin mumbles, "You're just . . . like Shorty. No brains. . . . It's hot in here, hot in the jungle." This brief flashback to the war helps Gagin slough off his rage and resentment: in "becoming" Shorty, Pila both revives Gagin's friend and midwifes his own rebirth.[20] Pancho, too, revivifies Gagin's trust by taking a beating from Hugo's hoodlums rather than betraying his friend. These somewhat stereotyped characters help Gagin rediscover his lost innocence, controverting the mercenary values embraced by Hugo and his girlfriend Marjorie (Andrea King).

In the end Gagin yields to Retz, despite Hugo's taunting that Retz will "give you a lot of gas about duty and honor. Fill you with fancy words like *responsibility, patriotism. . . .* And what're you gonna have? Nothin'." Words that Gagin could have spoken earlier in the film now bounce off him. He returns the good luck figurine to Pila, having incorporated it within himself. Gagin achieves restitution. Like the men in *Best Years* and Morrison in *The Blue Dahlia*, he is able to forget the war, remodel himself, and start anew with the support of a woman and a friend.[21] By forgetting, Gagin re-members himself: he recalls his past, restores his missing heart, and rejoins the human race. His restoration is thus more complete than that of most soldiers in the squad of noir vets, who are tortured by memories they can retrieve only in moments of extreme stress. Although these characters don't use prostheses like Homer Parrish, some are able to emulate him by learning to work with others, adapt to new conditions, and integrate their old and new selves—or even produce a third identity, a phoenix figure who combines the best of both. Gagin thus embodies a Franklinesque faith in Americans' powers of self-making, albeit tempered by a recognition of trauma's hardening effects.

Forgetting

"Even if you wipe out a man's memory, doesn't it stand to reason that his brain is the same, that his . . . standards are the same?" Or does "three years of war . . . change a man" irrevocably? These questions, asked in Joseph L. Mankiewicz's *Somewhere in the Night,* offer opposing possibilities: on the one hand, that amnesiacs retain their original selves; on the other, that the self is infinitely changeable, and that experiences alter one's identity and values in an ongoing process. Beneath them is the question I posed at the outset of this study: is identity an essence to be discovered or a malleable set of behaviors and beliefs? Though a second set of vet noirs asks this question directly, its answer is ambiguous.

Whereas the first platoon of ex-soldiers exposes the entrapping effects of unassimilable but ineradicable memories, the second explores the spaces of forgetting. In these vets the noir themes of alienation and isolation are given a material cause: along with their names or pasts, these ex-soldiers have lost all connection to the friends, lovers, and enemies who once defined them. Yet each is haunted by his forgotten past and might echo Ole Anderson's words, "I did something wrong—once."[22] Though these vets suffer from disabilities different from those discussed above, their narratives follow the same arc, as they encounter their pre-war selves and relive their traumas, while attempting to give restitution to those they have harmed, redeem themselves for wrongdoing, and either integrate their new and old identities or reinvent themselves entirely. The selves these amnesiacs at once seek and flee from, notes Santos, are "uncanny doubles, 'others'" whom they must "assimilate or destroy in order to reach psychological wholeness" (67). Indeed, these vets seek to re-member themselves in several ways: recall their previous lives; reattach that former self, like an amputated hand or leg; and rejoin humanity and American society.

As John Belton observes, "these amnesiacs epitomize the social estrangement and psychological confusion that has settled in the formerly healthy American psyche after the war. Audiences establish a troubled identification with these heroes . . . whose identity crises mirror those of the nation as a whole" (189–90). The United States was, of course, settled by immigrants who had abandoned their previous lives and built new selves unburdened by the past. Like the missing person films, then, the veteran-amnesia noirs probe the American ideals of self-reinvention and the pursuit of happiness. As "Immigrants in Their Native Land" (Waller 180), these former soldiers serve as synecdoches for postwar America's efforts to recreate itself and as test cases for the viability of the American Dream.

Reinvention

As *Somewhere in the Night* opens, the camera floats through a hospital ward in Honolulu, then hovers over a bandaged man lying on a bed. We hear the faceless man in voice-over: "I don't know my name. You—talk to me. Act like I was alive, not just somebody with eyes and no name. Think of a name. Taylor. Think of another name; there must be other names. Taylor. No. Taylor. No. Taylor. Taylor." The voice is that of one George W. Taylor (John Hodiak), who has lost his memory owing to a war injury, his identity verified only by his wallet and a far from heartening letter. "I despise you now," it reads. "I'm ashamed for having loved you. I shall pray as long as I live for someone . . . to hurt and destroy you, make you want to die, as you have me." Later we learn the full story: Taylor failed to show up at his wedding with a woman named Mary; the jilted bride was then struck by a car while crossing the street. If Taylor was such a heel, perhaps his amnesia is a blessing.

Taylor explores his old LA haunts, repeatedly encountering the friends and enemies of a Larry Cravat, who left Taylor $5,000. The more we know of Cravat, the less we like him. He was a low-level but honest detective, until "somebody dropped two million clams right in his lap"—money that the Nazis had stolen. Cravat was also wanted for murder. As the characters' names imply, the film explores identity via a clothing trope, eventually revealing that Taylor *is* Cravat, having borrowed his new name from the label inside his coat: "W. George, tailor." Like Johnny Preston in *Dead Reckoning,* Cravat camouflaged his past by joining the military. Ironically, his plan has turned into a grim joke on himself: the man who intentionally gave himself "amnesia" now truly doesn't remember anything.[23]

Though Cravat was a shady character, Taylor seems earnest and well-meaning, which implies that Cravat has changed more than his coat and tie. Nor can we help but sympathize when he bares his soul to Christy (Nancy Guild), a nightclub singer who was the late Mary's best friend and who now falls for Taylor. Although his amnesia may have handed Taylor what he calls a "brand new scorepad," it also makes him an alien—one of Waller's immigrants in his native land. "Do you know what it's like, Christy," he asks, "to be alone in the world? Really alone in the whole world? A billion people and every one of them a stranger." Santos speculates that Taylor epitomizes "the ultimate existential hero" (or antihero) who can "create any identity he wishes" (82; Taylor later gives his name as "Tom Carter" to a police detective pursuing Cravat). But it's not so simple, which becomes clear as Taylor continues, "Or what's worse, not a stranger. Somebody maybe who knows you, hates you, wants you to die." In other words he is not really alone, because his retailoring hasn't removed the threads tying him to Cravat. Like other noir veterans, Taylor/Cravat is dangling between past and future, old and new selves. Christy (who, like Joyce Harwood and Gagin's Pila, endeavors to redeem and renew her troubled vet) voices his condition in a song: "I'm in the middle of nowhere / I'm in betwixt and between."

As he seeks an exit from nowhere, Taylor/Cravat feels he is "chasing shadows," which the film illustrates by showing his enlarged shadow accompany him wherever he goes. In fact, the phrase fits all of noir's amnesiac vets, each one chasing the shadow of his former self (who may also be his own bête noire), while attempting to flesh out his new silhouette. Taylor/Cravat's chase leads him to a man named Conroy (Houseley Stevenson), who witnessed the 1942 murder of which Cravat is accused but was then run down by a car and has been incarcerated in an asylum ever since. Taylor/Cravat interviews Conroy's daughter, Elizabeth

(Josephine Hutchinson), who speaks for Taylor/Cravat in confessing that she has always pretended that "I wasn't dead, that I was alive. I wanted so to make believe that somebody loved me once." He consoles her: "I know a little bit about being lonely." Such empathetic connections may permit Cravat/Taylor to banish his shadow—or merge with it. But he is nearly denied the chance: on leaving Elizabeth's apartment, he is nearly run down by a truck, only narrowly avoiding replaying Mary's and Conroy's fates. Conroy himself has anterograde amnesia: unable to form new memories, he believes it's still 1942. An inverted Cravat, he is the shadow Taylor must banish before he can unite his new and old personae. Fortunately, before Conroy is stabbed to death by another shadowy figure, Taylor—who has retained Cravat's detective skills—gains a key bit of information: the murdered man left a suitcase on the dock.

In the film's most effective sequence, shot night-for-night on the docks, Taylor and Christy find the suitcase containing the money and the coat revealing his identity. Then they flee to a storefront mission, where the film appends a religious element to Taylor's quest for redemption, and where Christy utters the lines about identity quoted at the beginning of this section. George Taylor isn't capable of murder, but what about Larry Cravat? Does amnesia change a person irrevocably, or does one's essential nature endure? Has Taylor, because of his war injury and resulting amnesia, discarded his Cravat and fashioned a new, improved identity? Or is our protagonist neither Taylor nor Cravat but a third self who blends Cravat's savvy with Taylor's honesty? The rather contrived resolution, in which Mel Phillips turns out to be the murderer, doesn't provide answers. It is clear, however, that Taylor, with Christy's help, achieves redemption, first by forgetting and then by remembering himself. *Somewhere in the Night,* then, ultimately affirms the ideology of self-recreation, proposing that, rather than recovering their prewar selves, Americans are better off tossing them aside like suits of outdated clothing.

Made three years after *Somewhere in the Night, The Crooked Way* is a virtual remake that is immeasurably enriched by John Alton's striking cinematography. It opens at Letterman General Hospital in San Francisco, where amnesiac veteran and Silver Star awardee Eddie Rice (John Payne) is being interviewed: "Where were you born, Eddie? Who were your parents? . . . Are you rich? Poor? Got a girl? Married?" Situated to the far left of the frame, Eddie is lit only with a small light source on one side, as if reduced by amnesia to a silhouette. He hopes to meet someone who will fill in his outline, but Alton casts doubt by scoring Eddie's face and body with shadowy lines that suggest entrapment. His doctor goes on to distinguish between psychological and organic amnesia, noting that Eddie's is the latter—a piece of steel lodged in his brain has erased his memory. But actually he has both kinds: like Larry Cravat, he joined the service to escape his former identity as Eddie Riccardi, who was involved in a 1942 murder but turned State's evidence against his old friend, gangster Vince Alexander (Sonny Tufts).

After Eddie pays a visit to his ex-wife, Nina Martin (Ellen Drew, another nightclub singer), she informs Alexander that Eddie has returned, and, in a scene recalling *The Killers* and foreshadowing Alton's later work in *The Big Combo,* Vince and his thugs rough Rice up as neon lights flash outside his room, perhaps representing the flickering lights of Eddie's memory. On receiving Alexander's ultimatum—disappear within twenty-four hours or else—Eddie stares into a mirror, which, as in *Best Years* and *Crossfire,* indicates his coexisting but unintegrated identities. Although Nina refuses to help him, she does gaze longingly at the engraved cigarette case he gave her years earlier, inscribed "NINA / With All My Love / Till The Day I Die. / EDDIE." This item tangibly links him to his former self; yet it also suggests that, like Montgomery, Gagin, and noir's other disabled vets, Eddie has become a ghost or zombie. A witty moment in the film develops this metaphor. After Vince frames him for the murder of Detective Lieutenant Williams (who had determined that Eddie was innocent of the earlier crime), a fleeing Eddie is picked up by a hearse. But perhaps he still has a chance to be resurrected rather than embalmed.

Indeed, Eddie eventually persuades Nina to help him; she even takes a bullet for him. As he nurses her, she says, "You're far away. How far?" From her point of view we see Eddie's visage enveloped in shadow, illustrating his self-erasure. When he answers, "Five years. A lifetime," his face is suddenly illuminated, and he wonders "what it would be like if there'd only been an Eddie Rice." Nina responds, "Oh, you're good, Eddie. You're good." If she believes in him, it must be true. Again a woman's love redeems a disabled vet by affirming his goodness. But in this case redemption can happen only if the vet entirely erases his former self.

At last Eddie turns for help to Petey (Percy Helton), an old acquaintance who runs a war surplus store—an appropriate place to cast off his prewar persona. Instead of reposing on the bed Petey provides, Eddie packs a blanket with an army fatigue jacket and helmet and places them on the bed. During a break in the ensuing gun battle (the first shots are fired at the camouflaged bedroll, metaphorically murdering Riccardi), Vince proposes that he and Eddie revive their partnership. While he considers the proposition, Eddie's face is half-shadowed to suggest Riccardi's potential resurrection, but he ultimately rejects the offer.

Vince then subdues Eddie and tries to use his limp body as a shield, just as he used to do with Riccardi—now merely an empty shell—but the tactic fails, and Vince is killed. We end where we began, with Eddie Rice in the hospital, where he and Nina agree that he'll remain Eddie Rice forever.

If George Taylor retains some vestiges (doggedness, street smarts) of Cravat, Eddie Rice is divorced from everything of Riccardi except his wife. Yet both *The Crooked Way* and *Somewhere in the Night* suggest that prewar identities are a hindrance in the postwar world, amnesia a necessary precondition for writing a new scorepad. Indeed, insofar as it frees these vets from louche associations and illegal activities and permits redemption, the war is a blessing. But they are not just isolated cases: in these amnesiacs postwar audiences not only witnessed their own anxieties—their alienation; their lost innocence and desire to recover it; the sense that the prewar world was irrelevant, even a burden—they also watched their dreams of self-renewal fulfilled. These two films endorse the American Dream in which alienation gradually yields to self-affirmation and in which a life's second act may redeem an original sin.

Reenactment

The final two vet noirs, however, emphasize that reinvention requires enormous sacrifices. These films' amnesiacs embody both the complex anxieties and ambivalences left from the war *and* a new set of fears—of invasion, of prying and super-powerful legal and medical institutions—typical of the emergent Cold War. Curtis Bernhardt's *High Wall* (scripted by Sydney Boehm and future black-listee Lester Cole) employs its disabled veteran to question the humanity of medical and legal institutions; this vet's restoration occurs only after he is tamed by powerful institutions. Fred Zinnemann's *Act of Violence,* scripted by ex-Communist Robert Richards, is a powerful, sophisticated study of guilt resulting from the collision of remembering and forgetting; it raises thorny ethical questions about loyalty and forgiveness. Both films' ambience of surveillance and fear evokes the paranoid atmosphere of the HUAC era, and each leaves behind a residue of anxiety.

Just after *High Wall* opens, a disheveled man, an unconscious woman sprawled beside him, wrecks his car. The man confesses to the police that the woman—his wife, Helen (Dorothy Patrick)—was already dead before the crash, because he had strangled her. But the man, ex-bomber pilot Steven Kenet (Robert Taylor) has previously had brain surgery, so he must undergo a psychiatric evaluation before he can be tried. His history is traumatic: wounded in the war, Kenet recovered as a result of surgery. Yet he still felt "restless," like many veterans with PTSD, and went to Burma to fly freight planes, leaving behind his wife and young son. Another "slight crack-up" there left him with a subdural hematoma that causes severe headaches, mood swings, and memory lapses; during one of these attacks he allegedly murdered his wife. But his memory of the murder has been rendered irretrievable by the hematoma. In short, Kenet is a man cut in half, a vet who can neither remember *nor* forget. The doctors, including the beautiful Ann Lorrison (Audrey Totter), insist that Kenet undergo further surgery, but he refuses, thereby reinforcing the district attorney's suspicion that he is malingering to avoid trial.[24]

Kenet's resistance isn't merely a delaying tactic: he recognizes the grim calculus of this institution, where twenty-five hundred patients are served by a paltry twelve doctors, and where patients with a wide array of illnesses are thrown together randomly. The hospital, one of Foucault's "carceral/therapeutic" networks, thus engenders new "procedures of individualization" (305), giving inmates institutionalized identities that strip away their agency and replace it with scientifically classified data. In this world psychiatrists have donned the robes of judges; each person under their aegis "subjects to it his body, his gestures, his behaviors, his aptitudes, his achievements" (Foucault 304).[25] Thus we may read Kenet's resistance as a desire to preserve his guilt and thereby his humanity, even if doing so permits his debilitating condition to persist and subjects him to a criminal indictment.

But after the death of Kenet's mother, who had cared for his six-year-old son, Dickie, Dr. Lorrison coldly informs him that the boy will be sent to the county orphanage. "Do you know what life is like for an orphan in a public institution?" she asks threateningly. Having experienced a taste of institutional life, Kenet recoils in horror. She has recognized his hidden motive for resisting—shame. If he never stands trial, he'll never have to face the son he abandoned. And so Kenet agrees to the surgery, which does palliate his headaches. But the doctors aren't finished; next he must undergo "narcosynthesis"—injection with sodium pentothal—to uncover the truth about the murder they believe he is concealing.[26] During the interrogation Kenet is pushed into the corner of the frame and filmed from behind the questioner's shoulder, so that his head appears to sprout from the doctor's body: he is now their creature. Kenet doesn't deny his guilt; he merely wishes to preserve his own "rights" to provide for his son's future. Yet when the doctors offer to bring Dickie to him, a panicked look crosses Kenet's face, followed by irate shouting: "You can't push people around like this! What kind of doctors are you?" At his words the camera rises and pulls back, leaving him diminished and alone at the edge of the frame—one of many shots in the film that invoke the title and expose how institutions squash human autonomy.[27]

Under the drug's influence Kenet recalls visiting the apartment of Helen's employer, religious publisher Willard Whitcombe (Herbert Marshall), where Kenet found her in a compromising position. From Helen's point of view we see Kenet's haggard face, its right side bathed in shadow, then a close-up from his point of view of her terrified face. Kenet began to strangle her but desisted when his headache became too intense and then passed out. A now-familiar expressionist montage shows a whirlpool image, which dissolves into a spinning merry-go-round, along with tinkling music. Awakening, Kenet found the room in disarray and Helen lying dead. This flashback both disrupts and propels the narrative, at once knocking a hole in the story and providing it with a motive, as Kenet must prove he didn't kill his wife in order to convince his son he is a good man. So he and Dr. Lorrison return to Whitcombe's apartment so that Kenet can reenact the crime—with the doctor playing Helen. As Nadelson reminds us, Kenet is attempting to "repeat the experience to achieve mastery, *this time*" (88). The reenactment yields missing evidence: a carousel music box and Helen's monogrammed night bag.

Kenet's amnesia derives from a paralyzing double-bind: he wants to be both guilty and innocent, yearns both to remember and to forget. He wanted to kill his wife, but Whitcombe did it for him. Both of them have "amnesia": Whitcombe pretends not to remember killing Helen.[28] Earlier in the film, Whitcombe served as both Kenet's guilty conscience and his satanic tempter, urging him to plead temporary insanity and then taunting him that any accusation against Whitcombe would be ridiculed as the "ravings of a pitiful lunatic." At the film's conclusion, however, Kenet and Lorrison capture Whitcombe and, with the aid of sodium pentothal, induce him to confess to Helen's murder.

Though the film ends with the promised father-son reunion and a kiss between Kenet and Ann, it leaves a sour aftertaste. Kenet ultimately remembers his past and is re-membered into society, but he has left large parts of himself behind. And his "redemption" occurs only after he has submitted to the combined forces of the medical establishment and the police, whose enforcement technologies—depicted in a montage of teletypes, radios, and phones during the pursuit of Kenet—appear omniscient. Indeed, compared to the potency and ubiquity of these medical and legal institutions, Whitcombe's sordid little murder seems tame. And though our hero achieves the American dream of a reconstituted home (complete with son and psychiatrist wife to care for him), we have peeked behind the curtain to glimpse what the dream hides: oppressive technologies that regulate and shape desire in socially acceptable ways. Although this atmosphere of suspicion may owe a good deal to director Bernhardt's experiences in Nazi Germany, the film's aura of surveillance and control also heralds the Cold War, when citizens (including one of the film's writers) were monitored and punished for alleged subversion.[29] *High Wall*, then, tells a story of containment in which a disabled body—its impairments the product of an increasingly forgotten war—is segmented, disciplined, and fixed so that its possessor can be remolded into a docile bourgeois subject. He achieves the American Dream but only by subjecting himself to forces that undermine the Dream's celebration of individual liberty.

Although the ostensible topic of Fred Zinnemann's *Act of Violence* is the ethics of forgiveness, it also expands the paranoid atmosphere of *High Wall*. And if its theme of loyalty and the morality of informing is germane to World War II, it is even more pertinent to the mood of the late 1940s and early 1950s, when leftist filmmakers were encouraged to inform on each other, and when many were afflicted with "amnesia" about their previous political activities.[30] Further, Joe Parkson's sinister invasion of Frank Enley's home strikingly stages Americans' fears of being invaded or spied on by former wartime allies. These elements provide unmistakable subtexts for a story about the confrontation between veterans Enley (Van Heflin) and Parkson (Robert Ryan) over an incident that occurred when both were German POWs.

Parkson suddenly appears at the Memorial Day parade in Enley's California hometown, limping a perpendicular path through the marchers. The moment illustrates his condition: for him the war isn't over, so he is immune to these rituals of reconciliation and commemoration. In another sense, however, Parkson is a living Memorial Day—an embodiment of wartime trauma, a walking corpse. The bleak mise-en-scène immediately lightens when we cut to Enley, a civic leader looked on as a war hero. Whereas Parkson is bathed in shadows, often shot in singles, Enley is surrounded by a crowd of smiling admirers. Indeed, as a contractor who builds new homes, he seems to epitomize the bright postwar future. But his image is a lie constructed on willful amnesia about his term in a prison camp, when he informed his Nazi keepers of his fellow POWs' escape plan.

After spotting Parkson stalking him on his fishing trip, Enley returns home terrified ("I remembered something," he tells his friend). Turning off the lights and closing the blinds, he cowers in the dark with his wife, Edith (Janet Leigh).

But they can't silence the ominous drag-scrape of Parkson's leg, damaged because of Enley's wartime action. The sound is the echo of Enley's crime, his guilt come to life: Parkson's leg embodies Enley's moral disability.[31] Just as his son Georgie is seldom seen outside his barred crib, so his father's seemingly happy domicile is really a prison, his American dream home a fraud constructed on a crime. Because he has never come to terms with his past, he has purchased a false contentment by erecting a high wall in his mind. Both he and Parkson, in short, are still prisoners of war.

In a harrowing scene set on the staircase of a hotel where Enley is attending a convention, Edith hears her husband's confession. Bars and rails dominate the shadowy mise-en-scène, and Zinnemann shoots the sequence with very few cuts, to concentrate our attention on Enley's anguished words. As the senior officer in his bunkhouse, Enley had told the Nazi commandant about his men's imminent escape because he knew it was doomed to fail and hoped that by informing he could prevent his men from being killed. But he no longer believes in his rationale. "I was an informer," he concludes. "It doesn't make any difference why I did it. I betrayed my men. . . . The Nazis even paid me a price. They gave me food and I ate it. . . . I hadn't done it just to save their lives. . . . Maybe that's all I did it for: to save one man, me. . . . There were ten men dead, and I couldn't even stop eating." As he speaks, his immense shadow looms over him: his past, in pursuit. Considering the atmosphere in Hollywood at the time (the film was shot less than a year after the first HUAC hearings), one cannot help but hear in these lines a stark outline of former communists' dilemma as well: should one inform on one's peers if it means saving one's career? The film's screenwriter, Robert Richards, faced this dilemma; rather than inform, he took the Fifth Amendment (Navasky 169).

Still, perhaps Enley is too hard on himself. In retrospect he believes he informed only to save his skin, but the circumstances were complicated, indeed, impossible: the Nazis withheld food from prisoners precisely to divide them from each other and make individual survival paramount in each one's mind. They induced Enley to violate the soldiers' code, which, as Nadelson describes it, reshapes the self so that "'I' passes insensibly into 'we,' 'my' becomes 'our' and individual fate loses its central importance" (23). Enley committed the grievous crime of turning "we" back into "I," putting his own life above those of his men. In cutting himself off from the group, he branded himself a coward, one of those soldiers who, in the words of J. Glenn Gray, cannot escape death because "death is within." The coward is doomed, writes Gray, because "the more he struggles to

In *Act of Violence,* Frank Enley (Van Heflin) confesses to his wife, Edith (Janet Leigh), that he informed on his fellow POWs during the war. *Kobal Collection / Art Resource, NY.*

escape the greater is his captivity" (115). This is exactly Enley's predicament: not merely a prisoner, he is, in fact, already dead.

Both of these traumatized ex-soldiers try to reenact their trauma in order to master it at last (see Nadelson 88).[32] Though spiritually dead, Enley may, para-doxically, be resurrected by sacrificing himself, by restaging the traumatic cir-cumstances and accepting the consequences he originally eschewed. Conversely, Parkson, at the mercy of his obsession (which Zinnemann illustrates by constantly placing him in doorways or pushing him into the corner of the frame), has sought release, perversely, by *becoming* a kind of Nazi, determined to punish a man he deems unfit to live. The men are counterparts, as Zinnemann indicates with two lap dissolves late in the film, the first from Enley to Parkson, the second from Parkson to Enley. Each is his own worst enemy, his own bête noire.

Women again serve as voices of civility and restraint. Edith reassures Frank that he "only did what [he] thought was right." Parkson's girlfriend, Ann (Phyllis Thaxter), rebukes him. "Are you the law? . . . He's lived a decent, useful life ever since. But what have you done? What are you going to prove anyway with your vengeance, your violence? . . . You're just gonna smash a few more lives." Even Pat (Mary Astor), the frowsy barfly who befriends Enley after he rushes in despair from the convention hotel into a seamy section of LA, observes that he made "just one mistake. . . . Everybody makes mistakes." But these men can hear only the voices of the past—literally, in Enley's case, as he descends into a personal hell, dashing through darkened streets into the arms of Pat, who brings him to the corrupt lawyer Gavery (Taylor Holmes) and his minion, the assassin Johnny (Berry Kroeger). Gavery panders to Enley's selfishness and self-hatred—the same weaknesses that victimized him during the war—to persuade him to have Parkson killed: "You're the same man you were in Germany," he purrs. "What do you care about one more man? You sent ten along already. Sure, you're sorry they're dead. That's the respectable way to feel. Get rid of this guy and be sorry later. . . . It's him or you." Is Enley innately weak and selfish—"born that way"—or a good man who made a mistake? Can he discover his better self, or transform himself into a man capable of dying for others?

What follows is one of the most powerful scenes in the noir canon as Enley, stumbling from Gavery into a tunnel, relives his nightmare, hearing Gavery's insinuations, the voices of the POWs planning their escape, and that of the Nazi commandant assuring him that his men will be treated leniently. He recalls pleading with Parkson, "Don't do it, Joe!"—words he now screams, his agonized voice echoing off the walls. The hollow tunnel amplifies Enley's torture. Why a tunnel? Because the men he betrayed had dug a tunnel to freedom. Enley has dug his own tunnel, but its walls have collapsed, and he is about to be buried alive in this nightmare alley. Reeling toward the railroad tracks, he halts, intending to let an oncoming train smash him. At the last minute he leaps away, unable even to muster the courage to commit suicide, which, in any case, would merely prove Gavery's accusations. Finally succumbing to Johnny's blandishments, Enley tells him where to find Parkson and arranges to meet him on the Southern Pacific tracks at 9:00 p.m.

In the climactic sequence Zinnemann uses the clock (as he does in *High Noon*) to ratchet up suspense and the approaching train's whistle to express the men's anguish. The wide shots of the tracks and walking men reiterate the design of the tunnel scene, implying that this reenactment—in which Enley again sets up

Parkson to be shot—will eliminate Enley's problem forever. But instead Enley dives into the bullet's path and then attaches himself to the running board of Johnny's car, causing it to crash into a light pole and kill them both. Is Enley's death a just punishment for a war crime? Or is it an expiation—a cathartic reiteration of the camp incident in which he, at last, does the right thing, sacrificing himself for his fellow soldier and mastering the event? Whatever answer one proposes, the ritual of reenactment seems to close the narrative circle: Enley's amnesia is erased, along with Parkson's posttraumatic memory and vendetta. Yet Enley's re-membering is only partial: his recollection may permit restitution, but he can never regain what he has lost nor become a member of the postwar world. Remembering may restore the missing parts of a human or social body, but that healed body is never quite the same.

Beneath this story we may discern two related political allegories. One poses the same ethical questions raised by the HUAC hearings, when the government and "patriotic" groups worked hard to rebrand the act of informing from a breach of loyalty to a patriotic duty. The second is this: a former ally, disabled by the war, invades the dwelling place of an American who shrinks in fear, blankets his home in secrecy, and enlists shady accomplices to eliminate the invader. If we read Parkson as the Soviet Union, the film acquires a new meaning: our onetime friends are now enemies threatening our way of life. They remind us of our wartime compromise—turning a blind eye to one tyrant in order to vanquish another. Even if our fear of this enemy is justified, can we end the threat without debasing our own values and becoming just like them? These questions preoccupied American politics throughout the next three decades, and the film suggests, via Parkson, that we were already imitating the very values soldiers had fought so hard to eradicate. Our fears led us to jail thousands of citizens for exercising their constitutional rights, to destroy or damage the careers of many citizens, to form alliances with dictators, and to build and maintain massive arsenals of destructive weapons. Like Frank Enley, in pursuing complete security we instead generated a pervasive sense of insecurity.

Is defending our home worth the price of constant anguished vigilance? Can informers be forgiven if they sacrifice themselves? Is "amnesia" about one's former associations acceptable so long as one confesses them or dies trying to rectify them? *Act of Violence* doesn't answer these questions. Yet it does imply that both the loss of memory *and* its extraordinary persistence prevented postwar Americans from living authentically and fruitfully. In all of the vet noirs, indeed, remembering and forgetting are depicted as equally daunting obstacles to personal and national integrity and well-being. In these films one must recall the past but only as a pre-lude to forgetting it all over again. The American dream of self-reinvention, they suggest, cannot be accomplished without traumatic sacrifice. The disabled cog-nition of these veterans thus exemplifies postwar America's crisis of memory and guilt, which never really found resolution but merely metamorphosed into a different set of fears. Noir veterans' healing or reintegration could occur after they were broken down and then rebuilt. But into what sort of world were they reborn? Into a new America, purged of its history of violence and trauma? Or into a world shadowed by the fear of atomic destruction, a world haunted by a past that had been forcibly remolded by institutions that, in seeking to prevent history from repeating itself, instead reenacted it over and over?

4

Framed
Forging Noir Identities

"Every painting is a love affair," according to cashier and Sunday painter Chris Cross (Edward G. Robinson), in Fritz Lang's *Scarlet Street*. Cross is explaining his aesthetic principles to Katherine "Kitty" March (Joan Bennett), who later conspires with her lover, the slimy Johnny Prince (Dan Duryea), to sign Cross's paintings with her name. Cross's words resonate beyond this film; indeed, they could provide the epigraph for a group of early films noir that depict men falling in love with a woman's portrait.[1] Three films in particular—*I Wake Up Screaming, Laura,* and *The Dark Corner*—feature fetishized female images that males use to bolster their own identities or to fashion new ones. These women's portraits become, in effect, mirrors or self-portraits of the men. In these retellings of the Galatea/Pygmalion myth each man ends up creator and forger of the woman and of himself. The pictorial representations in the films also generate two types of self-reflexivity. First, in employing the typical noir device of the framed narrative or flashback, the films analogically replicate the fashioning of these characters' framed identities within exploitative perspectives. Second, their stories of fabricated female identities invoke Hollywood's own fabrication of female stars in the studio system.

A second triad of painting films—Lang's *The Woman in the Window* and *Scarlet Street,* and the film on which the latter was based, Jean Renoir's (nonnoir) *La chienne*—employs painting to explore problems of originality, authorship, and replication. In testing the relation between unconscious desire and waking life, *Woman* explicitly depicts its female portrait as an aspect of the male psyche. Here the lines between representation and viewer become nearly invisible: the portrait is less a painting than a mirror. *Scarlet Street* multiplies the reflections, at once repainting Lang's *Woman* and forging a copy of Renoir's film. The latter two films also stage a debate about cinematic authorship and record the filmmakers' concerns about their position in a culture that devalues art in favor of commerce. Finally, the little-known 1946 film *Crack-Up* uses an art-forgery plot to complicate further these problems of authenticity, originality, and subjectivity, posing anxious but ultimately unresolved questions about the reliability of memory and pictorial representation.

These films also enrich the discussion of self-reinvention and individualism that I have been pursuing. Whereas the dream films, missing-person movies, and vet noirs test the virtues of self-reinvention and the pursuit of happiness, ultimately finding them vexed but viable—albeit requiring immense sacrifices and often limited by social institutions and personal and national traumas—the forgery films' complex aesthetic offers a more pointed challenge. In blurring the lines between originality and forgery, subjectivity and objectivity, real and representation, these films imply that human character is too malleable and complex to be framed within a single subject or explained by a single narrative. They advance the idea that identity is not an entity but a never-ending process. They thus turn upside down Franklin's optimism about self-creation, implying that self reinvention may occur not as a result of individual choice but as an inevitable by-product of the gap between humans and our representations. Their critique of individualism is less political than philosophical and ontological, as they propose that all identities are, to some degree, forgeries.

Dream Girls

In *I Wake Up Screaming* the murder of model Vicky Lynn (Carole Landis) precipitates a search for her killer. Four witnesses recall, in ten flashbacks, the circumstances leading to her death. Promoter Frankie Christopher (Victor Mature) relates how he "discovered" Vicky while she was working as a waitress and collaborated with washed-up actor Robin Ray (Alan Mowbray) and columnist Larry Evans (Allyn Joslyn) to create her as a "face." Christopher—real name, Botticelli—aims to paint her as a goddess. Yet the flashback structure suggests that each narrator has imagined a somewhat different Vicky: Ray, for example, testifies that "the very sight of her gave me new hope" that he might revive his career. Vicky's image would refresh *his* image. Although Vicky insists to Frankie, "I'm a very attractive girl. You didn't create that. I'm no Frankenstein, you know," Frankie implies (as does the film) that she is just that—a synthetic creature pasted together from fragments of others' aspirations. Like Charles Foster Kane she remains a puzzle, a mirror within a mirror—a canvas on which others paint their own desires and values.

Vicky has always known she would be somebody, and now she has a chance to pursue her version of the American Dream ("Over the Rainbow" is played when

Christopher first takes her on as a client). But her sister, Jill (Betty Grable), is less sanguine and reminds Vicky of her class origins: what do people like Frankie Christopher, she asks, have to do with "people like us?" She also warns her that "one week your face is on the cover of a magazine, and the next it's in the ashcan." Vicky dismisses the admonition. "From that moment on," Jill recalls, "life became just one great dizzy world for her"; before long she even "fancie[d] herself as a chanteuse." Grable's presence injects a curiously self-reflexive note into this examination of celebrity. Her career followed a path similar to Vicky's, largely because her mother, Lillian, pushed her toward stardom at an early age and insisted that her daughter "make as many publicity and personal appearances as possible" (Billman 3). Like Vicky, Betty was groomed to be a singer, despite her so-so voice. Lillian's promotion paid off: after a series of lightweight roles in the 1930s, Grable grew wildly famous as one of the GIs' favorite pinups during World War II. She became identified with—even subsumed by—an iconic picture of herself in a bathing suit, her back to the camera, peeking flirtatiously over her shoulder. Betty Grable *became* a pinup photo.[2] The performance in *I Wake Up Screaming*, Grable's second and last dramatic role (Pastos 56), exposes her limitations as an actress: her picture doesn't fit this frame. Yet her presence also obscures the lines between the real and the representation, reminding us of the artificiality of all actors' personae and inserting a mirror into the film's pictorial frame.

In a sense Vicky's death scarcely matters, so long as her picture lives on. This fact becomes clear when Jill later recounts how she found Vicky's body. Christopher bends over the corpse, a circular portrait of Vicky behind him; Jill then moves upstage so that her face is next to Vicky's portrait. The juxtaposition reveals a real woman next to a two-dimensional one, Betty Grable beside her cinematic mirror image. Frankie, who had pursued but failed to win Vicky, protests to Jill that he never loved her, that "when a man really loves a woman, he doesn't want to plaster her face all over the papers and magazines. He wants to keep her to himself. Right in here." Another man—Inspector Ed Cornell (Laird Cregar)—wants to do both: it's his job, he asserts, to "look at people." Throughout the film he doggedly pursues Frankie, apparently convinced that he is the murderer. Near the end, however, we discover that Cornell has covered his apartment walls with photos of the dead woman, turning it into a creepy Vicky Lynn shrine. Christopher "took her away from me," he laments. Cornell had wooed her, but when she became a minor celebrity, "she started gettin' too good for me." In death she is his alone. "I'm a sick man," he admits, before taking poison. Yet his pathological obsession is merely an enlargement of the other males' attempts to portray a Vicky who might enhance their own images or help them forge a new one. Each of them shares the guilt.

During Cornell's confession Vicky's portrait remains in the frame between the two men: she is both the link and the wedge between them. The composition links two brands of framing, connoting that Cornell's attempted framing of Frankie follows from his fetishistic framing of Vicky. The narrative flashbacks enact a similar process: each narrator puts Vicky together piece by piece, yet the parts never quite cohere, and she remains fragmented, two-dimensional. Through her, however, *I Wake Up Screaming* encourages us to reflect on its status as constructed artifact, a series of pictures mirroring the audience's and the Hollywood production system's forging of idealized identities. Like Grable and (as I show below) Gene Tierney, Vicky allows herself to become a commodity. As such she exists only as a function of others' belief in her—of audience members who not only consume the creations of real-world Frankie Christophers but who also partake of Ed Cornell's fetishizing impulses.

Made at the same studio, Fox, and by the same producer, Darryl F. Zanuck, *Laura* is an elaborate repainting of *I Wake Up Screaming* that similarly calls attention to its own fictional status. Detective Mark McPherson (Dana Andrews) and columnist Waldo Lydecker (Clifton Webb) fall in love with competing portraits of aspiring (and murdered) advertising executive Laura Hunt (Gene Tierney). McPherson and Lydecker form two parts of a single male psyche: the investigator and the murderer, the one who will love her and the one who has loved her, the macho detective and the ambiguously gay snob.[3] To Lydecker Laura was a prize objet d'art for his collection; to McPherson her mysterious death makes her intriguingly enigmatic.

Like *I Wake Up Screaming, Laura* opens on the day after the subject's murder, then presents a flashback account—in this case, Lydecker's—of the narrator's relationship with the victim. The framed narration again functions analogically: just as the act of narration seeks to pin Laura to Lydecker's vision of her, so the story recounts his attempt to mold her into his desired form. They met when Laura ingenuously asked him to endorse a pen for an ad campaign. After Lydecker snidely rejected her, she chided him for his callousness and fraudulence; he replied that he was only interested in money, but Lydecker lied: he is really an obsessive romantic. Later he apologized and signed his picture with the pen, in a single gesture endorsing both the pen and the new Laura he began to fashion. "Her career began with my endorsement of the pen," he relates. "I secured other endorsements for her." But he actually endorses *his* portrait, not hers; Lydecker's Laura is a forgery, a picture made in *his* image, designed to enhance his prestige and help him project a heterosexual identity. And though he fancies himself Laura's Pygmalion, she created him as much as he created her: for her sake, he tells McPherson, "I tried to become the kindest, gentlest, most sympathetic man on earth." As their similar apartments also suggest, the two are alter egos, mirror images, each the other's artist and subject.

During his investigation McPherson rifles through Laura's drawers, sniffs her perfume, and stands before her dresser mirror while staring at the large portrait that looms over the room. Critics have argued that the portrait seems to fetishize and entrap Laura.[4] Yet throughout this sequence it remains almost constantly in view, often at the center of each shot, attesting to the power her image exerts over McPherson—and the viewer. As McPherson paws and ponders, variations on David Raksin's *Laura* theme play on the soundtrack, its changing arrangements reflecting the detective's shifting moods: initially unfocused and agitated, it gains clarity when he sits beneath the portrait and a piano restates the melody against a string background; as he dozes, a muted trumpet voices his isolation and longing.[5] What follows changes the tune and interrupts McPherson's mooning: the living Laura opens the door and stands framed within it. Perhaps, as Richard Ness points out, the variations on the theme reflect "her refusal to be contained," just as her sudden reappearance proves her capacity to escape the "fixed image created by her portrait" (60).

Just before her reappearance, director Otto Preminger dollies toward McPherson's face, holds, then dollies back out, using the conventional method of introducing a dream sequence (Kalinak 165). It is as if the rest of the story—in which Laura and McPherson fall in love and the killer is exposed—were a dream. Or perhaps the *first* half, depicting Laura's "death," is merely Lydecker's, or McPherson's, fantasy.[6] Either way, as McPherson declares, "Somebody was murdered in this room." Certainly: Diane Redfern, a model who resembled Laura, was the actual victim. Diane may have been a lesser, or forged Laura, yet the film implies that they are virtually indistinguishable.[7] In a sense, then, several Lauras *have* been killed: Lydecker's picture of her as his Galatea is erased, along with McPherson's mystified icon. And though Lydecker is the one who shot Diane (mistaking her for Laura), Laura understands that by having acquiesced in Lydecker's manipulation, she is nearly as "guilty as he is. Not for anything I did, but for what I didn't do." In a sense, it seems, Laura killed herself.

Detective McPherson (Dana Andrews) dreams of the eponymous Laura (Gene
Tierney). *Kobal Collection / Art Resource, NY.*

Nor is her resurrection complete. For although she announces to Lydecker
that "no man is ever going to hurt me again," her attitude and actions are ambiguous or inconsistent. As Liahna Babener observes, Laura remains "caught in a series
of contradictions: claiming to want freedom from overbearing men but clinging
to" them anyway (92). The film depicts her plight in the climactic sequence, as
the camera focuses on her brushing her hair before a large mirror: the two Lauras—
living woman and dead icon—remain inseparable yet never truly merge. But
Lydecker cannot allow a new Laura to be born and, having failed to frame both
Carpenter and Laura for Diane's murder, tries to kill Laura again. As a radio recording of his voice rhapsodizes that "Love is stronger than life. It reaches beyond the dark shadow of death," the incarnate Lydecker enters the apartment
bent on murder. He has become his own double, his life a deck of lies. As the recording intones Ernest Dowson's "Vitae Summa Brevis"—

> They are not long, the days of wine and roses;
> Out of a misty dream
> Our path emerges for awhile, then closes
> Within a dream

—the bodily Lydecker is killed. His dream is over.

Is Laura's? Does she escape her frame? It's possible to read the film as silencing her and thereby replicating the male characters' reifications. Babener argues that because Caspary's Laura narrates the fourth section of the novel, she "assumes authority over her life—she constitutes herself as subject" (85).[8] It is true that Caspary's Laura is more devoted to her work and generally a stronger, though equally complex, character than the movie's ethereal presence. But Laura doesn't get the last word, even in the novel: McPherson ties up the loose ends and concludes by quoting Lydecker. Nor does the film endorse Lydecker's version of the story: his narration ends a third of the way through. Hence, Laura escapes Lydecker's narrative frame—his attempt to control and silence her—just as she defeats his attempt to frame her for murder and thereby silence her again.

Nevertheless, as Sheri Chinen Biesen reminds us, "Laura's character is . . . manufactured not only by the men in the narrative but also by the male production executives involved in making the film" (160). Just as each male character believes his Laura to be the true one, so did the filmmakers who altered Caspary's novel to fit their vision. They, too, are Lydeckers—tricksters who let us believe Laura is dead and imply that part of their film is only a dream. Their *Laura* is perhaps as much a forgery—a falsely endorsed picture—as Lydecker's or McPherson's Lauras. These reinventions of Laura were eerily recapitulated in the life of Gene Tierney, an emotionally fragile woman who had just given birth to a multiply disabled daughter but was pressured by the studio to accept the part of Laura. Tierney became identified with the role; indeed, her performance as what she calls "the movie's key prop" overshadowed her later career just as Laura's portrait overshadows her living self (Tierney 113). In Tierney's autobiography (entitled *Self-Portrait*) she admits that her "problems began when I had to be myself" (114). *Laura*'s plot foreshadows how Tierney was elevated and then effaced in favor of an unchanging, two-dimensional icon (Rita Hayworth was similarly oppressed by the constant conflation of herself and Gilda). *Laura* thus presents a disturbing portrait of the mystification and reification of women's images in Hollywood films. Alas, Tierney's afterlife—which included several hospitalizations, a suicide attempt, and electroconvulsive treatments—was even more troubled than Laura's.

Lydecker's resurrection was more prompt, though no happier: he was reborn less than two years later as art collector Hardy Cathcart (again played by Clifton Webb) in Henry Hathaway's *The Dark Corner*.[9] This reiteration is perhaps fitting, for *The Dark Corner*'s plot is all about self-reinvention. It tracks private investigator and ex-convict Bradford Galt (Mark Stevens) through his attempts to foil Cathcart's plan to frame him for the murder of Galt's former partner Tony Jardine, who once framed Galt for manslaughter and is now having an affair with Cathcart's wife, Mari (Cathy Downs). Cathcart fetishizes Mari to the point of purchasing an expensive painting only because it resembles her. Thus, although this film does not include a frame narrative, it dramatizes framing in a number of ways. First, Cathcart's attempts to dominate his wife are shown by the way he tries to frame her as a painting he can possess—an expansion of his incarceration of her within his luxurious marital prison. Second, he tries to frame Galt for a murder that he himself commits. Third, the film employs numerous internal frames—boxes created by doors, windows, and the like—to embody Galt's and Mari's entrapment in Cathcart's machinations. The film's visual tropes thus illustrate its themes of identity and possession.

Early in the film, for example, Galt is reflected in a mirror, the two images of himself sandwiching his loyal secretary, Kathleen (Lucille Ball), who is helping him fashion a new self-portrait as an honest man. A little later he is visited by Cathcart's agent, a mysterious man in a white suit (William Bendix); after Galt roughs him up, the two are shown in a balanced, split-frame composition, with Galt to the right in silhouette, and White Suit to the left: framer and framed as doubles. Later, when White Suit kills Jardine with a poker and places it in the unconscious Galt's hand, these visual frames are enacted on the level of plot.

Cathcart's attempted framing of his wife emerges early in the film, when he tells her, "I never want you to grow up. You should be ageless, like a Madonna, who lives, breathes, smiles, and belongs to me." Mari understandably feels stifled, lamenting to Jardine that Cathcart "gives me everything a man can give a woman. It still isn't enough. . . . I just keep sitting, listening to his paintings crack with age." As she delivers these lines, the soundtrack plays the Warren/Gordon standard "The More I See You," whose lyrics could be Cathcart's credo:

The more I see you
The more I want you. . . .
My arms won't free you
And my heart won't try.

To possess her more fully, Cathcart has purchased a painting he has long and ardently coveted, a portrait of a woman gazing seductively at the viewer. Its resemblance to Mari "isn't pure accident," he admits. "It was as if I'd always known her. And wanted her."[10] The more he sees her . . .

As for Galt, he understands after he wakes up beside Jardine's body that "I could be framed easier than Whistler's mother." To escape this frame, he visits Cathcart's gallery and pretends to buy a Donatello sculpture.[11] Cathcart emerges from the shadows holding a gun, and then Galt tells him he's really interested in a piece of modern art "finished the night before last" but now "stiff as a statue. . . . A Tony Jardine." Cathcart: "Nonsense. I never handle anything as worthless as a Jardine. . . . It was found in your apartment." Galt: "Actually, this Jardine really belongs to you. You paid to have it done. . . . Somebody had to pay that muscle artist to brush him off." As the dialogue indicates, Cathcart cannot distinguish between human beings and objects: if his murders are a form of collecting, likewise

In *The Dark Corner,* Hardy Cathcart (Clifton Webb) tries to control his wife, Mari (Cathy Downs), through a painting that resembles her. *Kobal Collection / Art Resource, NY.*

his collecting is a form of murder. The sequence ends with Galt standing on one side of a door frame, Cathcart on the other; between them, at the far end of the room, hangs Cathcart's beloved portrait. A reverse shot shows Cathcart, gun in hand, framed by the doorway. All the frames break when Mari (offscreen) shoots her husband, leaving Galt free to remake himself as a law-abiding citizen.

These three films all portray forged identities, not only those of the women whom the males mold into objects but of the males themselves, who use these female images to fabricate or reinforce their identities as lover, worthy husband, or intellectual. Yet the males don't merely define themselves against femininity; they also try to incorporate it. They recreate themselves, in other words, *as women* in order to *become men*. The films' power struggles and gender crossings may signify what many film historians have detected in noir's femmes fatale: the likelihood that, as I noted earlier, they embody anxieties about wartime and postwar gender roles.[12] Yet these characters—both framers and framed, victims and killers—also represent the deeper questions about American values that noir repeatedly poses: is the American Dream of self-reinvention, of playing a new role in life's second act, still viable? And does such reinvention ever occur without violence, exploitation or commodification?

The portrait noirs suggest that identities are *always* in flux, always a matter of performance. In so doing, they invoke the conditions of their own making, not only reminding viewers that their characters are actors staging their own fabrication but even referring to and remaking earlier versions of the same story. Thus, *I Wake Up Screaming*, itself an adaptation of Steve Fisher's hard-boiled Hollywood-insider novel, is transformed (by the same producer) into *Laura*, one character of which is then revived (with alterations) for the same studio's *The Dark Corner*. But that's not the end: in 1953 *I Wake Up Screaming* was remade by Fox as *Vicki*, with Jean Peters in the title role, Jeanne Crain as Jill, Elliott Reid as Christopher (his first name changed to Steve), and Richard Boone as Cornell. The story is a near-copy of the first adaptation, but the dialogue lacks its snap, and the film is missing most of the 1941 version's witty edges. Cornell (who doesn't kill himself in this version) is portrayed as pathetic rather than creepy. *Vicki* also acknowledges the first adaptation: at times Boone seems to be channeling (the by-then deceased) Laird Cregar, and several shots replicate those in the earlier version.[13] Because by 1953 the theme of celebrity fabrication was less novel, *Vicki* is more explicit about the title character's artificiality and more unforgiving in its ironies. For example, Christopher boasts that he can sell Vicki "like a brand of coffee," and as Christopher and Jill enter his car on their first date, a billboard featuring Vicki's face promoting Caress beauty products is visible behind them, at once slyly acknowledging Christopher's creed and indicating the deceased sister's contribution to their romance. Given the story's self-reflexive elements—exposing how promoters and audiences create portraits of women as fantasy figures and thereby kill them—*Vicki* seems to undermine itself even as it unwinds, simultaneously eliciting viewers' fascination with these processes and criticizing them. Less a forgery than a cover version of *I Wake Up Screaming, Vicki* adds another layer to what seems not merely a set of movies but an infinite regress of mirrors within mirrors. The next group of films brings us even closer to that condition.

Mirror Images

"Some dreams require solitude. . . . At times the illusion of love may outlast the image of a dingy room, but awaken we must." These are the words of Maurice Legrand (Michel Simon), the protagonist of Renoir's *La chienne*, but they also describe Professor Wanley of *The Woman in the Window*, and Chris Cross of *Scarlet Street*. These three films reflect one another in multiple ways. As Oliver Harris observes, because Fritz Lang's two films employ the same lead actors (Robinson, Bennett, Duryea) performing in similar stories, they induce "a kind of vertigo of déjà vu, cross-reference and pure confusion" (7). The effect is heightened by Lang's tendency to create a "sealed-off environment," where, in Foster Hirsch's description, there seems to be "no world outside the frame" (6). When we add to the mix *La chienne,* not a film noir, of course, but an earlier adaptation of *Scarlet Street*'s source material (both were based on a novel by Georges de la Fouchardière), the trio becomes a hall of mirrors filled with reverberating themes and visual echoes, all illustrating plots that also involve frames, doubles, mirrors, and portraits. In all three "the project of desire discovers itself to be within a frame, in a potentially infinite *mise-en-abîme*"—one that even swallows the viewer (Gunning 287). Together they constitute a triangular dream text revealing their directors' reflections on the art of filmmaking and the nature of authorship.

Early in *The Woman in the Window*, psychology professor Richard Wanley (Edward G. Robinson) laments the "stodginess" that has engulfed him and his friends. With his wife and children out of town, he has a chance to break out but instead spends the evening reading the Song of Solomon. When, a bit later, he gazes through a shop window at a woman's portrait (his friends had earlier called her their "dream girl"), his cage begins to crack. We regard the portrait from

Wanley's point of view; in the reverse shot a faint reflection of the portrait appears to emerge from his shoulder. Lang cuts back to the painting, now juxtaposed with an actual woman's face, before returning to Wanley and the reflection. Another shot of the painting follows, and then the camera pans left to rest on a smiling Alice Reed (Joan Bennett), the portrait's model. As the scene continues, the portrait is placed between Wanley and Alice in every two-shot: he can't see around the portrait to the actual woman. Wanley's painting is not a love affair; his love affair is a painting.

As the multiple images of Alice suggest, she plays several roles in what follows—siren, victim, accomplice. When she invites Wanley into her mirror-filled apartment, he follows her through the looking glass into Lewis Carroll terrain, where he plays a topsy-turvy chess game in which his every move is wrong and where authorities hound him until he is finally cornered. Yet in the wonderland of his unconscious Wanley also becomes a dashing hero, a man who would yield to

Professor Wanley (Edward G. Robinson) is entranced by a portrait of his dream girl (Joan Bennett) in *The Woman in the Window. Kobal Collection/Art Resource, NY.*

temptation instead of just reading about it—a man who would, like Harry Quincy, even kill if necessary. That's what he does when Alice's lover, Claude Mazard (Arthur Loft), breaks in on them and attacks Wanley, provoking the professor to stab him repeatedly with the scissors Alice provides. As they clean up, the two are repeatedly framed by mirrors to represent the redoubling of identities in the aftermath. If Alice is both a portrait come to life and a mirror of Wanley's desire, Mazard also embodies Wanley's impulses: as Gunning notes, "killing Mazard [is], in a sense, killing himself" (302). Later, Mazard's former bodyguard, a man named Heidt (Duryea), blackmails Wanley and Alice until they try to poison him with Wanley's medication. They fail but inadvertently set up Heidt to be killed and identified as Mazard's killer. In short, not only does Wanley frame Heidt; in an important sense Wanley *is* Heidt.

Wanley also frames himself. Throughout the investigation he makes incriminating "mistakes" when discussing the case with his friend, District Attorney Lalor (Raymond Massey): he knows the killing occurred at night; knows the body was dumped over barbed wire; almost leads the police directly to the scene; and even shows Lalor the arm he scratched on the fence. Certainly Wanley wants to be caught, but these inculpating acts are not merely a guilty conscience at work: to be recognized as the killer would also validate him as an adventurous and virile man. But, ironically, instead he must efface his identity by burning his coat and hiding his monogrammed pen.

Distraught over his failure and certain of his guilt and its imminent discovery, Wanley poisons himself. As he sits in his chair at home, slowly losing consciousness, Lang dollies in and holds on Wanley's face (meanwhile, his breakaway robe is removed and the "wild" home set is replaced by the club set), then pulls back as a club employee wakes him.[14] The whole experience was Wanley's dream. The gimmick (similar to those in *The Strange Affair of Uncle Harry* and *The Chase*) is hokey, as Lang himself recognized; yet its thematic and psychological plausibility largely redeems it, as Wanley and the others are retrospectively transformed.[15] For example, we now realize that the portrait's appearance as Wanley's appendage had already told us she was a projection of his psyche. Like Heidt, Mazard, and the rest, Alice is Wanley's self-portrait. He is their author—and they are his.

Yet in this film the frame is invisible—if it exists at all. The absence of cuts in the awakening scene, that is, implies that no line exists between the dream and waking worlds.[16] Slavoj Žižek thus argues that the ending means not that it was all a dream and Wanley is a normal man but that "in our unconscious, in the real of our desire, we are all murderers." He continues: "we do not have a quiet, kind, decent bourgeois professor dreaming for a moment that he is a murderer; what we have is . . . a murderer dreaming . . . that he is just a decent bourgeois professor" (16–17). But this formulation is too dualistic: Wanley is *simultaneously* a bourgeois professor and a murderer. Just as Alice is both inside and outside of the portrait, so Wanley exists in two realms at once. We may feel cheated by the ending. But if so, Lang has caught us doing what Wanley does—conflating the real and the imaginary. As Harris puts it, "Like him, we too have passed through the window: *in our unconscious, we are all naive spectators*" (8–9; emphasis his). The ending, then, both invokes the power of cinematic authorship—as if Lang were announcing, "I can change this all into a dream, for a movie is just a dream anyway"—and its limitations: "this is *merely* a fantasy that ends when you exit the theater." Wanley's face is a portrait of ourselves watching it—an image of how film pulls us through the looking glass, inviting us to dream new selves as a professor or murderer or model or prosecutor, or all of them at once.

La chienne likewise evokes its own artificiality and elides it. It begins with puppets disagreeing about the story to come, until the last puppet declares that it's "neither comedy nor drama" but a realistic tale depicting "plain people like you and me." On one hand the film's cluttered mise-en-scène, constant ambient sounds, and cramped living spaces lend it a meticulous verisimilitude. On the other hand a curtain comes up at the beginning and goes down at the end, drawing our attention to the story's theatricality, and its plot contrivances and emphasis on the constructed nature of truth insinuate that we should be skeptical about all representations. Renoir thus both pulls us into this world and holds it at a distance, warning us neither to believe in fantasy nor to trap ourselves in Legrand's brand of cynicism.

Shackled to his shrewish wife, Adele, who calls him "the laughingstock of the neighborhood," Legrand has good reason to be cynical. The compositions show his entrapment: as she chides him about his painting hobby, he stands to the left of the frame facing her; between them looms a large oval portrait of her first husband, Alexis Godard, a hero killed in World War I. He was "a *real* man," she asserts, adding later, "a regular lady killer." Legrand will never match this smug, uniformed icon. Yet he tries to enlarge his male identity after he meets Lulu (Janie Marèse), a prostitute he believes he has saved from a beating by her pimp, Dede (Georges Flamant). A month later Legrand has set her up in an apartment and let her believe he is a wealthy, successful artist.

Soon we watch Legrand paint a self-portrait. As we observe, three Legrands become visible—his reflection in the mirror, his image in the unfinished painting, and his body, shown from the rear (a similar composition is used in *Hollow Triumph*'s scarring scene). Split between his identity as a cashier (we've already seen him working in his cage) and his new self as Lulu's sugar daddy, Legrand is now painting a picture of himself *as* a painter. Yet he remains surrounded by frames, including the one revealed as the camera pulls back to disclose a window through which we can see a neighbor.[17] Legrand doesn't notice the neighbor; he prefers his narcissistic obsession. More important, perhaps, this camera movement invites us to recognize that the entire scene has been created by a painter named Renoir.

This self-reflexive layer unfolds further after Dede's friend instructs him about capitalizing on Legrand's work: "the only thing that counts in art is the signature. And since you can't use a famous signature, you'll only get chicken feed." The two then come up with "Clara Wood" as the pseudonym with which Lulu will sign Legrand's paintings. Voila—they have made a painter! But Lulu must endorse this picture, as she does soon after, by signing over a check to Dede; her signature now ensures both aesthetic and economic value. This moment reminds us that the essence of forgery lies not in the act of copying but in the act of signing (otherwise the thousands of "art prints" for sale online would be subject to prosecution). It also raises broader questions about the nature and limits of authorship and identity. As K. K. Ruthven observes, every signature is to some extent a self-forgery, in that no two are exactly identical (156). Furthermore, a signature may always be close to a forgery because to sign a document is to endorse the notion of a consistent, essentially unchanging self (Thwaites 6)—a notion that all these films (as well as much modernist and postmodernist art) challenge.

But are the paintings really forgeries, since Legrand consents to the scheme? And are they his creations, or hers, or even Dede's? After all, Dede invented Clara. And upon seeing Legrand's paintings, a dealer boasts, "We can make painters, you know." In a sense, then, he also "makes" the paintings. Renoir here insinuates that artworks are collaborative products of painters and the entrepreneurs who turn the artifacts into commodities. This matrix encompasses filmmaking as well. Who is a film's author? The director? Or is it the screenwriter, actors, production company, or all of them at once? In effect, the film offers a critique of auteur theory avant la lettre. But when Dede induces Lulu to romance a wealthy man who wants her to paint his portrait, Renoir unveils the darker side of collaboration: by permitting others to write over his name, an artist becomes a prostitute.

As both a forger and a forgery, Legrand shares this distinction with M. Godard, who suddenly reappears with a false name and no money. Through a farcical stratagem, Legrand reunites him with Adele, leaving himself free to marry Lulu. But when he goes to break the news to her, he catches her in bed with Dede. As Legrand opens the door, Renoir cuts to outside the bedroom window. The camera moves right, then holds Legrand within the window frame, and the next two shots frame him within the door. The meaning is evident: Legrand is trapped within the picture he helped to paint. Thus, when he confronts Lulu the next day as she lies in bed cutting the pages of a novel, she replies, "Take a look in the mirror." He berates and beseeches her; she laughs at him. Then he takes up Lulu's knife and . . . Renoir takes up his, cutting to a shot outside the apartment, where a crowd gathers around some musicians. We don't need to see the murder to understand that Legrand has at last matched Godard: he has now become a lady killer.

Dede, who imagines himself as one, now drives up in his flashy convertible, goes upstairs and returns, all in full view of the crowd. He is quickly charged with the murder. Who is guilty? Like that of the paintings, the murder's authorship is shared. Renoir even identifies Lulu's two lovers through a brilliant camera movement in the police station. We see Dede, his back to the wall, lamenting his fate; then the camera pulls back and tracks right to reveal Legrand in the same position on the other side of the wall: they are two faces of the same portrait. But Legrand lets the police and jury view only one side and permits Dede to be framed for his murder. Ironically, he has at last come into his own as a painter—one capable of forging convincing representations of himself as a dupe and of another man as murderer.

In the epilogue Legrand meets Godard again, both of them now homeless derelicts. Though Legrand says he "wouldn't mind" being dead, and admits to being a murderer, he doesn't seem guilt-ridden: the two jocosely share a smoke and gaze at some paintings through a store window. Legrand briefly spots his self-portrait being loaded into a car but is more interested in twenty francs that have fallen to the sidewalk. He snatches the cash, and the two depart for a feast. As the opened-up mise-en-scène indicates, in losing his bourgeois identity Legrand has been liberated from his constricted life and lethal fantasies. It doesn't matter that he no longer paints; he has found a soul mate. By yielding control, Legrand discovers a new self.

To remake this story, Fritz Lang teamed with Walter Wanger (who had produced *The Woman in the Window*) and Wanger's wife, Joan Bennett, to form

Diana Productions. The notoriously autocratic Lang usually treated collaboration as interference and clashed by night and day with his American producers.
On this film, however, he was afforded a great deal of freedom. Ironically, Lang
used this freedom to direct an allegory about losing it. He told Peter Bogdanovich that Chris Cross's fate is that of "an artist who cares much more for his paintings than for gaining money" (205). Thus we may read *Scarlet Street*—the story of
an artist whose works are appropriated by a prostitute and her pimp—as the self-
portrait of a director harnessed to mercenary producers and studio heads who
"steal" his pictures and put their names on them.

Patrick McGilligan (*Fritz Lang* 321) writes that Lang and screenwriter Dudley
Nichols failed to find a print of *La chienne,* and Lang recalled that they tried to be
"absolutely uninfluenced by it" (Bogdanovich 205). But close scrutiny reveals that
he imitated or carefully revised *La chienne* in pivotal scenes. Indeed, with its borrowed plot about lost identity and forged paintings, *Scarlet Street* is itself a kind
of forgery or plagiarism, a painted-over Renoir to which Lang signs his own name.
Yet despite his debts to the French master, Lang displays a quite different attitude
about authorship and forgery.

Protagonist Chris Cross's unlikely name introduces an important set of motifs. First, it presages a series of double crosses: Kitty March betrays him by stealing his words, name, and money; Chris double-crosses Adele and her first husband, Homer Higgins, by forcing them to reunite; he crosses up Johnny by framing
him for the murder of Kitty. These crossings constitute a series of exchanges:
Chris for Kitty, Chris for Johnny, Homer for Chris. Perhaps more significant, the
name signifies Chris's erasure. Kitty rubs out Chris's identity as a cashier and a
painter and replaces it with hers; in complying with the forgery scheme, Chris
commits self-erasure. In the end he even exes out his dream by testifying that
he's not a painter at all.

In a sense, however, Chris's erasure scarcely matters, for he is a nonentity
from the start. In the opening scene, for example, his reward for twenty-five
years of service to the firm of J. J. Hogarth is a watch—an appropriate present for
a "fourteen-carat, seventeen-jewel cashier." The metaphor—a trope for authentic
representation and value—captures Cross's mechanical existence. In this he resembles Professor Wanley: both are bored with their humdrum lives but too
timid to escape.[18] When Chris tells his friend that he once dreamed of being a
painter, the friend replies, "When we're young we have dreams that never pan
out. But we go on dreaming." Unlike Legrand, he doesn't mention waking up.
Though the lines are not delivered by Chris, they nonetheless pinpoint a primary

difference between him and Legrand: whereas Legrand is fettered by his sense of superiority and finds release in being humbled, Cross seeks restoration in fantasy. After all, he is, like the immigrant Fritz Lang, an American, and he believes in self-remaking. Thus, when his paintings are later sold for a tidy sum, he enthuses, "It's just like a dream!" No, it's a nightmare, one that begins, as in so many noirs, with a single act—his "rescue" of "actress" Kitty March from a beating by her boyfriend, Johnny Prince.

That night Chris explains to Kitty his aesthetic principles. He doesn't paint what he sees, but merely puts "a line around what I feel." And what he feels is love: "every painting is a love affair." Gunning describes Chris's aesthetic as "semi-Expressionist" (327)—one similar to that of the American version of Fritz Lang. Indeed, Chris's quasi-primitivist paintings are visual allegories that resemble Lang's heavily symbolic films, a symbolism exemplified when Chris's body is dissolved over an image of the wilting flower he brings home from the meeting with Kitty.[19] In his painting, however, the wan bloom is large and erect. His imaginary love affair has already begun to restore his potency—at least in his imagination.

In the real world of home, however, he remains emasculated; in one scene he even wears a frilly apron while doing the dishes—an abject image of the castrated male. But if Chris is a fake wife, so is Adele, despite being addicted to a radio show called *The Happy Household Hour*. The scene in which Adele castigates Chris about his paintings also proves that Lang viewed *La chienne* closely, for the composition and framing of the two versions are nearly identical. Like Renoir, Lang places Adele and her current husband on opposite sides of the frame (he left, she right); between and over them hangs a large oval portrait of the proudly smiling first husband (this time a cop who allegedly died while saving a woman's life), his chest out, his arms akimbo. Homer is to Adele as Kitty is to Chris—an image of the ideal mate. But this portrait is as enhanced as Chris's flower: as we learn later, Homer faked his death and stole money from the drowning woman. In copying this scene, Lang thus casts himself as Cross, with Renoir the heroic forerunner to be overcome.

Kitty's lover wields his own phallic power by wangling money from her and romancing her—whenever he's not roughing her up. It's Johnny's idea to sell Chris's paintings, and his idea—after they attract the attention of an art dealer named Janeway—to attribute them to Kitty. For these two as for Lulu and Dede, paintings are merely commodities, and an artist is just a prostitute. Lang none-too-subtly depicts Johnny's values in a characteristic lap dissolve: skulking outside

Kitty's apartment, he is superimposed over Chris's painting of a snake. But if the dissolve conveys Johnny's potency and sliminess, it also implies that he is a product of Chris's imagination. That is, by endorsing the painting scheme, Chris *creates* Johnny, just as he later frames him for the murder of Kitty. The snake, like the flower, is Chris's imaginary self-portrait.

Still, if Chris's paintings are forgeries, it's not because they are copies of another painter's work but because they are signed "Katherine March." Hence, whereas Renoir implies that Lulu—the signer—is the forger, Lang assigns the role to Chris: he's the one, after all, who makes a career, in Hillel Schwartz's formulation, by "standing invisible behind names or styles in demand" (315). Indeed, his imaginary love affair embodies art critic Francis Sparshott's explanation that "the primary erotic analogue of artistic forgery is the substitution, in conditions of desperation or poor visibility, of an alternative sex object for the loved one" (254). Chris tries to stand in for Johnny and Homer; like Cornell, Lydecker, Cathcart, and Wanley he loves not a woman but a portrait of one. Sparshott also contends that original art shows us something about the person who created it; forgery, by contrast, is a lie about the self (252–53). In that regard Chris, who pretends to be an unmarried, successful painter, is a forger from the moment he meets Kitty. And Kitty—more plagiarist than forger—perpetuates the fraud by parroting Chris's aesthetic principles to Janeway; ironically, this lie ratifies her earlier lie to Chris that she is an actress (Janeway gushes that talking to her is "like talking to two people"). Likewise, Johnny pretends to be the boyfriend of Kitty's roommate, Millie, and Homer pretends to be dead. All of them are self-forgers, their Franklinesque remodeling achieved for dishonest ends.

Peter de Bolla observes that "forgery . . . inserts the possibility of multiple personality, or no identity at all, into the paper-thin circulation of trust in a speculative society," thereby destabilizing "self, society and certainty" (73). In short, forgery severs the relation between object and representation, thus releasing the anchor of social relations—the belief that people are who they claim to be, that a signature belongs to the signer. Chris's consenting to the forgeries casts him adrift in a world of floating signifiers. For Lang this is his most damning self-betrayal: a denial of the authorship that confirms and cements an artist's identity.

Chris's plight, like that of *Hollow Triumph*'s John Muller, epitomizes the dilemma of the forger—the only artist whose success depends on *not* being recognized. His paintings, that is, acquire value *because* they are signed by a young attractive woman rather than by a meek male nobody. Ironically, only by effacing his identity as a painter does Chris actually become one: his lie allows him to assume what he thinks of as his "true" identity. But Chris's identity is very much in question, as evinced by his "masterpiece"—a painting of Kitty entitled *Self-Portrait*. As Chris reads about Kitty's solo exhibition in the newspaper, this painting dissolves over a medium shot of Chris in his cashier's cage, sitting beneath his name. For a moment "Cross" is written across Kitty's face, the *o* covering her mouth. Earlier Chris had told her, "It's just like we're married, only I take *your* name." Now she takes his. Who is crossing out whom? In painting Kitty, Chris paints his own self-portrait not just as a painter and forger and lover but *as a woman*. As in *Laura*, the creation of a forged identity is linked with gender transgression. Gunning speculates that Chris's identification with a woman "could be seen as a revolt against the hypocritical ideal male identity embodied in the portrait of Homer Higgins," and that his "cross-gendered identity" enables him to trick Homer (331–32). Seen from another angle, however, this gender crossing sends him to a limbo between an unformed feminine self and an inchoate adventurous, passionate male self. Though no longer himself, he can't be Kitty. Chris can't cross.

Flushed with his victory over Adele, he rushes to tell Kitty he is free to marry her. But as Chris stands outside her window, he witnesses her embracing Johnny (to a recording of "Melancholy Baby" that repeatedly sticks on the line "in love"). Here Lang revises Renoir's rendering, in which Legrand is the focal point of the internal frame. We see Lang's lovers from Chris's point of view, boxed in by the window to resemble a painting. This portrait of the Freudian primal scene shocks Chris, whose subsequent effort to claim Kitty is even more pathetic than Legrand's. Laughing derisively, she berates him as "old and ugly." As she begins her diatribe, she turns away from the camera, so that we see her face only in the mirror's reflection. It is as if her head has been severed from her body, just as her real intentions have long been separated from her ostensible ones. Kitty is two people again—only one of whom Chris kills by stabbing her four times with an icepick, finally enacting the piercing lust he has kept caged.

With remarkably bad timing, Johnny drives up in a light convertible. In contrast to Renoir's busy street, however, only one person sees him, but he is enough to verify Johnny's presence and get him indicted for the murder. In the swift trial scene montage, testimony establishes that (1) Kitty was an artist, (2) Chris is not an artist but a forger and thief, and (3) Johnny is a low-down son of a bitch and pathological liar. Yet in framing Johnny, Chris must frame himself, for his life depends on disavowing his identity as a painter. The newspaper headline sums it up: "Famous Painter Slain." Chris's painter self dies along with the lover and the cashier. The shell, however, endures a death-in-life, superbly rendered in a chilling, expressionist sequence in which Chris enters his dark hotel room, whistling "Melancholy Baby," then is driven to (unsuccessfully) hang himself by the taunting voices of Kitty and Johnny. As a reporter told Cross after the trial, "Nobody gets away with murder," because we all carry a little court room "right in here. Judge, jury and executioner."[20] Like Joe Wilson in *Fury,* or child-murderer Hans Beckert in *M,* Cross is tormented by ghosts. Worse: Johnny still possesses Kitty, and Chris is denied even the relief of suicide. There is no escape from his self-made frame.

Lang's epilogue contrasts starkly with Renoir's. It's Christmastime, but Chris's present is a lonely afterlife. Homeless and doddering, he watches incredulously as Katherine March's *Self-Portrait—his* self-portrait—is sold for $10,000 and loaded into a truck. "Well, there goes her masterpiece," remarks the dealer, as "Melancholy Baby" plays on the soundtrack. "Why do you grieve? / Try to believe," the lyrics recommend, but there is no silver lining here. Whereas Renoir was at pains to define his characters—and partly redeem them—by placing them within a lively social context, Cross's plight, as Kaplan notes, is an "individual tragedy" ("Ideology" 36). Cross reenacts Wanley's strangulating self-enclosure, as Renoir's vision of radical freedom is transformed into "powerlessness . . . not once but twice" (Welsch 61). Far from being liberated by his self-reinvention, Cross, like John Muller, Ole Anderson, and Vincent Parry, merely moves from one prison to another. As he gazes at Kitty's picture, we are drawn back to the opening of *Woman in the Window:* the same actor stares at a portrait of the same actress through what could be the same window on the same street. We watch ourselves watching him watch. We have stepped through the looking glass, but it's no longer clear which side we're on.

Though *La chienne* depicts Legrand as a dupe, he is at least freed from the prison of self and permitted to exercise his creativity by living rather than by painting. *Scarlet Street,* in contrast, dramatizes a world of obsessive reiteration and implacable fate where Chris's best instincts—his capacity for love, his artistic passion, his integrity and credulity—are ruthlessly exploited and then utterly obliterated. Chris, seduced by the American dream of starting over, loses everything; worst of all, he is stripped of his agency. For Lang, any artist who allows his work to be overwritten by others also loses his soul. In remaking *La chienne,* however, he avoids Chris's fate because in repainting Renoir's masterpiece, he signs it not as Chris Cross but as Katherine March—the one who fashions a self-portrait by appropriating the work of another.

A Little Fractured

"All of a sudden I don't know myself," admits George Steele (Pat O'Brien), the disoriented art critic of *Crack-Up,* who has become the target of a forgery ring. Steele's confusion isn't his alone. *Crack-Up* also dramatizes its makers' ambivalence (or confusion) about their own aesthetic aims: while the film purports to champion a realist, near-documentary aesthetic of "truth"—the kind found in representational art—it also presents forged works as authentic ones. And while the film diagnoses cracks in American ideals, it leaves them unhealed: like the portrait noirs, *Crack-Up* does not resolve the questions it raises about originality and identity.

The film opens with a bang, as Steele shatters the window of a museum and knocks over a large sculpture before being subdued by a guard. On coming to, he can't remember how he got here and admits to being, like the male sculpture he toppled, "a little fractured." He then launches into an account of his day for the onlookers, which include the curator and a Dr. Lowell (Ray Collins). Steele's flashback—his framed narrative—is, we eventually discover, also the narrative of a frame designed by forgers seeking to discredit him. They know he's smart: during the war he was Captain Steele, famous for finding "all those forgeries" in the Nazis' collections.[21]

Steele had proved himself a menace earlier in the day by delivering a lecture mocking modernism and advocating the use of X-rays to detect forgeries. First unveiling Jean-Francois Millet's 1858 painting *Angelus*—which depicts two peasants praying over a basket of potatoes—he declares that it's not the judgment of "phony" critics and collectors that make it valuable but the fact that "people like you over the centuries appreciate it. Because Millet was successful at communicating what he felt was a beautiful moment."[22] Steele's populist aesthetic principles are based on a commonsense notion of "truth"—emotional honesty and representational verisimilitude. Modernist art, in contrast, is associated with European radicalism and disdained as "nonsense."[23] This contrast is dramatized when he scornfully displays a surrealist painting (a pastiche of Salvador Dalí) at which the audience laughs derisively—all except one man with a foreign accent, who charges that Steele lacks "sensitivity to abstract emotional values." The foreigner is jeered and thrown out. Yet the introduction of Dalí cracks open a window into a fascinating corner of art history. Steele earlier noted that the old masters sometimes painted over images they had originally placed in a work. Though he doesn't mention it, that is what happened with *Angelus.* Dalí, a great admirer of Millet's painting, long insisted that it was really a portrait of grief, that the couple were originally praying over a child's coffin.[24] An X-ray of the canvas confirmed his suspicion: Millet painted the basket of potatoes over a shape resembling a child's coffin ("Jean-Francois Millet"). As the film proceeds, similar erasures are repeated in Steele's lapses of memory, just as forgery comes to represent the blanking out and rewriting of history itself.

Steele reminds his audience—in what seems a veiled critique of commercial filmmaking—that although a forgery can be as old as an original, "a good technician with nothing to say is a very dangerous man." Art critic Mark Sagoff offers a more sophisticated version of this argument. A painting, he writes, advances "a theory concerning the way we see things or the way they can be . . . seen. . . . In this sense a representational painting is an experiment." A forgery, however, lacks "cognitive importance: it merely repeats the solution to a problem which has already been solved" (146). But why is that dangerous? The answer lies in Leonard Meyer's contention that forgeries undermine "our most fundamental beliefs about the nature of human existence: beliefs about causation and time, creation and freedom" (92). Similarly mistaken beliefs about time and causation also lurk behind the fracturing of Steele's identity. In a sense, we learn, Steele is himself a forgery, a man whose past has been painted over by skillful, dangerous technicians.

Steele remembers being called away from dinner with his friend Terry (Claire Trevor) by a message that his mother was ill. On the way to visit her, he became convinced his train was about to collide with another one. As the second train approaches, we see Steele and his reflection in the window: visually he is "a little fractured." A series of quick cuts shows Steele from outside the window in full-face and in profile, both images tightly boxed within the window so that he resembles nothing so much as a portrait—of overpowering terror. He pulls the brake cord, stops the train, and collapses. But his mother was not ill, he has no train ticket, and no train wreck occurred yesterday. Perhaps, hypothesizes Lowell, his traumatic war experiences have affected his cognition. Steele is like those cognitively disabled veterans discussed in chapter 3: he can neither fully remember his traumas nor completely forget them. Yet his visual fracturing also links him to the cubist shapes and terror-ravaged faces portrayed by European modernists. Hence, his false memories indicate a rupture in his own realist aesthetic, based as it is on a congruence between representation and shared reality. Can we trust what we see or recall, especially if others don't share our perceptions? "All of a sudden," he confesses to Terry, "I don't know myself. In twenty-four hours everything has become unfamiliar."

When Steele reenacts his train trip, looking for a clue, director Irving Reis repeats Steele's visual fracturing, again resorting to expressionism. As the second train approaches, Steele's face is again confined within the window frame as the train whistle grows louder; his eyes widen and he appears to panic. This time the train passes without incident, but then the entire frame surrounding his face goes black, and he recedes rapidly into an abyss and disappears. Then the shot reverses itself, and his face grows to refill the frame. Like Laura and Wanley, Steele has died and been reborn; he has fallen back through the looking glass.[25] The reenactment of his flashback helps him recognize that he is "in somebody's way": in replaying the frame tale, that is, he discovers that he is being framed in someone else's crime story.

Steele learns that a Gainsborough painting, allegedly lost at sea, and the museum's Dürer—*The Adoration of the Kings [Magi]*, which he had displayed during his lecture—are both forgeries. Locating the Dürer on a ship's hold just as a fire starts, he rolls up the painting and flees with it.[26] After gaining access to an X-ray machine with the help of Terry and a museum employee, he examines the painting. In the original *Adoration*, he explains, Dürer painted over an unfinished figure in the upper left; Steele compares its X-ray to one of an eighteenth-century forgery that has no such figure. He then examines the X-ray of a second forgery, the "Scola copy," which is different yet. Placing that X-ray next to that of the museum's *Adoration*, he realizes that the museum has been exhibiting the Scola forgery.[27] As these images fill the frame, the film itself becomes an X-ray, proposing that cinema is the sole reliable vehicle for discovering truth. But of course the film's paintings and images are forgeries—in fact, forgeries of forgeries, since there never was a "Scola copy." Once again the film authorizes realist representation on one level while undermining it on another.

With the forgeries destroyed, Steele explains, the forgers will possess the original Dürer and Gainsborough paintings. Thinking the originals destroyed, other dealers and collectors will stop searching for them. But this plot twist seems dubious: if art dealers believe the originals destroyed, the originals would be perceived as forgeries—and hence would be unsellable! This seeming incoherence, however, does suggest a set of intriguing complications. First, in such a case the authenticity of a painting would matter less than its mere uniqueness. Further, the case suggests that a forgery *always* matters as much as its original, because the former validates the latter. That is, since only valuable paintings are forged, the existence of forgeries amounts to a backhanded way of recognizing an original's value, even as the forgeries seek to appropriate that value. A forgery thus enhances the value of the original by certifying it as worthy of protection. As Schwartz argues, "an object uncopied is under perpetual siege, valued less for itself than for the struggle to prevent its being copied. . . . It is only within an exuberant world of copies that we arrive at our experience of uniqueness" (212). A unique painting is unique—and valuable—only insofar as it faces the possibility of being forged. Thus, if an original's existence ensures a forgery's value, the reverse is also true: a forgery ratifies the value of the original.

But just as Steele makes his discovery, he is captured by the forgery ring, whose leader turns out to be Dr. Lowell. To determine what Steele knows, Lowell injects him with sodium pentothal, the same drug administered to *High Wall*'s Steven Kenet and to several other noir characters. "Odd, isn't it," Lowell asks, "that truth should be a by-product of war," so infamous for spawning lies and myths. This drug has "placed honesty on a scientific basis" and generated a "direct method of communication with a man's true self." The ironies multiply: a forger promises to uncover Steele's "true self" and integrate his fractured psyche with a truth serum in order to cover up *his own falsehoods*. Where does the truth lie?

Lowell explains his motives. "Did you ever want to possess something desperately that was unobtainable, that you couldn't buy?" He is defending great art from "dolts who can't differentiate between trash and these masterpieces." The truth is out: these forgers are elitists, the kind who, as Steele earlier defined them, want to turn art into a "private tea party." Lowell's words echo those of Lydecker and Cathcart: here is another collector who prefers artworks to people and treats humans as objects. According to Lowell, however, forgers are not criminals but guardians of the canon: his copies are designed to preserve the beauty and value of the originals. Far from criminals, forgers are the true art lovers.

The original paintings are hidden right in the house, but Lowell will no longer enjoy them, for he is shot by Traybin (Herbert Marshall), a Scotland Yard inspector who then pulls the previously unseen Gainsborough from its hiding place. It is *The Painter's Daughters* (1758), a dual portrait of Mary and Margaret Gainsborough as children. But not exactly: the painting he displays depicts only one daughter. In fact, this "original" is a copy of a copy—a replica of a nineteenth-century imitation of the Gainsborough portrait—which portrays only Mary.[28] Again, even as it condemns forgery, the film commits it: like Lowell and his gang, the filmmakers have created copies in order to defend originality. And like the creators of *Laura* and *The Woman in the Window*, these cinematic tricksters invite us into a realistically rendered world only to remind us that it is a fabrication.

To further complicate matters, at the end Steele believes he has taken another journey, that "everybody's nuts around this place" but himself. He remains suspended between his failure to remember what has happened to him and his inability to recover from his war injury. Here *Crack-Up* augments the other vet noirs' challenge to the American ideal of self-reinvention. If Steele, a war hero and famous exponent of truth, can't start over, then can anyone in postwar America do so? And from what fragments will we paint our new self-portrait? Neither the shards of demolished European high culture nor embattled pictorial realism seem quite up to the task. The split portrait thus comes to represent America's fissured psyche as well as the film's—and indeed, film noir's—divided aesthetic. All are a little fractured.

While purporting to expose the differences between originality and forgery, then, *Crack-Up* instead reveals a symbiotic relationship between them. Further, its depiction of Steele's divided psyche exposes an unresolved ambivalence both about the war (which, as I argued in chapter 3, Americans wanted both to remember and to forget) and about representation and modern art: though ostensibly condemning European modernism, the film incorporates it. Even so, the portrait noirs dramatize the power of pictures to make their subjects, frame expectations, and unsettle conventional ideas about gender, selfhood, and memory.

More broadly, the painting noirs validate the Emersonian quest to find and defend one's "aboriginal" self even as they dramatize, with Franklinesque ingenuity, the near-impossibility of such an enterprise. These films remind us that self-reinvention may not be the result of individual choice but of the gap between reality and our representations of it. The multiplication of these forged selves raises the possibility that the ideal of self-fashioning relies on an untenable assumption about originality. In short, these films suggest that all identities are forged. In them, for better or worse, there is no cohesive subject, no Emersonian essence; there are only self-portraits that we paint and repaint, identities that we invent—or that are invented for us—again and again.

Noir's Cars
Automobility and Amoral Space

Los Angeles. Night. A gray coupe careens down a dark street, hurtles through a stoplight, barely missing an oncoming truck, then pulls up unsteadily before a tall building. A wounded man emerges: Walter Neff (Fred MacMurray), narrator/protagonist of Billy Wilder's influential 1944 film noir, *Double Indemnity*. The speeding, out-of-control car in fact symbolizes Neff, whose life has gone crazy ever since the day he first visited half-dressed, anklet-wearing housewife (and murderer) Phyllis Dietrichson (Barbara Stanwyck), ostensibly to sell auto insurance.

Cars serve both as the pretext for the plot's insurance scam and as part of the film's broader transportation motif. Recall, for example, the witty double-entendre dialogue between Neff and Phyllis, in which he suggests he needs to drive her name "around the block a few times," to which Phyllis offers the flirtatious put-down that he's exceeding the "speed limit." "How fast was I going, officer?" Neff asks. "I'd say around ninety," she answers, and so on. Recall, too, that Neff impersonates Mr. Dietrichson on a train to set up the actual murder. And remember the words of Neff's mentor, claims investigator Barton Keyes (Edward G. Robinson), that murderers ride a trolley car "all the way to the end of the line and it's a one-way trip and the last stop is the cemetery." If the train and trolley represent fate, the auto exemplifies the desire to flout history, destiny, and law, signifying freedom from rules and the American dream of forging a new self.

One might argue that film noir begins with *Double Indemnity*'s opening scene.[1] That would be appropriate, for cars figure prominently throughout the noir cycle. And though they sometimes appear in what Edward Dimendberg calls "centripetal" or "downtown" noirs (108) such as *Side Street*, they figure much more centrally in those set in the West and Southwest. According to Paul Fotsch it is no accident that so many noirs take place in Los Angeles, for the city's design—a centerless string of suburbs—engendered a sense of isolation and loneliness that "created instabilities for domestic relationships" (107) which, in turn, "facilitate[d] crime" (113). The profound sense of privacy and isolation fostered by geography extends to citizens' cars, which in films noir become not only alternative homes but amoral spaces where laws and social arrangements—marriage, class hierarchies—are suspended. Thus, for example, in *Double Indemnity* Neff uses his car to establish his alibi for a murder that—committed by him but engineered by Phyllis—takes place in the Dietrichsons' sedan.[2] The camera holds on Phyllis's face as, out of the frame, Neff strangles her husband: in more ways than one Phyllis is in the driver's seat. The murder of Dietrichson inaugurates a pattern: the remarkable number of violent crimes that occur in noir's cars.

In these films automobiles also become overdetermined symbols of characters' aspirations and disappointments. For example, Tay Garnett's adaptation of James M. Cain's *The Postman Always Rings Twice* illustrates the entrapment of adulterous lovers Cora Smith (Lana Turner) and Frank Chambers (John Garfield) through their lack of a car. As they try to hitchhike their way out of Twin Oaks, the roadside diner owned by Cora's husband, Nick (Cecil Kellaway), Frank explains why they have to thumb: "Stealing a man's wife, that's nothing. But stealing his car, that's larceny"—it means taking his identity and hope.[3] But without wheels the lovers are soon soiled, saddened, and dispirited, as Cora's increasingly smudged white outfit graphically indicates. Hitchhiking, she complains, will only lead "right back where [she] started": the "hash house." In Cain's novel Cora even describes their stunted hopes in terms of auto makes: "We had all that love," she tells Frank, "and we just cracked up under it. It's a big airplane engine, that takes you through the sky, right up to the top of the mountain. But when you put it in a Ford, it just shakes to pieces. That's what we are, Frank, a couple of Fords" (Cain, *Postman* 70). Their "make" forever brands them as ordinary, dooming their aspirations to crack up on the class ceiling. Hence their scheme of self-elevation or "rebranding" via murder culminates in Nick's car, where Frank clubs Nick to death with a bottle, while Cora sits behind the wheel. The car seems to carry the weight of karma: after getting away with Nick's murder, they sit in the front seat and exchange a "kiss with dreams in it," but the kiss so distracts Frank that he drives into a bridge, killing Cora and condemning himself to death row for her "murder."

Cora's words demonstrate how Americans internalized their identification with cars, commodifying themselves through automotive self-extension. The selling of autos in the aftermath of World War II, when automobility was promoted as a solution to economic and social malaise, encouraged this process. During the war, passenger car production had halted as factories and workers were enlisted in the war effort. Hence, when the "government rescinded wartime curbs on car production, gasoline purchases, and speed limits," writes Katie Mills, driving a new car became a "way to celebrate winning the war" (36). As millions of veterans returned home, landed jobs, and started families, their newly purchased cars became signs of restored consumer power and renewed possibility—of a refurbished American Dream (see Mottram 107). The material gain encoded in cars, as Ken Hillis notes, was thus "directly connected to acquiring greater agency and social status" (4). Exploiting these phenomena, some postwar writers turned road stories into a "declaration of independence," creating from highway narratives a "broader vision of autonomy and mobility for all" (Mills 2). These two linked qualities—autonomy and mobility—unite in narratives of "automobility" (Mills 18), in which the automobile's "synthesis of privacy and mobility" (Field 61) promised a means of bypassing class and gender barriers. Noir's cars likewise frequently represent the propulsive aspirations of disenfranchised people who turn to crime, embodying the possibility of social mobility through automobility.

As Kris Lackey observes, the postwar auto also offered ways of "surmounting biological limitations" and "challenging both nature and nurture" (12). In expanding the self, the car "loses its mechanical identity . . . and becomes a kind of bionic prosthesis" (32). Cars contributed to that conception of human identity as "a shiny commodity without a past" (Hillis 9) outlined in my introduction. It makes sense, then, that in many noirs the main car is a convertible, associated since its invention with youth, freedom, and rebellion.[4] Convertibles symbolize the American belief in mobile identity: convertibles, that is, represent the very promise of convertibility. Convertibles embodied the pursuit of happiness; they were a vehicle in which to chase the American Dream. Yet in film noir the convertible's positive aura is repeatedly shadowed by defeat and disillusion, as drivers make reckless decisions, crash against class barriers, and become victims of law-abiding citizens' guilt over their own transgressive desires. For noir's characters convertibility is usually a chimera, automobility a flywheel leading nowhere.

Unlike convertibles, whose open tops encourage visibility, most new postwar cars were "mini-arsenal[s]—of privacy, seclusion and isolationism on a par with our national thinking—and a vehicular deterrent to invasion by others" (Wieder and Hall 32). The car's symbolic power lies in its representation as a commodity identified with its owner. The figure of the hitchhiker, who appears in a number of significant noirs, challenges this aura of ownership by personifying risk, the intrusion of chaos, and the fragility of the postwar prosperity and security that automobiles embody. Though they are often loners who seem to epitomize frontier individualism, hitchers are also those who can't afford a car; using their thumbs, they seek to attach themselves to the automobility of more prosperous citizens. Whether vagabonds, drifters, psychopaths, or simple thugs, hitchhikers both exemplify the American Dream's individualist ideology and challenge its faith in unlimited upward movement.

Later noirs more dramatically depict the risks of automobility. In noirs produced after the Cold War had become a pressing concern, the automobile is portrayed as a Trojan horse: a false gift whose promise of freedom from obligation actually signifies a system—enforced by government institutions that also use automotive technologies—that transforms drivers into automatons. In these films cars are metonymies for a commodified world gone mad, a realm of utter insecurity propelled by internal and external explosions that may end in the largest explosion of all—the atomic bomb. These films warn that our addiction to automobility may have turned us *into* machines

Lamming It

A linked set of early noirs mobilizes autos as potent symbols of their hapless characters' desperation and restlessness. In these "outlaw road movie[s]" (Laderman 20) the lovers wish to break away from oppressive social circumstances yet long for a respectable domesticity they can never achieve. Postwar automotive conditions again influence these narratives. As William Beverly notes, the rapid expansion of roadways in the Southwest, where these films are set, rendered the fugitive criminal "just another face on the highway" (117); given such anonymity, the car becomes an amoral space, and a driver's permit a license to do anything at all. Postwar cars were also much roomier than earlier vehicles: advertisements touted them as a "total environment on wheels, rivaling home for comfort and luxury" (qtd. in Mottram 107). As if inhabiting this consumer fantasy, these films' fleeing lovers treat their cars not only as sexual fetishes, symbols of identity and murder weapons, but as living rooms, bedrooms, and nurseries. These young fugitives' cars replace "the normative American home and its various constituents" (Beverly 141), just as the lovers themselves expose the criminal impulses lurking inside law-abiding, apparently domesticated citizens. Yet their improvised mobile domesticity never lasts: the loss of their auto adumbrates the loss of liberty and often the loss of life.

The primary examples of this subgenre are *Desperate, They Live by Night, Shockproof,* and *Gun Crazy,* but their progenitor, Fritz Lang's *You Only Live Once* (1937), introduces the major motifs. Lang repeatedly displays ex-convict Eddie Taylor (Henry Fonda) and his wife Joan (Sylvia Sidney) being hounded by suspicious citizens such as Eddie's bigoted boss, who fires him for tardiness when he takes an hour to go house-hunting with Joan. As Tom Gunning writes, here Lang, like the makers of films such as *Caged* and *High Wall,* depicts "American society as mimicking and reproducing the structure of a prison in its suspicious surveillance and inhuman maintenance of disciplinary protocols" (246). Eddie and Joan are the victims of a panoptic environment that, paradoxically, prevents them from becoming like everyone else. Yet the film's ordinary citizens are fascinated by crime and criminals: wanted posters are ubiquitous; an innkeeper keeps a stash of true crime magazines; and bit-players exchange envious dialogue about the fugitives' allegedly luxurious lifestyle. Nor do allegedly law-abiding types really abide it: we see a cop steal an Italian grocer's apple, and two gas station attendants pilfer money from the till, then blame the theft on Eddie and Joan. These ordinary folks fit the description given them by the bank robbers in Edward Anderson's contemporaneous novel (the source for *They Live by Night*): they are all "thieves like us." The lawful need outlaws to express their own antisocial urges but repress their guilt by gleefully cooperating with the police.

After he is wrongly accused of an armored car robbery, Eddie sneaks up on the house he and Joan have purchased and gazes at her through the window. After a cut, he's seen from inside the house, his face trapped within the window's box, cramped by cage-like bars. Though no longer physically in prison, Eddie is forever barred from the bourgeois domesticity he desires and has little choice but to create an alternative domestic space seemingly immune from the prejudices of those who condemn and glorify his exploits—a car. And once Joan, a straight-arrow who works in a law office, picks up Eddie in the car she "borrows" from her boss, she becomes his accomplice. "We have a right to live," she proclaims, standing at the car door; in the next scene we see her pumping stolen gas. The car's need for fuel acts as a metonymy for the lovers' need for freedom; it is as if automobility itself—the desire to elevate Eddie from the criminal class to the honest working class—pushes Joan into criminality. Though they try to pass as regular citizens, features such as the bullet holes in the car window "tell too much": the car remains associated with the criminal identities they can't shed. After Joan (implausibly) delivers her own baby, their auto becomes their mobile home, complete with nursery, living room, and kitchen. Yet they still yearn for ordinary domesticity. "We were inside a house once, for a few minutes," Eddie recalls wistfully. "Lots o' people in love get to live inside a house." "Anywhere's our home," Joan assures him. "In the car, out there on that cold star, anywhere's our home." But their home isn't mobile enough: directly after this conversation Eddie drives into a police roadblock. Machine-gun fire pours through the back window, wounding them both and forcing them from their car, whereupon they both die. Narrow-minded people, the film suggests, will always sacrifice those like Eddie and Joan, less for their criminal deeds than from envy of the threatening (anti) social mobility and freedom figured by their speeding car.

Director Douglas Sirk's little-known *Shockproof,* scripted by Helen Deutsch and Samuel Fuller, is a distaff version of the same story. This time the man, Griff Marat (Cornel Wilde), is a parole officer in love with an ex-convict named Jenny Marsh (Patricia Knight), who cannot sever her tie to oily gambler Harry Wesson (John Baragrey). After Griff receives a mysterious phone call from Harry that ends in a gunshot, Griff picks up Jenny in his car. During the drive she tells him that she accidentally shot Harry: here, as in several other noirs, the car serves as the engine of narrative itself.[5] When she finishes her story, Griff turns both the car and himself around and takes Jenny on the lam. During their journey cars become symbols of sexual license (though they allegedly marry in secret offscreen, this is an unconvincing nod to the Breen Office) and shifting identities. Those two meanings ingeniously converge when Griff and Jenny steal a newlywed couple's car, its hanging cans and "Just Married" sign covering the license plate. Though not literally a convertible, the car nevertheless represents their mobile identities: Jenny dyes her hair (back to its original brunette shade), and Griff assumes a nom de guerre. But as we saw in the missing-person noirs, the freedom to become any-body eventually turns them into nobodies, as represented by their increasingly humble modes of transportation: car, bus, then freight train. Their downward flight briefly comes to rest in an oil driller's shack that, for Griff, proves that they're "living like pigs." Unable to bear the thought of a life of perpetual downward mobility, the lovers turn themselves in. Griff had unwittingly forecast this pros-pect while earlier explaining a western movie to his younger brother: criminals, he explained, usually give up when "corrosion" sets in. When he decides to give up, Griff cites this line, suggesting that the lovers' flight has transmuted them into worn-out car parts. As in *You Only Live Once,* cars' amoral space devolves into amorphousness, and unending automobility becomes a traveling prison cell.

Nicholas Ray's *They Live by Night* opens with an overhead shot of a car hold-ing three escaped convicts: young Bowie Bowers (Farley Granger) and his mentors

Chicamaw (Jay C. Flippen) and T-Dub (Howard Da Silva). The car gets a flat, and while fixing the tire, Bowie talks of his dream of owning a gas station with Keechie (Cathy O'Donnell), the grubby daughter of an accomplice. At once Bowie's conscience ("fine company you're runnin' with," she admonishes, standing above him in the frame) and his motive for mobility, Keechie hopes to fix Bowie as he does the tire. Alas, as an escaped convict with no money or prospects, Bowie has little choice but to drive the getaway car for his partners, who understand that their criminal identities are embodied in their getaway cars and thus always burn them after heists.

Soon, however, Chicamaw's reckless driving causes a crash that injures Bowie, implicates him in two murders, and forces him temporarily to exit the motorway. Nursed back to health by Keechie, Bowie falls in love and marries her. Whereas Keechie's blossoming is blatantly displayed in Cathy O'Donnell's flattering new makeup and clothes, Bowie's rebirth is illustrated by his postnuptial car—a dashing convertible, which embodies his wish to convert from impoverished ex-convict

In *They Live by Night,* Bowie (Farley Granger) and Keechie (Cathy O'Donnell) fall in love as he changes a tire. *Author's collection.*

to up-and-coming man about town. As in *You Only Live Once,* the convertible becomes a mobile home, complete with dining room and, of course, bedroom (Keechie soon becomes pregnant). After a final job results in the death of his cronies, Bowie and Keechie flee to New Orleans, where they try to impersonate ordinary newlyweds. But a sequence depicting their outing to a park and a night-club (they are mystified by golf and disdain dancing) dramatizes their status as permanent outcasts. At evening's end a chanteuse sums up their condition: they're just two kids in a "red wagon," she sings, and even if it's "all [their] own," it's going nowhere. Bowie, the song continues, cannot forever use Keechie as his "spare tire," for eventually "you get burned when you play with fire." As in *Shock-proof* and *You Only Live Once,* the end of automobility (here, in a motel) signals the end of the male's life (in the novel both die). Their convertible provided only the illusion of transformation; its mobility was merely geographic, never social, and even that movement was circular. Little more than children, Bowie and Keechie were merely play-acting in their wagon, briefly enacting a fantasy of rising from poverty.

Even more innocent than Ray's characters are truck driver Steve Randall (Steve Brodie) and his pregnant wife, Anne (Audrey Long), in Anthony Mann's *Desperate.* Mann and his director of photography George Diskant underline this ingenuousness by juxtaposing their bright apartment with gangster Walt Radak's gloomy hideout, where a single bulb provides the only illumination. (In an eerily effective scene early in the film, Radak's men beat up Steve as the bulb swings, lending a nightmarish quality to his predicament.) But the barriers between their worlds break down once Steve is enlisted to deliver "perishables" for Radak (Raymond Burr) and then wrongly implicated in the murder of a policeman. This turn of events reminds Steve and viewers that, as Dennis Broe points out, "working-class mobility is tenuous and can just as easily lead downward" (57).

And so, when he and Anne go on the lam, the car they drive is not a convertible but a beat-up jalopy. After offering to fix and then buy it for ninety dollars, Steve is duped by a crooked dealer who, realizing that Steve is in a hurry and probably in trouble, ups the price as soon as it is roadworthy.[6] When Steve returns to persuade him to sell it, he finds the dealer gone and steals the car, which, initially representing the Randalls' marginal economic position and victimization, now embodies Steve's conversion into a shady character. But Steve doesn't want to be converted; he wants to affirm his authenticity as an honest man. And unlike the other lamming lovers, the Randalls thrive only when they stay put: while living with Anne's aunt and uncle, for example, Steve gets a new job, and the couple are remarried by a minister. Would they be better off eschewing upward mobility for rustic stability? Radak's appearance at the farmhouse (where the thugs' dark trench coats, fedoras, and gangster argot contrast jarringly with the farm's rural domesticity) renders the question moot and forces another departure.

After Anne gives birth, the lovers formulate a plan entertained by a surprising number of male noir protagonists: to own a "filling" station.[7] Popping the baby's bottle into her mouth, Anne fantasizes about "Steve Randall's gas station." But after sending Anne and baby away to claim the station, Steve becomes the police's bait for Radak, who captures and arranges to kill Steve at the very moment Radak's brother is being executed for the cop's murder. Their tense wait for midnight to strike (punctuated by imposing Eisensteinian close-ups) is interrupted when a neighbor knocks on the door to borrow cream. The contrast between domesticity and mobility, innocence and evil, is thus rendered in terms of fuel—milk versus gas. But despite abundant indications of his milky innocence, Steve dirties himself by killing Radak. And the Randalls' dream of domesticity remains harnessed to the auto economy: they can provide milk for the baby only by selling fuel for others' cars. By the end of the film, these innocents have been soiled by road grime, infected by the auto's amoral space, altered by automobility.

Unlike Ray's or Mann's ingénues, lovers Bart Tare (John Dall) and Annie Laurie Starr (Peggy Cummins) in Joseph H. Lewis's sensational *Gun Crazy* never try to settle down. And unlike Keechie, who tries to dissuade Bowie from his criminal career, trigger-happy Laurie entices weak-willed Bart into ever more reckless capers: robbing diners, then hitchhiking so as to rip off lecherous male drivers. For them, cars are like guns—erotic machines that enable them to evade the fate embodied by Bart's sister, who represents (to Laurie) the living death that is small-town domesticity (see Wager, *Dangerous* 101). They prefer the nearly infinite play of convertibility enacted during their crime spree, when they adopt a series of outrageous false identities and vehicles: in one scene they wear conservative suits and glasses; in another Bart dons his old army uniform. In the film's most celebrated sequence—which unfolds for three and a half minutes without a cut—the lovers sport ludicrous carnival cowboy outfits while robbing a bank. Lewis places us in the backseat of their car as Bart and Laurie, like teens on their first date, make nervous conversation, and the camera remains in the car as Bart executes the robbery.[8] Lewis thus makes us their passengers and accomplices, brilliantly evoking suspense and sympathy by inviting us to inhabit their amoral space. Indeed, as Laurie and the cop she encounters suggestively fondle their guns, we become voyeuristic partners in the lovers' erotic escapades. Their car is now both camera and gun: it not only moves—it shoots! Not surprisingly, their string of sedans and coupes ends with a convertible.

Though Bart professes his unwillingness to continue—"everything's going so fast, it's all in such high gear. It doesn't feel like me"—Laurie persuades him to pull one last heist. And so the lovers take straight jobs with Armour in order to rob the packing plant's safe, but the caper goes wrong when Laurie shoots two employees. The sequence ends in a striking scene depicting the two racing through a refrigerated chamber filled with dangling carcasses. Jim Kitses reads this scene as a "caricature of the ideal of social mobility enshrined in the capitalist trajectory" (48), but it may also be Lewis's (and the film's blacklisted cowriter Dalton Trumbo's) sardonic commentary on the lovers' consuming amorality, whereby other humans are merely carcasses serving a cold, hedonistic lifestyle in which, as Bart almost comically puts it later, "two people [are] dead just so we can live without working."[9]

In *Gun Crazy*, Bart Tare (John Dall) and Annie Laurie Starr (Peggy Cummins) part at their convertible. *Author's collection.*

The fugitives had originally planned to split up afterward and drive separate convertibles in different directions, but in the end they can't do it: their car, after all, represents their bond and the incessant mobility that is the essence of being gun—and car—crazy. Despite their violent natures, there is something childish about their attitude, an idea borne out during their final fling, when they ride a roller coaster and merry-go-round like youngsters out for a lark.[10] But these vehicles move only in circles, just as their lam ends where it began—in Bart's hometown of Cashville. Significantly, they have to hop a freight car to get there, and even after they steal Bart's sister's car (*not* a convertible), they can't escape their fate, the inevitable outcome of being car and gun crazy.

By portraying lovers who test their society's tolerance for extreme mobility, these lam films imply that the American dream of convertible identity can be lived only briefly, often at the cost of death. Whereas the vet noirs imply that permanent self-reinvention is possible (if only by experiencing trauma and painful recovery), and the missing-person films suggest that one cannot truly change one's nature because it is molded by others, these lovers' pursuit of upward mobility through automobility is presented as a speed trap contrived by a society that craves yet finally cannot abide the antisocial impulses of young lovers. And despite the fugitives' challenges to the economic and social system that confines them, they cannot evade their own commodification as glamorous criminals in hurtling cars. Even so, the thrill of riding with Eddie and Joan, Griff and Jenny, Bart and Laurie, Bowie and Keechie seems infinitely preferable to the pedestrian lives of Cora's husband and Bart's boyhood friends—and even, perhaps, to the compromised stability of the Randall family. If the lamming lovers' restlessness ends up imprisoning them, at least they felt briefly the rush of air on their faces, the passing delight in driving—indeed, *being*—convertibles. And if they finally have no particular place to go, at least they've gone there fast.

Thumbing a Ride

The lamming lovers temporarily exercise freedom through automobility. The hitchhikers who figure in many films noir might seem even less encumbered. But hitchhiking is a dangerous game, if we believe Al Roberts (Tom Neal), the protagonist of Edgar G. Ulmer's brilliant B picture *Detour*. As Paul Cantor points out, this film "revolves around the automobile": not only does much of the story take place during Al's thumbing trip from New York to LA, but his journey ultimately brings him to "two distinctively American" automotive spaces: the used-car lot and the drive-in restaurant (complete with those other archaic roadside icons, car hops; see Cantor 154). Like Frank Chambers, Al is a kind of picaro, a vagabond living on the edge of society.[11] Yet if Al's westward journey seems at first a plausible means of freeing him from his humiliating gig as a saloon pianist and a "perfect symbol of [American] mobility" (Cantor 154), in fact Al, like those missing persons analyzed in chapter 2, merely swaps one form of confinement for another. The film sardonically parodies Depression-era tales of escape through westward movement by presenting Al's dream as a nightmare—a "meaningless circle or trap" (Naremore, *More Than Night* 148; see also Polan 270).[12] Owning (or driving) a car may generate a feeling of sovereignty and autonomy, but thumbing testifies to a lack of control: it is mobility without autonomy. Hitchhiking places Al at the mercy of drivers such as Charles Haskell, a big talker whose nice suit, wad of cash, and fancy convertible can't save his life.

While Haskell sleeps, Al gets behind the wheel. But he's not really driving; fate is. Haskell's untimely (though apparently natural) death in his convertible catalyzes Al's conversion from disgruntled musician to victim of destiny.[13] After discovering that Haskell is dead, Al stands beside the car in a driving rain and makes the first of several tragically foolish decisions: to hide Haskell's body and then take his money and driver's license. It's almost as if the car forces the transformation: had it not been a convertible, Al wouldn't have had to stop to put up the top; Haskell wouldn't have fallen out, may not have died; and Al might have fulfilled his original plan (although, as I suggest in chapter 6, he may not have really wanted to join Sue in LA in the first place).[14] Al's new plan is foiled when he picks up the hitchhiking Vera (memorably played by Ann Savage), the "dangerous animal" responsible for the gruesome scratches Haskell earlier displayed ("What kind of dames thumb rides?" he'd asked Al. "Sunday school teachers?"). More important, she is a person who knows Al isn't Haskell. And so Vera becomes Haskell's "ghostly reincarnation" (Naremore, *More Than Night* 149)—as if, Al tells us, he were "sitting right there in the car laughing like mad while he haunted me." Vera first demands that Al sell Haskell's convertible to avoid having it traced but then arrives at a more ambitious scheme: to collect Haskell's inheritance from his dying father. How will Al prove he's Haskell? With his car and driver's license, of course. But though they keep the convertible, Al still isn't in the driver's seat and ends up (semiaccidentally) strangling Vera with a phone cord. Al's hitchhiking—he's doing it again at the film's conclusion—determines his character: he will remain forever subject to the wishes of others, whether they be club patrons or conning car owners. Al's American dream is foiled by his lack of agency; he can't remake himself because he has so little self to begin with. Not everyone is truly convertible.

In *Detour*, hitchhiking subjects the thumber to vicissitudes of the road, whims of fate, and eruptions of coincidence. In most subsequent noir hitchhiking films, however, the roles are switched: the hitchhiker is an invader who seizes control of the car, thereby embodying the fears of Cold War Americans—their terror of invasion and loss of freedom—as well as the recognition that their new prosperity cloaks a churning desire for lawlessness. In *The Devil Thumbs a Ride*, for example, the handsome gray 1941 convertible owned by traveling salesman Jimmy Ferguson (Ted North) seems to express his willingness to pursue the upward mobility—represented by Emerald Products (a line of ladies' lingerie)—urged on him by his wife. In contrast the car represents the possibility of escape for Jimmy's hitchhiker, psychopathic robber and murderer Steve Morgan (Lawrence Tierney), as well as for the two women, Agnes (Betty Lawford) and Carol (Nan Leslie), who later hitch a ride with them. But the car apparently doesn't satisfy Jimmy, who is drunk throughout most of the film and seems well on his way to alcoholism. Indeed, the ease with which Morgan persuades Jimmy to let him take the wheel indicates a thirst for adventure running beneath Jimmy's dream of conventional success; the convertible embodies Jimmy's unspoken desire to defy the law and live, like Morgan, on the fly. This desire is played out after Morgan—a much better salesman, in his way, than Jimmy—convinces him to hole up at a friend's beach house, then punctures the car's tires to prevent their departure. After Morgan murders Carol (who has learned that he's on the lam) and the sheriff appears, Morgan uses Jimmy's driver's license and car keys to convince the lawman that *he's* Ferguson. The doubling of the two characters thus becomes explicit—Morgan incarnates Jimmy's own lawless impulses—with the convertible again acting as catalyst.

Eventually a detective and his deputy (a gas station attendant named Kenney) expose the true identity of Morgan, who is apprehended and killed, thereby restoring order. At the end Jimmy's wife reveals that she is pregnant and drives the convertible toward home. But though the car now seems to indicate Jimmy's reconversion to uxorious husband and law-abiding lingerie vendor, its weaving progress in the concluding scene suggests that Jimmy's transgressive impulses are merely quiescent, liable to resurface as soon as he fails to please his grasping wife. Jimmy's convertible, first a sign of his mobility and then a vehicle for Morgan's, represents the instability of conventional values and the fragility of Ferguson's middle-class male identity.

The figure of the hitchhiker as a threat to middle-class values and masculinity appears even more forcefully in Ida Lupino's *The Hitch-Hiker* (its taut screenplay was cowritten by Lupino and Collier Young). This film begins with a precredit introduction establishing its veracity: "This is the true story of a man and a gun and a car. The gun belonged to the man. The car might have been yours—or that young couple across the aisle. What you will see in the next seventy minutes could have happened to you. For the facts are actual." By grounding the tale in documentary detail, the prologue heightens the eruptive force of the hitchhiker. What follows—a series of montages showing the hitchhiking psychopath Emmett Myers (William Talman) at his deadly work—reinforces a sense that cars automatically generate the risk of invasion. The next sequence depicts the back of a Dodge convertible pulling up beside a man and picking him up. Darkness falls. A second car pulls up to the same man; we hear gunshots and a woman screaming, see the hiker's hand as he examines books and papers that have fallen from the car, then his walking feet. Another car picks up the hitchhiker, who appears again only as feet and hands. Finally, we're riding with ordinary guys Gilbert Bowen (Frank Lovejoy) and Roy Collins (Edmond O'Brien), who (without telling the folks at home) decide to take a detour from their fishing trip to pursue happiness by gawking at the decadent sights in a Mexican border town. The introduction thus triangulates the characters: Myers, who views human beings as body parts, as objects of demonic automotive fishing, is the sinister alter ego of Bowen and Collins, whose outlaw urges are channeled into guilty, giggling voyeurism.

Myers seems to have been conjured to punish them for their foibles. As he rides in their backseat, his face pokes into the light, revealing a paralyzed eye and a pistol barrel: "face front and keep driving," he snarls. With the gun and commandeered car, he now possesses the full trinity of masculine power. So armed, he proceeds ruthlessly to strip away the fishermen's defenses and masculine strength. First he plays humiliating mind games, forcing Bowen to shoot at a can Collins is holding. Then he mocks their values, calling them "suckers" who are "up to [their] neck in IOUs," and boasts that he doesn't "owe nobody": he just takes the things he wants. "I didn't need any of 'em. . . . If you got the know-how and a few bucks in your pocket, you can buy anything or anybody. 'Specially if you got 'em at the point of a gun." This consummate individualist exposes the limitations of that venerated American ideal. And in appropriating their auto, Myers robs them of the sense of sovereignty cars are designed to produce. They are now prisoners in their own vehicle—ironically, a Plymouth, a brand named after an icon of American liberty. Thus Myers stands as a grotesque exaggeration of the principles by which these men live. His power reaches its apex when Bowen and Collins try to escape, and Myers finds them by using the car's headlights. The point of view given him as he spotlights the men suggests that the car has indeed become his prosthesis, a mechanical extension of his evil eye. Myers, in short, *is* a car, a Frankenstein's monster assembled from the prized technologies and ideologies of postwar America.

That Myers, like Steve Morgan, also represents the fishermen's repressed subversive impulses (the same impulses that impel policeman Cal Bruner to steal in the Lupino-Young script for *Private Hell 36*) is displayed when he forces Collins to exchange clothes with him. Indeed, as the film proceeds, Collins—angry and embittered, dragging his left leg—comes more and more to resemble Myers. Near the end of the film he glowers at the hitchhiker and seethes, "You stink, . . . just like your clothes. . . . You haven't got a thing except that gun. You better hang on to it, because without it, you're nothing." Later he punches Myers in the face

Psychopath Emmett Myers (William Talman) abducts fishermen Bowen (Frank Lovejoy) and Collins (Edmond O'Brien) in *The Hitch-Hiker. Author's collection.*

while the police hold the erstwhile hitcher. In this film, then, the car becomes a stage where the men enact a crisis of masculinity that, I have argued, appears in so many noirs. By abducting them, Myers forces them to discover previously hidden portions of themselves, to abandon the masks of civility they weren't brave enough to discard on their own. Myers's presence reveals that guns and cars, those prosthetics with which American males bolster their identities, are signs not of power but of anxious vulnerability. In short, here guns and cars function like the extra wife acquired by Harry Graham in Lupino and Young's *The Bigamist*—an ineffective means of empowering himself and of restoring his wounded masculinity. Unlike Graham's second marriage, Myers's ominous existence forces an inner conversion: a mobility that is not social but psychic.

Like *The Hitch-Hiker,* Andrew Stone's *The Night Holds Terror* presents the hitcher as a synecdoche of lawlessness, and the car as a masculine prosthesis, but the film links these qualities to an insecure economic status and to postwar technologies that entrap as much as they liberate. Here again an introduction establishes the factuality of events: an abduction perpetrated against the Courtier family in 1953 (we even see a photo of the real-life family). In the film, when Courtier (Jack Kelly) realizes that young Gosset (Vince Edwards), who has thumbed a ride in his convertible, wants to rob him, he laments in voice-over: "Why, why had I stopped to give that guy a lift? I was taking a chance; I knew that. Yet nearly everyone's picked up a hitchhiker at one time or another. Haven't you?" Courtier's very friendliness (a quality, it is implied, shared by many American males) and his car's mobility and openness render him (and it) more subject to invasion.

Gosset has assessed Courtier's wealth from his car but has mistaken his humble Mercury for a Lincoln. "You sure picked the wrong car," comments Courtier, who is carrying only ten dollars. The thugs—led by John Cassavetes's intense Batsford—then force Courtier to sell his Merc for the $2,000 he claims it's worth. Unfortunately, they can get only $500 from the dealer and must return the next day for the balance. So they spend the night in the Courtiers' home, where Gosset makes a pass at Mrs. Courtier (Hildy Parks) and the others make free with his possessions—Batsford, for example, dons Courtier's smoking jacket. Equipped with a gun and Courtier's car, the thieves prove again that stealing a man's car is stealing his male identity. Relieved of these accouterments of masculine power, Courtier is reduced to sputtering ineffectuality.

The film thus presents automobility as inherently risky: the convertible that seems to empower Courtier by displaying his affluence actually makes him more vulnerable. Nor is his car a ticket to the open road; instead, it signifies his confinement in domesticity and debt. Hitchhikers, in turn, aren't merely criminals but subversive forces who undermine and reveal the limitations of the values—autonomy, prosperity, domestic security—that cars are employed to represent. These hitchhikers and the cars they thumb down embody the buried restlessness in the males who own them: their desire to escape, to convert from, say, engineers (Courtier) or gas station owners (Collins) into lone wolves who owe nothing to anyone. The cars' amoral spaces do not appease their longing for freedom so much as fuel it: it is as if the cars drive *them*.

Bombing Around, or The Trojan Car

Like most pseudodocumentary noirs, *The Night Holds Terror* sides with law enforcement, stressing its mastery of surveillance technologies such as radio, television, and teletype, as well as its control of information. The second half of the film thus tracks the police's attempt to apprehend the thugs without letting them know (though the outlaws have access to police radio frequencies). But if the hitchhikers are frightening, there is something equally ominous about the police's panoptic power, which reaches all the way into the Courtiers' home to show Mrs. Courtier some mug shots. And when we recall that Mr. Courtier was abducted while returning home from his job at an airbase, we realize he is already imbricated in this same system of information, his car merely the visible tip of a vast technomilitary complex that culminates in bombs and missiles. And if subversive forces such as hitchhikers can commandeer our cars, they might also steal other, more dangerous technologies—as, in fact, Soviet spies had done a few years earlier. This association of automobiles and secret technologies becomes blatant in other postwar noirs where cars are portrayed as Trojan horses—boons whose promise of freedom distracts citizens from the presence of more lethal technologies. In these films cars are no longer merely guns; they are bombs.

In *White Heat,* for example, cars are associated with "heat"—with contained, automated combustion. By using cars in his crimes, gangster Cody Jarrett (James Cagney, in a legendary performance) would seem to participate in this mechanized world. But Cody produces heat of a different sort: far from a machine, he is a force of nature, subject to headaches and explosions of temper, and requires "tons of specialized equipment to get him cornered" (Shadoian 168). Indeed, Cody always seems hemmed in by machines, from the opening train-robbery sequence to the prison machine shop where he's nearly killed, to his apocalyptic demise at an oil refinery. It makes sense, then, that the FBI traps him by using electronics technician Hank Fallon (Edmond O'Brien), who, as Vic Pardo, worms his way into Jarrett's confidence and ultimately switches off his power. Where Cody is ebullient, impulsive, psychotic, Fallon/Pardo is canny, emotionless, machinelike: an embodiment of chilly technologies designed to dampen and smother outlaw impulses (Shadoian 169).

Nor are Cody's cars convertibles, for he is no youngster forced into crime by poverty, nor is he a working-class guy on the make, but a hardened criminal who craves secrecy. For Jarrett autos are hiding places. Thus, in one remarkable sequence, Jarrett; his wife, Verna (Virginia Mayo); and his (overly) beloved mother (Margaret Wycherly) take cover in a drive-in movie (the film: *Task Force*), where Cody decides to give himself up for a lesser crime to avoid a murder rap. Later, after his mother dies, he escapes from prison by hiding in a car's trunk. But though cars and trucks permit the gang to make bigger hauls and move from place to place, they also leave tracks that enable the police and FBI to apprehend them. Cars seem to be a criminal's best friend, but, like Pardo/Fallon, they are really Trojan horses, rats on wheels.

These themes converge in the final sequence when Jarrett and the gang (explicitly citing the *Aeneid*) hide inside an empty tanker in order to steal the refinery payroll. The scenes shot within the tank make Cody look small and cramped, suggesting that though he believes he is in charge, he is actually just a cog in Fallon/Pardo's machinations. For he never suspects that his own Trojan horse has been signaling the police with a radio transmitter. Curiously, Fallon displays not even a hint of ambivalence about betraying a man with whom he has grown intimate. Hence, while viewers may fear Jarrett's psychopathic violence, we likely root for him over Fallon, who seems to embody the soulless technologies increasingly used to exterminate the Cody Jarretts of the world and whose role as informer invokes the presence of "friendly" witnesses—that is, those who informed on their former friends—in midcentury Hollywood. And if the famous final apocalyptic explosion amid the refinery's Hortonspheres alludes to the larger threat looming over the world—the atomic bomb, as I have argued elsewhere—Cody Jarrett seems less responsible for these explosions than do the police who fan his white heat.[15] For although Cody's heat is like the gas of a speeding automobile, the government's pervasive and intense heat—artificial, passionless, ubiquitous, and, above all, secretive—might very well lead to an all-consuming conflagration.

The apotheosis of noir's cars occurs in Robert Aldrich's *Kiss Me Deadly*, where the automobile's amoral space collides, almost literally, with new explosive technologies. Machines are everywhere in the world of the protagonist, "bedroom dick" Mike Hammer (Ralph Meeker), with his telephone answering machine and flashy Jaguar roadster. From the opening scene, when the mysterious Christina (Cloris Leachman) flags Hammer down by standing in the middle of the road and holding up her arms in an X-figure, we seem to be riding in a speeding car. Even the opening titles crawl backward (from bottom to top) as if we're reading them from the passenger's seat. And if Christina is a hitcher, so are the film's viewers, barely hanging on through the film's careening narrative, which (filled with odd camera angles, sequence shots, and strange characters) seems to swerve and dart like Hammer's car (Silver, *"Kiss Me"* 209) as it drives us ever closer to "The Great Whatsit," a radioactive device desired by a gang of criminals led by the mysterious Dr. Soberin (Albert Dekker).

Hammer is far from a sympathetic hero: after nearly running Christina down, he callously responds, "You almost wrecked my car!" She immediately parses his personality: "You're one of those self-indulgent males who thinks about nothing but his clothes, his car, himself. . . . You're the kind of person who never gives in a relationship." As she astutely discerns, Hammer's car, far from signifying convertibility, embodies his hammer-like, inflexible character, which Shadoian compares to a "hard rubber object" (222). A man who pimps out his girlfriend/secretary, Velda (Maxine Cooper), to catch wayward husbands and whose motto is "what's in it for me?," Hammer has accepted as fait accompli the commodification of everything. He has also internalized the automobile's amoral space: agile but robotic, Hammer *is* his roadster.

Cars also symbolize the rootless amorality that pervades his world. Indeed, most of the film's characters act like automatons, Los Angeles having mutated from the sleepy suburbia of *Double Indemnity* into a city filled with human bumper cars. As a mover's assistant puts it in the film, "people . . . never stand still." Hence we hear traffic sounds constantly, even during interior scenes such as the eerie sequences set in the room of "Lily" (actually named Gabrielle, played by Gaby Rodgers), whom Hammer interrogates and then attempts to aid. The soul-destroying hollowness of Hammer's Los Angeles indeed exemplifies Anthony Giddens's description of modernity as "a runaway engine of enormous power which . . . we can drive to some extent but which also threatens to rush out of our control and which could rend itself asunder" (139). This engine lies inside the automobile, which is once again figured as a Trojan horse—a gift whose autonomy and mobility engender amorality and anomie. *Kiss Me Deadly*'s cars signify a world where humans have become machines.

Hammer undergoes conversion, however, after Soberin's gang runs him off the road and nearly kills him. He symbolically dies twice more, once when the gang plants a bomb in his new convertible and again when they drug him to learn what he knows about what Velda dubs the Great Whatsit. His cars symbolize this capacity for resurrection, his ability to imitate "Lazarus rose out from the grave," as Hammer's mechanic, Nick (Nick Dennis), names him. In fact, Hammer has at least three lives: his first life as a sleazy private eye, represented by his first car (a Jaguar XK120 roadster); his transition from roadster to quester, embodied by a convertible that he briefly drives (probably an MG TD); and his final, slightly more humanized, self, symbolized by the Corvette convertible given to him as a phony peace offering by Soberin's gang. Another Trojan horse, this car carries not one but two bombs, the first designed to explode on ignition and the second when the car reaches a certain speed. That would be a "sweet little kiss off," explains Hammer to Nick, for whom cars and pretty women prompt identical expletives: "Va-voom! 3D pow!" Pow indeed: cars are deadly weapons. Nick himself is murdered automotively when Soberin (identified only by the expensive shoes we earlier saw when his gang tortured Christina) releases the jack holding up a car under which Nick is working. Viewers are implicated in this murder through a brief shot taken, as it were, from the falling car's point of view. In the aftermath we ride shotgun in Hammer's Corvette as he kills and tortures people to avenge Nick's death and to solve the mystery of the Great Whatsit.

The crucial item in this quest is a key that Christina hides on her body before dying; it's the key to a locker, but it may as well be an ignition key, for the film suggests that cars are just the leading edge of a continuum leading inexorably to the atomic bomb. Like the device inside the roaring, blindingly shining box that Gabrielle opens despite Soberin's warning, cars change everything. They even alter human bodies, as the film illustrates through its constant shots of detached hands, feet, legs. Like the bomb itself—the result of splitting atoms—automotive technologies and the capitalism that sells them as expansions of selfhood instead convert human beings into aggregates of colliding parts. No longer mere convertibles, cars have become converters transforming people into atomized automatons. Cars and bombs are both Great Whatsits whose advanced technologies paradoxically expose our most primitive impulses—terror, violence, selfishness,

Opening "The Great Whatsit" in *Kiss Me Deadly. Author's collection.*

and greed. In *Kiss Me Deadly* automobility fosters a restless amorality that ultimately consumes everyone.

Noir's cars seem to speed the characters toward liberation, with their promise
of automobility and convertibility, but instead inevitably crash into roadblocks.
They trace an arc that mimics that of postwar American society and culture:
beginning as an emblem of rebirth and a remodeled American Dream, they become vehicles for a set of pervasive anxieties: the mixed desire for and dread of a
convertibility that is almost invariably smothered by envy and amorality; the

fear that the machines that seem to liberate and expand us actually render us vulnerable both financially (we incur debt in order to "own" our cars and houses) and physically (by subjecting us to invasion and violence that may end in a conflagration). In these films the world has become a speeding car. But who, they prompt us to ask, is really in the driver's seat?

6

Nocturnes in Black and Blue
Memory, Morality, and Jazz Melody

A sharply creased fedora rests atop the oiled hair of a smart-talking detective, whose steely eyes gaze at a seductive blonde smoking a cigarette. When they kiss—as they inevitably will—a slinky jazz saxophone plays. Hat, blonde, smoke, jazz: to many twenty-first-century viewers these tropes are identified with film noir. But there's a problem with this scenario: the jazz wasn't really there. As David Butler has shown, not a single 1940s noir and only a few from the 1950s actually featured a jazz soundtrack. Our popular contemporary association of noir with jazz is, he writes, a "retrospective illusion" (166), a dream of the postmodern era.[1]

One reason for this illusion may be that, as Claudia Gorbman notes, most film music is "inaudible" (77): it reinforces the narrative, furnishes emotional effects, and outlines characters without consciously registering in viewers' minds.[2] But jazz in noir is inaudible in a different sense, which derives partly from the invisibility of African Americans in midcentury cinema. Although black characters are no more prominent in noirs than in other Hollywood movies of the period, this whitewash took place only on the surface, leaving blackness intact beneath and allowing it to surface in the form of jazz. Noir filmmakers employed jazz as a gateway to invisible segments of society, in the process unveiling various suspicious character types and exposing hidden corners of postwar cultural consciousness. Jazz, I propose, gave noir filmmakers a means to explore shifting attitudes about race relations and equality; to dramatize anxieties about disability, sexuality, and gender; and to analyze American ambivalence about violence.

In noir, as in other midcentury Hollywood movies, jazz is, as Kathryn Kalinak has argued, a symbol of otherness (167). Racial otherness is sometimes displayed in noir's nightclub scenes. Often the sole moments when African Americans appear, these scenes introduce viewers to an alternate America, one characterized by liberated sexuality, drug use, racial mixing, and violations of orthodox gender roles and sexual orientations. This otherness colors the depiction of white male jazz musicians, who are almost invariably portrayed in noir as fragile *(The Man I Love)*, sexually suspect *(Nocturne)*, or ultrasensitive and unreliable *(Nightmare)*—or all of these traits at once. Alternately hypersexual and effeminate, noir jazz musicians are prone to madness, drugs, and violence. Yet the films betray a lingering respect and fascination with these geek-like figures who enact viewers' repressed impulses, including an attraction to blackness. These white jazz musicians are, in short, "noired"—made into surrogate African Americans.

But if noir jazz registers the dissonances of a changing postwar world and provides a key to the American cult of violence, it also offers a glimpse into a new world in the making, one that challenges prejudice and convention and trumpets progressive ideals such as hybridity, emotional liberation, racial equality, and self-creation through improvisation. At its best, noir jazz hints at a reformed American identity composed from previously silenced strains of the social melody.

The Whole USA in One Chorus

Jazz in midcentury Hollywood was fraught with mostly negative meanings. Sometimes it stood for the dehumanizing urban environment (Butler 193); elsewhere it represented sexual urges that surfaced only at night, when taboos were broken and drugs were taken.[3] For white audiences of the period, notes Kalinak, jazz was perceived "as an indigenous black form" that represented the "urban, the sexual and the decadent" (167). Hence, jazz was coded as black even when (as was almost always the case) the musicians on display were white. Eric Lott has persuasively argued that classic noir, by borrowing blackness and subsuming it into the "untoward aspects of white selves," constitutes a "whiteface dream-work of social anxieties with explicitly racial sources" (551). It does so, I would add, less through the rare black characters shown onscreen (as Lott proposes) than through the music itself, which shades white characters by lending them traits stereotypically attributed to African Americans.

There is another side to this phenomenon. Jazz is a quintessentially American music because of its improvisational nature, because it blends European harmonies with African rhythms, and because it supplies a medium for marginalized groups to "signify" upon the norms of the dominant culture. It promotes the individual soloist within a group context, thus uniting individual and collective achievement. Indeed, not only did jazz provide a path for African Americans' upward mobility; it also served as a whitening force for Jewish musicians and composers such as Al Jolson, the Gershwins, Benny Goodman, Artie Shaw, and many others. In addition the music furnished an arena for interracial cooperation, such as when, in the 1930s, Benny Goodman hired African Americans Teddy Wilson and Lionel Hampton for his band, and Billie Holiday briefly fronted Shaw's all-white orchestra. As Lawrence Levine has argued, jazz also expresses the "side of ourselves that strove to recognize the positive aspects of our newness and our heterogeneity" (433). Jazz can be an "emblem of American liberalism's capacity for flexibility and innovation" (McCann 116) and thus, writes Peter Stanfield, help "to construct and negotiate the boundaries of American cultural identity" (*Body* 5).

These ideals underlie the depiction of musicians in *Blues in the Night,* a significant nonnoir jazz film from 1941. Early in the film a group of young men, jailed for starting a brawl, respond excitedly to the exhortations of pianist Jigger Pine (Richard Whorf) to play "blues, real blues, the kind that come out of people. Real people. Their hopes and their dreams. What they've got and what they want, the whole USA in one chorus. . . . And that band, they ain't guys just blowin' and poundin' and scrapin'. That's five guys . . . who feel, play, live, even think the same way. That ain't a band, it's a unit. One guy multiplied five times . . . like a hand in a glove." For Jigger, to play the blues is to pursue the American Dream. His speech, written by Communist (and future blacklistee) Robert Rossen, makes it sound as though Jigger's ideal group ain't a band but a labor union; nevertheless, a group of black inmates responds with, "We all got the miseries in here" and begin to sing "Blues in the Night" as if it were "real low-down New Orleans blues" (as Jigger claims) rather than a pop tune written only a year earlier by Harold Arlen and Johnny Mercer (Stanfield, *Body* 110).[4] The song continues nondiegetically beneath a stock montage of black workers balin', sweatin', eatin', and sleepin'; because they like black music, Jigger and his white friends are included in the cadre. At the end of the song we dissolve to a white trumpeter named Leo (Jack Carson) playing stratospheric high notes, then find the band at a club enjoying Jimmy Lunceford's all-black orchestra. Boasting that he can blow them out of the joint, Leo begins to play, and Lunceford's men yield the floor to him. Apparently white musicians are better than black players. Yet when told to get back to work by their employer, clarinetist Nicky (who claims to know "the anatomy of swing, not only musically but theoretically") responds, "We're coming, massa Sam." In other words, Jigger's boys are black when it suits them and white when it doesn't.[5] But they adhere to Jigger's principles, acting out the title song's

lyrics by traveling from place to place and maintaining the carefree spirit de-
noted in their other theme song, "Hang on to Your Lids, Kids."

It's not difficult to predict what happens next. After the band lands a steady
gig at a club called The Jungle, we watch them rehearsing "This Time the Dream's
on Me" in the garage, then performing it in the club—but without Leo, whose
horn rests on his empty chair. He is upstairs, gambling and flirting with singer
Kay Grant (Betty Fields), who, Jigger complains, is "bustin' up the unit!" Once
Character (Priscilla Lane), the band's vocalist and Leo's wife, becomes pregnant,
Leo's conflict shifts to Jigger, torn between band loyalty and a burgeoning obsession with Kay. He even asks her to replace Character as the band's chanteuse: a
bad idea, as illustrated in a montage of the two rehearsing "This Time the Dream's
on Me" that includes a shot upward from the keys implying that the piano itself
is resisting her. Alas, Jigger cannot: despite numerous warnings about two-faced
women (including the title song's), he abandons the band to join the Guy Heiser
(read Kay Kyser) Orchestra. When the old outfit takes in a Heiser show, their
faces freeze in horror at the insipid novelty act in which Jigger is trapped. Disgusted, Jigger quits Heiser; disappointed, Kay quits him. Jigger spirals into depression until, unable to remember how to play his "new" tune (actually a quasi-
classical arrangement of "Blues in the Night"), he collapses at the keyboard. An
expressionist montage, underscored by dissonant strains from the title song, displays Jigger's diagnosis ("neuropsychiatric disorder"), and then a series of grotesque images from earlier in the film: Jigger grimly shouting his ideals; a sweating
black man proclaiming that he has "got the miseries"; large, clumsy hands; a
grinning Kay playing the violin, bassoon, and tenor saxophone while fronting an
all-female band; a disturbing shot of Jigger as a monkey dancing to the organ-
grinding Heiser; a final overhead shot of Jigger at the piano, superimposed over
the black man's face. Clearly, Kay has made a monkey of him. The montage also
identifies the African American singer, the monkey, and the pianist, as if to confirm that our hero is, indeed, a Jigger—a counterfeit black man.[6]

Thus is introduced a characterization that will become familiar: the male jazz
musician as idiot savant—childlike, unstable, and easily victimized by a scheming woman. Jigger is a set of hands with no head, his talent a gift, not a craft developed through rigorous discipline. But with the help of jazz ("my medicine, my
prescription") he recovers and is next seen performing a flashy, Art Tatum–esque
version of "Blues in the Night" to an adoring crowd at The Jungle. No longer
an egalitarian project, the music has devolved into personal therapy. After a

melodramatic climax (Kay kills the club owner, and Jigger's bandmates prevent him from following her), the film closes with the reunited band riding freights "From Natchez to Mobile, from Memphis to St. Joe, / Wherever the four winds blow." Jigger's lofty aspirations were a chimera, for musicians aren't artists; they aren't even adults. They're just kids living a dream they can sustain only by enveloping themselves in a protective cocoon, away from the adult sexuality and economic compromises that would threaten to knock off their precarious lids.

Jive Crazy

For all its silliness, *Blues in the Night* at least presents jazz as a positive force. That is seldom true of noir jazz. Although jazz-club scenes appear frequently in the films, they rarely feature African American characters, and even when they do, they register no "traces of the social ferment" (Wager, "Jazz" 226) of the postwar period, when African Americans had begun agitating strongly for civil rights. Sometimes these club or jam-session scenes comment on the main story, as in *They Live by Night,* when Bowie and Keechie visit a New Orleans nightclub and listen to a black songstress deliver "Your Red Wagon," whose lyrics offer them coded advice. In later noir films certain characters' affiliation with jazz and African Americans lends them an aura of hipness. In *Kiss Me Deadly,* for instance, the crass Mike Hammer is humanized when comforted in his cups by a black bartender and African American singer Madi Comfort's rendition of "Rather Have the Blues." Most often, however, jazz-club scenes arrive laden with louche associations: sexual obsession, decadence, loss of control, violence.

Oddly, although bebop was flourishing in the late 1940s, bop is never heard and rarely mentioned.[7] Butler explains that bebop musicians' "desire for intellectual status" rendered the style too intimidating for Hollywood (83). But race is a far more likely reason for this exclusion, for bebop, which emerged in the 1940s out of late-night jam sessions in New York clubs, was created almost entirely by young black musicians as a modernist alternative to swing. These musicians eschewed the affable, eager-to-please manner that made artists such as Louis Armstrong palatable to whites, instead adopting no-nonsense, even arrogant postures designed to challenge white audiences and project an image of serious artistry.[8] New Orleans–style jazz, then undergoing a revival led largely by white musicians (dubbed "moldy figs" by disdainful bop aficionados), was a more comfortable choice for Hollywood. Yet even nonbop jazz in noir is represented as insidiously intoxicating and dangerous.

The earliest noir jazz sequence occurs in *Phantom Lady* (directed by Robert Siodmak, produced by Joan Harrison and adapted from a Cornell Woolrich novel), after engineer Scott Henderson has been convicted of murdering his wife, and his secretary, Carol "Kansas" Richman (Ella Raines), entices jazz drummer Cliff Milburn (Elisha Cook Jr.) into giving her information about the murder. Popping her gum and tarted up in a tight skirt and heavy makeup, Kansas pretends to be a "hep kitten" named Jeannie and makes eyes at Cliff during his regular gig backing a Carmen Mirandaesque singer. After the show they attend a basement jam session. Though all the musicians are white (an extremely unlikely situation in real life), they are amply blackened by shadows and by choke shots of their grimacing faces. Cliff's notoriously suggestive drum solo is the work of a stereotypically hypersexual jazz tomcat. First planting herself directly in front of Cliff (letting him leer at her legs), Jeannie then stands over him and eggs him on throughout his increasingly frenzied solo; meanwhile Siodmak cuts to ever closer shots of his sweaty, straining visage. Although the censors dictated that Raines never move provocatively on camera (Butler 65), we don't need to see her hips to be hip to what's going down. As Porfirio and Butler note, she seems to be playing the solo through Cliff (Butler 66; Porfirio, "Dark Jazz" 181), exhorting him to intensify his gymnastics, until at last she motions for them to leave and finish with their bodies what Cliff has begun on the skins.[9]

Though the film omits Woolrich's explicit references to drugs, the scene's debauched atmosphere (and some suggestive dialogue about how Cliff spends his money) make their existence plain enough.[10] Cliff himself is an instrument played by Kansas, as well as a proxy for the real murderer, insane sculptor Jack Marlow (Franchot Tone). Cliff's hands are prosthetic extensions of Marlow's hands—the same hands that strangle Henderson's wife and later the hapless drummer himself. *Phantom Lady* thus splits the traits of the disreputable artist figure between Cliff, a walking id, and Marlow, an effete megalomaniac afflicted with headaches and dizzy spells. Jazz embodies the seedy urban domain that Carol/Kansas must navigate to save her boss. Despite her avowed distaste, however, she seems to relish the evening of slumming that enables her to unveil and exploit the sexuality that she otherwise hides: after the jazz scene her formerly restrained hair is allowed to fall freely about her shoulders.

Siodmak uses jazz similarly in *Criss Cross,* when protagonist Steve Thompson (Burt Lancaster) flashes back to his encounter with his ex-wife, Anna (Yvonne De Carlo), in a nightclub where Esy Morales and His Rhumba Band are performing. Steve stares at Anna, writhing to a hot Latin vamp, the burr in the flute soloist's tone beautifully conveying Steve's passion; after they rendezvous, the flute becomes increasingly staccato, as if channeling her voice. The solo bespeaks Anna's sexual charms, as well as Steve's obsession with the woman who later lures him to participate in an armored car heist, break his arm, and eventually die.[11] *Criss Cross* presents jazz as a sexually transmitted disease, and Steve has a terminal case.[12]

The trope of jazz as infection recurs in Rudolph Maté's *D. O. A.* in a remarkable scene set in The Fisherman Club, where protagonist Frank Bigelow (Edmond O'Brien), on a brief vacation (without his fiancée) in San Francisco, has accompanied a group of partying conventioneers. An all-black quintet led by tenor man Illinois Jacquet performs a hot jump blues number before a serpentine painting of a saxophone and a raucous crowd. Inserts show white audience members shouting encouragement: "Cool, really cool!" As the music grows more frenetic and the crowd more frenzied, Maté films the sweating musicians in choke shots that render them grotesque and fearsome yet sinfully appealing. Beasts with bulging eyes, these caricatured jazzmen pass blackness and sexual energy on to Bigelow (Butler 70; Porfirio, "Dark Jazz" 179).

After the tune ends, Frank chats up a "jive crazy" rich "chick" named Jeanie, as a bluesy B-flat minor ballad plays in the background. The tune's lyrics ("I wanted to kiss you / I tried to resist you") reveal the real point of their coy conversation. But although Frank knows he's fishing, he doesn't realize he's also bait: distracted by Jeanie (Virginia Lee), he fails to notice a mysterious man in a distinctive scarf and hat meddling with his drink. When a hungover Bigelow awakens the next morning, we hear the ballad again, but now it sounds tinny and hollow, indicating both Frank's self-disgust and his incipient illness: having been dosed with "luminous toxin" (a radioactive chemical), he will die within days. The song thus serves as the audible residue of the club and of Frank's desired (though incomplete) infidelity. We hear the tune twice more: when Frank finds a Fisherman Club matchbook in a deserted warehouse and again when he confronts Halliday (William Ching), the mysterious personage who poisoned him because he once notarized a bill of sale for an iridium shipment. Inadvertently, Bigelow is acting out the tune's lyrics: "And when I met you, I tried to forget you / But you whispered, 'Darling, I know.'" His knowledge is deadly. Robert Porfirio points to the ballad's "lethal potential" ("Dark" 180). But it's not just this song that carries that potential; it's jazz itself. Thus Bigelow is punished not merely for notarizing a document, or for sowing some wild oats, but for yielding to the enticements of jazz, depicted as an aural toxin and the very voice of Satan. Though the poison itself is a luminous white, Bigelow, like Jigger Pine, has been blackened by the touch of jive.

D. O. A. links two of the period's pervasive cultural anxieties. First, it dramatizes the allure and fear of African American culture, which, in the form of jazz, emancipates the primal impulses of the world's Frank Bigelows. As an instrument for blacks to repay whites for commodifying and sexualizing their bodies, jazz offers a more insidious brand of rebellion than the riots and protests that eventually yielded progressive social changes. Second, jazz is associated with the anxiety about atomic energy, materialized in the luminous poison.[13] In sum, the Fisherman band embodies the mix of desire and dread that marked American attitudes toward two dangerously intoxicating entities: blackness and the Bomb. Far from fusing the "whole USA" into one chorus, here jazz splits the nation into two camps: infected victims and poisonous perpetrators.

So Black and Blue

"That tune! . . . Why was it always that rotten tune? Knocking me around, beating in my head, never letting up. Did ya ever want to forget anything? Did ya ever want to cut away a piece of your memory or blot it out? You can't, ya know. No matter how hard you try." Thus speaks the hapless Al Roberts, erstwhile saloon pianist in *Detour*. The tune that makes him feel so black and blue is "I Can't Believe That You're in Love with Me," an innocuous pop song from 1927 that is forever associated in his mind with his ill-fated journey to Los Angeles to meet his fiancée, Sue, and the nightmarish events that followed: the death of Charles Haskell and his unfortunate decision to assume Haskell's identity, his killing of Vera, and his subsequent flight. But whereas Al wants to forget this song, other noir musicians can't remember important songs. Just as the ballad in *D. O. A.* becomes a vestige of the night of Frank Bigelow's murder—a memory of an ineradicable but mysterious trauma—so in many noirs melodies provide mnemonic clues to the plot's initiating events, which are often the protagonist's own crimes. In these films jazz is linked to violence, fear, and rage.

Gorbman demonstrates how romantic/classical film scores establish "motifs of reminiscence" that enable audiences (unconsciously or consciously) to link disparate moments of the narrative (28). According to Caryl Flinn, musical themes often signal "temporal disphasures, especially those associated with the flashback"

(109), which express a wish to "reach back from an unlovely present to the past, and therefrom to construct a lost beauty." This "utopian function" of film music, she argues, creates a "conduit to connect listeners . . . to an ideal past" (50). Noir likewise employs musical motifs to indicate temporal disphasures; however, rather than revealing "lost pleasure and stability" (Flinn 117), these films record their impossibility. In noir jazz films traumatic events—occurring before the narrative itself or at its outset—become repressed memories that can be retrieved only through nightmares, posttraumatic flashbacks, or forced reenactments similar to those plaguing disabled vets. These half-remembered melodies violate the principle of inaudibility by invoking memories both for the audience and for the characters.

In *Detour* "I Can't Believe That You're in Love with Me" prompts the flashback that frames the narrative. A sign of both a utopian past and a lost future (Flinn 124), the song embodies Al's mistake in believing that he could escape his club gig and start a life with Sue in Hollywood. Its lyrics don't promise love or success but rather profess incredulity that someone so wonderful could love the song's speaker; even so, Al balks at serving as Sue's accompanist and playing for little money (a ten-buck tip is a "jackpot") and less respect at the Break o' Dawn Club. He should complain, for he is clearly possessed of great talent, displayed when he ingeniously transmutes Brahms's "Waltz in A Major" into an improvised boogie-woogie. Flinn writes that this scene indicates that jazz signifies failure for Al (125).[14] But it also shows Al using improvisation the same way that the black inventors of jazz did: to turn confinement into liberation. Al's hitchhiking (geographic improvisation) further indicates that he enjoys playing things by ear. Perhaps sensing that life with Sue would be as insipid as the song, he doesn't really want to join her. His ambivalence is suggested in a shot that occurs just before his nightmare begins, as he gazes into the rearview mirror of Haskell's convertible and pictures Sue in Hollywood, singing "I Can't Believe" before a shadowy band. The shot's placement within the mirror implies that Al will never achieve his dream, the song and all it stands for immuring him, as Flinn suggests, "in much the same way that the film's claustral visual style and narrative structure confine him" (127). Later, while waiting in a stifling hotel room with the predatory Vera, Al tries to phone Sue; as he waits to speak, "I Can't Believe" swells, only to dissolve into dissonant fragments as he hangs up, unable to complete the call. Al really *can't* believe that Sue's in love with him; moreover, he probably prefers his improvised life to the suffocating future promised by "I Can't Believe." Although the tune haunts him as a symbol of his fatal detour, this restless musician would never have been satisfied playing Sue's sideman for life.

Most noir jazz musicians share Al's self-contradictions and instability. Of course, the association between musical talent and mental disturbance is hardly new to noir; musicians have long been deemed unreliable and threatening by conventional folk. Traveling from town to town, whether alone or with other suspicious types, musicians seldom establish ties to a single locale. After sleeping much of the day, they work at night inviting audiences to lose inhibitions. Musicians thus become scapegoats for audiences' guilt, as well as focal points for their longing to escape. Further, as Susan McClary observes, "the whole enterprise of musical activity is . . . fraught with gender-related anxieties." For example, the "charge that musicians are 'effeminate' goes back as far as recorded documentation about music, and music's association with the body and with subjectivity has led to its being relegated . . . to what was understood as a 'feminine' realm" (17). Musicians often dress stylishly and create art that evokes emotions, yet they are also widely perceived to be sexually predatory, using their sensitivity and exoticism to entice semiwilling partners.[15] Male musicians are thus viewed simultaneously as androgynous and hypermasculine. Jazz musicians carry even more baggage, since they are coded as at once black *and* white, gifted *and* disabled, stars *and* geeks. Hence, as jazz historian Ted Gioia writes, male jazzers are a sonata of dissonances: "world-wise yet innocent; hard-edged yet wearing their hearts on their sleeves," they are "flip and cynical, yet firmly committed to their calling" (77). In short, the postwar jazz musician bundled together anxieties about race, masculinity, and productivity, embodying conflicting traits that appear throughout noir jazz films, where musicians' scandalous characters and sensitive natures create what Gioia calls a "fascinating series of 'anti-hero' contradictions" (77).

Midcentury Hollywood's stereotyping of musicians and the affiliation between music and memory are both exemplified in the neglected whodunit *Nocturne* (directed by Edwin L. Marin and produced, like *Phantom Lady*, by Joan Harrison), in which music and lyrics (by Leigh Harline, Mort Greene, and Eleanor Rudolph) play pivotal roles. The film begins with a high overhead shot of composer Keith Vincent's house, then cranes down and seems to pass through the large picture window into the room where he is playing the piano for a partially hidden woman. Vincent (Edward Ashley) cavalierly lists the various songs he has written for his paramours: a Latin number for a compliant señorita; a jolly swing tune for a Sun Valley girl, and so forth. For the listening woman he has written a piece called "Nocturne," which he plays while talking through the lyrics—

> Nocturne, you are my nocturne
> You are the words I sing
> The notes I play

—and ending with these lines:

> When it's over and done
> You're no longer the one
> For that was yesterday.

She may be his muse, but only for about three minutes; women are fine for brief nocturnal activities, but there shall be no strings attached. Ironically, "Nocturne" is also Vincent's swan song: as the final chords resound, a shot rings out and he falls dead.

His death is officially called a suicide, but Lt. Joe Warne (George Raft) believes it's a murder and becomes obsessed with solving the crime, even after being suspended from the force for doing so. The crime is linked in his mind to the melody of "Nocturne," which, early in the investigation, he plinks out on the piano: A, A, up to C, down to F, then G, then A; A, A, D, F, G, A. On the sheet music is written, "For Dolores," but this clue is no help, for Vincent called all his women "Dolores." That night Joe dreams of these Doloreses, oneirically scanning the photos on Vincent's wall as the title tune plays: it's his nocturnal edition of Vincent's song. Following a montage of interviews with the Doloreses, we watch a photo emerge from the developing bath, then dissolve to the face of its subject, Frances Ransome (Lynn Bari), a bit actress with a firm alibi and a soft kid sister, Carol Page (Virginia Huston), a nightclub singer who works with pianist Ned "Fingers" Ford (Joseph Pevney). Soon after they meet, Joe and Frances visit a club where Fingers essays "I Couldn't Sleep a Wink Last Night" (too many nocturnes, perhaps). But when Joe asks him to play "Nocturne," Carol becomes upset, arousing Joe's suspicions. Though the sisters are hot, Warne is lukewarm: after kissing Frances, he immediately turns her off with persistent accusations.

The next morning he visits Fingers and Carol as they rehearse "Why Pretend?" and Fingers admits that after he cowrote three songs with Vincent, the latter dumped him. However, the key clue comes from another set of fingers—those of Joe's mother and her friend Queenie, as they discuss how powder burns showed up on Vincent's head and hands.[16] While demonstrating, Mrs. Warne accidentally fires Joe's gun, leaving powder burns on the head of her son, who has intervened at the last moment. Fortunately, the pistol was loaded with blanks, which explains Vincent's powder burns: someone fired blanks at him after his death. Two other incidents provide further clues: Joe finds Charles Shawn, the man who photographed every Dolores, hanged in his own studio; then at Frances's place he discovers the gas on and Frances lying unconscious. In the latter sequence "Nocturne" plays, as it should, for the scene reenacts the first murder. Indeed, all three deaths are staged suicides, melodramatic tableaus designed to be misinterpreted. "Nocturne" plays again when Joe finally confronts Carol and Frances: a long pan left reveals Fingers, who confesses that he is married to Carol and was cuckolded by Vincent. He murdered the composer, then set up the fake suicide. The pianist's fingers pull out a gun, but Joe has already removed the slugs.

The title tune is associated with murder as well as with the promiscuous lifestyle of Keith Vincent, who used women and then tossed them away, as his lyrics describe. "Nocturne" is also the aural emblem of Fingers's dirty hands. More interesting than these associations, perhaps, is the triangular relationship among Vincent, Fingers, and Warne, each of whom plays the theme song on the piano: Vincent sardonically, Fingers passionately, Warne haltingly. Each man's ability to play mirrors his ability to "play": Vincent, though portrayed as an epicene dandy by Edward Ashley, is an inveterate womanizer; Fingers is ineffectual, perhaps impotent (his gun was, remember, loaded with blanks). But what of Warne? What did he do to be so black and blue? Why does he risk his career on this case? Perhaps he gets a thrill from vicariously living Vincent's decadent life. After all, he only halfheartedly romances Frances, and we can't help but wonder about the sexuality of a man in his forties who lives with his mother and can't stir up ardor for any woman. In this regard George Raft's wooden performance is appropriate, for Warne's stiffness may signify either a man married to his job or a closeted homosexual. Or perhaps Joe would like to be Vincent but actually resembles Fingers: his gun may also be filled with blanks. In any case, though Joe tries to stay clean, he is dirtied by the black powder burns that indicate his noir impulses. The title song, then, not only symbolizes the fake suicides, but, as its occurrence during Joe's "Dolores" fantasy sequence implies, also represents the inauthentic life of Joe Warne, who seems doomed to remain his own nocturnal companion.

Though the songs in *Nocturne* are closer to 1940s-era pop than to jazz, the film exemplifies how jazz is represented in early film noir: as evidence of decadent sexuality, as a reminder of forgotten trauma or violence, as an instrument of "noiring" that darkens even those charged with regulating those impulses. A similar set of motifs characterizes *Black Angel,* a film made concurrently with *Nocturne* and adapted, like *Phantom Lady,* from a Cornell Woolrich novel. Its narrative also resembles that of *Phantom Lady:* a man—this time it's pianist Marty Blair (Dan Duryea)—can't remember the night his estranged wife (singer Mavis Marlowe [Constance Dowling]) was murdered; again the wrong man (this time it's one Kirk Bennett) is arrested and convicted of the crime, despite the attempts of a woman—Bennett's wife, a singer named Cathy (June Vincent)—to clear him. As in *Nocturne,* a melody signifies a murder: in *Black Angel* the tune is "Heartbreak," a song Marty wrote for Mavis, and which is playing on her phonograph when Bennett enters her apartment and finds her dead. A moody beguine, the song is the musical correlative to the other major clue, a heart-shaped brooch that Marty presented to Mavis the night she died. "Heartbreak" is not just a song; it captures the tortured identity Marty assumed after his marriage failed and he became an alcoholic.

Suspecting that nightclub owner Marko (Peter Lorre) is behind the murder, Cathy enlists Marty's help, and the two audition to become the club's featured entertainers.[17] Marko hires them. Convinced that Cathy has enabled him to stay sober, Marty tries to woo her with a song called "Time Will Tell." But she brushes him off, prompting a binge, and during the bender montage, dissonant strains of "Heartbreak" are heard, as if Cathy has become Mavis. During his spree Marty spots a bargirl wearing the heart-shaped brooch; a fight starts, and Marty lands in a prison hospital. There he flashes back to the night of the murder and recalls that he wasn't passed out in bed that night as he'd believed but had returned to Mavis's apartment and strangled her. During Marty's flashback the images swim and sway to reflect his drunken perspective, and dissonant fragments from "Heartbreak" swirl through the score: she broke his heart, so he broke her neck. Marty escapes, only to collapse in Cathy's apartment ("Time Will Tell" is heard on the soundtrack). As he awakens, a shot from his point of view dissolves Mavis's face into Cathy's: the bad wife gives way to the good wife, each one representing a side of Marty's tortured psyche. He confesses in time to save Bennett's life, and at the end "Time Will Tell" plays over a shot of the sheet music.

At first the key to Marty's buried memory, "Heartbreak" is then transposed from a lament over lost love to a symptom of mental illness. As the symbol of Marty's alcoholism, ruined marriage, and capacity for violence, it is counterpointed with "Time Will Tell," the theme song of his redemptive relationship with Cathy: Marty murdered his wife out of heartbreak, but time will tell if he proves himself worthy of his good angel. Marty's duality is deep: his angelic talent is inextricable from the "blackness" of his addiction, self-pity, and rage. Marty, then, is the black angel of the title, another sensitive white artist noired by jazz, a performer whose talent seems only marginally more useful than that of *Night-mare Alley*'s chicken-biter.

The patterns found in *Nocturne* and *Black Angel* are amplified in Maxwell Shane's *Nightmare,* a 1956 remake of his earlier *Fear in the Night,* both adapted from "Nightmare," another Cornell Woolrich story.[18] In the later film's striking opening sequence, New Orleans jazz clarinetist Stan Grayson (Kevin Mc-Carthy) experiences a nightmare—all canted angles and eerie music—in which he is trapped in a mirrored room and about to be strangled; a woman hands him an icepick with which he stabs his assailant to death. Upon awakening, however, he finds evidence—a button, a key, his own bruises and scratches—that he actually committed the crime. Equally potent is his memory of a dissonant melody—D, up to B♭, down to G♭, then G, A, played over a D augmented chord, a "slow, crazy melody, like a tune from another world"—that convinces him of his guilt.

Music is essential to the story. This nightmarish jazz melody again represents objects, particularly a key Stan finds; indeed, the tune *is* the key to the crime, and in an effective montage sequence Stan roams Bourbon Street, playing the tune for every musician (some of them black) he encounters. No one recognizes it. Stan then flirts with a woman who resembles his dream's icepick lady while a black pianist plays for them. As they retire to her apartment, the couple are serenaded by an unseen female singer's rendition of "A Woman Ain't a Woman (Unless She's Got Herself a Man)." But this woman ain't really got one, for once Stan gazes at himself in her mirror, he finds himself unable to play his part in the promised sexual duet, as if the icepick has replaced his clarinet.

In other scenes Stan's steady girlfriend, Gina (played by singer Connie Russell), belts out the bluesy jazz numbers "What's Your Sad Story?" and "The Last I Ever Saw of My Man." The latter includes these lines: "Keep one eye open as you sleep / Or your man will get away." The former, arranged New Orleans style, is heard during Stan's later flashback to the night of the murder, which occurred on the same night that their band leader, Billy, rejected Stan's arrangements for the up-coming recording session as "far out" and "not commercial." Obviously Stan is too imaginative, too sensitive for his own good. As his brother-in-law, homicide detective Rene Bressard (Edward G. Robinson), observes, Grayson is a "high-strung" man with an "artistic temperament"; or as Billy more bluntly puts it, he is a "screwball." Stan exemplifies Hollywood's jazz musician: passive, unstable, and easy to manipulate, a geek tortured by his talent and unable to adapt to the work-aday world.

But Bressard doesn't believe he's guilty, and the two begin to piece together the facts when—with Gina and Stan's sister Sue (Virginia Christine)—they seek shelter from a deluge in a large mansion. In the house Gina puts on a record, inadvertently switching the turntable setting from 33⅓ to 16 rpm; abruptly the lighthearted tune becomes Stan's nightmare melody. It is (coincidentally!) the same house where the murder took place. Stan enters the mirrored room where his key opens a closet door; inside the closet is a blood stain. Convinced of his guilt, he passes out at the police station, then tries to commit suicide by jumping from a window—variations of the "nightmare" theme stabbing in the background—before Bressard wrestles him back into the room. Ultimately, through a series of flashbacks, Stan realizes that Dr. Belknap, the psychiatrist who owns the mansion, had hypnotized him to kill Belknap's wife and pin it on her lover.[19] Wearing a wire, Stan returns to the scene and gets Belknap to confess: just as sound once condemned him, it now sets him free.

Nightmare's highly melodramatic plot boldly colors in the outlines sketched in *Phantom Lady, Nocturne,* and *Black Angel;* like the latter two films, it places an unstable jazz musician at the heart of a half-remembered murder and uses a melody as the residue of a violent trauma. But if the hazy details of the murder are eventually explained, Stan is never cleared, for his association with jazz and the African American musicians who chaperone his encounter with the bargirl indelibly "noir" him. Like those of *Phantom Lady*'s Cliff, his hands have been appropriated by a more cunning artist—the hypnotist. This pattern suggests that beneath the jazz musician's racial attributes lies another stain: that of disability. Jazz musicians, indeed, share many traits with noir's disabled veterans, and their emotional and cognitive dysfunctions resemble nothing so much as posttraumatic flashbacks. These musicians permitted Hollywood filmmakers to transpose into another key the anxieties about readjustment, masculinity, and productivity at play in the vet films.

Though Stan's nightmare is over, the dark cloud Hollywood casts over jazz is not. Indeed, jazz melodies represent guilt even in films where musicians play minor roles. For example, in Fritz Lang's *The Blue Gardenia* the title song represents the guilty, fractured memory of its female protagonist, Norah Larkin (Anne Baxter). After receiving a "Dear Joan" letter from her soldier boyfriend, Norah rashly accepts a date with the wolf Harry Prebble (Raymond Burr). We first hear the title song suavely performed by Nat "King" Cole in the Blue Gardenia restaurant during Norah's date with Prebble. An inebriated Norah (having drunk too many Polynesian Pearl Divers) then accompanies Prebble to his apartment, where he spins a record of "The Blue Gardenia" and tries to rape her. Norah fights back, and as she struggles, the soundtrack switches from the diegetic recording to a nondiegetic arrangement that turns the tune into a discordant whirl of confusion and fear. The visual elements are equally disorienting: we see Norah grasp a poker, then images of a shattered mirror, after which she passes out. Awakening, she flees, and the next morning Prebble is found dead, his head bashed in with a poker, surrounded by "petals" from a broken mirror.

The film is a scathing portrait of the sexual marketplace. Every man keeps a little black book and treats every woman as a number; every woman (not coincidentally, Norah and her roommates work for the phone company) seems desperate to capture a man—any man. The double standard is ubiquitous: everyone (including Norah) assumes that any woman who would enter Prebble's apartment is a slut. Hence, as Krin Gabbard observes, the song signifies "Norah's status as a fugitive and a fallen woman" (248). But its lyrics suggest not rampant sexuality but rueful memory:

> Love bloomed like a flower.
> Then the petals fell.
> Blue gardenia,
> Thrown to a passing breeze,
> But pressed in my book of memories.

The song also represents memory in the film. Thus, as *Chronicle* columnist Casey Mayo (Richard Conte) exploits the case by writing an open letter to the "unknown murderess" whom he has dubbed "The Blue Gardenia," phrases from the song are heard whenever the murder is mentioned: orchestrally when Norah first listens to a radio report of the crime, again in a rhumba arrangement during the "blue gardenia" newspaper montage, again when Norah reads Mayo's open letter urging her to trust him, and again when she phones him. After she agrees to meet Mayo, he plays the tune on the jukebox at Bill's Beanery, and a portion of the melody is detectable when Norah's roommate, Crystal (Ann Sothern), guesses the truth about her. It is last heard just after Norah is arrested.

Norah is neither a slut nor a murderer. Yet Mayo is duped by prejudice. At first treating her merely as a story (when she meets him in his office, a flashing sign over her head reads "Chronicle"), he soon falls for her, but only because he thinks she can't be the (black and) blue gardenia. Ultimately it is revealed that Prebble's girlfriend, Rose (Ruth Miller), killed him in a fit of anger, the presence of her favorite classical record proving to be the pivotal clue. We never hear the title song again, perhaps because, Gabbard suggests, "the song's codes no longer apply to her or to the film" (249). But the codes never change; only Norah does. So hardened is she by repeated male betrayals that at the film's end this former ingénue plays hard to get to lure Mayo into chasing her. Far from resisting female commodification, she embraces it. No one is immune from the cutthroat sexual marketplace, from stifling gender roles, or from the public's insatiable appetite for lurid sex crimes. The title song, then, betokens Norah's lost innocence, her unhealed psychic and emotional bruises, and the dark taint of illicit sex that ultimately enhances her value. She remains a blue gardenia, stained by her association with the song (performed, we recall, by a black singer), a fallen petal pressed to fit into patriarchy's little black book.

To Build a Dream On

Two 1950s noirs perpetuate the stereotype of musicians as overgrown children. Yet these films also present—implicitly, at least—the potential for new American identities founded on jazz's optimism and tolerance, while sharing with *Blues in the Night* a belief that the racial divide is not impervious. One of these films even presents jazz as the foundation for a remodeled American Dream.

The earliest noir with a jazz score, *The Strip* features Mickey Rooney as Stan Maxton, a talented but callow drummer (at thirty years old, Rooney looks sixteen) who becomes a suspect in the shooting of gangster Sonny Johnson (James Craig) and his girlfriend Jane Tafford (Sally Forrest). After the shootings, Stan narrates much of the story in flashback to a police lieutenant. A Korean war vet suffering from PTSD, Stan left the hospital and headed to Los Angeles, where he immediately took a job with the oily Johnson and found his way to Fluff's nightclub, where he was treated to delightful performances of "Shadrack" and "Basin Street Blues" by Louis Armstrong and his seasoned interracial band (Jack Teagarden, Barney Bigard, Earl Hines; Fluff [William Demarest] often joined them on piano).[20] After closing time one night, Stan sat in with Fluff and was offered the gig on the spot. But he was more interested in pursuing Jane, a dancer at the club, and besides, he was already earning "good dough" with Sonny. The fatherly Fluff asked Jane to persuade Stan to join.[21]

The conflict is an ancient one: money versus artistic fulfillment. Indeed, the lyrics to "Shadrack" describe Stan's dilemma. In the song (as in the book of Daniel), King Nebuchadnezzar attempts to use the music of horn, flute, and clarinet to entice Shadrach, Meshach, and Abednego to worship his golden idol; when they resist, they are cast into a fiery furnace (God saves them). Similarly, despite Sonny's disdainful remarks about jazz ("you came out here to beat your brains out with a lot of slap-happy jive men and maybe in ten or twenty years you'd end up with your own club"), Jane's kisses persuade Stan to abandon Sonny. Stan even tells Fluff that "money isn't everything when you're doing what you want to do." His motives, however, are less pure than Shadrach's: he wants to woo Jane, even though she is merely using him to get close to Sonny, who she believes will advance her movie career. Recognizing Stan's predicament, Fluff tells him of a girl he lost and sings the song he allegedly wrote for her, which is actually the 1935 Kalmar/Ruby/Hammerstein standard "A Kiss to Build a Dream On": "Give me a kiss to build a dream on / And my imagination / Will thrive upon that kiss." It's a corny moment (as the two croon in harmony, we seem suddenly to be watching an outtake from an Andy Hardy picture), but the song is appropriate, for Stan is indeed seeking his American dream. Alas, his version—upward mobility culminating in a steady job, kids, and a home—doesn't jibe with Jane's vision of a glamorous career in show business. As Fluff tells Stan, Jane is a girl who aims every act at "accomplishing her [career] goals." She's hardly alone. In this Los Angeles, where everyone claws for success, Stan's ingenuousness is refreshing; even so, his foolishness becomes annoying, as he ignores Edna (Kay Brown), another of Fluff's employees, who is crazy for him, barely pays attention to his drumming, and eventually misses a gig after he gets beaten up by Sonny's thugs for refusing to leave Jane alone.[22]

Though at first Rooney seems miscast, his diminutive stature fits this foolish kid who prefers a woman who doesn't love him to his art.[23] In this respect he follows the pattern set in *Blues in the Night*. But in other ways he differs from earlier noir jazz cats: far from being an alcoholic or murderer, Stan is just an ordinary guy who happens to play the drums, and the music he plays is unfailingly upbeat and genial. Hence, when a devastated Stan returns to Fluff's after Jane's death, the band switches from "A Kiss to Build a Dream On" (which Stan associates with her) to a fast number, and as soon as Stan begins to play, his blues vanish. Gabbard asserts that *The Strip* diminishes jazz by portraying it as "strictly for good times, providing at best a little solace now and then" (223). But compared to the films that precede it, that represents progress. Nowhere in this film do we find the unsavory connotations the music bears in *D. O. A.* or *Phantom Lady,* and although Stan is literally made black and blue, it's not music that roughs him up; it is, rather, the balm for his bruising. Still, *The Strip* is a minor film, and Stan never entertains, let alone attains, the lofty artistic goals that drive and torment

Marty Blair or Jigger Pine, nor does he achieve the depth that, as I demonstrate below, belongs to Ida Lupino's torch singers. Nevertheless, the film implies that playing jazz can be a legitimate way to make a living and that musicians may find in the jazz community a surrogate family and an identity that exemplifies positive American values—values reinforced by working relationships with musicians who might be black.

Armstrong was a safe choice for *The Strip:* by 1951 he had long ago refined his persona as a smiling, nonthreatening musical ambassador. Far from a glowering bebop gunslinger, he presented the image of a clown (though his actual views on race and music were more complex). A much less amiable black musician appears as a noir protagonist for the first (and last) time in Robert Wise's 1959 *Odds against Tomorrow,* in which Harry Belafonte plays singer/vibist Johnny Ingram.[24] Belafonte, an astonishingly handsome man whose light skin and suave demeanor helped him to fashion a successful crossover career, allows his portrayal of the desperate Ingram to darken his image considerably.[25] In this film the theme of race, an underground strain throughout classic noir, is made explicit via a bank robbery scheme that collapses because one member of the gang, Earle Slater (Robert Ryan), is a bigot who won't trust a black man with the key to their getaway car. Indeed, the plan itself is founded on the alleged inability of whites to tell two dissimilar black men apart: by dressing as a food delivery man, Ingram enables the gang's after-hours entry.

The film constantly juxtaposes Slater and Ingram, at first highlighting their differences as each one visits the scheme's mastermind, former cop Dave Burke (Ed Begley). Slater patronizes the African American kids running around outside Burke's hotel (in a cringe-inducing moment he calls one little girl a "pickaninny"), wears drab clothes, is usually alone in the frame, and snarls at the friendly black elevator operator. Ingram, by contrast, distributes gifts to the kids, jokes with the elevator man, and impresses him with his fancy duds. Likewise the film's unobtrusive jazz score, composed by Modern Jazz Quartet pianist John Lewis, employs dissonant minor seconds on the vibes and close brass harmonies in Slater's scenes but waxes flamboyant during Ingram's.[26]

The film, however, gradually reveals the two men's similarities. Jobless and supported by his girlfriend Lorry (Shelley Winters), ex-soldier Slater is emasculated and filled with rage. Wise depicts his feelings of oppression by constantly shooting him within doorways or windows, or from a slightly low angle that makes his head seem to bump against the ceiling. As he and Burke gaze out a hotel window at their prospective target, a bank in the small town of Melton, Slater growls, "You didn't say nothing about the third person bein' a nigger." As he utters these words barred shadows slash his face: he is imprisoned by his anger and hatred.

Ingram is just as angry. Just after Slater's words, Wise cuts to Ingram singing a blues tune in the club where he works. "Believe me, pretty mama, / It's not just me I know," Belafonte proclaims in his signature hoarse tenor; "I just can't make that jungle outside my door." Ingram may be protesting, but he is doing nothing to free himself; though possessed of a lovely wife and daughter, he is a gambling addict who owes a huge debt to the gangster Bacco. On an outing with his daughter, he spends most of his time phoning creditors and dodging Bacco's men instead of paying attention to his child. One evocative shot shows him surrounded by spinning merry-go-round horses, illustrating both his entrapment and his immaturity. Ingram's flaws become clearer after he is roughed up by Bacco's men and, instead of employing music to emancipate himself, as Stan Maxton does, he interrupts the marvelous Mae Barnes's song "All Men Are Evil" by pounding the vibes out of time and singing badly, as if confirming the truth of her accusation. Though Ingram has the blues, he doesn't practice the blues philosophy, famously described by Ralph Ellison as the ability to "keep the painful details and episodes of a brutal experience alive . . . to finger its jagged grain, and to transcend it, not by the consolation of philosophy but by squeezing from it a near-tragic, near-comic lyricism" (79). Ingram can muster neither lyricism nor transcendence. In a similar vein, jazz critic Albert Murray describes improvisation as not merely a musical style but as a "survival technique . . . suitable to the rootlessness and discontinuity . . . of human existence in the contemporary world" (113). In this light, one might observe that what dooms the bank job is the men's inability to improvise: as soon as they are forced to depart from the script, they panic and turn on each other. In short, Johnny may play jazz, but he doesn't live it.

At the film's end, after the heist falls apart and Burke is killed (here the score becomes quasi-classical, eliding its jazz elements just as Ingram erases his identity), Slater and Ingram face off in a gun battle that ends in a conflagration as they blow up an oil refinery. A rescue worker looks at the two charred bodies and asks, "Which is which?" Answer: "Take your pick." Racial hatred has destroyed them both and, the film suggests, may do the same to the allegedly United States.[27] We may also see in this fiery conclusion a dramatization of Langston Hughes's famous questions about the African American dream of equality:

What happens to a dream deferred?
Does it dry up like a raisin in the sun?
Or fester like a sore—

.   .   .   .

Or does it explode?

Two earlier scenes, however, hint at alternatives. One takes place in the In-
grams' apartment, where Mrs. Ingram (Kim Hamilton) is hosting a PTA meeting for white and black parents; when her husband interrupts them and sneers at
her alleged attempt to pander to bourgeois "ofays," she repudiates him. And during
the park scene, Ingram leaves his daughter briefly in the care of a white woman—
thus reversing stereotypical roles. A nation where blacks and whites work together, attend school side by side, and treat each other as equals is adumbrated in
these sequences, which contradict the suspicion and fear that destroy Slater and
Ingram. In such moments *The Strip* and *Odds against Tomorrow* suggest that
Americans might find in jazz a foundation—if not a kiss, at least a handshake—to
build their dreams on.[28]

Moral Twilight

Brassy big band arrangements, swaggering saxophones, a heavy swing rhythm,
and a loping minor-key theme: these are hallmarks of so-called crime jazz, a brand
of musical scoring that became popular in mid-1950s film and television. Composers such as Shorty Rogers *(Private Hell 36)*, Henry Mancini *(Touch of Evil,* and
a multitude of TV themes, including *Peter Gunn)*, Duke Ellington *(Anatomy of a
Murder)*, and Pete Rugolo *(The Strip)* created important scores in this style.[29] Was
jazz being divested of its disreputable connotations? Yes and no. For example,
when asked to furnish a score for Otto Preminger's adaptation of *The Man with
the Golden Arm*, Nelson Algren's novel about a heroin-addicted drummer, Elmer
Bernstein sought a style that, he said, spoke of "heroin, hysteria, longing, frustration, despair and finally death: in a word, jazz" (qtd. in Butler 130). Yet in films
such as Wise's *I Want to Live!* and Preminger's *Anatomy of a Murder,* jazz scores
lend intellectual sophistication and an aura of hip urbanity to characters as different as *Live*'s convicted murderer Barbara Graham and *Murder*'s defense attorney
Paul Biegler. Jazz scores still came equipped with conflicting connotations.

These meanings are perfectly exemplified in David Raksin's remarkable score
for Joseph H. Lewis's powerful noir *The Big Combo.* The film opens with an aerial

shot of an unnamed city, behind which a soprano saxophone wails a swanky, languidly swinging D-flat minor theme that, according to Edward Dimendberg, "would not be inappropriate . . . for a striptease performance" (87).[30] The film does feature a stripper, Rita (Helene Stanton), the on-again-off-again girlfriend of the intense protagonist, police Lieutenant Leonard Diamond (Cornel Wilde). Yet the musical theme is more often associated with the other major female character, Susan Lowell (Jean Wallace), a beautiful but tormented woman attached to Diamond's nemesis, the mobster Mr. Brown (Richard Conte), whose "combo," the Bolemac Corporation, has extended its reach into legitimate businesses. Early in the film, Susan dines with Brown's minions, the gay couple Mingo (Earl Holliman) and Fante (Lee Van Cleef), as the restaurant pianist plays the title theme. When her former piano teacher encounters her, he asks if she still plays. Susan answers, "The only thing I play now . . . is stud poker." The aural equivalent of poker, jazz signifies Susan's fall from grace.

Diamond has vowed to destroy Brown, but though the film leaves no doubt that Brown is a sociopath (he coldly kills his own assistants when they get out of line), Diamond is no jewel, and he fixates on Susan as the symbol of Brown's success: his vendetta seems motivated less by righteousness than by jealousy. In one scene Diamond asks Rita why any woman would fall for a criminal. As they talk, a version of the theme melody swells up on tenor saxophone to show that Diamond (a tenor, not a soprano) is thinking about Susan. "Hoodlums, detectives," Rita answers. "A woman doesn't care how a man makes his living. Only how he makes love." The next scene proves her point: Brown enters Susan's apartment and, even while she protests that she "hate[s] and despise[s]" him, the ecstatic look on her face as he kisses her neck and shoulders and then moves downward, out of frame, shows why she stays with him. The jazz theme thus represents Susan's ambivalence about this sadomasochistic sexual relationship: although Brown turns her black and blue (at least emotionally), she is addicted to his bruising. A bit later Diamond follows Susan to a classical music concert, where he brutally announces that her mink wrap isn't made from animals but from the skins of Brown's victims. As he speaks the music grows agitated to reflect the inner state of Susan, who answers that she lives in "a strange, blind, and backward maze, and all the little twisting paths lead back to Mr. Brown."

And so, apparently, does the music, for Brown's gang is identified with big band jazz. In one of the most brutal scenes in all noir, the thugs use the hearing aid of Brown's lieutenant, Joe McClure (Brian Donleavy), to torture Diamond with loud, frantic jazz. As the tune plays, Mingo forecasts a "real crazy" drum solo that will render Diamond insensible. Clearly Brown and jazz are associated with pain—Diamond's and Susan's—as well as with transgressive sexual practices. Susan, Mingo, and Fante, and even Diamond, are all thereby noired, or at least thoroughly browned. Because the title melody is the sound of Brown's power, it all but disappears when he is absent or weakened—for example, while he softly recalls his first wife, Alicia (Helen Walker). And though we hear the melody when Susan persuades Alicia to testify against Brown for killing his former boss, in that scene it is only played softly on violin. Both women have felt Brown's bruises, but his aural power is softened by Susan's feminine timbre.

Ultimately Brown is captured by Diamond, with the help of Susan, who shines a spotlight on him as he skulks, ratlike, in the corners of an airplane hangar (John Alton's cinematography enhances the atmosphere immeasurably). Lit from behind, so that they appear as silhouettes against the cloudy white background, Susan and Diamond walk into the murk, the soprano sax keening the moody theme as the film closes. But since Brown has been brought down, why does his melody linger? The answer is that although the film explicitly endorses law and order, its latent content tells a different story. Throughout the film Diamond envies Brown, who taunts him unmercifully: "The only trouble with you is you'd like to be me. . . . You think it's money. It's not. It's personality. You haven't got it, Lieutenant." He's right: Diamond (remember, this is a cop whose girlfriend is a stripper) would love to possess Brown's sexual and financial power, instead of breaking his back for $96.50 a week. More broadly, the film implies that no law can quell the darker impulses represented by jazz, which Susan, Diamond, and the film's viewers (many of whom, I've learned, find the charismatic Brown more interesting than the plodding Diamond) carry within. And although the theme melody modulates to a more optimistic A major in its final cadence, it seems less triumphant than resigned, as if implying that all who live in this city are as black and blue (and brown) as the protagonists. The suffering doesn't vanish; Brown lingers in the music just as his combo has been woven into the city, and just as all that Brown represents forever resides in human hearts.

The Big Combo suggests that jazz—and only jazz—adequately captures the complex emotions and motivations of contemporary urbanites. No longer consigned to basement jam sessions and out-of-the-way clubs, it is imbricated in the intimate lives of modern Americans. The music thus both emerges from and expresses the black, blue, brown—and fallen—twentieth-century world. This world is fully displayed in the scintillating late noir *Sweet Smell of Success,* in which big band jazz again serves as the aural equivalent of urban corruption. Elmer

Bernstein's bluesy, minor-key title theme (its triplet figures recalling "Blues in the Night") specifically represents the domain of sadistic, Winchellesque columnist J. J. Hunsecker (Burt Lancaster) and Tony Curtis's weaselly publicist Sidney Falco.[31] Like the film's sardonic, crackling Clifford Odets/Ernest Lehman script, its score bespeaks a world as corrupt as Brown's (indeed, Brown kills people, but Hunsecker destroys souls). Yet Bernstein's main theme is not the only jazz in the film. When Sidney is on the make, we hear a peppy motif that reflects his unflagging energy. More significantly, the Chico Hamilton Quintet performs in a couple of club sequences and exemplifies a more progressive image of jazz.

Hamilton's biracial group features an unusual front line of guitar (Martin Milner, as guitarist Steve Dallas) and Fred Katz's cello; its modernist modal music is the polar opposite of the retro big band orchestrations in Bernstein's score.[32] *Sweet Smell* is thus the first film noir to include a jazz group performing music that was cutting edge at the time of its release. Guarded, cool, and serious, its musicians are also as far removed from the frenetic grinders of *D. O. A.* and *Phantom Lady* as New Orleans is from New York. Steve Dallas has nothing but contempt for the Sidney Falcos of the world. As for Hunsecker—whose sister, Susie (Susan Harrison), is dating Dallas—Steve deems him "some kind of a monster." The film thus sharply distinguishes between the jazz of Hamilton and Dallas—an advanced, highly intellectual art—and the brand that underscores Hunsecker's city of lies and innuendoes, a realm that lives by what one character calls "the theology of making a fast buck."[33]

Not that Hunsecker and Falco don't try to spread this gospel. The film's plot revolves around Hunsecker's attempt to smear Steve so that Susie, with whom Hunsecker has a creepy, quasi-incestuous relationship, will break up with the guitarist. To keep his own hands clean, Hunsecker enlists Falco to do his dirty work. A hustler who has buried his conscience beneath mounds of smelly ambition, Sidney is a willing proxy, despite his jealousy of J. J. Believing that nearly everyone else is as much a whore as he is, Sidney even pimps out his girlfriend, Rita, to rival columnist Otis Elwell, then passes on to Elwell Hunsecker's lie that Steve is a Communist and pothead, in exchange for J. J.'s promise of future columns. Steve is then forced to request Hunsecker's help in clearing his name—in exchange for being "good" to Susie. Oddly enough, Falco actually respects Steve and doubts he'll accept the favor from J. J., who asks (his face half in shadow), "What has this boy got that Susie likes?" Sidney: "Integrity. Acute, like indigestion." J. J.: "What does this mean, 'integrity'?" Sidney: "A pocketful of firecrackers, waitin' for a match." Even Hunsecker asserts that he'd never let Susie date a man like Falco, who, he says, lives in "moral twilight." But Falco at least feels a twinge of remorse for his acts: if he's in moral twilight, Hunsecker is shrouded in total darkness. When Falco angrily informs J. J. that Steve had accused Hunsecker of planting the smear, J. J. feigns outrage. Yet Steve holds his ground, asks the intimidated Susie to speak for herself, and when she can't, cusses her brother out.

That outburst seals his fate: Susie promises never to see Steve again, and her brother gives her a patronizing kiss. J. J. seems to have won. Yet at that moment the main musical theme is played on cello, as if to indicate that Dallas's jazz (and integrity) has begun to challenge Hunsecker's. And though Falco puts marijuana in Steve's coat and gets him arrested, both he and J. J. are defeated after Susie faces down her brother, who then turns in Falco for planting the cannabis on Steve. Butler concludes that "the 'taint' of the decadent corruption that surrounds Steve and his band is so overpowering that the film's audience can easily recall Steve's progressive jazz as being emblematic of the corruption and not an antidote to it" (136). His reading is exactly backward. The film clearly presents Dallas and Hamilton as the antithesis of Falco and Hunsecker, and though the brassy Hunsecker theme plays at the end, its swaggering swing has been replaced by a determined marching thump that propels Susie's hopeful walk into the morning, suitcase in hand. Falco and Hunsecker lose the jazz war to Steve Dallas, as moral twilight gives way to dawn.

The stolid Dallas contrasts starkly with the grimacing, sweaty jazz musicians of 1940s noir. He is no petulant, oversensitive kid like Johnny Ingram or Stan Maxton; nor an addict, weakling, or womanizer, like Keith Vincent, Marty Blair, or Stan Grayson; nor a fatuous "jigger" who just happens to have a gift. In his person jazz is an island of integrity in a sea of corruption. Though "noired" by his association with the music, Dallas is never befouled and never merely black and blue, for he hands out as many blows as he receives. Of course, Steve Dallas is a white man. How different would the story be if Susie were dating Chico Hamilton! Hence, despite laudable progress in presenting jazz and its musicians as real artists, both this film and *The Strip* still depict African Americans as instruments for the refashioning of *white* identities and relationships. The promise of true equality in the films—as in real-world America of the late 1950s—remains mostly a dream deferred.

As African Americans were gradually incorporated into the mainstream of American life, noir's jazz musicians began to lose their degrading traits. When blackness needed not be translated into mental illness, addiction, or violent rage, it began to be heard as an essential—perhaps *the* essential—voice in the American chorus. In most 1940s noir, jazz musicians represent the secret fears and fascinations of a nation grappling with race relations and changing notions of masculinity, productivity, and gender: jazz cats were a focal point for the nation's dreams *and* nightmares. In 1950s noir, however, jazz musicians are more often presented as working professionals—regular Stans or Steves—refining their art and pursuing a modest version of the American Dream. Increasingly recognized as a music requiring discipline and rigor, jazz gained respectability even as its popularity waned. It must be said, however, that Steve Dallas is a less interesting character than Marty Blair: he has shed his complexity along with his complexes. Perhaps, then, it is no accident that the music he plays betrays few traces of the blues. In serving up jazz musicians as paragons of authenticity and integrity, filmmakers risked stripping them of the depth that makes such characters so fascinating. Indeed, the blues is not only a key influence on the birth of jazz; it is also an essential element that, in two other 1940s films, permits musicians to transmute their bruises into badges of courage.

A Kind of Poet

In Raoul Walsh's *The Man I Love,* named for the Gershwins' famous song, torch singer Petey Brown (Ida Lupino) languidly delivers the title song's lyrics during a late-night jam session at the "39" club in New York:

> Some day he'll come along
> The man I love
> And he'll be big and strong
> The man I love
> And when he comes my way,
> I'll do my best to make him stay.

Though she sings the song "as if she has lived it" (Stanfield, *Body* 136), her no-nonsense manner belies its endorsement of submissive domesticity.[34] As Stanfield notes (138), it's not Petey who is a "soul in torment" but pianist San Thomas (Bruce Bennett), the title character whose "emotive piano workouts" evince a tumultuous inner life. When Petey fails to capture San, she is not devastated by the experience, as the lyrics would suggest. Instead, though bruised by life's knocks, she emerges with her integrity and artistry intact.

Petey is a figure frequently seen in film noir: the female nightclub singer.[35] But though her songs lament lost loves in tones "dreamy and sad" (to quote "One for

My Baby," a song Lupino performs in *Road House*), she herself is pragmatic and resilient. Indeed, Petey gains strength through her voice: as Adrienne McLean notes, women who sing in Hollywood films thereby become "active communicating" subjects rather than passive, acted-upon objects, as their songs permit them to tell their stories and master their experiences (4). Two films in which Lupino plays singers, moreover, provide counterpoint to noir's troubled male musicians by presenting jazz as a path to liberation through artistic labor. Lupino's chanteuses extend the tradition founded by classic blues singers such as Ma Rainey and Bessie Smith, whose style turned black-and-blueness into female empowerment. As this lineage implies, Lupino's singers are "othered" through association with blackness (also indicated by the prominent blue notes in the melodies of "The Man I Love" and "One for My Baby"); but unlike their male counterparts they are not ruined by their noiring. Instead they use it to model a progressive identity built on improvisation that embraces life as an extended jazz solo.

Though directed by Raoul Walsh, *The Man I Love* is a female-centered and -coauthored picture, with a script by Catherine Turney (and male writer Jo Pagano), adapted from the novel *Night Shift* by Maritta Wolff.[36] It presents several realistic scenes of women working together, supporting each other, and showing strength (the exception is a woman named Gloria [Dolores Moran], who cheats on her husband, Johnny, and neglects her baby). But at the center of the film—which lies on the fringes of noir—is Petey, a sharp-tongued, sardonic woman who seems to need nobody.[37] After Petey travels to California to visit her sisters Sally (Andrea King) and Ginny (Martha Vickers), she becomes involved with shady club owner Nicky Toresca (Robert Alda), for whom her brother Joey works, and eventually with San Thomas.[38] Petey wants to help them but also aims to advance her career and auditions for Toresca by singing the Kern/Hammerstein standard "Why Was I Born?" in a jaunty style that contradicts its gloomy lyrics about dreaming of a lover but waking up "all by myself." Though both this song and "The Man I Love" confess creamy romantic yearnings, Petey is more concerned with hard cheese—practical matters such as staving off Toresca's advances and monitoring her brother's illicit activities.

After she meets San, the couple take a romantic stroll on the boardwalk as the title song plays on the soundtrack. Later San performs it in a flashy, two-handed arrangement (Bennett appears to be actually playing sections of the piece). But alas, he tells Petey, his recording of the song never caught on. "You were ten years ahead, that's why," she replies, though it offers nothing that Art Tatum and Earl Hines hadn't already been serving up for more than a decade. San "ran down like a clock" because he "tried to make the piano do a lot of things I guess no one guy can do." After his wife, Amanda, left him, he started drinking and lost his muse. Here is the now-familiar figure: a male jazz musician too sensitive to function in the real world. Although San claims to be comfortable with his "blank" life, the theme music contradicts his assertion by swelling extradiegetically, as if coaching him to tell Petey that she might give him back his "spark." Sure enough, even after he warns her that he'll make her "sing the blues," they melt together in a kiss. Petey seems to be living out the title song's lyrics after all. But ten days later, San stands her up for a date, and, on returning home, Petey hears him play "Body and Soul" on her piano. The tune's famous lyrics—

> My heart is sad and lonely
> For you I sigh for you, dear, only.
> Why haven't you seen it?
> I'm all for you, body and soul.

—might suggest that he has fallen for Petey, but in fact he's still carrying the torch for Amanda.[39] The two embrace by the fire, but when he admits that he has tried to see Amanda, Petey breaks off the relationship.

The film detours into a noirish plot in which Nicky uses Joey to get rid of the obnoxious Gloria, which results in her being run down by a car. Having discovered Gloria's infidelity, her husband confronts Nicky with a gun. But Petey talks sense to him, knocks the gun from his hand, slaps him around, and calls the police. As her name indicates, she is a terrific blend of big sister and tough guy, equally able to sooth feelings and rough up villains—all while wearing a glittering evening gown! During this scene a dark, dissonant version of the title tune plays, representing the bitterness that frustrated romantic longing may engender— especially for San, for although the film's other males are healed, San isn't. After he departs, Petey walks alone on the pier, weeping—but only a little. She may be doomed to loneliness, but she repudiates the song's portrait of dependency: this film is not about finding the man she loves but about giving him up to retain her autonomy. *The Man I Love* thus counterpoints the stereotypical depiction of San with the progressive figure of Petey, for whom music is not the sign of a nature too sensitive to survive but an indispensable means *to* survive. Her mastery of song signifies her mastery of the blues philosophy: an ability to remain independent and be only mildly bruised by the sexual marketplace.

Lily Stevens, Lupino's character in *Road House,* is even tougher: when we first see her, newly arrived from Chicago in the small town of Elton, she sprawls, a cigarette hanging from her mouth, one shapely leg resting on a table, playing solitaire and trading quips with Pete Morgan (Cornel Wilde), the manager of Jefty's Roadhouse. A few minutes later we find her at the bar beneath a stuffed deer's head, illustrating her recognition that "this is a moose trap all around." The club's spoiled owner, Jefty (Richard Widmark), certainly thinks of her as his prey and, to make her easier to capture, agrees to pay her $250 a week to sing. Lily downplays her abilities, informing Jefty that she has a "small voice." She isn't being falsely modest. Early in the film Lupino plays piano and sings "One for My Baby" in a voice that is okay, according to the barmaid Susie (Celeste Holm), if you "like the sound of gravel." Yet Lupino's raspy voice and unsentimental delivery generate a compelling authority and authenticity; even Susie (who has a crush on Pete) admits that she "does more without a voice than anybody I've ever heard."[40] Lily seems to have lived the world-weary lyrics of Arlen and Mercer's saloon song, as well as its stoic attitude toward the world's slings and arrows: as Jefty affirms, she *is* "a kind of poet" with a "lot of things to say." Better than any other noir jazz figure, she enacts Ellison's blues impulse, keeping "the painful details . . . of a brutal experience alive" but transcending it by "squeezing from it a near-tragic, near-comic lyricism" (79).

Lily expresses this philosophy through her sexuality and clothing. A striking sight in Elton with her sophisticated mien and alluring garb (evening gowns, tight halter tops, short shorts), she draws big crowds—but doesn't appeal to Pete, even when she sings the film's hit, "Again," directly to him. She has better success during a "fishing" outing with him and Susie. Having neglected to bring a swimsuit, Lily disappears behind a bush only to reappear moments later clad in a brief two-piece outfit she has fashioned out of scarves. Lily likewise crafts her identity from scraps and ad libs. Such performances can be misinterpreted: when Dutch, a burly roadhouse habitué, thinks she's singing "The Right Kind of Love" just for him and Lily rebuffs him, he starts a brawl. But at least Dutch is honest about his urges, unlike both Pete, who pretends not to be falling for Lily, and Jefty, who camouflages his sadism with jokes and phony bonhomie. Yet the brawl brings Lily together with Pete, with whom she shares her painful life story: her "old man" pushed her to become an opera singer, so she practiced every night while working by day in a factory, until overwork destroyed her voice. Since then, Lily has treated life as a tragicomic jazz solo, as a constant process of improvisation.

Insanely jealous of Pete, Jefty frames him for stealing money from the club, but after his conviction Jefty volunteers to supervise his parole—so he can prevent him from possessing Lily. There will be no more improvisation now that Jefty

Lily Stevens (Ida Lupino) improvises with Pete (Cornel Wilde) in
Road House. Kobal Collection / Art Resource, NY.

calls the tunes. But even he recognizes that under his direction Lily's "voice
doesn't sound the same": absent autonomy, she can't sing. And once Jefty arranges a "little vacation" for the four of them to celebrate his dominance, Lily is
reduced to relying on Pete, until the film's climax, when she guns down Jefty. This
act is not out of character. As one commentator in the DVD featurette explains,
Lily is in many respects the film's "male-coded character"—the stranger who
comes to town and shakes things up. Unlike *The Blue Gardenia*'s Norah Larkin,
she resists becoming prey. Even more than Petey Brown, Lily Stevens offers a
powerful, positive alternative to the weak, tormented male jazz musicians who
populate noir. Like Petey she overcomes professional and personal obstacles by
employing her wit and husbanding her emotional resources. Her success stems

not from musical technique but from inner strength and flexibility. More complex than Steve Dallas and more successful than Johnny Ingram, Lupino's singers best exemplify how jazz can be not merely a way of playing but a way of living, a poetic enterprise founded on the principle of improvisation, that "survival technique . . . suitable to the rootlessness and discontinuity . . . of human existence in the contemporary world" (Murray 113). Petey and Lily jazz the world instead of being jazzed by it.

At once resilient and resistant, Lupino's torch singers model a realistic but inspiring American identity that incarnates a spectrum of blackness, whiteness, and blueness. Hybrids who epitomize the American values of equality, flexibility, and freedom of expression, they sing of Franklinesque self-fashioning. Neither disabled nor pathetic, they embody how improvisation may foster individual achievement within a collective and demonstrate how Americans of any race or gender could endure through the blues. These tough but sensitive artists' improvised lives show how jazz can indeed encompass "the whole USA in one chorus."

Femmes Vital
Film Noir and Women's Work

"One night she started to shim and shake, / That brought on the Frisco quake," sings the shimmying Rita Hayworth in *Gilda*. "So you can put the blame on Mame, boys, / Put the blame on Mame." Gilda's sarcastically delivered lines describe the quintessential femme fatale—a character type, embodied in women like Kathie Moffat and Phyllis Dietrichson, that has become identified with film noir. However, as Julie Grossman has shown, such femmes fatale appear less frequently than casual viewers of noir may believe. Overinvested in this stereotype, critics have ignored the wide array of women's roles that noir actually presents (5).[1] Noir does offer its share of amoral seductresses and conniving criminals, but it also gives us wives, mothers, and nurses; businesswomen and writers; secretaries, singers, sleuths, and social workers; psychologists, physicians, prison guards, wardens—and even professors. In fact, most women in film noir work, and their forms of labor closely reflect the actual postwar US female workforce.

Just as important as the women working in films noir, however, were the women working on films noir—the females who performed in, wrote, produced, and even directed the movies. Their presence is one reason why noir portrays so many working women and why the films address many of postwar women's chief concerns: sexism; the conflict between traditional domestic duties and newfound labor power; the anxieties and possibilities implicit in shifting gender roles; changes in courtship, marriage, and motherhood. The films on which these women worked—which I'm calling *femme noirs*—furnish complex, critical, and generally progressive analyses of American mores and institutions. While facing the same obstacles dramatized in the films, these female filmmakers nudged Hollywood toward more enlightened views about gender and, in one case, helped to redefine cinematic authorship. Far from femmes fatale, these women were *femmes vital*: indispensable presences whose creative labor modeled an alternative to traditional female labor—childbearing and -rearing—and injected a protofeminist note into male-oriented genres.

In Labor

Women went to work with a vengeance during World War II: more than six million took new jobs, increasing the female labor force by more than 50 percent (Renov 40). By 1944, women composed more than 36 percent of the total labor force, up from 25 percent in 1941 (Walsh 1, 53). Defense jobs spelled "significant social mobility," as many women traded low-paying employment in restaurants or laundries for wartime production work that as much as doubled their wages (Blackwelder 124; Walsh 57). Rosie the Riveter notwithstanding, the majority of working women held clerical positions during the war: for every female factory worker there were two women in office employment.[2] These conditions changed rapidly once the war ended: in 1946, although 80 percent of wartime women workers were still employed, only 40 percent still held their wartime jobs, and overall employment declined from 19.5 to 15.5 million, with wages plummeting along with employment (Walsh 78). Michael Renov notes that by late 1944 government agencies were encouraging female withdrawal from the workforce (33). Nevertheless, the war permanently altered women's expectations: polls showed that almost 75 percent of women workers wished to remain employed after the war (Walsh 75). Perhaps more significantly, the *kind* of women who worked had permanently changed. Whereas before the war single women outnumbered married workers, by 1947 more married than single women worked, a pattern sustained ever since (Blackwelder 124).

But it would be a mistake to believe that the increased presence of working women by itself overturned prevailing ideologies; rather, it fostered dissonance and contradiction. Thus, although more women expected to work, movies and magazines continued to stress domestic obligations. Analyzing a wide range of popular periodicals, Joanne Meyerowitz finds that "domestic ideals coexisted in ongoing tension with an ethos of individual achievement that celebrated nondomestic activity, individual striving, public service and public success" (231). Although a great many of these portrayals presented marriage and motherhood as proper women's roles, a significant minority (anticipating Betty Friedan) depicted domesticity as "exhausting and isolating, and frustrated mothers as overdoting and smothering" (Meyerowitz 242). Perceptions of marriage, too, underwent renovation: in women's magazines, marriage was often depicted, perhaps wishfully, as "an equal partnership, with each partner intermingling masculine and feminine roles" (243). The war and aftermath intensified trends toward companionate marriage and serial monogamy, and increased expectations about intimate communication and friendship between spouses (Walsh 67). Yet, as I noted about the vet noirs, most men who had spent the war years without women reentered civil society with their prewar ideas about gender intact or even exaggerated.

Of course, working women weren't working all the time; among other activities, they were also attending movies. Then, as now, women made up more than half of the viewing audience. To attract this audience, studios increasingly turned to the so-called woman's film: melodramas set in bourgeois domestic spaces, featuring female protagonists struggling with complex moral questions and competing emotional bonds (see Walsh 24).[3] One subgenre aimed at women (and often female-authored) was the Gothic, in which a female protagonist is confined to a house, menaced by a mysterious male figure, and oppressed by a secret from the past. Though usually perceived as a masculine genre, noir is not entirely distinct from Gothic: the two forms overlap stylistically, narratively, and thematically. In addition to their dark visual styles, both frequently employ retrospective narrations, deal heavily with questions of guilt and complicity, incorporate sexual violence, and involve investigation.[4] Several films I have discussed (e.g., *The Strange Affair of Uncle Harry, No Man of Her Own, My Name Is Julia Ross*) employ Gothic conventions. Hence, as Steve Neale declares, "any absolute division between noir and the gothic woman's film is unsustainable" (164). More important for our purposes is that, as Lizzie Francke points out, hybrids of melodrama and film noir "became a staple genre for female screenwriters" (51). Femme noirs—that is, films noir written, produced, or directed by women—share many traits with the "woman's film": female protagonists; gender anxiety; ambivalence, or downright cynicism, about marriage.[5] In addition to treating women's issues, then, these films blurred generic boundaries and brought strong women characters into formerly male territory.

One of those issues is motherhood. Most noir mothers exist primarily to shed light on the male protagonists: Cody Jarrett's smothering ma exposes his Achilles heel in *White Heat*; Bart Tare's sister, Ruby, in *Gun Crazy*, serves as Annie Laurie Starr's foil. Even less evident than mothers are children, who also function as plot devices or symbols: Dave Bannion's daughter provides a pretext for his revenge campaign in *The Big Heat*; Frank Enley's toddler son, in *Act of Violence*, mirrors his own entrapment. In the femme noirs, children still appear in mostly symbolic roles—as measures of the mother's morality, as signs of attachment to the past, as emblems of fresh beginnings, as psychological scars—and rarely as real people. Most often, children—those products of female labor—represent the conflict between domesticity and nondomestic work. Femme noir's many dead or damaged children not only motivate the action; they also indicate conflicting views about a woman's place.

A Woman's Place

"Writers are the women of the film industry" (qtd. in Francke 2). This quip, overheard by screenwriter Eleanor Perry, both indicates the low prestige of writers in Hollywood and points to a prime reason why women were the writers of the film industry. As "middle-level executives in a large collective enterprise," writers earned much less than directors or actors (Ceplair and Englund 8); female writers generally earned less than their male counterparts (Ketti Frings, whose work I discuss below, was an exception). Studios could use these women's expertise without threatening the male power structure. This pattern was well-established by the 1930s and explains why even film scholars may not recognize all of these names: Marguerite Roberts, Lenore J. Coffee, Ketti Frings, Silvia Richards, Catherine Turney, Sally Benson, Lucille Fletcher, Lillie Hayward, Gertrude Walker, Leigh Brackett, Virginia Kellogg, Bess Meredyth, Dorothy Hannah, Eve Greene, Muriel Roy Bolton. Yet each of these women wrote at least one screenplay or original story for a completed film noir, and almost nothing has been written about any of them.

A case in point is Turney, who wrote scripts for MGM in the 1930s (including the one for Dorothy Arzner's *The Bride Wore Red*) before being hired by Warner Bros., which boasted a roster of female stars who sought roles "in which they weren't just sitting around being a simpering nobody." Turney, whose forte was writing stories about women "battling against the odds," could provide them, as she did for Ida Lupino in *The Man I Love* (Turney, qtd. in Francke 47). At Warner Bros., where she was the only woman writer on-site, Turney was charged by ambitious young producer Jerry Wald with adapting James M. Cain's novel *Mildred Pierce*. Wald, who went on to produce several femme noirs, was eager to capitalize on the loosening of censorship signaled by *Double Indemnity*, and he hoped to transform Cain's chronicle of a female restaurateur and her monstrous daughter into a murder mystery with a flashback narrative.[6] Resistant to both changes (no murder or flashback exists in the novel), Turney was more intrigued by the story's female characters and relationships but after three months was removed from the project; after Albert Maltz beefed up the murder plot, she was brought back with strict instructions to follow his outline (Francke 51). Although Turney eventually left to write the Bette Davis vehicle *A Stolen Life* (leaving the credit to Wald favorite Ranald MacDougall), her stamp remains on the film's female-centered workplace, supportive female friendships, and its complex portrayal of Mildred's ambition and resilience (traits that also appear in Turney's script for *The Man I Love*).[7]

Biesen attributes the finished film's blend of women's melodrama and noir to its having been "rewritten, produced, and directed by males to reinforce a macho crime ethos" (138–39). Yet Cain himself believed that the story was about "one woman's struggle against a great social injustice—which is the mother's necessity to support her children even though husband and community give her not the slightest assistance" (qtd. in Biesen 139). Joan Crawford, who won the role after Davis and Barbara Stanwyck had turned it down, perceived Mildred not only as her ticket back into the Hollywood pantheon (MGM had dropped her after several flops) but as an alter ego, for Mildred's life mirrored that of poor young Lucille LeSueur, who remade herself through grit and relentless energy into a Hollywood icon. *Mildred Pierce* displays both the conditions of its creation and the period's ambivalence about a woman's place. Hence, the noir mise-en-scène— sharp diagonal lines, heavy shadows, an aura of doom—dominates the first few minutes, as Mildred's playboy husband, Monty Beragon (Zachary Scott), is shot in her (actually Curtiz's) beach house, after which Mildred attempts to frame her associate Wally Fay (Jack Carson) for the crime. But the rest—comprising Mildred's recollections at the police station—adopts a more orthodox style.

With or without the murder the film is a piquant study of social mobility and a scathing critique of capitalism. When Mildred's first husband, Bert (Bruce Bennett), loses his real-estate job and admits his affair with a Mrs. Biederhof, Mildred kicks him out, leaving her without money or skills, aside from her well-developed homemaking prowess ("I felt as though I'd been born in a kitchen and lived there all my life," she proclaims).[8] Doggedly seeking work despite numerous rejections, Mildred finally lands a waitressing job, but wearing a uniform and taking orders from others offends her bourgeois sensibilities. Yet that job launches her rise to successful owner of a restaurant chain. Even before her success, however, Mildred pushes daughters Veda (Ann Blyth) and Kay (Jo Ann Marlow) to take ballet and piano lessons and dress above her means. Although Mildred disavows Veda's pretensions, early in the film Curtiz cuts from a montage of Mildred at work directly to the girls at their lessons to suggest that Mildred is fashioning a new identity for herself through them. The girls are a vehicle for *her* self-expression; like the restaurant she buys, they are her properties.

Poor little Kay, who dies of pneumonia contracted while Mildred spends a romantic weekend with Beragon, is sacrificed for her mother's aspirations; Veda becomes an insufferable snob who sneers at the smell of grease. She is sacrificed in a different way, as her humanity is scorched out of her by Mildred's burning drive: not only does Veda hurl insults at Mildred, but she extorts $10,000 from a wealthy boyfriend by claiming to be pregnant and eventually has an affair with Beragon. In the film, as Veda is sent to jail for murdering Monty, she insists to her mother that "It's your fault I'm the way I am." Perhaps Mildred has been too busy to notice that her daughter has become a gorgon or is simply too weak to say no to her. A more likely explanation is that she cannot separate Veda from herself, for she is Mildred's class aspirations come to monstrous life. Mildred says she loves Veda more than herself, but, as Haskell observes, her love masks a "hatred so intense it must be disguised as love" (32): a hatred, I would add, not just of Veda but of herself.

Why does Mildred hate herself? Because she is torn between the myth of domesticity, in which a woman's worth is certified by her credentials as wife, homemaker, and mother, and the emerging postwar ethos that encouraged women to boost their self-esteem (and independence) through nondomestic labor. Just as Mildred's homemaker self despises the ambitious entrepreneur, so Veda's snotty remarks about grease express Mildred's own self-disgust. The film is similarly riven. Thus Mildred's restaurants are depicted as lively, collegial, female-dominated environments—welcome respites from men and her stifling home. The restaurant also lets Mildred find her voice: when she tries to purchase the restaurant property from Beragon, Wally, who has engineered the deal, won't let her speak; only when she makes her own plea does Beragon agree to sell. Soon after that scene, however, Curtiz dissolves from Mildred's face to Mildred's place: she *becomes* the restaurant.[9] By commodifying herself, the film suggests, she loses both her femininity and her humanity. Veda's fake-pregnancy scheme thus reflects lessons learned from her mother: to get ahead, you must sell yourself.

Indeed, everyone is a commodity in *Mildred Pierce.* Not only does Mildred turn herself into a restaurant; she also buys Monty, gradually increasing her "loans" to him until he becomes little more than a gigolo, then purchasing him as a present for the estranged Veda ("Sold. One Beragon," Mildred remarks). Veda uses her body to get money; Wally betrays Mildred for money. By working outside the home, the film implies, Mildred merely exchanges one form of objectification for another; in prostituting Beragon, she also prostitutes herself. In short, her American dream is self-sabotaging: as Cain commented, the story proposes that "a dream come true may be the worst possible thing that can happen" (qtd. in Als 111).

Both forms of female labor, then, seem poisonous in *Mildred Pierce*. At the conclusion Mildred is back with Bert, and as they walk from the police station, they pass two cleaning women on their knees—images of a woman's proper place, perhaps. Several critics therefore argue that the film condemns Mildred and demonstrates Hollywood's efforts to "rechannel working women back into the home" (Biesen 143).[10] The film is, however, as Walsh points out, far from univocal (133). After all, Mildred is as much victim as perpetrator. Because males exploit her, her business fails. Because society is suspicious of female entrepreneurs, Mildred must work twice as hard to succeed. Because the community stigmatizes divorcees, she gets no help in raising her daughters. Yet despite these obstacles, she bounces back again and again. Indeed, the restaurant scenes, with their female workers bursting with industry and purpose, resonate beyond the chastening conclusion. *Mildred Pierce* epitomizes Jeanine Basinger's argument that even retrograde or ambiguous films can foster progressive ideas. To convince women that marriage and motherhood were desirable, she writes, Hollywood had to show women doing something else. "By making the Other live on the screen, movies made it real. By making it real, they made it desirable. By making it desirable, they made it possible" (6). By asking what women should do, Hollywood implied that there was more than one answer. *Mildred Pierce* thus demonstrates how female artists and protagonists, even when supervised by males, exerted pressure on Hollywood's industrial system and generic conventions.

Female Properties

Other women managed to exercise more creative control. Two women—Joan Harrison and Virginia Van Upp—even became producers. The Oxford-educated Harrison began as Alfred Hitchcock's production assistant, learning the business from Hitch and his wife, writer Alma Reville. Harrison earned cowriting credits on five Hitchcock films before striking out on her own as a screenwriter. She eventually became a producer at Universal and RKO, where she supervised several noirs, four of which I have already discussed. Because I treat her films at length elsewhere in this book, here I will merely glance at her work.[11] I have already pointed out how films such as *Nocturne, Uncle Harry,* and *Ride the Pink Horse* challenge gender norms and macho posturing by harnessing these themes to crime stories. Indeed, Harrison insisted that she was "proud of being a [crime] specialist" (qtd. in Francke 57), but despite her hard-boiled oeuvre, news stories and studio publicity releases invariably emphasized her "ah-inspiring legs," "wavy blonde hair, dimples and . . . 24-inch waistline" (qtd. in Francke 59). More insidious was the institutional sexism she faced: as Harrison confessed to the *Boston Sunday Post* in August 1944, studio heads "simply do not want to give a woman authority. . . . They recognize women writers but prefer to keep us in prescribed groves [*sic*]" (qtd. in Francke 60).

One of those "groves" was the Gothic, and in this grove resided Harrison's first post-Hitchcock script (cowritten with Marian Cockrell), *Dark Waters,* a moody piece about a woman named Leslie Calvin (Merle Oberon), who recovers from posttraumatic stress after a shipwreck kills her family, and later must fight off criminals impersonating her relatives with the help of Franchot Tone's Dr. Grover. The success of *Dark Waters* gave Harrison the clout, when Universal asked her to adapt *Phantom Lady,* to insist that she be allowed to produce the film as well. More typical of Harrison's productions, *Phantom Lady* offers a somewhat more enlightened, though still conflicted, view of gender, as represented by Ella Raines's protagonist, Carol "Kansas" Richman, who, in becoming a sleuth, plays an array of roles that test and enhance her strength and flexibility. Grossman proposes that Carol embodies the "resourcefulness, flexibility and aggressiveness of the *femme moderne*" and enacts the "subversive potential of the hard-boiled female protagonist" (35).[12] But not too subversive: at the end she happily receives employer Scott Henderson's marriage proposal via Dictaphone. The film thus challenges gender norms only to reinstate them at the end. If Carol's roles mirror those played by the writer-producer who helped create her, the film's conclusion points to the compromises she had to make to achieve success.

A child of Hollywood (her mother had been an editor for Ince), Virginia Van Upp rose from assistant casting director to secretary for writer Horace Jackson at Pathé and Paramount, where her gifts (she reportedly finished some of Jackson's scripts when he was too drunk to work) were soon recognized (Francke 62). Working mostly with director E. H. Griffith, she specialized in crafting sharp parts for actresses such as Madeleine Carroll. By 1941 she was one of only five screenwriters in Hollywood earning more than $75,000 per year (Ceplair and Englund 3–4).[13] Seeking someone to propel newcomer Rita Hayworth to stardom, Harry Cohn wooed Van Upp to Columbia, where she wrote *Cover Girl* for Hayworth and oversaw her performance. Their relationship culminated in *Gilda,* the career-defining role for Hayworth, which she accepted with the condition that

Van Upp produce the film (Francke 63). The screenplay, credited to (male writer) Marion Parsonnet but supervised (and much of it written) by Van Upp, displays a skeptical perspective on gender and relationships and mocks the sexism that permeates noir. *Gilda* is indeed a key film in the noir canon, for it reveals how men create femmes fatale out of femmes vital and use marriage to regulate female sexuality.

Down-and-out gambler Johnny Farrell (Glenn Ford) is saved from a mugging in Argentina by casino owner Ballin Mundson (George Macready), with the help of Mundson's "faithful and obedient" friend, a phallic cane-cum-knife. When he hires Farrell as his right-hand man, Mundson warns him that "gambling and women do not mix"; Farrell swears that he is "no past and all future." Presumably, Johnny would kill for Mundson, just like his other little friend, so the three form a tight little trio. As this scene's dialogue and blocking imply (Farrell is placed below Mundson or seems to grow from his body), their relationship is sadomasochistic as well as (at least latently) homosexual.[14]

But the geometry changes once Mundson marries Gilda. In the scene of her introduction to Farrell, she quips that Johnny's name is "so easy to forget," but in fact she can't forget her earlier failed relationship with him (so much for Johnny's "no past and all future"). She married Mundson on the rebound, or perhaps to torture Farrell, who angrily reminds Mundson, "I thought we agreed that women and gambling didn't mix," to which Mundson replies, "My wife does not come under the category of women." No, she comes under the category of property. As Doane remarks, in *Gilda* women and money are "substitutable objects within the same system and logic of exchange" (*Femmes* 99). But Mundson hasn't won Gilda; he has merely bought her. Only when Farrell enters the picture does Gilda become a chip. Throughout the film, indeed, she serves as a medium for the men to work out their conflicted relationship: a stand-in for Johnny to simultaneously disguise and express his sexual attraction, his love/hatred, for Mundson; a means for Mundson to whet and cloak his sadistic feelings for Johnny. Farrell despises the man he works for and loathes himself for kowtowing, yet through Mundson he can inflict revenge on Gilda. Thus after that first meeting, Farrell says in voice-over that he wants to "go back up in that room and hit" both of them, yet he also wishes to "see them together with me not watching." He craves humiliation, and maintaining his attachment to Mundson keeps him harnessed in hatred to the couple. A bit later, Mundson proposes a toast to "the three of us," but Farrell refuses. The original "three," adds Farrell, included a "her" (the knife/cane). How does he know? "Because it looks like one thing, then right in front of your eyes it becomes another thing." Another *thing,* indeed: Mundson's blatantly phallic cane hardly seems female, yet the line suggests that Farrell has conflated Mundson and Gilda and remains attached to them so he can be repeatedly pricked.

Farrell's line also points to the film's second extended trope: masquerade. The metaphor becomes explicit when the casino throws a costume ball (Gilda is a cowgirl, complete with whip; Mundson appropriately dresses as a vampire). Earlier, Mundson explained that "hate can be a very exciting emotion"; it's "the only thing that has ever warmed" him. It also warms Farrell and Gilda, whose frequently expressed mutual hatred barely masks their passion: Farrell hates her so much that he can't "get her out of [his] mind for a minute"; she "hates" him so much that she would "destroy [herself] to take [him] down" with her. When Gilda begins to date other men, Farrell monitors her activities, fetching and carrying her for Mundson, "exactly the way I'd take and pick up his laundry." He tells himself he is protecting Mundson, but Gilda snidely notes that "any psychiatrist would tell you that your thought associations are very revealing. . . . Who do you think you're kidding, Johnny?" She recognizes that Farrell is jealous of Mundson *and* of her, that he punishes himself by obsessing about her lovers, hiding his guilty masochism and loathing for Mundson inside his "hatred" of Gilda.

The script thus deftly exposes Farrell's self-deceptions, Mundson's cruelty, and Gilda's pain. Director Charles Vidor also presents the triangle's complexities visually. Perhaps the most telling scene occurs when Mundson, catching the two returning after Gilda's date with another man, appears as a featureless silhouette, his head cut off by the top of the frame. Farrell, looking much smaller than Gilda and Mundson, is placed between them. As the dialogue (in which swimming substitutes for sex) continues, Mundson walks left, so that Gilda is placed between the two men. At the end of the scene Gilda, in shadow, walks upstairs, leaving the men alone. A cut then places the two men on the same level, with Mundson still a silhouette.[15] This brilliantly staged scene reveals their shifting allegiances and power relations: if initially Farrell is the third party between Mundson and Gilda, by the end Gilda mediates the relationship between the males. Yet the emotions can be read in opposed ways. Gilda and Mundson are vying for Johnny, yet he also interferes with their connection; the two men duel for Gilda, even as she enables their friendship. While Mundson remains in the foreground, his featurelessness (and the dialogue) imply that he is no more than a chip in Farrell and Gilda's game. Yet Mundson seems to hold the trump card, since he is her husband,

and he shows what that means on the night of the costume ball by forcing her to close her window, reminding her that she remains his property.

Farrell and Gilda's relationship comes into focus when Mundson catches them in a kiss ("I hate you so much," she tells Farrell, "I think I'm going to die from it. Darling!"), then fakes his death by flying his plane into the ocean. Johnny "inherits" all of Mundson's property, including Gilda, whom he marries; but, like an adolescent boy, Johnny confuses himself with his father-figure—mistakenly calling Gilda "Mrs. Mundson"—and emulates Mundson's imprisonment of her. Though Gilda flees Buenos Aires for Montevideo, where she lands a performing gig, it's not clear whether she truly desires freedom or only wants to make Farrell jealous. In any case, after Farrell fetches her back, Gilda slaps him and begs him to let her go. Falling at his feet, she restages, as Doane notes, Johnny's position in regard to Mundson at their first encounter (*Femmes* 114–15). Johnny has become Mundson. At last Gilda taunts him with a legendary mock-striptease (only a single glove is removed) while singing "Put the Blame on Mame," whose lyrics explain how men attribute all the world's evils to women.[16] The song also exposes Farrell's "thought associations": he scapegoats Gilda for his own masochism, self-delusion, and confused sexuality. "Now they all know what I am," Gilda exults. "The mighty Johnny Farrell got taken and that he married a—" (the line is interrupted by his slap). What is the difference between a wife and a prostitute? Answer: nothing.

The policeman Obregon (Joseph Calleia), who has been covertly investigating Mundson's (and now Farrell's) involvement with a tungsten cartel, recognizes the truth beneath the masquerade: "You two kids love each other pretty terribly," he tells Farrell. "Gilda didn't do any of those things you've been losing sleep over. . . . It was just an act. . . . But I'll give you credit. You were a great audience." When at last Farrell sees the light and pleads with Gilda to return to the States with him, Mundson reappears, explains that he faked his death out of jealousy (whether for Gilda or Farrell is not clear), and advances toward the lovers holding a pistol, only to be stabbed with his other "little friend" by Uncle Pio (Steven Geray), the bathroom attendant who functions as chorus and sage throughout the film. Obregon declines to prosecute; Gilda and Johnny stay together. Many critics find this ending unsatisfying.[17] I do as well, but for a different reason than others do: having exposed marriage as a method for males to control women's sexuality, the film now wants us to accept it as an egalitarian romantic institution. How, after witnessing these lovers' self-deception and cruel games, could one believe that honesty and compassion will suddenly prevail?

Rita Hayworth as Gilda ironically urges us to put the blame on Mame.
Kobal Collection/Art Resource, NY.

Despite its eyebrow-raising denouement, the film forcefully exposes the
femme fatale as a male fantasy. Yet Van Upp herself seems to have been conflicted about marriage and work. Before producing *Gilda,* she wrote and produced two films, *Together Again* and *She Wouldn't Say Yes,* about career women
who resist marriage only to accept it at the end. She resigned her position at Columbia in 1947, purportedly to focus on her marriage to Ralph Nelson, only to
divorce two years later. Asked about the cause of the breakup, Van Upp re-
marked, "I am going to marry my work—I think that's safer" (qtd. in Francke 65).

Although Van Upp's struggles mirror those of many postwar American women, *Gilda* remains as biting an analysis of marriage and gender as midcentury Hollywood ever offered. Deconstructing masculinity and the conventions of the Hollywood love story, *Gilda* presents a complex love triangle in which Mundson serves as the object of desire for Gilda and Farrell, Farrell the desired object for Gilda and Mundson, and Gilda the prize for men who both desire her and use her to enact their own sexual conflicts. Each character is a chip in the others' game. Of the three, however, only Gilda is denied agency and must resort to torturing the men through (largely feigned) promiscuity. Can we really blame her? As female property, Gilda has no choice but to use her sexuality.

Ethel Whitehead, protagonist of *The Damned Don't Cry,* possesses a more hard-boiled view of feminine power than either Gilda or Mildred. As adapted by Jerome Weidman and Harold Medford from a story by Gertrude Walker, *Damned* seems at first a remake of *Pierce,* with Jerry Wald again producing and Joan Crawford reprising her leading role. But unlike Mildred, Ethel would never let a mere teenager get the better of her; instead this once-impoverished protagonist ruthlessly exploits her sexuality and reinvents herself as a socialite and underworld figure. In the end, however, she is victimized by her gender, and though she plays the males' game remorselessly, she lacks real power. This multiauthored film also displays an ambivalent attitude toward its female protagonist, yet its documentation of the forces constraining ambitious females likely issues from Gertrude Walker, whose work is populated by strong but morally questionable women.[18]

At the film's opening we learn that socialite Lorna Hansen Forbes has disappeared after the death of crime boss George Castleman (David Brian). But why does her history go back only two years? Because Mrs. Forbes is really humble divorcee Ethel Whitehead, who has fled to her parents' small house, where she recalls her career. Ethel ended her loveless, brutalizing marriage after her son, Tommy, was killed while riding a bike Ethel bought for him against her domineering husband's wishes. If she had only had money, she believes, her son wouldn't have died. As in *Mildred Pierce,* a dead child signals the death of a marriage and the demise of the protagonist's original identity; it also propels her to find other work.[19] After a frustrating search, she eventually takes up modeling, learns that she is more valuable merchandise than the clothing, and memorizes the motto that becomes her credo: "the customer is always right." Soon she becomes involved with meek accountant Martin Blackford (Kent Smith), pushing him to join the ruthless Castleman's criminal gang. When Blackford, shocked by

Castleman's activities, pleads that he wants to preserve his self-respect, Ethel responds, "The only thing that counts is that stuff you take to the bank, that filthy buck that everybody sneers at but slugs to get. . . . You gotta kick and punch and belt your way up," because "nobody cares about us except ourselves." She sells this cynical version of the American Dream to Blackford. But as soon as he signs on, she dumps him for Castleman (birth name Joe Cavendy) an erstwhile small-time hoodlum who has remade himself (through crime) into a cultured businessman. Though put off by her rough edges and cheap perfume, Castleman is impressed by Ethel's guts and brains; aware that they are two of a kind, he offers her a place in his organization. What place? she asks. "It's too soon to judge yet. We'll have to see in which direction your capabilities lie," he purrs. But she already knows her capabilities and plans to use them to "drain everything out of" the years she has left, to "squeeze them dry." Ethel is merely doing what her education has taught her: assess her value and then sell herself to the highest bidder.

But that education is still incomplete. Using Castleman's money and the guidance of Patricia Longworth (Selena Royle), Ethel relearns how to dress and speak (replacing her gum-smacking "tough" lingo with broad vowels), and assumes a new identity as the mysteriously wealthy Mrs. Forbes (of course, the newly remodeled Lorna drives a convertible). In that guise she's perfect for her new job: ingratiate herself with Nick Prenta (Steve Cochran), one of Castleman's minions, and find out how he plans to challenge his boss. This scheme is a way for Castleman to make his "investment" in Ethel pay off. Though she protests, she knows the rules of the game: "the customer is always right." But the plan goes awry when "Lorna" seems to fall for Prenta (Lorna/Ethel has been faking emotion for so long that she seems unable to distinguish between real and counterfeit love). Castleman sends Blackford to clarify her role: she must set up Prenta to be killed. When she demurs, the hardened Blackford brutally lays out the facts: this "isn't a party you can leave when you get bored," for the money that converted her to Mrs. Forbes comes from "a hundred killings."

Betraying Prenta is difficult for Ethel because he is, like her, a lower-class striver. So instead of setting him up, she tries to warn him. But Castleman finds out, slaps her around, and then kills Prenta as a "lesson in political science."[20] "Lorna" metaphorically dies with him, and as Ethel drives off in her convertible, we're driven back to the beginning. The circular narrative structure indicates the lesson that noir protagonists never seem to learn: as Emerson reminds us, no matter what name you assume, you always end up in bed with yourself. Lorna/Ethel's story is one of failed reinvention, but not just because she can't shed her aboriginal self. No: although she can imitate the ruthless grasping of powerful males, and can change her name, she can't change her sex. Thus she remains subject to the law that a woman's only real property is her body, which is transferred to the male who purchases (or marries) it. A distaff *Nightmare Alley, The Damned Don't Cry* reveals how pursuing the American Dream drives the disenfranchised into criminality. But its ultimate lesson in political science is this: when a woman becomes a commodity, she relinquishes agency.

Complicity

Ethel Whitehead doesn't qualify as a femme fatale, for she is, like Mildred and Gilda, as much victim as violator (the film was in fact first submitted to the Breen Office under the title *The Victim:* PCA file). In the work of screenwriter Ketti Frings, the lines between victim and violator are blurred even further. Frings (nee Katherine Hartley) wrote two provocative noirs for Hal Wallis at Paramount that depict strong but self-divided women hemmed in by social and gender roles and forced into crime.[21] Their guilt is shared by the equally conflicted men with whom they are involved. Frings's scripts exemplify how, according to Walsh, moral choices are typically presented in women's films as "complex . . . and as embedded in a network of interpersonal relations" (43). Indeed, the key theme in the two films I discuss, *The Accused* and *The File on Thelma Jordon,* is complicity.[22] In the former, Dr. Wilma Tuttle (Loretta Young) kills a man who tries to rape her and then must wrestle with her conscience and confront her sexuality; in the latter, Thelma Jordon (Barbara Stanwyck) entices assistant district attorney Cleve Marshall (Wendell Corey) into abetting a murder plot but is a reluctant party to the scheme, which is engineered by her lover, Tony (Richard Rober). Though the plan succeeds, Thelma's emotions are torn to pieces.

Cleve Marshall is a willing victim. As the film opens, he is drunk, wallowing in self-pity and feeling emasculated by his wife, Pam, and her wealthy, domineering father. Thelma exploits his craving for liberation. As she sits in the driver's seat, preparing to depart from his office, Cleve thrusts his head through the car window and declares, "I'm harmless and I'm lonesome." Soon the car becomes the lovers' alternate home, their amoral space where all rules are suspended. The next evening, Thelma intimates that she, too, is "tired of being on the outside looking in," and the following night they park in the woods and make out "like a couple of teenagers." But they can't stay in the car forever, so Cleve, fearful of his reputation, assumes a series of phony names—Thompson, Johnson—whenever he calls on Thelma. We learn later that Thelma first mistook him for his boss, Miles Scott, who was the original target. Cleve isn't the only person with multiple identities: after her date with Cleve, Thelma kisses a man named Tony Laredo, even though she has just told Cleve that Tony is her husband but no longer in her life.

Cleve's identity becomes the key missing piece in the subsequent crime—the murder of Thelma's rich Aunt Vera—and investigation. The murder sequence, with its spidery staircase, deep shadows, nail-biting suspense, and shrewd use of sound (we hear the old lady fall but don't see the murder) displays director Robert Siodmak's skills. But the screenplay is ingenious in its own right, as it depicts Cleve, pretending to be Mr. Johnson, phoning Thelma, then helping her alter evidence. He believes her story that Tony, without Thelma's help, killed Aunt Vera for her emeralds. The next day Thelma is interrogated by the police, who know about her phone call from "Mr. X"; they also inform Cleve that Tony was in Chicago that night and that Thelma was never married to him. Despite this evidence of Thelma's mendacity, Cleve anonymously hires high-powered defense attorney Kingsley Willis (Stanley Ridges) to represent her. The canny Willis describes criminals as having split personalities so that their "left hand never lets the right hand know what it's doing." As the right hand to Thelma's left, Willis doesn't want to know if she's guilty. Of course, these words also fit Cleve who, after giving Willis information that forces Cleve's boss to recuse himself, now must argue the case against his own lover. His left hand defends; his right hand prosecutes.

At the trial he works at cross-purposes, antagonizing jurors while also presenting damning evidence against Thelma. Willis exploits Cleve's ambivalence, evoking reasonable doubt by raising the specter of Mr. X, who, he shows, could have committed the murder. Cleve's alter ego (his defender self) thus undermines his case, and Thelma is acquitted.[23] But Mr. X *is* guilty of a crime: Cleve is an accessory to murder after the fact. His responsibility becomes clearer in the aftermath, when Tony, pleased with his "lifelong annuity," celebrates with Thelma. But she remains as conflicted as Cleve, first refusing to leave with Tony, then telling Cleve (perhaps to protect him) that she has always loved Tony and that she killed her aunt for her jewels. "You were the fall guy, Cleve, right from the beginning." Cleve knew, but didn't want to know; hence, when he threatens to indict Tony for "complicity," he is also naming his own crime. But Thelma recognizes her own complicity (Tony remarks in an early version of the script that she is a "chameleon" who "changes colors" depending on which man she is with), and, as she and Tony drive away, she burns him with the car's cigarette lighter, causing a wreck that kills him.[24] On her deathbed Thelma describes her lifelong struggle: "Willis said I was two people. He was right. You don't suppose they could just let half of me die." The old Cleve—the attorney—dies as well; his divided self exposed, he is disbarred but does finally acquire integrity.

Like Phyllis Dietrichson, Thelma Jordon elicits the antisocial impulses lying dormant in her victim. But unlike Phyllis, Thelma is herself under the sway of a powerful man and therefore not completely responsible. An embodiment of complicity, she doesn't know what she wants.[25] The same is true of Dr. Wilma Tuttle, the psychology-professor protagonist of *The Accused*. In that film's opening sequence we watch a guilty-acting Wilma return to her apartment (staring into the mirror, she seems not to recognize herself), then recall administering a quiz, the previous day, about conditioned reflexes.[26] "Think of your needs, your hungers, your fears," she advises her students, for these "rule most of us."[27] One student, Bill Perry (Douglas Dick), needs no encouragement to think of his hungers: he ogles Wilma, copies her gestures, and violates her space. She agrees to meet him in her office (along the way speaking with another student, Susan, whom Bill is harassing), but when he doesn't show, she leaves him a note, then encounters him outside. Their chat causes her to miss her bus—a pretext for Bill to give her a lift home in his convertible. On the drive she analyzes him as a divided soul: overindulged by one parent and overdisciplined by the other, he lacks balance. The drive leads to a drink, Bill's sharing of his passion for hunting abalone ("it's the fight they give you that's important"), then to parking at the palisades above the beach, where he proposes a moonlight swim. "You're even more unbalanced than I thought," Wilma declares. Bill manhandles her, tries to kiss her; Wilma flees, briefly resists, then kisses him back. "You little firecracker. Don't pretend you don't like it!" he exults. But when Bill squeezes her arm and hurts her, Wilma grabs a metal spring (used for opening abalone shells) and beats him to death.

The screenplay contains no hint that Wilma returns Bill's kisses; nonetheless, it's clear that Wilma's diagnosis of Bill applies to herself, for she too is conflicted, unable to recognize her sexual feelings: at first passive, she becomes willing, then abruptly turns aggressive.[28] As the investigation, led by Lt. Dorgan (Wendell Corey), proceeds, the police read Bill's exam, in which he describes a certain woman as a "cyclothymiac" who "swings wildly from one side to the other" and whose long hair comes undone "because her emotions are coming undone. She'd like to break loose but she can't."[29] His diagnosis of her (like his earlier comparison of her to a shell-bound abalone) is as accurate as hers of him. Although she tells herself in voice-over that the killing was justified and that she has nothing to feel guilty about, she covers up her actions, writing a second note to Bill when the first one vanishes and changing her hairstyle so as not to fit Bill's description. Like that other psychologist/killer, Prof. Wanley of *The Woman in the Window,* Wilma "accidentally" incriminates herself by arguing with the forensic expert investigating the case, Dr. Romley (Sam Jaffe). He speaks so callously about Bill's body that Wilma bursts out with "you miserable ghouls!" (the harsh lighting on Jaffe reinforces the description) and accuses them of falsifying evidence. In short, Wilma acts guilty.

Bill's guardian, attorney Warren Ford (Robert Cummings), aids the investigation and begins a relationship with Wilma. Dorgan, too, is attracted to her but nevertheless begins to suspect Dr. Tuttle once he rereads Bill's exam.[30] But she is "so nice, so intelligent!" Romley adds, "so tense, so emotional." After researching cyclothymia Dorgan realizes that Wilma fits the bill, and plans to trap her by inciting her anger. Ford does it for him, however, by bringing Wilma to a boxing match where one of the pugilists resembles Bill and the bloodthirsty crowd evokes memories of the crime. As a woman behind Wilma screams, "Kill him, kill him, kill him!," a shot from Wilma's point of view shows the young fighter being pounded into submission, his face dissolving into Bill's. "Bill, you're hurting me," Wilma shouts, then dazedly adds, "I didn't mean to!"[31] Though Ford suspects the truth, he protects her, then asks her to go away with him. He can't comprehend why she demurs: why would a woman's "two-penny job" matter?[32]

The next morning, Dorgan asks her to play the role of "juror number one," while he restages the murder with miniatures and a mannequin. After Wilma grabs the spring and whacks the mannequin Bill's head viciously and repeatedly, Dorgan reveals that her attempt to hide the crime by writing a second note confirmed her guilt: only the murderer would have known that Bill didn't see the note and would have written a second one. In other words Wilma incriminates Dr. Tuttle. But both of them have a good lawyer in Ford, and their case is compelling: it was self-defense, her only crime being concealing evidence. Ford helped her conceal it: like Cleve Marshall he is complicit, an accessory after the fact. In his closing statement Ford intones, "Out of fear she killed. And out of fear she concealed and evaded. But if we're to hold Wilma Tuttle accountable in fear, then the world must be held accountable. For these fears are not born in us; they are man-made." This speech, devised by Frings (it doesn't exist in the novel or in others' drafts: see *The Accused* final draft), seems to excuse Wilma, yet its "fears" remain vague. Does he mean her fear of sex? Rape? Lost reputation? We can't be sure because, like Thelma Jordon, Wilma Tuttle doesn't testify at her own trial; a man speaks for her. Indeed, though Warren wins Wilma by rescuing her, his insistence that she quit her job and marry him seems only a gentler version of Bill's brutal advances. Speaking for her, using the force of the law to save her from herself, Warren is like a father curbing his daughter's sexuality through marriage. He is his nephew's counterpart—a Bill who won't bite. This denouement also squashes the fascinating questions that the film has raised about Wilma's conflicted character and her complicity in her own victimization. Bill would have raped her, so her violent response was justifiable. Yet we sense that the murder was as much a reaction to her own repressed sexual feelings as to her fear of Bill, for a part of her was flattered by, and welcomed, Bill's attentions.

Yet unlike *Thelma Jordon*, *The Accused* places us inside its female protagonist, evoking sympathy for her plight while exposing her lack of self-knowledge. Frings's early drafts take pains to analyze and empathize with Wilma's self-contradictions (though they don't make it into the film; see *Strange Deception*, 20). Like the novel, albeit more subtly, the film suggests that Dr. Tuttle relies too much on her brains, so when her emotions are aroused, she has no idea what to do with them. These implications echo the patronizing assumptions made about *Spellbound*'s Constance Petersen and reflect the mistrust of intellectuals (especially psychologists) evident in the films discussed in chapter 1.[33] But though the key situations and events are found in Truesdell's novel, Frings's screenplay not only improves the story's narrative (by changing the flashback's placement and cutting extraneous material); it also nudges the story in a more progressive direction by showing respect for Dr. Tuttle's career and by loosening the novel's traditional views of gender. In the finished film Wilma is mostly guilty of not knowing herself. Frings, by contrast, did know her worth: she not only earned more for her work than any of the male writers who contributed to the script. She deserved it.[34]

It is useful to compare *The Accused* to another movie about rape made the following year—*Outrage*, cowritten and directed by Ida Lupino, who effectively uses overhead shots and silence to depict the entrapment of Ann Walton (Mala Powers) by the rapist. Ann does nothing to encourage the rapist, and *Outrage* portrays more explicitly than *The Accused* the sexist culture in which she lives.[35] Her controlling father, for example, loathes her fiancé, Jim (Robert Clarke), and objects to their marriage plans, and Jim can't understand why Ann, after being raped, finds his too-insistent advances "filthy." In the aftermath Ann is subjected to rude stares and whispered comments. The stamping of papers and the drumming of nails at her workplace seem unbearably loud, and her shame compels her to run away. The message is clear: rape merely exaggerates the oppressive sexism that underwrites her world.

The second half of the film, however, retreats from this provocative opening and repeats the trajectory of *The Accused:* Ann is rescued and sent back to her parents by a man, Bruce Ferguson (Tod Andrews), a minister who seems immune to sexual feelings. But after Bruce has helped Ann recover, another man, Marini (Jerry Paris), makes a pass at her and insinuates that Ferguson just wants her for himself. As Marini plays with Ann's hair, Lupino moves to a close-up of his mouth, which, from her POV, becomes the rapist's mouth. Because Marini's mouth uttered the unspeakable—that she and Ferguson may harbor sexual feelings for each other—Ann grabs a wrench and brains him.[36] Certainly Marini is too aggressive, but the traumatized Ann overreacts because sexual feelings have become anathema to her. Like Wilma Tuttle in *The Accused,* at her judicial hearing Ann doesn't speak for herself; Bruce makes the case that she suffered from "temporary insanity" and blames society for not providing help for the rapist, who has spent half of his life incarcerated, and for its "criminal negligence" toward Ann. He pleads for better methods of turning "human scrap back into useful human beings." After the prosecutor drops the charges, and a psychiatrist recommends that Ann undergo treatment, she returns to Jim and her parents. Thus, as Pam Cook comments, "every move Ann makes to take control of her destiny is punished or refused" (66). Moreover, what Ronnie Scheib calls the "juiceless, deadpan Army" of male doctors, ministers, judges, and lawyers absolve themselves of guilt (61) by attributing the blame to a vague entity called "society," without recognizing their own complicity in the silencing of women.

It's not clear whether Lupino et al. mean this denouement to be as ironic as it may seem to contemporary viewers. Several of the Lupino/Filmakers' pictures, including *The Bigamist* (see below), feature similarly wishy-washy endings. But we may read the film as indicting not just rapists but patriarchy's continuing violations of Ann: in the end the rapist's gaze is merely replaced by the equally invasive surveillance of legal and mental health institutions, which will decide when, if ever, she is to be freed. To compare this film to *The Accused,* then, is to understand the degree to which women artists' perspectives on female victimization were constrained by prevailing attitudes about sexuality and gender, and by a trust in institutions that more radical films might condemn. There's no hint of complicity in Ann's conscience, but complicity exists—on the part of a society that cannot integrate female sexuality, and by filmmakers who cannot conceive of alternatives.

Inside, Looking Out

Early in *Possessed,* a catatonic Louise Howell (Joan Crawford again) is admitted to the hospital. As a machine scans her body, the doctors speak of her in the third person. He hasn't even talked to her, but Dr. Willard (Stanley Ridges) already knows that she is "frustrated, just like all the others we've seen," and he is "thrilled" to use "narcosynthesis" (that familiar noir treatment) to induce her to tell her story. As he did in *High Wall,* director Curtis Bernhardt exposes how psychiatry steals patients' agency. But it matters that this patient is a woman, for, even more than Ann Walton, Louise is a victim of patriarchy.[37] As adapted by Silvia Richards and Ranald MacDougall from a *Cosmopolitan* novelette by Rita Weiman, *Possessed* presents a "schizoid" America that hides behind legal and clinical discourses while it turns women into objects.[38] As in *High Wall,* the asylum is not separate from the world outside but an extension of it.

Louise's flashback is prompted by the memory of a Schumann piece that her former lover, David Sutton (Van Heflin), loved to play on the piano. Louise confesses to Sutton that she "just existed" before she met him, but he gets defensive the minute she mentions marriage: "I like to play solo," he protests. Louise pleads, "I just can't go back [to] being on the outside of people's lives looking in." He replies, "We're all on the outside of other people's lives, looking in." These lines evoke both our voyeuristic role as spectators of Louise's gradual dissolution and the film's master trope of barriers and bars. We don't know why Louise clings to Sutton so tightly, for no background is provided, but clearly she has learned that her worth depends on being valued by a male. Louise is already doubly in thrall, being further tyrannized by Pauline Graham (Nana Bryant), the invalid for whom she works as a live-in nurse. Not only does Mrs. Graham constantly ring Louise's buzzer, but she is certain that Louise has designs on her wealthy husband, Dean (Raymond Massey). Ironically, before long Louise becomes Mrs. Graham—both literally, for she marries Dean after Pauline's death, and metaphorically, in that she too becomes disabled by jealousy and paranoia.

After a pause the flashback resumes with Louise's memory of Mrs. Graham's suicide by drowning. The doubling of Louise and Pauline begins at the coroner's inquest, when Graham intones, "She did it deliberately" (the two "shes" seeming to blend) and Graham's daughter Carol (Geraldine Brooks) angrily charges, "She killed herself because of you," then announces to her father that "Miss Howell has taken my place, just as she took mother's place!" Months later, Louise has become Graham's son's nanny and moved to Washington with them. When Sutton visits them, she is at first cordial, then shaky, and finally, as he boasts of his conquests, nasty: "Your love affair with yourself has reached heroic proportions," she declares, before slapping him. Mortified, she resigns. But Graham proposes marriage on the spot, and Louise accepts. If, like Julia Ross, Louise seems to have everything a woman could want, in becoming Mrs. Graham, she, like so many other noir escapees, merely swaps one form of servitude for another.

Louise mends fences with Carol, but their relationship is strained again when Sutton begins to woo the girl. Carol invites him to a piano recital, where the soloist plays the Schumann piece, sending an upset Louise back to the mansion. Alone in the house, she is tormented by sounds real and imagined—echoey piano music, high-pitched shrieking, a loud clock, even her own heartbeat. Louise shuts the barred window, but her enemies are not outside; they are inside her own mind. When Carol returns and again accuses Louise of killing her mother, Louise admits it; the women struggle, and Louise knocks Carol down the stairs to her death. Then, as the perspiring Louise gazes down in horror, Carol's body vanishes, and Carol, quite alive, reenters the house: the argument and murder were all Louise's fantasy. This waking dream reveals that Louise's jealousy of Sutton is tangled up with her guilt over Pauline's death. Her motives and pathologies converge in the "murder" of Carol: she at once eliminates a rival for Sutton's affections, enacts her own guilty wish to have murdered the first Mrs. Graham, and—since Pauline is her alter ego—kills herself.

Calling herself "Mrs. Smith," Louise seeks help from a physician, who diagnoses schizophrenia and compares her to a person who can't wake from a dream. Then Mrs. Smith asks Dean for a divorce. But he has his own cure in mind: she must *face* her illness by returning to the lake estate where Pauline died. Once there, Louise sees a hand close the window of Pauline's room, then hears her buzzer and a tinny voice calling, "Louise!" She enters Pauline's bedroom, and we hear a series of screams. Racing upstairs, Dean finds Louise standing in the corner, a shadow slashing her middle. "It's Pauline," she declares. "She wants me to kill myself like she did." Louise indeed seems "possessed" by the spirit of the first Mrs. Graham, just as she has been possessed in marriage by Mr. Graham. He calms her, but Louise's torments aren't over, for she remains fixated on David Sutton. After Carol announces her engagement to Sutton, Louise coldly informs her that Sutton is still in love with her and vows to prevent the marriage at any cost. When Dean tells Louise that he has engaged a shrink for her, Louise screams, "You just wanna lock me up; you wanna put me away, I know!" Then she races to Sutton's place and points a pistol at him. The arrogant Sutton can't believe she would pull the trigger, but she does, repeatedly, killing him.

The flashback ends with Louise screaming, "I killed him! David! David!" Dr. Willard smugly concludes that Louise is what used to be called "possessed of devils" and (in a reprise of the epigraph to *Spellbound*) asserts that he must cast them out. He declares that Pauline's death triggered Louise's psychosis and that she is "neither mentally nor morally responsible for any of her actions."[39] But neither he nor Graham mentions the obsession with Sutton—the real catalyst for her illness—nor the servitude and emotional repression that fed her illness, nor the likelihood that their patronizing behavior exacerbated her disorder. Indeed, the real problem, as R. Barton Palmer observes, isn't psychological but ideological: that the David Suttons and Dean Grahams of the world are free to enact their desires, but the world's Louise Howells are not (166). She can revolt only by becoming insane, thereby refusing to be integrated or pacified. Alas, the hospital only multiplies the imprisonment, isolation, and alienation that Louise experienced outside its walls. Inside at last, Louise will never get out.

Similar themes are stressed in *Caged,* a hard-hitting hybrid of noir and social-problem film set in a women's prison and produced by Jerry Wald for Warner Bros.[40] Journalist Virginia Kellogg, who cowrote the screenplay, spent months visiting women's prisons and even stayed in one for two weeks to obtain material. Later she wrote that the club women who visit prisons never see the "rot" inside (qtd. in Francke 73; emphasis in original).[41] But *Caged* also exposes a more insidious rot at the core of American society. Like *Possessed,* it first distinguishes between the inside and outside only to conclude that there is little difference between them.

The film's first shot puts us inside a police van filled with female convicts, looking out the window with protagonist Marie Allen (Eleanor Parker). A frightened naif, Marie seems out of place among these hardened women. Her "crime" is, again, one of complicity: she and her husband, Tom, had moved in with her mother and stepfather, but the men couldn't get along. Desperate for cash, the out-of-work Tom held up a gas station, and when he was clubbed by the attendant, Marie tried to help him, which made her an accomplice. She received a fifteen-year sentence—all for a paltry forty dollars. "Five bucks less and it wouldn't be a felony," remarks the intake clerk. Clearly Marie is guilty of little more than weakness and of being a woman. Though her age is nineteen, her more important number is 93850: her new identity. Indeed, as the film proceeds, Marie is gradually stripped of everything she once called her own: privacy, free time, and—after she learns that she is pregnant and must bear her child in prison—control over her body. Her loss of agency is brilliantly rendered by director John Cromwell through a disturbing montage. A prison bell chimes, followed by a repetitive round of tasks: bell, work, bell, roll call, bell, chow, bell, end of work. Their time totally regulated, the inmates become machines.

According to head matron Evelyn Harper (frighteningly played by Hope Emerson), however, the inmates are just animals and should be treated as such. She puts Marie to work scrubbing the floor: "Just like the big cage in the zoo; only you clean it up, instead of the keeper." At the other extreme is prison superintendent Ruth Benson (Agnes Moorehead), whose well-meaning liberal aims and empathy for the inmates are impotent to overturn the power structures inside and outside the prison. The inside is ruled by Harper and inmate Kitty Stark (Betty Garde), who recruits inmates to become "boosters" (shoplifters) for her gang, promising phony legit jobs and paroles for those who cooperate. She advises Marie to "wise up before it's too late," but Marie declines the offer. Despite these hierarchies, the prisoners unite to help one inmate, June (Olive Deering), dress up for her parole hearing, and they defend each other against informants and brutality. And whenever a train passes by, all of them stop, listen, and gaze longingly out the barred windows at the "free side." They're all alike in another important respect: "if it wasn't for men," June concludes, "we wouldn't be in here."

When June is denied parole and hangs herself, the shock induces labor for Marie, who delivers her baby boy prematurely. Afterward Benson threatens to fire Harper for not informing her of June's depressed state, but Harper, who knows a highly placed politician, is immune. As she and Benson argue, the camera rests behind Harper, so that Benson's tiny head appears to grow out of Harper's shoulder, showing us who really holds power. Harper's view of the inmates is also shared by the world outside, represented by the smug Senator Donnelly (Taylor Holmes), who pays a visit after an obstetrician reports the infirmary's filthy condition, sneering at Benson's pleas for more rehabilitation services and a bigger budget. After he departs, Benson gazes out her barred window at the street below: she is as caged as the prisoners. The fact of female confinement becomes even clearer when Marie's mother visits. Marie implores her to take her baby, but her stepfather won't allow it. Her mother can't leave him, or "there'd be no one to take care of me till you get out." So Marie must put the baby up for adoption. This lost child signifies her disconnection from the outside and the loss of control over her body and her circumstances. Mother and daughter—one outside, the other inside—are equally imprisoned by their gender.

Marie Allen (Eleanor Parker) is *Caged. Kobal Collection / Art Resource, NY.*

Marie's parole hearing further illuminates her plight. The board members—all men—won't look at her. Nor do they want to hear her story (one of them even wears a poorly functioning hearing aid), for they have already made up their minds. Deeming her "hardly more than a child," they refuse to let her live on her own. Yet Marie's stepfather won't take her in. Ironically, then, Marie's youth and innocence work against her, despite her protest that she's not like the other inmates. Denied parole because she lacks "beneficial influences on the outside," Marie is trapped in a Catch-22: if she is corrupted, she must stay; but if she remains innocent, she is powerless to create favorable conditions for parole. Under the guise of protecting her, then, the parole board further dehumanizes her, meanwhile sitting smugly beneath a copy of The Declaration of Independence. After Marie hears their decision, the prison bell rings loudly, and a siren sends her screaming down a corridor and into the yard, where she ineffectually tries to climb the barbed-wire-topped wall.

In the aftermath Marie is hardened, exchanging her former breathy tentativeness for a clipped delivery. The entrance of "vice queen" Elvira Powell (Lee Patrick), who gets Kitty Stark exiled to solitary confinement, disrupts the inmates' hierarchy, and Marie's foolish attempt to adopt a kitten prompts a riot and earns Harper's wrath: Marie's reward is a shaved head and a stint in solitary. Having already lost her identity, her baby, and her hope, Marie has left only her will; this new punishment crushes that as well, and we watch her weep hopelessly in the darkness. But what finally breaks Marie isn't punishment but a simple look. When a group of "club women" visit the prison, Marie is arrested not by their rude comments ("it smells like a zoo") but by the pitying stare of the youngest visitor—a woman like the one Marie might have become. Her stare mirrors our own emotions—prurient interest, followed by horror and pity—but it is cut off before it can change into moral outrage. The glare that Marie returns to the woman is also directed at us, as if to say, "Judge me if you dare." So Marie joins Elvira's gang. As she does, the inmates sing "Amazing Grace," but there is no grace for Marie. There isn't even the kind of rough justice that Kitty renders on Harper by stabbing her to death with a fork. There is only conforming. Ironically, only when Marie is finally corrupted does she receive parole. Aware that her outside job is a fraud, Benson reminds her that in a couple of months she might have been paroled and preserved her "self-respect and dignity." Marie snarls, "What did those things ever get me? . . . From now on what's in it for me is all that matters," and sardonically concludes, "for that forty bucks Tom and I heisted I certainly got myself an education." Marie has come of age; she has acquired a new identity, though hardly the sort promised by the Declaration's ringing phrase about the pursuit of happiness. Prison has also taught her the same lesson Ethel Whitehead learns: use others before they use you. Marie sells out. But what choice does she have? In *Caged* it matters little whether one lives inside or outside the walls, for a woman is imprisoned either way.

Both *Possessed* and *Caged*, as their titles indicate, share a grim vision of America as a vast carceral institution that, under the guise of helping women, strips them of their souls. Although each film fits into a Hollywood genre—the psychiatry film and the social-problem picture, respectively—they also reveal how their protagonists' gender exacerbates their ill treatment. Less hemmed in than Louise or Marie but still constrained by the studio system, writers Silvia Richards and Virginia Kellogg managed to fashion provocative feminist examinations of American ideologies and institutions.

For Richer, for Poorer

The institution perhaps most on women's minds, however, was marriage. Femme noir probes this institution in two films, *Caught* and *The Bigamist*, which are ideal test cases, not only for their content but also for their production histories. Both explicitly address postwar conflicts about the two kinds of labor, and both depict marriage in a myriad of guises: as an economic arrangement and a prison but also as a refuge and means of redemption. Each is also the offspring of a mixed creative "marriage." Loosely adapted from Libbie Block's novel *Wild Calendar* and told from a woman's point of view, *Caught* was created by a male writer, Arthur Laurents, and a male director, Max Ophuls (who took over from John Berry).[42] Conversely, *The Bigamist,* scripted by Collier Young and directed by Ida Lupino, is told from the (male) bigamist's point of view. Both were the brainchildren of independent production companies (*Caught* of Enterprise Studios, a consortium of leftist artists and businesspersons, *The Bigamist* by Filmakers, Inc.), two of several that sprouted in late-1940s Hollywood, providing artists with greater sovereignty and expanding the zone of permissible content.[43] Both films exemplify how progressive filmmakers developed alternatives to the studio system that enabled them to critique hallowed American institutions and beliefs.

"Look at me, look at what you've bought!" shouts Leonora Ames (Barbara Bel Geddes) to her husband, the wealthy (and much older) Smith Ohlrig (Robert Ryan) in *Caught*. But Leonora wanted to be bought: she molded herself into a commodity modeled after the pages of a fashion magazine. Early in the film, as she and her roommate fantasize about landing a rich husband and wearing mink coats, Maud (her original name) decides to enroll in the Dorothy Dale School of Charm, whose credo is "look your best" to win a husband. There she changes her name to Leonora (it's more "charming") and learns to walk, talk, and wear clothes, which leads to a modeling job. Clearly the mink coats she wears are not the only items for sale (Doane, *Desire* 157). Soon she meets Ohlrig, who, as he drives her to his mansion, quizzes her coldly about her life and assumes she'll sleep with him. Leonora declines, which only whets Ohlrig's appetite. The next scene, a session with his psychiatrist, reveals him as a pathologically insecure man driven by an insatiable need for omnipotence. His recurrent "heart attacks" are, according to the doctor, really panic attacks, pleas for pity issuing from the loneliness and fear he hides behind his imperious manner. When the doctor challenges him about his inability to form relationships, Ohlrig vows to prove him wrong by marrying Leonora.[44]

A year after the nuptials, we find the miserable Mrs. Ohlrig at home, with nothing to do but look stunning in her expensive clothing: she has indeed been flattened into a magazine photo. Ophuls and cinematographer Lee Garmes brilliantly use deep focus to stress the rooms' immense emptiness, as well as Leonora's isolation and diminished self-esteem. Not only does she never see her husband; she is tormented by his factotum, the oily Franzi (Curt Bois), who plays awful piano and responds to her laments with a brusque "tough." When Smith at last comes home, he treats her as a servant, then humiliates her in front of his associates when she has the temerity to laugh while he projects a self-aggrandizing movie about his accomplishments. As they argue, Leonora faces *away* from Smith, denying him the adoring gaze he desires and reversing her original position as spectator and consumer of idealized images.[45] After she shouts, "Look at what you've bought," Ohlrig notes that she's better paid than any of his other employees.

The next day she quits this "job" to seek one as a receptionist in the office of Doctors Hoffman (an obstetrician) and Quinada (James Mason as a pediatrician; the doctors' specialties point to her possible future), whose small, noisy waiting room contrasts starkly with Ohlrig's sterile Brobdingnagian manse. Leonora charms Quinada into giving her the job, only to quit two weeks later after he scolds her for parroting Dorothy Dale dogma to a little girl. A chastened Ohlrig visits Leonora's tiny apartment, imploring her to come back to him and pledging that things will be different (but as they speak, she is repeatedly framed in doorways that make her resemble a doll in a box). However, when she learns that the honeymoon Smith had promised is actually a business trip, she leaves her mink coat at the mansion, returns to Quinada, acquires secretarial skills, and accompanies him on a house call. Shocked at her lack of an overcoat, Quinada offers to buy her one; but this time she won't be lured by new clothes. As they talk, they stand before a store selling "New and Used Merchandise": used merchandise herself, Leonora has learned a few things. Soon the doctor proposes, but Leonora, pregnant with Ohlrig's child, must first get a divorce. Quinada follows her to Ohlrig's mansion, where he looks puny within its vast spaces, and where Ohlrig informs him that Leonora is still his "employee." As the men argue, the camera pans back and forth to track Leonora's pacing, illustrating her role as a shuttlecock in their battle for control. (The metaphor is apt, for Ohlrig is addicted to games.) Her husband seems to win by refusing to divorce her unless she gives him sole custody of the baby. He claims to despise her for her weakness, but what he really hates is his own weakness: his inability to *make* her love, honor, and obey him. Leonora shuts herself in her room and refuses to come out, despite Ohlrig's insistent phone calls and Franzi's blandishments. At last even Franzi grows fed up with Ohlrig's brutality and quits.

From her bed Leonora hears a crash and dashes downstairs to find Ohlrig lying helplessly beside his beloved pinball machine. She looms over him, then

In *Caught,* Dr. Quinada (James Mason) is dwarfed by Smith Ohlrig (Robert Ryan) and his mansion. *Kobal Collection / Art Resource, NY.*

walks away as he begs for water. In the aftermath, tortured by guilt—"I wanted him to die," she cries (though he doesn't die)—she goes into labor. Beside her in the ambulance, Quinada exultantly tells her that she is "free to start living again." Yet, as Doane observes, the blocking and camera movements contradict his words: as Quinada cheers her up, he moves closer and closer, finally nearly lying upon her, and the camera closes in on Leonora, as if to imply that she is "caught in the pincers" of marriage (*Desire* 172). The last shot of Leonora, lying in a hospital bed, writes Doane, depicts her as another Louise Howell, "a helpless, bedridden object of the medical gaze" (174). The film's tone, however, contradicts this reading; indeed, what is most disturbing here may be the cavalier, even jocular manner with which everyone treats the death of her premature baby, as if to acknowledge that the child was a mere plot (in)convenience in the first place. Along with the baby, "Mrs. Ohlrig" dies too. Perhaps she can now give birth to a new self.[46]

One would like to believe that Leonora has traded her alienated labor as Ohlrig's captive for Quinada's love and has cast off her shallow aspiration to be a magazine picture. But one need not entirely agree with Doane to find the film's conclusion unsatisfactory. Even putting aside the ending's rushed pace (perhaps owing to the demise of Enterprise midway through the shoot), Leonora still marries a man who is also her boss.[47] Her relationship with Quinada is based on the same conflation of roles that characterized her marriage to Ohlrig. As Doane remarks, she "becomes the object of exchange, from Smith Ohlrig to Dr. Quinada" (173). Hence, the film indicates that Leonora cannot be independent because marriage, even when motivated by love, remains an economic arrangement in which men control the purse strings.

A lost child plays a key role in another film made the same year: *Not Wanted,* a social-problem picture about an unwed mother, coscripted and produced by Ida Lupino for the independent company Emerald Productions, which she founded with producer Anson Bond and her then-husband, Collier Young.[48] This sensitive story concerns young Sally Kelton (Sally Forrest), who is impregnated by a jazz pianist but, while at a home for unwed mothers, gains the sympathy and solidarity denied to Marie Allen and Leonora Ames.[49] After giving up her baby for adoption, Sally finds love with Drew (Keefe Brasselle), a disabled veteran whose injury (like that of Bruce Ferguson in *Outrage*) renders him safely asexual. The film refrains from judging Sally, nor does it kill off the child as a plot convenience. In fact, Lupino sympathized with unwed mothers ("I think we owe them a new start") and aimed to "bring to the public a keener understanding of what it means to be not wanted" ("Eleanor" 8). In other words it's not just the babies who are not wanted. Thus, though we may protest the decision to have Sally rescued by a man (and may raise an eyebrow at the compromises Lupino and company made to the Breen Office), *Not Wanted* still manifests how the presence of a female auteur influenced both subject matter (this was the first Hollywood film about unwed mothers) and treatment.

More important than this single film, however, is Ida Lupino's body of work. Given that she was the only female director working in Hollywood at the time, it is shocking how little has been written about her. This multitalented woman, the scion of a renowned British theatrical family, became famous in the United States for tough, intelligent roles in such films as *Road House* and *The Man I Love.* The low-budget, socially conscious films that she directed, produced, and/ or wrote are even more distinctive: they analyze gender roles (and not just femininity; as we have seen, she turns a cold eye on masculine posturing in *The Hitch-Hiker*), motherhood (*Hard, Fast and Beautiful*), female sexuality (*Not Wanted, Outrage*), and marriage, all from an enlightened liberal point of view.

Lupino's work portrays ordinary people as "victims of an uncomprehending society who struggle to find an identity" (Cook 59): they are noir characters, in other words, casualties of the American pursuit of wealth. Yet, as Amelie Hastie writes, Lupino has been "relegated to the 'women's' room for feminists to reclaim, however reluctantly" (75). Very reluctantly: before Annette Kuhn's 1995 collection rehabilitated Lupino's reputation, the feminist view of her work was exemplified by Barbara Koenig Quart's condemnation of her "extreme obeisance to male wisdom and authority," and of her films' alleged repudiation of "the very values Lupino lived by" (27, 28). Lupino's films do tend to conclude by appealing to legal or medical authorities. Yet in *Outrage* and *Not Wanted* she addressed previously unmentionable subjects with sympathy and without sensationalism. A more generous view would echo Francine Parker, who lauds Lupino for "daring to be inventive in concept and technique; daring to do 'A' movies on 'Z' budgets long before it was fashionable, risking unknown faces, gambling on untried subjects; daring to shoot big while shooting fast; daring to direct at a time terrifyingly tough for women" (19).

Calling these films Lupino's, however, begs an important question—that of cinematic authorship. I have noted that screenwriters exercised little control over their products: even Van Upp, who supervised the production of *Gilda,* had to answer to Harry Cohn. As the "women of the film industry" writers have occupied a low position in studio hierarchies since the 1940s. Lupino's case, however, is different, for all the films she directed (aside from her last theatrical picture) were made for her own production companies, first Emerald, and then The Filmakers, Inc., which she cofounded and co-owned with Young and Malvin Wald.[50] This arrangement provided her with an unprecedented degree of creative control. Indeed, The Filmakers represents a radical approach to cinematic authorship. A survey of the credits tells part of the story: Lupino directed seven of the company's films, produced or coproduced two, wrote or cowrote five, acted in three, and, according to those who worked with her, also served in a variety of other capacities, from set design to prop management. In *The Bigamist* she was the first woman to direct herself in a Hollywood film. As Hastie observes, Lupino's authorship "proliferated in multiple directions" (22). Collier Young produced eight and wrote or cowrote four pictures, and the couple continued to work together even after their marriage ended. The Filmakers' collaborative approach thus helped to "transform the very ways that we understand how films are created" (Hastie 21). The company seems to exemplify a "feminine" approach to authorship, one emphasizing mutual support and community over hierarchy

and factory-style pigeonholing (see Kuhn 4). Most important, by blending entrepreneurship with collaboration, Filmakers offered an alternative to the patriarchal Hollywood system, making progressive films that examined women's issues
and questioned the American pursuit of wealth and happiness at any cost.

One of those issues, marriage, is the subject of *The Bigamist*, a blend of noir
and domestic melodrama told largely in flashback by bigamist Harry Graham
(Edmond O'Brien). When Graham and his wife, Eve (Joan Fontaine), decide to
adopt a child in San Francisco, they are investigated by the agency's Mr. Jordan
(Edmund Gwenn), who is bothered by Harry's diffidence during the interview.
Following Graham to Los Angeles (where he travels frequently) and appearing
unannounced at his modest home there, Jordan is shocked to hear a baby cry; he
learns that Graham is also married to Phyllis Martin (played by Lupino). *The
Bigamist* is, in short, the Flitcraft episode redux—except that this businessman
lives his two lives at the same time. But unlike Flitcraft's, Graham's lives are as
different as the two women he has married.[51]

In an early scene in San Francisco, Harry describes Eve as "the perfect wife,"
but he seems to be describing a stereotype, not an actual woman. In fact, as his
flashback makes clear, Harry feels intimidated by Eve, who is also his business
partner. When he returns home after meeting Phyllis, he finds Eve entertaining
business associates and displaying a more thorough knowledge of the refrigerators they sell than Harry possesses. When she asks Harry to serve brandy while
she plays poker with the boys, he feels she has usurped his masculine role in both
marriage and business.[52] The refrigerators may represent Eve but more likely
stand for their marriage—or for marriage itself (Seiter 113). In any case, the couple is unable to conceive a child: instead of a dead baby, we have a baby that never
exists. Seiter notes that the film recalls *Mildred Pierce*'s preoccupation with "the
instability caused by career women who neglect the domestic sphere and misdi-
rect their maternal energies" (109). Yet we must resist putting the blame on Eve;
Harry implies that she is at fault, but he is far from a reliable narrator.

Graham's transgression began one weekend in LA, when he felt particularly
alienated from Eve. It was "loneliness" that drove him to it, he claims; indeed,
throughout his narration Graham acts as though he had no choice in the matter.
But Harry is the one who initiates the meeting with Phyllis on a Hollywood "star
tour" bus, gently making a pass that prompts her world-wise response, "You're not
very good at pickups."[53] After a flirtatious conversation and a visit to her workplace, they part. On his next visit to LA he and Phyllis travel to Acapulco, where,

it is implied, they have sex. The guilt-ridden Harry stays away from Los Angeles for three months, then returns to find Phyllis pregnant, depressed, and bedridden. He proposes to her because, he tells Jordan, "for the first time I felt needed." His double life nearly comes to an end when Eve appears in Los Angeles and Phyllis learns that he has been with another woman, but even after she kicks him out, Graham still can't spill the beans, and Phyllis forgives him.

With Phyllis, Harry feels important, in charge, masculine. Because he can't reconcile the conditions of his first marriage with his values, he is self-divided and takes no responsibility: it is as if some other Harry Graham is married to Eve. Unable to bring himself to ask Eve for a divorce ("How could you hurt someone so much?") or to tell Phyllis the truth, he blames the women for his passivity. When he informs Jordan that he had planned to "help" Eve by staying with her until the baby was adopted, Jordan replies, "That was both a gallant and a foolish scheme." Wrong. It's a cruel scheme. By pretending that he is too kind to hurt either woman, he ends up hurting both. In fact, Graham projects his own deficiencies onto them, a different set for each: his sterility and emptiness onto Eve, his emotional neediness onto Phyllis.[54] Though he protests that his bigamy was a result of their needs, it's obviously a product of his own. At the end of his story Jordan remarks, "I despise you, and I pity you." He may be too generous: this is a man, after all, who enlists a friend to tell his wife about his bigamy.

Graham's attempt to reinvent himself fails because, as Emerson reminds us, no matter who is lying beside him, he still wakes up with himself. Harry wants to be punished, but there is no legal penalty; instead, as the magistrate declares at his trial, he will be punished by stigma and by the loss of his wives and son. According to his lawyer he is "an ordinary man that made one terrible mistake." This rather forgiving description of Graham's persistent deceptions does, however, point to the film's broader critique of marriage. As his lawyer notes (and the judge agrees), there is a "peculiar . . . irony" in the case: had Graham merely "kept" Phyllis as his mistress, other people would wink at it. But because he married her—because, in a bizarre way, he followed convention—ordinary folks condemn him. In seeking to preserve his marriage, Graham destroyed it. Hastie thus concludes that *The Bigamist* (and, I would add, the bigamist) "rebels against rebellion" (63).[55] I would argue, rather, that the film puts the blame on marriage itself, which entraps females by bringing them under male sovereignty and traps males by stifling their sexuality and enforcing rigid gender roles. Hastie is thus correct in stating that Graham's situation reveals "conflicting ideals about marriage in

[the] postwar USA" (7)—the tensions I outlined above, between traditional, hier-archical arrangements and an emerging ethos of equality.

The circumstances of the film's production add a curious element to this cri-tique. By the time *The Bigamist* was shot, Young had divorced Lupino and married . . . Joan Fontaine, who plays Eve. In other words Young was working with his current wife and his ex-wife on a film he had written about bigamy! The two actresses publicly maintained that they were good friends and that the situa-tion didn't bother them (see Hastie 14; Donati 201). But surely they were aware of the ironies involved in acting out (and in Lupino's case, directing a movie about) their husband's mixed feelings. They likely shared them: like many movie stars, both Lupino (who was by 1953 married to her third husband, Howard Duff) and Fontaine (for whom Young was the third of four husbands) engaged in serial monogamy. This web of relationships among the film's multiple creators is mirrored in its ambivalence about marriage and muted sympathy for Gra-ham. Hastie thus asserts that Lupino "was positioned between fictional and actual roles because of her personal and professional entanglements. The story in this way is less Harry's than it is hers" (81). It is also the story of her society, as it reveals the shifting moods and mores of a time when women's growing presence in the workforce—women such as Eve Graham and Phyllis Martin (and Ida Lupino)—produced anomie, anxiety, and alienation, as well as hints of liberation.

These vexed personal and professional relations aside, Ida Lupino and The Filmakers embody an alternative to a factory system that exploited writers and women. The Filmakers' approach to authorship endorsed collaboration over individualism, eschewed glamor in favor of social conscience, and abandoned moralizing for complexity. That the films end by softening their indictments of institutions and practices is regrettable but was probably necessary, given the power of the PCA and the conservatism of their audiences. Ida Lupino is, indeed, an ideal example of a noir femme vital: a woman who used her multiple talents to advance women's interests and model female creative labor. Along the way she also helped to pioneer a revolutionary approach to cinematic authorship.

It is evident that film noir is unthinkable without femme noirs and the women who made them. These female-authored pictures helped to redefine a woman's place, both through their content and through their production circumstances. While working behind the scenes on modestly budgeted films in an often op-pressive system, these female filmmakers trained a critical eye on sexist institutions, raised important questions about marriage, and reflected on the nature of guilt and responsibility as it affected women in particular. The femme noirs were a proving ground for major cultural shifts, a theater where Americans could witness their society dreaming for itself a new shape, as these women's labor helped give birth to a new set of cultural paradigms.

8

Left-Handed Endeavor
Crime, Capitalism, and the Hollywood Left

In *The Asphalt Jungle* the invalid wife of corrupt lawyer Alonzo Emmerich (Louis Calhern) confesses her fears. "When I think of all those awful people you come in contact with, downright criminals, I get scared," she tells him. "Oh, there's nothing so different about them," he replies. "After all, crime is only a left-handed form of human endeavor." A dissolve superimposes his face over that of Dix Handley (Sterling Hayden)—a downright criminal who, with Emmerich's backing, has helped to pull off a jewel heist. The wealthy lawyer and the hooligan are two of a kind, except that Dix, unlike Emmerich, is loyal to his comrades and believes in an undefiled world outside of the asphalt jungle.

In the context of John Huston's film, Emmerich's words sound like an excuse. But the line carries broader resonance for film noir, which, as many critics have recognized, was a haven for postwar Hollywood's radical leftist writers and directors. Their films repeatedly demonstrate, as McGilligan and Buhle note, that crime is "at its base about capitalism and capitalism about criminal greed" (*Tender* xx). Indeed, as Lary May observes, the idea that crime is but a left-handed form of endeavor "informed the thinking of an entire group" of radical film artists in the 1940s (225). Important noirs made by liberal activists such as Huston and by radicals such as John Garfield, Jules Dassin, Robert Rossen, Abraham Polonsky, Cyril Endfield, Dalton Trumbo, and Joseph Losey portray class, unfettered capitalism, and hypocritical institutions as obstacles to true American democracy. Dassin's *Thieves' Highway* delineates the plight of truckers who fall prey to a crooked capitalist. Rossen's script for *The Strange Love of Martha Ivers* anatomizes class envy and the depredations of industrial capitalism, and his *Body and Soul* (scripted by Polonsky) chronicles the commodification of a boxer (played by Garfield) through his association with a wealthy gangster. Polonsky's brilliant *Force of Evil* explicitly equates capitalism and organized crime with its story of two brothers involved in the numbers racket. *The Asphalt Jungle* evokes sympathy for its disenfranchised citizens, who view crime as the sole pathway to upward mobility and the only means of preserving authenticity. Endfield's *The Underworld Story* indicts the press for perverting its constitutional mandate into a moneymaking machine. Finally, as I show in my conclusion, Endfield's *Try and Get Me!* and Losey's *The Prowler* (scripted by Trumbo) portray the dissolution of the American Dream into an alibi for nihilist self-advancement.

Leftist filmmakers used noir to critique certain American values and to promote an alternative Americanism that emphasized equality, sympathy for the oppressed, and collectivity over capitalism and rampant individualism. Their left-handed endeavors criticized materialism and condemned the hypocrisies of the upper class while exposing the media's complicity with oppression. Some of their films—even those made before the House Un-American Activities Committee (HUAC) descended on Hollywood in 1947—also capture the period's paranoia through tales of secrecy and betrayal. These filmmakers' challenges to orthodoxies led to their blacklisting or forced emigration, but their critiques of self-interest and the depredations of big business, as well as their defense of liberty and equality, remain trenchant today.

Un-American Dreams

Many of the Hollywood Left were, or had been, members of the Communist Party. The majority of them joined during the period of the Popular Front—a coalition of radicals and liberals who fought fascism and championed the rights of workers in the 1930s—and hoped to advance the struggle for better labor conditions in Hollywood.[1] Quite a few left the party after the Hitler-Stalin pact or in disenchantment with the CPUSA's dogmatic devotion to Stalinism. The Hollywood reds were motivated, as Trumbo wrote in 1972 and Dassin repeated in a later interview, by a sincere desire to make the world better: to combat prejudice, work for communitarian ideals, fight fascism, resist corporate tyranny, bolster organized labor, and, not incidentally, give themselves ownership of their own creative work.[2] For these artists, communism was a means to preserve and protect cherished American values: equality, freedom of expression, resistance to oppression. Their alleged "un-Americanism" was motivated, in other words, by a faith in the American Dream.

Leftist filmmakers were out front in fighting fascism both before and during World War II, as the long, impressive list of their antifascist and/or patriotic war films attests.[3] They also contributed a good deal to the intellectual life of Hollywood, founding and sustaining the journal *Hollywood Quarterly,* the only venue in which working filmmakers could discuss technique and theory.[4] Many were involved in the labor agitation that swept Hollywood in the mid-1940s and that drew the attention of reactionary elements inside and outside of government.[5] Rightly perturbed that the rank and file had seen little evidence of the vast profits studios had earned during the war, the guilds and unions struck for better pay and working conditions (Broe 9). Though they won some early battles, they lost this war once the radical-led Conference of Studio Unions was overwhelmed by the more conservative International Alliance of Theatrical Stage Employees (IATSE). Ronald Reagan was elected president of the Screen Actors Guild, and, with the help of conservative Hollywood organizations such as the Motion Picture Alliance for the Preservation of American Ideals (MPAPAI), vehement anticommunism won the day. The Screen Writers Guild, long the bastion of Hollywood reds, fell apart. Soon business moguls united with Republican lawmakers, using the Taft-Hartley Act of 1947 (which severely regulated labor unions and prevented Communists from leading them) to expose and fire leftist labor leaders.

HUAC swooped down to complete the job. As Trumbo wrote, the committee attacked Hollywood "to destroy the trade unions, to paralyze anti-fascist political action, and to 'remove progressive content from films'" (qtd. in Neve, *Film* 93).[6] At the forefront of the conservative backlash was Eric Johnston, a former president of the Chamber of Commerce hired as head of the Motion Picture Association of America in late 1945, who declared: "We'll have no more films that deal with the seamy side of American life. We'll have no more films that treat the banker as a villain" (qtd. in May 177). But, in fact, HUAC showed little interest in the content of films. Rather, the committee aimed to limit movie content to what fell within its own narrow definition of Americanism by preventing Communists or "pinkos" from working, simply labeling any movie made by a known Communist or former Communist, no matter how anodyne, as "subversive." Ceplair and Englund conclude that such charges "served as a pretext for silencing a cultural and humanitarian liberalism" (254). The strategy worked and by 1951 had permanently altered "the structure of power and ideology in Hollywood" (May 197) by emasculating the guilds and purging radicals from the studios (Ceplair and Englund 222).

But before the first hearings, in October of 1947, spirits were high among the nineteen subpoenaed radicals.[7] The group decided on a strategy of evasion, though many of them also prepared statements explaining why the investigation was unconstitutional and defending their First Amendment rights. A Committee for the First Amendment, formed by respected liberals Philip Dunne, John

Huston, Humphrey Bogart, and William Wyler, distributed press releases and statements defending the nineteen. But these plans quickly foundered as a stream of "friendly" witnesses cited long lists of alleged Communists; although HUAC allowed these persons to read statements, it not only cut off the "unfriendly" witnesses but, when they refused to cooperate, cited them for contempt of Congress.[8] Within days the CFA had collapsed out of fear of being painted red (Bogart even issued an abject apology in *Photoplay* a few months later). In November studio executives issued the notorious Waldorf Statement, which declared that no studio would knowingly hire a Communist.[9] With it the blacklist began.

Ten of the original nineteen subpoenaed radicals were jailed; but perhaps more significant than the jailings was the blanket of fear that immediately descended on Hollywood. HUAC withdrew between 1947 and 1951, but radicals—even if their involvement with the Communist Party had been minor or had taken place in the distant past—saw jobs vanish overnight: even Trumbo, the highest-paid screenwriter in Hollywood in 1947, was forced to use a "front" to sell his work. If the original hearings had been designed to flush out Communists and force the studios to police themselves, the 1951–53 hearings were mostly a series of what Victor Navasky calls "degradation ceremonies" (314): their purpose was not really to find or prosecute Communists (most names were already known) but to induce witnesses to name other radicals. That is, the committee's goal was to humiliate and convert those who testified, ostracize and stigmatize those who did not, and meanwhile drum up publicity for themselves. The committee also sought to transform the perception of the informer from that of "rat" to patriot. Those who named others and apologized were permitted to work again; those who refused to name others—even if they testified—were blacklisted. For the studios, however, it was all about money. Already hemorrhaging audiences in the wake of the *Paramount v. Loews* decision that stripped them of theater ownership, and fearing the advent of television, studios were less concerned about reds than about red ink.

Whatever the motives of its perpetrators, the blacklist cut a swathe through Hollywood. Loyalty oaths became de rigueur, as many radicals and former radicals—including Dmytryk and Rossen, along with Sterling Hayden, Elia Kazan, Silvia Richards, and many others—were paraded through the committee chambers and forced to cite names, thereby preserving their livelihoods but earning a lifetime of second thoughts and condemnation from those who refused to testify. The ritual was chillingly successful: as Navasky observes, no Hollywood Communist or former Communist who was called to testify and failed to name others worked under his or her own name again for many years (84). An estimated 350 creative artists lost their jobs, and only about 10 percent of blacklistees salvaged their careers (Broe 85; Ceplair and Englund 419).[10] The radicals' view—that HUAC's witch hunt was not only unconstitutional but un-American—was drowned out by the loud chorus of fearmongers (which included the American Legion and other hyper-"patriotic" organizations), publicity seekers, and media shills. Among the "recklessly mangled lives and careers" (Navasky 76) were those of some of the finest artists in Hollywood. According to Ceplair and Englund, blacklisted writers had scripted ten of the ninety-one top grossing films before 1952 and had accumulated 14 percent of available accolades while contributing 20 percent of the material on which recognition was based (333). And though several writers were able to sell screenplays using fronts, their earnings dwindled, and they relinquished any control over the outcome. The news was worse for directors and actors. Polonsky (not one of the Nineteen but an outspoken radical who had been involved in labor organizing before coming to Hollywood) was unable to direct a film between 1948 and 1969. Losey, Endfield, and Dassin emigrated, and though all three had success abroad, they were cut off from their communities and friends. Actors John Garfield and Canada Lee, two stars of *Body and Soul,* were hounded to death: as Navasky puts it, both men died "of blacklist" (340). In sum, the blacklist was a disaster not just for Hollywood's radical community but for the entire American movie industry.

Red Noir

Yes, they were skilled; but were they subversive? John Howard Lawson wrote in 1949 that "it is impossible for any screen writer to put anything into a motion picture to which the executive producers object" (qtd. in Ceplair and Englund 322). As we have seen, the writer in midcentury Hollywood exerted little control over the final product. Moreover, the Hollywood reds had little or no interest in subverting the United States government, as HUAC charged. Yet these writers and directors did critique certain American values in the crime films that we now call noir. James Naremore argues that "the first decade of American film noir was largely the product of a socially committed faction . . . composed of 'Browderite' communists . . . and 'Wallace' democrats" (*More Than Night* 104).[11] Paul Buhle and Dave Wagner likewise declare that noir was "the cinematic triumph of the Left's filmmakers . . . over adverse circumstances and ideological resistance from Communist aesthetic reductionism" (xvi); Philip Kemp has even suggested that radical ideas underpin the entire noir canon.[12] More plausibly, May divides noir into two types, one set focusing on authority figures who demolish evildoers, cure pathology, or ease adaptation to the middle-class dream, and a second group (created by the Left) that celebrates nonconformism and "perpetuate[s] the ideal of the hybrid rebel in quest of wholeness against an alienating society" (220). Broe further argues that the leftist slant of noir between 1945 and 1950 was supplanted after 1950 by a conservative wave (30). Although Broe's dates are questionable (*Try and Get Me!* and *The Prowler* were released in 1951; the right-wing pseudodocumentary *Walk a Crooked Mile* appeared in 1948), he is correct that radical style and politics were much harder to find in 1950s noir.

In his seminal 1985 essay "Red Hollywood," Thom Andersen lists thirteen films as exemplars of what he dubs "film gris," a subset of noir distinguished by greater emphasis on social "realism" (257; his list includes most of the films I discuss in this chapter). Expanding the list to sixteen, Joshua Hirsch outlines the sources and themes of this subgenre, which he describes as "the most radically leftist cycle of Hollywood pictures" before the 1960s (84).[13] But even Andersen seems embarrassed by the term *film gris,* so I propose a new name for these products of Hollywood radicals: *red noir.* Though indebted to the gangster films of the 1930s, as Joshua Hirsch argues, the red noirs turn those pictures' implied critique of capitalism into an explicit one (89, 85).[14] As he explains, this group scrutinizes three aspects of American society: the class system, capitalism, and the ideology of the American Dream (86). These categories provide a helpful template for the ensuing discussion.

Making a Killing: Noir's Class Critique

"You're Genghis Khan, Alexander the Great, Caesar! . . . Your every move is obvious. . . . Not cleverness, not imagination. Just force, brute force." Intoned by Dr. Walters (future blacklistee Art Smith), these lines not only cite the title of Jules Dassin's violent prison melodrama but also state its major theme and describe its villain, Captain Munsey (chillingly enacted by Hume Cronyn). Unfortunately, the lines also pinpoint the film's main flaw: though its heart is in the right place, its every move is obvious.[15]

In portraying the inhumane conditions that prompt inmate Joe Collins (Burt Lancaster) to lead a prison break, *Brute Force* presents an allegory of a fascist society, with Munsey as its Fuehrer and Collins (note his initials) as a Christ figure who sacrifices himself to take Munsey down. Dassin succeeds in making us hate Munsey, a sadistic martinet who listens to Wagner while torturing a prisoner and spouts neo-Nazi twaddle such as "weakness is an infection that makes a man a follower instead of a leader. . . . Nature proves that the weak must die so that the strong may live." Ultimately, the film's conflict boils down to a face-off between Hitler and Jesus.

Dassin's antifascist allegory is coupled with an equally heavy-handed class critique. The prisoners are shown laboring in factorylike conditions, and those Munsey disfavors are sent to the "drain pipe," a grimy, dark, dangerous place where inmates attempt, seemingly without stint or success, to clear muck. The inmates are lower-class workers enslaved to Munsey's tyrannies, which include extreme punishments for minor infractions and the cultivation of informers. The latter element—omnipresent throughout—looms especially large after Collins's escape scheme is doomed by the Judas among his apostles, "Freshman" (future black-listee Jeff Corey). Though it was released just before the first HUAC hearings, *Brute Force* nonetheless conjures the period's paranoid atmosphere. For a radical like Dassin the relationship between Munsey and the oppressed inmates may also have evoked the one between studio heads and the striking workers who risked the loss of careers and even imprisonment from their activities.

If *Brute Force*'s leftist politics seem ham-handed, Dassin's next film, *The Naked City*, suffers from the opposite problem: far from naked, its class critique is, as Rebecca Prime has shown, muffled by compromises.[16] After the shoot, Dassin made producer Mark Hellinger promise not to change anything while he was out of the country, but the pledge became moot after Hellinger died in December (Prime 149). Viewing the final version a few months later, Dassin was outraged that the film had been shorn of "anything connected with poor people or poverty or struggle" (qtd. in Prime 150). A muted class critique does linger in the opening sequences, which show ordinary folks hard at work while the idle rich—including playboy Frank Niles (Howard Duff) and his soon-to-be murdered girlfriend Jean Dexter—live off their labor (Broe 91). The plot, too, suggests that Dexter, whose working-class parents lament her obsession with wealth, was infected by a virulent version of the American Dream: ripping off the wealthy in order to become just like them. During the film's exciting conclusion we pass through the teeming streets of the Lower East Side as the police pursue murderer Willie Garzah (Ted de Corsia), yet the tenements are little more than a colorful backdrop. Hellinger's self-congratulatory voice-overs notwithstanding, the finished film does not "lay New York open" but diverts its gaze, turning radical politics into a run-of-the-mill police procedural.

A more successful exposure of the proletariat's plight appears in Dassin's next film, *Thieves' Highway*, adapted by A. I. Bezzerides from his novel, *Thieves' Market*. Nick Garcos (Richard Conte) returns from military service to learn that his father (future blacklistee Morris Carnovsky) lost his legs when corrupt produce wholesaler Mike Figlia got him drunk and, Nick believes, wrecked his truck and took his money. Seeking restitution, Nick teams up with Ed Kinney (Millard Mitchell) to drive a shipment of Golden Delicious apples to San Francisco. Because this is the first crop of the season, Kinney assures him, it's "like money in the bank." For Kinney the apples are wealth incarnate; for Nick they are embodied aspiration. In short, the apples are fetishized commodities that represent, in Marxian terms, the entire system of production: hence we see Kinney try to cheat the growers who load his truck. Yet for Kinney—so poor that he can't afford to fix his decrepit vehicle—their purpose is less to make him rich than to help him survive. And though he assures Nick that they'll "make a killing," it's a risky venture, as Kinney must race two other drivers, Pete (Joseph Pevney) and Slob (Jack Oakie), to reach the market first.

Arriving before the others, Nick meets Figlia (played with panache by future "friendly" witness Lee J. Cobb), who sends the prostitute Rica (Valentina Cortesa) to occupy him while his minions slash Nick's tires and thereby provide a pretext for Figlia to sell Nick's load.[17] Nevertheless, Nick charms Rica and negotiates shrewdly enough with Figlia to earn $3,900 for the apple shipment. Bursting with pride, he phones Polly, his hometown girlfriend, boasts that he "made a killing the first time out," and asks her to marry him in San Francisco. But when he takes Rica out for a celebratory drink, Figlia's thugs beat him up and steal his earnings. Meanwhile, Kinney's prediction about making a "killing" comes true when the U-joint of his truck breaks while descending a hill, causing his death in a fiery crash. As the truck burns, the apples bounce down the hill, mutely mocking the trucker's aborted dream. Pete and Slob, who witness the wreck, do reach the market, only to be rooked by Figlia. Worse, Pete agrees (to Slob's disgust) to help Figlia scoop up Kinney's dumped apples for fifty cents per box. No matter that the fruit represents their dead friend: the apples are now money, which has no smell. The fruit here symbolizes how, as Marx famously wrote, capitalism transforms human relations into "a relation between things" (*Capital* 1:321).[18]

Rica, too, represents the commodification of human beings via the "cash nexus" (Marx and Engels 475–76). But at least she is straightforward about her goals, declaring to Nick that she wants "money, lots of money." Polly is no better: as soon as she learns that Nick has lost his wad, she curses him and departs. "The only difference between you and Polly," Nick asserts, is that "she's strictly an amateur." Figlia, however, is no amateur: he now has both the apples and Nick's hard-earned money. The personification of capitalist oppression disguised as free trade, Figlia, like one of Marx's factory owners, transmutes apples into surplus value by exploiting the labor of those who produce and transport them.

In the film's hokey conclusion Nick and Slob catch up to Figlia at a diner, where Nick beats him into submission and avenges his father. The police arrive and lecture Nick about letting them take care of people like Figlia. Added by producer Darryl Zanuck after Dassin had left the country to escape the blacklist, this scene violates the film's tenor and theme (we already understand that Figlia's fiefdom operates with the tacit approval of the authorities) but does not erase its broader implications.[19] *Thieves' Highway* could scarcely be more direct in equating capitalism and criminality: although honest dealers are mentioned, we don't see any and instead witness the wealthy steal from the proletariat and force them to exploit each other. Like the cars discussed in chapter 5, the men's trucks are potential engines of upward mobility (it's not an accident that Kinney crashes while cresting a hill) on a permanently blocked road. Hence, even as the film celebrates Nick's success in achieving his American dream through individual enterprise, it more forcefully underlines the obstacles to such attainment.

Class is also the theme of *The Strange Love of Martha Ivers* (directed by Milestone and scripted by Rossen), a film that, according to the MPAPAI, contained "sizeable doses of communist propaganda" (qtd. in Buhle and Wagner, *Radical* 377).[20] Propaganda or not, the film dramatizes "how class oppression had hardened since the Depression" (Broe 64) via a melodramatic tale of a love triangle involving Barbara Stanwyck's Martha, the niece of a wealthy factory owner; Walter O'Neil (Kirk Douglas), the weak son of a middle-class striver; and Sam Masterson (Van Heflin), a lower-class boy Martha once loved.[21]

As a child in 1928, Martha, after being caught trying to run away with Sam, bludgeons her snobbish aunt (who has just killed Martha's cat) and causes her to fall down the stairs to her death.[22] Although Walter had snitched on Martha and Sam for running away, he stays mum about the murder and, with his father's help, worms his way into the Ivers family by keeping the secret. Their shared information perfectly fits Georg Simmel's description of the secret as a form of "inner property"; it is at least as valuable as the tangible property that Martha inherits (331). But, as Simmel reminds us, secrets are also "surrounded by the possibility and temptation of betrayal" (333): though it connects Martha and Walter, it also, like the secret in *No Man of Her Own,* places a barrier between them. Hence, if the secret gives Walter power over Martha, it also ties him to her in perpetuity and makes him her minion—and gradually converts him into a drunk who can't enjoy his success. The secret also granted Walter's father the leverage to "see all his dreams come true": using the threat of blackmail, he sent his son to college, married him to an heiress, and participated in the framing of a homeless man for the murder.

When Sam, who left Iverstown the night of the murder, returns eighteen years later, he finds Martha married to Walter, who is running for reelection as district attorney.[23] Hearing about his campaign, Sam addresses the poster of O'Neil: "You still look like a scared little kid to me." Beneath the poster is his own reflection in a mirror. Is he referring to Walter or to himself? Sam is also scared, and he is, moreover, divided about his class allegiances, his feelings for Martha, his attitude toward money—about everything. His ambivalence is embodied in Toni Marachek (Lizabeth Scott), an ex-convict who shares his working-class background and with whom he becomes romantically involved. Yet Sam also remains fascinated by Martha, even after she and Walter get Toni arrested and try to scare Sam away with a beating. Martha, too, is divided: she wants Sam because he represents her father's working-class origins and her innocent childhood, but she also hopes to prevent him from spilling the beans about her childhood crime.

Walter and Martha believe that Sam plans to blackmail them; in fact, they seem to *want* him to blackmail them, for doing so would assuage their guilt and reinforce their belief that everyone is as dishonest as they are. To test him, Martha brings Sam to her office overlooking the factory. Sam sardonically remarks that when he was a kid, he couldn't even get past the gate. Surveying her domain, she recalls that her father was a mill hand there before marrying her wealthy mother and boasts that she has expanded the business tenfold "all by myself." But now Sam wants half of it. Later, during a hilltop tryst above the city (Martha is invariably shown looming over others or perched above the town), she tells Sam of the sensation of power she feels from owning all this, and, ignoring his warning ("you know what happened to Lot's wife when she looked back, don't you?"), she professes to wish that she had married him instead of Walter. Sam then reveals *his* secret: he wasn't even present during the murder and only that day investigated the killing and trial. Enraged at her self-incrimination, Martha tries to brain Sam with a fiery stick, then pleads with him to stay with her, admitting that she feels trapped. This is Martha's "strange love": she loves money and power but hates herself for having them; she loves Sam but hates him for making her feel guilty.

In the film's final confrontation at her mansion an intoxicated Walter tells of Martha's affairs, her soulless immorality, and his own cowardice. Stumbling drunkenly, he falls down the stairs, as if to reenact—or undo—the original crime and the class elevation he received as a result of it. Martha urges Sam to finish Walter off, to "set both of us free." A wide shot shows her gazing down the stairs at the men, like a puppeteer with her marionettes. But Sam carries Walter to a chair. "Now I'm sorry for you," he says to her. "Your whole life has been a dream." Taking up a pistol, Martha sneers, "What were their lives compared to mine? . . . A mean, vicious, hateful old woman who never did anything for anybody" is worthless compared to Martha, who has donated to charity, built schools and hospitals, and put thousands of people to work. Martha here reveals her true nature: she is a fascist. "And what was he?" she continues, referring to the man she framed. Sam's answer to both questions: "a human being." After Sam departs in disgust (Martha having been unable to shoot him), Walter excuses them. It's nobody's fault, he tells her. "It's just the way things are. It's what people want and how hard they want it. And how hard it is for them to get it." Broe calls this speech a "direct concentration on the structure of class inequality" (66), but it isn't that, for it blames their crimes on universal appetites rather than on economic circumstances. In the end Martha induces Walter to shoot her. Dying, she utters her birth name, "Martha Smith," and then Walter kills himself. Thus do the capitalists—their wealth a product of murder—dig their own graves, as Marx and Engels promised. When Sam and Toni leave Iverstown (passing the sign for "America's Fastest Growing Industrial City"), he quips, "Don't ever look back. You know what happened to Lot's wife, don't you?"

As is so often the case in noir, individuals are fated to repeat the actions that entrapped them. Milestone alludes to the specters haunting Iverstown through setting and mise-en-scène. For example, both the opening sequences and the scene of Sam's return take place during rainstorms, as if to suggest that he personifies the past. The concluding scenes on the stairway also replay the murder scene, as if to imply that Martha's and Walter's lives have been irrevocably molded by that single childhood act. In these images and in the concluding lines we may also sense postwar Americans' ambivalence about their Depression past and, perhaps, the filmmakers' fears that their own pasts, their own secrets, might return to make them pay. Overpowering these themes, however, is the film's argument that wealth is criminal and capitalism a brand of soul murder. These sentiments lie at the heart of red noir, as *Body and Soul* further reveals.

Capital Crimes

"Ya gotta be businesslike, Charlie. . . . Everybody dies." The speaker is Mr. Roberts (Lloyd Gough), a gangster who owns boxer Charlie Davis (John Garfield) and wants him to throw his next fight so Roberts can make a killing by betting against him.[24] Business is not only Roberts's creed; it's his only reality, as he declares in one of many memorable lines in Polonsky's script for *Body and Soul*: "Everything is addition or subtraction. The rest is conversation." Like Garfield a working-class Jewish kid from the inner city, Charlie believes in the American Dream of upward mobility, which he hopes to achieve through boxing, but in the course of the film he is transformed from an aspiring young man into a thing.[25] This sharply written fable of a young man who sells his soul was the only hit for Enterprise Studios, which teamed with Roberts Productions (co-owned by Garfield and Bob Roberts) to produce the picture. Strongly invoking 1930s social realism (Naremore, *More Than Night* 103; Buhle and Wagner 390), the film is among red noir's finest achievements, as well as a tribute to the collaborative, artist-first ethos of the short-lived Enterprise.[26] It also initiated a new round of boxing pictures, including *Champion* and *The Set-Up*, as the ring proved a useful setting for tales of moral combat, as well as a handy way to depict the symbiosis of crime and "legit" businesses.[27]

In Charlie's dressing room, just before his title fight, Roberts speaks the lines quoted at the beginning of this section and then reminds Charlie that he must lose in fifteen rounds. Not only has Roberts bet against him; Charlie has wagered on his own defeat. Tortured by second thoughts as he lies on his pallet awaiting the opening bell, he flashes back to the beginning of his career when he met his girlfriend, Peg (Lilli Palmer), an art student, and shared his dreams with her. "You mean you want other people to think you're a success?" she asked. "Sure," he replied. "Every man for himself." Charlie's response reveals a confusion that becomes deeper as the film proceeds. To illustrate it, early in the film Rossen and cinematographer James Wong Howe place Charlie in small, cluttered spaces surrounded by others to show how he is defined by his friends and relatives: Shorty (Joseph Pevney), who first promotes him; Peg; his mother and father; his neighborhood. Yet Charlie clings to the fantasy that he is an individual striver—a "tiger," as Peg calls him, quoting Blake's poem and drawing him with fur on his legs.[28] Yet this trait also stems from his environment, as his mother (Anne Revere) laments: because they live in a jungle, he can only be a "wild animal." Above all, Charlie dreads becoming his father (Art Smith), who runs a dinky candy store before being killed in gang-battle crossfire. His mother exhorts Charlie to "fight for something, not money," and encourages him to go to night school, but the only thing Charlie values is money. In a scene just after his father is killed, Charlie stands before the empty store, a "for rent" sign behind his head: he is available for lease or purchase, a piece of merchandise like the Coca-Cola advertised beneath the rental ad. Charlie's conflict between financial goals and emotional ties is also invoked after Alice (Hazel Brooks), one of Roberts's hangers-on, claims to be "nobody." Peg quips, "Nobody is anybody who belongs to somebody. So if you belong to nobody, you're somebody." What does it mean to belong? To be the property of someone, or to be emotionally attached to someone? Charlie's dilemma revolves around these conflicting connotations: does he belong to Peg and his family and friends, to Roberts, or to himself?

Offended when a social worker interviews them to determine if they qualify for welfare, Charlie, with a push from Shorty, sells himself to Quinn (William Conrad), Roberts's underling, and starts to box in earnest. Bursting with magnanimity after winning several fights, he brings his entourage to a lavish hotel room. There Shorty implores Peg to marry Charlie right away to save him from becoming "a money machine, like gold mines, oil wells." Roberts, he warns, is "cutting him up a million ways." Sure enough, shortly afterward Charlie agrees to give 50 percent of his earnings to Roberts, who has promised a bigger pie, with "more slices, more to eat for everybody." But not for Shorty, who is cut out—he's now one of Charlie's "expenses"—and will get only Charlie's crusts. Despite his fantasy of independence, Charlie has become an alienated laborer whose talent and effort are surplus value for Roberts. He's not the only one: African American boxer Ben Chaplin (Canada Lee) has already passed through this stage. Left with a head injury from his previous fight, he has been warned not to box again but agrees to fight Charlie with the understanding that he (Ben) will lose. Unfortunately, Roberts and his partners don't let Charlie in on the plan, and he pummels Ben mercilessly. Celebrating his tainted victory, Charlie learns that his opponent threw the fight and has been severely injured. No matter, says Roberts: "Everybody dies." Shorty is enraged: "We didn't win. He [Roberts] won." Charlie is not "just a kid who can fight; he's money. And people want money so bad, they make it stink; they make you stink." When Shorty is killed by a speeding car, Charlie's conscience seems to die as well; Peg also urges him to quit, but he won't give up the dream. "I can't stop now," he tells her. "It's what we wanted. . . . I'm the champ!" "You mean Roberts is," she answers. "I can't marry you; that'd just mean marrying him." The Johnny Green title song plays in the background: Charlie belongs to Roberts, body and soul.

In the ensuing montage Charlie fights and spends in a fury; Roberts is in every shot, sometimes superimposed over the action, and Alice has supplanted Peg. No longer a tiger, Charlie has become a prize horse that Alice rides to win her own animal—the mink coat Peg once wore. Human relations, as Marx warned, have devolved into relations between things. Aware that his animal will soon wear out, Roberts gives Charlie a final job: accept $60,000 to lose to Jack Marlowe. "Why not live the easy life?" he cajoles. "You got a million friends, Charlie; you can't miss." He backs this soft-soap with a hard punch: "Nobody backs out now." Charlie goes along, but Ben, who has become his trainer, refuses Roberts's patronizing payoff. "Take the money," Charlie urges him. "It's got no memory. It don't think." Charlie should know: he *is* money. However, he *does* have a memory, and it prompts him to beseech Peg to take him back; after all, he'll be rich. "Don't tell me what you can buy," she says. "You've got nothing to buy." Against Roberts's cash nexus Peg represents Charlie's soul bonds. Guilt pangs further buffet Charlie after a neighbor praises him as a credit to Jews, and even Charlie doesn't seem to believe his explanation to Peg and his mother that throwing the fight is "an investment, a sure thing." But the turning point comes in the next scene, when Roberts fires Ben, who falls backward over the ring ropes, then goes berserk, collapses, and dies. His sacrifice revives Charlie's moribund conscience.[29] Perhaps, as Buhle and Wagner state, Ben's death forces Charlie for the first time to glimpse "something beyond himself and [he] comes to terms with the pain of another human being" (*Dangerous* 115). But he also realizes that Ben's fate is likely to be his own.

The frame closes as Charlie opens his eyes on his pallet. He was "dreamin'," he says, but now he has awakened. And so the climactic fight begins. Or rather, the match begins, but no fighting happens for several rounds, as the athletes stall, following Roberts's plan. Then, in round thirteen, after being knocked down four times, Charlie decides to defy Roberts, and his frantic comeback scares even his opponent. "Like a tiger stalking his prey," according to the announcer, Charlie chases Marlowe around the ring until he knocks him out. Afterward he throws Roberts's words back at him: "Whaddaya gonna do? Kill me? Everybody dies."[30]

Even more directly than *Thieves' Highway, Body and Soul* equates crime and business, with sweating bodies replacing golden apples as fungible objects. Roberts, who speaks solely in terms of business and mathematics, turns people into commodities. Desperate to rise out of the ghetto, Charlie jumps at the chance to earn big money but instead becomes it. Yet the film doesn't really scorn the American Dream: it endorses the version voiced by Charlie's mother—the same one pursued by Polonsky himself. How, the film asks, does one navigate the path between individual achievement and social/communal obligations? It suggests that Charlie's most grievous error is replacing his loved ones with parasites like Quinn and Alice; when he is finally all alone, he must decide to whom he will belong and in what sense. In this respect *Body and Soul*'s values are not leftist so much as humanist. What really matters, it implies, is not money but one's soul—not wealth but honor and loyalty. These latter values were hard to find in HUAC-era Hollywood, where many witnesses, as Dassin starkly put it, chose career over honor ("Jules Dassin" 213). Although the trials and blacklist were still in the future (the film was shot in April 1947 and released that August: Silver and Ward 38), *Body and Soul* adumbrates the choices that would soon face Hollywood progressives.

"At Enterprise, I was God, thanks to *Body and Soul*," remembered Polonsky in 1997 ("Abraham Polonsky" 486). As the writer of the studio's sole hit, he was afforded a chance to direct his first film, *Force of Evil*, which he adapted from Ira Wolfert's novel *Tucker's People*. Whereas *Body and Soul* traces the commodification of an individual and crime's parasitic relationship to sports, *Force of Evil* attempts a more sweeping indictment. As Polonsky observed, the film uses the numbers racket to represent the entire American system of business (qtd. in Neve, *Film* 133)—a system that oppresses its workers, corrupts its leaders, and hides its depredations behind patriotic platitudes and "everybody's doing it" excuses.[31] The evil force in *Force of Evil* is capitalism itself. Yet the film is far from a dull didactic tract. Its crisp cinematography (George Barnes modeled the mise-en-scène after the paintings of Edward Hopper; "Abraham Polonsky" 489), powerful acting, and poetically evocative dialogue make it one of the most thoughtful, incisive noirs in the canon. These features also render its critique of American values all the more persuasive.

The film's exposure of capital's crimes begins from its opening overhead shot of Wall Street, where Joe Morse (Garfield, in a riveting performance) explains in voice-over that he will make his first million dollars tomorrow, July 4, as the lawyer for Ben Tucker's numbers racket. Every "sucker" will bet on the number 776 out of sentimental attachment to the American Revolution. There's one born every minute: according to Morse, citizens spend over $100 million daily betting on numbers. Ordinarily, all of these sentimental bettors would lose, but this year Tucker plans to fix it so the number wins, thereby driving out of business all the "banks" (the betting concerns are "like banks because money is deposited there" but "unlike banks because the chances of getting your money out were a thousand to one"). This scheme will not only give Tucker's "combine" a monopoly; it will also increase public sentiment to make the numbers racket a legal lottery and vastly increase Tucker's—and Joe's—earnings. The only problem is that the scam is "slightly illegal"—but no more so, Joe implies, than Wall Street's other activities. He dismisses a colleague's warning about a new prosecutor, Hall, insinuating that working with criminals is just business and that his own hands are not dirty because they're merely hired.

Joe does retain the vestiges of a conscience. His brother, Leo (Thomas Gomez), whom he hasn't seen in years and who sacrificed to put Joe through law school, operates one small bank, which will go broke along with the others on July 4. Against Tucker's wishes Joe warns Leo and offers to bring him into Tucker's fold, only to be met with Leo's hostile response: "I'm an honest man here, not a gangster. . . . I do my business honest and respectable." His brother scoffs: "Don't you take the nickels and dimes and pennies from people who bet just like any other crook? . . . They call this racket 'policy' because people bet their nickels on numbers instead of paying their weekly insurance premium. . . . It's all the same, all policy." According to Joe, Leo is a hypocrite, the numbers racket being no different from the racket called "insurance." Since all business is robbery, why not make it more efficient? According to Leo, Joe is a soulless, amoral shill; unlike Tucker's employees, Leo's are members of his family—closer to him, indeed, than his brother. Leo believes his "legit" brother to be more crooked than he; Joe believes all crooks are the same. As Joe later explains to an associate, Tucker lends money to those he likes and lets the rest go belly-up: "we're normal financiers." Their plan to create a monopolistic conglomerate conforms, indeed, to postwar trends among lawful corporations, which bought out or overwhelmed small businesses to increase profits and eliminate competition.[32] The trend continues: is there really much difference between Tucker's tactics and those of, say, twenty-first-century Walmart?

What happens next seems to confirm Marx and Engels's contention that capitalism degrades family relations by turning them into money relations (Marx and Engels 476): Joe tips off the police to raid Leo's bank, hoping to force him to join Tucker's combine. But instead Leo vows to quit the business—tomorrow, which will be too late to salvage his bank. "People have bets in my bank. That's a debt," he declares. He wants to be able to "look in the mirror and see my face, not [Joe's]." As becomes clear during the raid sequence, Leo is a kindhearted man who tries to spare his employees. The blocking also suggests that he may be morally superior to his brother: during the scene in which Leo vows to quit the business, for instance, he is constantly placed above Joe—reversing the arrangement of their first scene together, in which Joe tries to muscle Leo. But Leo soon echoes Joe's views. When Leo's wife reminds him that he used to own legitimate businesses, he sputters, "Real estate business: living from mortgage to mortgage, stealing credit like a thief. And the garage! . . . Three cents overcharge on every gallon of gas. . . . Well, Joe's here now. I won't have to steal pennies anymore. I'll have big crooks to steal dollars for me." Real estate, numbers, a gas station: just different forms of theft. Munby observes that Leo's speech reveals the "hallowed American space of individual private enterprise . . . to be just another form of graft" (129). But Leo's screed isn't cynical, as Munby's reading implies; rather, it expresses the Marxian dictum that private property ineluctably leads to oppression (Marx and Engels 484–85).

Meanwhile Joe woos Leo's secretary, Doris Lowery (Beatrice Pearson), asserting that her alleged innocence is a pretense, that she wants him to be wicked so that he'll bowl her over. When he admits that he would love to give her a "million-dollar ruby," she replies that he's like a magician with his "ruby words."[33] Later he resumes his blandishments, claiming that Leo planned to join the combination all along but wanted to be coerced "in order to maintain a moral superiority over me which doesn't exist. . . . He pretended to be forced. Is that what you want to do?" Lifting her and placing her on a mantelpiece, he declares that she doesn't know what she really wants. He may be correct: as we have seen, Leo's claim that his criminality is cleaner than Joe's is self-deluded, and Doris clearly enjoys consorting with the powerful, "wicked" Joe Morse. Yet Joe believes that everyone who works in the rackets is just as left-handed as he. In an earlier conversation, after Doris had told him that it's not wicked to "give and want nothing back," he answered, "It's perversion. . . . To go to great expense for something you want, that's natural. To reach out to take it—that's human, that's natural. But to get your pleasure from not taking, from cheating yourself deliberately, like my brother did today, . . . don't you see what a black thing that is for a man to do? How it is to hate yourself, your brother, to make him feel that he's guilty, that I'm guilty. Just to live, and be guilty." First articulating a fundamental American principle—that it is one's *duty* to satisfy one's appetites—as well as a prime tenet of American business—that it is wrong *not* to take a profit—Joe's speech ultimately exposes his dawning self-awareness. Beginning as a defense of his "everyone is crooked" ethos, the speech turns into a self-accusation (that by forcing Leo to admit his guilt, Joe was trying to reassure himself of his own innocence) and a confession. Joe is starting to grasp that his excuses mask a hypocrisy more dangerous than Leo's.

When Leo's bank is engulfed by the combine, its labor practices abruptly change. As one worker says to another: "See this nickel? It belongs to Tucker, and so do we." The film thus charts how, as stated in *The Communist Manifesto*, capitalism transforms workers into wage slaves (Marx and Engels 476). Whereas Leo's small-time operation made them all feel like contributors, Tucker's people might as well be working in a factory: they become estranged, as Marx argues, from the process and products of their work, as well as from other workers. Perhaps most important—as shown by the figure of the bookkeeper, Freddie Bauer (Howland Chamberlain)—each worker becomes alienated from his or her own humanity.[34] Thus, on entering Leo's bank and hearing that the profits are now channeled to Tucker, Bauer angrily quits: "I'm not your slave!" But Tucker won't let him quit, so Bauer uses the method that trapped people often employ: he becomes an informer, keeping the police apprised of Tucker's activities. After his first call to the cops, Bauer is accosted by Wally, a minion of Bill Ficco (Paul Fix), one of Tucker's competitors, who proposes that Bauer give him a list of all the banks. "I don't want to have anything to do with gangsters," says Bauer. Wally replies, "Whaddaya mean, 'gangsters'? It's business."

Wally's mock indignation echoes the protests of Joe Morse, who has all along mouthed two conflicting interpretations of his activities: that his hands are clean because he's just a lawyer, not a gangster, and that this doesn't matter anyway because all business is exploitative. His conflicted nature is represented by the phones in his office—one above his desk for legitimate business; a second phone, used for shadier activities, hidden in a drawer: right-handed and left-handed endeavors, respectively. This second phone, with which he reports to Tucker and tells the police about Leo's bank, substitutes for his hands and serves as a switching point between plans and their execution. The phone had allowed him to make a killing from a distance, but now it becomes the nexus where loyalties lapse and secrets become betrayals. Thus when Tucker's slinky wife informs Joe that his phone is probably tapped, he realizes his "hands" are dirty, his words potentially incriminating. As Joe slowly approaches his desk, the camera, placed just behind the drawer containing his phone, seems to entice him to make a call. Picking it up gingerly, as if it might explode, he hears the telltale click that means someone is listening. These scenes of Bauer's whistle-blowing, Ficco's request for lists of names, and Joe's tapped phone eerily forecast the blacklist period. Indeed, the phone-tapping device is not merely a prediction: during the making of *Force of Evil*, Polonsky's phone was tapped by the FBI![35]

Now Joe is further conflicted: he wants Doris, who represents the better part of himself, but can't truly believe in her (or his own) innocence; he wants to save Leo but can't do so without betraying Tucker and endangering himself. But after Bauer's snitching gets Doris arrested again, she breaks off with Joe, telling him that Leo will "die of this. . . . Well, I don't wish to die of loving you." Delivering these words in a phone booth, she exposes Joe's hypocrisy by invoking the instrument that enables it. Returning to his office in the dark, Joe walks toward matching doors that symbolize his choices: stay or quit. Peeking through the skylight of the right-handed door, he views his office on the left, where an FBI agent is using Joe's own phone to report on him. After the agent leaves, Joe opens his safe, removes his money and a gun, then trudges alone down a deserted Wall St. But it's too late for Leo: Bauer has set him up to be captured by Ficco. As Leo is taken away, Polonsky dissolves from him to Joe: the older brother will die for the younger one's sins.

Ficco meets with Tucker and agrees to join Tucker's combination but wants Joe removed. Interrupting their meeting, Joe learns that Leo has been killed, his body dumped in the Hudson River. Suddenly the phone rings, but nobody answers—at first. Then, as Joe recounts their criminal schemes, he lifts the receiver so that whoever is on the line can hear him implicate Tucker and Ficco in the murders. Ficco fires his gun and the lights go out. A shot of Joe crawling across the room cuts to a shot of the phone; the next shot shows a man, his features immured in shadows, creeping toward the door. Since we have just seen Joe crawling, we assume it is he; Ficco shoots the man and is killed himself. As he dies, a pair of feet kick the gun from his hand and a hand picks up the phone. Only then do we see that the survivor is Joe Morse, who tells the listener he is turning himself in. The shadows imply, of course, that Joe, despite his lawyerly excuses, is indistinguishable from Ficco or Tucker. All are guilty of capital crimes.

In a final gesture of penitence Joe descends a long series of steps ("it was like going down to the bottom of the world") to retrieve Leo's body. A shot of him against the wall, then beneath the George Washington Bridge, illustrates his diminishment. In voice-over he speaks: "He was dead—and I felt I had killed him.

I turned back to give myself up . . . because if a man's life can be lived so long and come out this way—like rubbish—then something was horrible and had to be ended one way or another, and I decided to help."[36] Though anchored in a specific location in New York, the descent is also symbolic: tunneling into his conscience, Joe finds his dead brother—the one he helped to kill—as well as the old Joe Morse. The bridge further suggests that Joe, the "legitimate" lawyer, crossed to the other side by working with a gangster; Leo, the good-hearted crook, crossed back over to appeal to his brother's loyalty and morality. Each one forced the other to face his own self-deception: thus, as Polonsky asserted, in this film "every act of love is also an act of betrayal" ("Abraham Polonsky" 488). Perhaps most ironic of all: Garfield's character becomes what Garfield died trying *not* to be: an informer.

The personal story is political. That is, although Joe's concluding speech (created to satisfy the Breen Office) suggests that the special prosecutor will clean everything up, the rest of the film implies that neither gangsters nor slimy lawyers are the real problem. Rather, it argues, the fault lies with capitalism itself, which is not only criminal but inevitably leads to other crimes. This is not a critique of American ideals so much as an indictment of their perversion: the numbers racket baldly dupes those gullible enough to believe that they alone would think of "776" on July 4, but "legitimate" businesses cloak their thefts more cleverly behind phony patriotic slogans about free enterprise.

The City under the City

A small band of men, each with some extraordinary power, team up for an important mission. They plan with meticulous care, each member playing his assigned role. Because their organization aims to challenge a sovereign power, the plan must remain secret. One mistake, however, undermines the mission, and one member betrays the others; the team unravels and one or more members die.

This plot could be that of a superhero tale or medieval quest romance, but it also describes the stories of a noir subgenre that emerged in 1950: the heist picture.[37] Films such as *The Killers* and *Criss Cross* feature collaborative robberies as part of their stories, but the true heist film places a "caper" or collective theft at its center. One of the first such films, *The Asphalt Jungle* challenges the emerging law-and-order ethos by enabling viewers to empathize with a gang executing a jewel robbery.[38] Although direct leftist critiques were rapidly vanishing from Hollywood (*Try and Get Me!* and *The Prowler*, the two last blasts of the Left, were released in 1951), Huston's film shows that anti–status quo messages were still possible if camouflaged in a pro-law-and-order framework. Released between the initial HUAC hearings and the second round, *The Asphalt Jungle* not only smuggles in critiques of corporate crime and red-baiting; it also dissects the ethics of secrecy and betrayal that lay at the heart of the blacklist era. J. P. Telotte asserts that the heist film questions the dominant culture's "efforts to codify, to impose conformity, . . . to eliminate the enigma of individuality from society" ("Fatal Capers" 165). But *Asphalt* is less about individuality than about teamwork, loyalty, and honor—paramount values in societies under repression.

The gang's mastermind, Doc Riedenschneider (Sam Jaffe), just released from prison, recruits Louie Ciavelli (Anthony Caruso), Gus Minissi (James Whitmore), and Sterling Hayden's Dix Handley for the caper. Two others are involved as well: Cobby (Marc Lawrence), a high-strung bookie who provides seed money, and crooked lawyer Emmerich. This team plays a high-stakes game.[39] Moreover, like most gangs in heist films, they display the characteristics of a secret society, as brilliantly anatomized by Simmel. Such groups, he writes, create a "second world alongside the manifest world" (330)—or, as the film has it, a "city under the city." The secret plan endows each member with "inner property"—an enormous boon for these lower- or working-class men, who possess little tangible property. Yet secrets also carry the seeds of betrayal, as each one contains a "tension that is dissolved in the moment of its revelation" (Simmel 333). The secret, that is, simultaneously exists to prevent betrayal *and* creates the possibility for it: a secret at once unites and divides those who hold it. Hence, as Telotte notes, multiple double crosses "are the ultimate law" of heist movies ("Fatal Capers" 165): the secrets in these pictures seem to exist *in order to be betrayed*. Simmel speculates that secret societies such as criminal gangs are a by-product of the money economy itself: modern money's compressibility, abstractness, and "effect-at-a-distance" promote alienation that fosters the growth of secret societies (335). Further, Simmel suggests, "the secret society emerges everywhere as the counterpart of despotism and police restriction" (347). Thus, as HUAC cracked down on Hollywood and the red scare swept through America, subversive groups were pushed underground. The repression of radical organizations created criminals by relabeling once-lawful activities as illicit. Just as secret societies in the noncinematic world bubbled up like the return of the repressed, so heist pictures emerged when direct challenges to capitalism and law and order became taboo. And yet, as Simmel astutely observes, secret societies often become a "counter-image of the official world" and end up imitating the structures and values of the society they had aimed to repudiate (360). As gangs fall apart, solidarity is supplanted by greed, loyalty by betrayal, teamwork by retribution. In *The Asphalt Jungle* not only does the underworld both mirror the legit world and permeate it; ultimately, the film suggests, there is no difference between the two.

The film's opening minutes establish the setting in an unnamed midwestern city where crime is said to be out of control yet where police track Dix as he walks the streets and enters Gus's "American Food" diner (situated next door to the "Pilgrim House").[40] Dix's rap sheet paints him as a career small-time criminal. But even if he is guilty of some recent holdups, he is less corrupt than Lt. Ditrich (Barry Kelley), who is on the take from bookie joints (including Cobby's) and under pressure by Commissioner Hardy (John McIntire) to solve the crimes. The police seek Riedenschneider, but he eludes them long enough to introduce his plan to Cobby; during their conversation Dix, who owes Cobby $2,300, interrupts to ask Cobby for more time. Later, when Dix complains to Gus that owing money to the slimy bookie damages his "self-respect," Gus lends him $1,000; a call to his friend Louie—whose tiny apartment houses him, his wife, and baby— yields another thousand. Soon Dix is visited by Doll Conovan (Jean Hagen), who has lost her job and apartment; he agrees to put her up at his place, no strings attached. Clearly these criminals are actuated by humane values such as loyalty and generosity. Yet they are also trapped: Gus in his seedy diner, Louie in his cramped apartment, Dix by his gambling addiction.[41] They are thus ripe for the promise of quick money.

Doc outlines his plan to Emmerich: $1 million in jewelry is waiting to be taken from Belletiere's; all he needs are the right men and some seed money. Because "men get greedy," the "helpers"—a "boxman" (safecracker), driver, and "hooligan"—will each receive a flat wage rather than a cut of the take: $25,000; $10,000; and $15,000, respectively. Reynold Humphries aptly notes that this scene resembles nothing so much as a corporate board meeting "from which the workers and their representatives have been excluded": the proletariat are neither involved in the planning nor partake of the profits (237). The class difference between the owners of the means of production and the workers extends even to the underworld. As mere "functional units" in a "Fordist division of labor" (Mason 99), the boxman (Louie), driver (Gus), and hooligan (Dix) (their descriptions indicate their low status) become alienated workers. Doc and Emmerich, however, share a taste for elegant apparel and young women (Emmerich's mistress, Angela, is played by a ravishing young Marilyn Monroe). Huston also provides parallels between Emmerich and the other criminals: he has an invalid wife and

The heist gang plans a "left-handed endeavor" in *The Asphalt Jungle. Kobal Collection / Art Resource, NY.*

Louie a sick kid; both Emmerich and Cobby wear bow ties (Humphries 237). Although the underworld and the "legit" world mirror each other, the lower-class criminals are more honorable than the smug, slippery Emmerich.[42]

This "antiphrasis" (J. Hirsch 85) is most obvious in the case of Dix. According to Doc, hooligans are necessary but repellent figures, and Louie declares that they all have "a screw loose somewhere." Yet we have already seen that Dix, though ragged and gruff, is kind. What drives him is not greed but a nostalgic dream involving a "tall, black colt" named Corncracker that he rode back on his ancestral Kentucky farm, Hickory Wood. Dix's obsession with gambling on horse races is the residue of his pastoral fantasy: he hopes to use horses to make a killing and buy back the farm. When he gets there, he tells Doll, the first thing he'll do is "take a bath in the crick, and get the city dirt off me." His American dream is not of Franklinesque self-invention but a romantic, Emersonian vision of recovering his aboriginal self through nature and of undoing the asphalt jungle's contamination. Self-deluded though he is, Dix is honorable (he pays Cobby back) and strong; that's why Doll, who "never had a proper home," loves him. Unlike the lovers in the lamming noirs, then, this pitiable pair turn to crime not as a path to upward mobility but as a road to rediscover a lost innocence and sense of belonging.[43]

Doc carefully outlines his meticulously conceived plan to his crew. Similar planning scenes appear in every heist film to emphasize that to succeed, the men must behave like machines, as if they were, indeed, working in a factory. Although the planning scene's single-source overhead lighting casts shadows on the men's faces and doubts on their success, once they enter the jewelry store by way of a manhole—"the city under the city"—the robbery comes off almost perfectly, except that a security guard, alerted by alarms going off nearby, comes to the door as the men are escaping. Dix punches him; the man's gun falls and shoots Louie in the gut. With this mishap the scheme begins to unravel. In fact, as Simmel would predict, the gang's solidarity had started to disintegrate even earlier. The loose thread is Emmerich, who is broke and plans to double-cross the others, take the jewels, and disappear. But when Doc and Dix meet him and his co-conspirator, a private eye named Brannom (Brad Dexter), afterward, they don't buy Emmerich's story. Brannom pulls a gun and wounds Dix before he himself is killed.

Soon the police arrive at Emmerich's house, inquiring about Brannom, whose body was found in the river; Emmerich claims he was with his mistress that night. After they leave, he reassures his wife with the words about "left-handed endeavor" quoted above. In their proximate context, as I have noted, the words seem a feeble alibi for amorality, but they express red noir's larger theme that crime and capitalism, crime and law enforcement, are not just mirror images but symbiotic enterprises. About to be arrested, Emmerich kills himself. Things go further downhill from there: Louie dies from his wounds and Cobby, after Ditrich slaps him around, turns stool pigeon, leading to Gus's arrest.[44] So much for solidarity.

That leaves only Dix and Doc, who has the jewels but no way to turn them into money. Yet he is mostly upset that all his planning has gone for nothing ("What can you do against blind accident?") and blames himself for not killing Emmerich: "Greed made me blind." Far from greedy, Dix gives Doc $1,000—but he never has a chance to spend it. Lingering in a diner to ogle a dancing teenaged girl, Doc is arrested. The brilliant, meticulous planner is foiled not by blind accident but by simple human weakness. Yet he scarcely matches the picture of criminals painted by Commissioner Hardy, who delivers a speech to the press after Doc's (and Ditrich's) arrest. "People are being cheated, robbed, murdered, raped. . . . It's the same in every city of the modern world. But suppose we had no police force, good or bad? . . . The battle's finished, the jungle wins. The predatory beasts take over." Most dangerous of all, he insists, is Dix, a "hooligan, a man without human feeling or human mercy." His words ring hollow, for we already know that Dix is generous and loyal (indeed, if anyone seems to lack human feeling or mercy, it's the commissioner, with his brusque manner and obsession with order). A dissolve to Dix's final moments further undercuts Hardy's pronouncement. Although (according to the doctor who diagnoses him) Dix "hasn't got enough blood left in him to keep a chicken alive," he makes it back to Hickory Wood, only to collapse in a pasture. In the film's powerful concluding shots the camera rests on the ground next to Dix's body; his unseeing eyes stare up at the sky while a mare and colt nuzzle him. A long shot shows his tiny figure dwarfed by the vast expanse. Dix has made it home—but it's too late to wash off the city dirt.

The film implies, however, that Dix's pastoral dream, his vision of an unspoiled America, has been besmirched not by crime but by urbanization and the cynicism of people like Emmerich. And when we recall the rapid collapse of Huston's Committee for the First Amendment after the first HUAC hearings, *The Asphalt Jungle* seems to reflect his loss of faith in collective action. The gang has power *only* as a group, but fear and mistrust, along with the cash nexus, break them up. Even so, the film's criminals—like those labor agitators who became criminals only when the laws changed—are more honorable than Ditrich, the sole policeman we see up close. Above all, the film affirms Doll's touchingly unconditional love for Dix. They are more victims than villains, as are Louie and Gus, disenfranchised lower-class urbanites who lack even Dix's nostalgic vision. The city has borrowed nature's teeth and claws, and in this jungle those without education or resources inevitably end up as prey.

The Blacklist Disguised

Leftist filmmakers were themselves prey for red-baiters, greedy studio heads, reactionary politicians, and their own peers. If Dalton Trumbo's placating 1970 pronouncement that "there were only victims" (qtd. in Navasky 371) in the blacklist period failed to distinguish between those who stood on principle and those who elected to save their careers, it also implied that the artists didn't fight back. But the blacklistees did appeal to civil liberties organizations (to little avail) and endeavored to continue their careers. Of course, given that they were unable to work, it was difficult for them to respond through cinema itself. Yet one radical director, Cyril Endfield, made two films in 1950 and 1951 that attacked the blacklist as explicitly as was possible. The first, *The Underworld Story,* has been virtually ignored in noir criticism; I analyze the second, *Try and Get Me!* in the conclusion. It is remarkable that Endfield was able to get these brave films made, even as independent productions, for both movies criticize the blacklist and indict the press for contributing to the red scare by pandering to readers' worst impulses and serving as mouthpieces for reactionary corporate interests.[45]

When reporter Mike Reese (Dan Duryea) writes a story causing District Attorney Munsey (Michael O'Shea) to be shot, Reese is blacklisted by newspaper magnate E. J. Stanton (Herbert Marshall). Unable to find a job with another city paper, he borrows money from gangster Carl Durham (future blacklistee Howard Da Silva) and buys a share in the small-town *Lakeville Sentinel.* Reese, however, is no hero but a cynical operator who lies about his motives to co-owner Cathy (Gale Storm). Then a break comes: Stanton's daughter-in-law, Diane, is found murdered in Lakeville. To Cathy she was a friend, but to Reese she is just a story, a lucrative one: he immediately sets up a wire-service exclusive and starts to milk it for all it's worth, especially after Molly Rankin, an African American servant who pawned Diane's jewelry the day of her murder, becomes the prime suspect.[46] Molly appears at the *Sentinel* office and appeals to Cathy and Reese; he persuades her to turn herself in and tell her story to reporters and to Munsey, who, he assures her, is a "pal of mine." The shadows on Reese, however, imply that he's not to be trusted, and in fact he is maneuvering to get the $25,000 reward for her capture. He even tells Munsey she is guilty but cautions him about speaking by phone: "Don't you think your phone's being tapped, just like everybody else's around here?" The comment doesn't make sense in the context of the film (it is too early in the story for Reese's phone to be tapped) and was likely dropped in to remind viewers of the real-life surveillance occurring at the time. Munsey refuses to give Reese the reward, but Reese doesn't give up: he forms a Save Molly Committee, enlists townspeople (including Mrs. Eldridge, the banker's wife), and solicits donations.[47] He even hires expensive lawyer Becker (Roland Winters) to defend her. But Reese doesn't give a damn about Molly; he plans to use her "human interest" story to make money and split it with Becker.

Immediately the *Sentinel* starts running stories with headlines such as "Lakeville Community Doubts Rankin's Guilt." We more than doubt it, for we learn early on that E. J.'s son, Clark (Gar Moore), murdered his wife out of jealousy. Though appalled and angry after Clark's confession, the senior Stanton vows to save his son. But that shouldn't be difficult, Clark assures him: "Who'll believe . . . the word of a nigger against ours?" His views are echoed by the town's reactionary elements, represented by a character called The Major. And so Stanton smears Molly in his newspapers with headlines such as "An Eye for an Eye" and "State Claims Airtight Case."[48] Even Becker believes that "the verdict's in. If she was white, she wouldn't stand a chance." Thus, Reese's defense committee initially rakes in donations and attracts volunteers, but after a cabal of bankers and businessmen exerts covert pressure, donations dry up, committee members resign, and a rally for Molly is canceled. This, we see, is how blacklists work: nothing is out in the open, and money talks silently. Reese and Becker approach Molly with a deal: plead guilty to manslaughter and get a light sentence (so they can salvage the remaining committee funds). Becker will argue that Molly killed Diane in justified rage after her boss called her lazy and shiftless. "Think of yourself," Reese advises her. "Like you did when you were ready to sell me for $25,000?" she retorts. "That's a high price for a human being. I had a great-grandfather who was sold for much less." In rejecting her commodification, she exposes Reese's slimy tactics. He returns to the *Sentinel* office to find the printing press smashed. Parky, the printer, comments, "Looks like they're burning witches again." Turn Molly from black to red, alter Becker's advice from pleading guilty to naming names, and the allusions are as clear as a mountain lake.

Molly's scolding prompts a change of heart for Reese, but on learning of evidence exonerating her, he foolishly shares it with Clark Stanton and agrees to meet him at his office. Clark, however, has hired Durham to silence Reese in exchange for a lifetime of positive publicity from the Stanton newspapers. Extortion, blackmail, and murder? Just business. The now-righteous Reese meets with Stanton and his staff and pleads, "Here's your chance to make those words on the Stanton mastheads about ethics and truth really mean something." But Stanton refuses, and as he departs, Reese reads a wall engraving: "This building is dedicated to the cause of true industrial freedom and liberty under the law." The words are a direct blast at the real-life press's rush to judgment and its craven yielding to red-baiters and corporate flunkies ("industrial freedom" refers to the freedom to strike, the very freedom that aroused Hollywood's right wing). But Reese's reflection is also visible beneath the words, which apply to him—the man who used murder as a publicity stunt and slanted the news as much as the Stantons, albeit for a better cause.

Durham, now working for Stanton, abducts Reese, but Cathy convinces Munsey—who had dismissed Reese's panicked phone call about Stanton as just another gimmick—to send the police after them. The police fool Durham's guards by pretending to be drunks (in another nod to the history of American race relations, the fake drunks sing "John Brown's Body"). But despite repeated beatings, Reese won't reveal whether he has told anyone else what he knows. Growing queasy at the violence, the elder Stanton asks Durham, "What are you?" Durham answers, "Same as you, only smarter." He thus reiterates a primary tenet of red noir: capitalists and criminals are the same, except that "legitimate" capitalists hide their depredations behind fancy houses and fine words. In the end E. J. Stanton shoots his son as he tries to escape, the truth comes out, and Reese is hailed as a hero. Yet this denouement matters less than the film's courageous stand against the co-optation of the press.[49] *The Underworld Story* demonstrates compellingly how free speech and equality under the law—values codified in America's founding documents—have been twisted into excuses for profit-taking. Truth is a matter of what we now call "spin," and accusations require no proof so long as they are repeated frequently and loudly enough. Public opinion is easily molded by appeals to fear, and corporations, including movie studios, will do anything to preserve profits. Hence the film's title, which initially seems a misnomer, is apt: as Humphries points out, the "underworld" refers not to ordinary crooks but to the "life-style, values and activities of the wealthy bourgeoisie" (235) who scapegoat the innocent and powerless to cover up their own crimes.[50] They are, the film argues, no better than slave owners.

It is now clear that red noir's makers were brave, committed artists who challenged American citizens and institutions to live the values they professed to endorse: an abhorrence of tyranny, freedom of speech and the press, equality under the law for all classes and races. They defended the dignity and humanity of the poor and disenfranchised and the rights of the working class to earn a decent living without being exploited. That these artists were harassed, jailed, humiliated, blacklisted, and hounded to death testifies to the power of fear and the fickleness of public opinion. Just as guilty as the witch hunters, however, were the studio heads: it was they, after all, who perpetrated the blacklist. The HUAC hearings and the Hollywood witch hunt are black spots in American history that, we sigh in relief, are safely consigned to the past. If only that were true. In fact, among the most striking features of red noir is that its challenge to uphold American values remains viable today. Substitute Muslims for Communists, and the similarities between 1951 and 2011 are striking. As I write, Americans are again beset by hysteria about "Socialists" and cowed by reactionaries spewing lies in the media about progressive citizens. Most chilling of all is that since September 11, 2001, we have replicated the violations of privacy and liberty that occurred sixty years ago. It is these violations, red noir reminds us, that are truly "un-American activities."

Conclusion
American Nightmares

"After Hiroshima, after the death of Roosevelt, and after the [HUAC] investiga-
tions, only then did one begin to see the complete unreality of the American
dream," observed director Joseph Losey in the late 1970s (qtd. in Ciment 96). As
is now clear, many, though not all, noir filmmakers shared his views. For example, certain vet noirs depict traumatized ex-GIs healing their wounds and fashioning new selves; a few jazz films hold out hope for interracial harmony and for
self-making through improvisation; women writers and directors modeled
female empowerment through creative labor. Other films noir criticize not the
values themselves but their perversion. Thus, for instance, *Body and Soul* endorses upward mobility and indicates that honest labor and the support of family
and community may enable a striver to fight capitalist exploiters—but only
through extraordinary sacrifice and tenacity. *The Underworld Story* dramatizes
how a free press can be a powerful instrument to combat corruption.

For the majority of noir's characters, however, the American Dream is a chimera. The noir canon shows that the American ideals of individual liberty and
self-invention are often at odds with true community. Hence, *Hollow Triumph*
implies that radical individualism engenders a world of alienated monads indifferent to each other's pain. The displaced, impoverished characters in the car
films—Bowie and Keechie, Al Roberts—find only small oases of freedom in the
autos that, ultimately, fail to provide security or social mobility. The film *Nightmare Alley* dramatizes how the pursuit of happiness is transformed into a shallow
consumerism by means of a therapeutic ethos that supplies cheap but ultimately
unsatisfying solutions to existential questions. Red noirs such as *Force of Evil*
depict capitalism as criminal exploitation. In general, noir's ordinary citizens are
at the mercy of powerful forces they have no chance of resisting.

I conclude this book by examining two late noirs by former Communists—
Endfield's *Try and Get Me!* and Losey's *The Prowler,* both from 1951—that powerfully depict how the Dream has been voided. In the first, working stiff Howard

Tyler, hemmed in by poverty, becomes a criminal and then a scapegoat for his community's rage and resentment. In the second, policeman Webb Garwood is enslaved to "false values"—a belief that material wealth is all that matters (Losey, qtd. in Ciment 100). Driven by a "monstrous, all-consuming class envy," he is a portrait of the American striver gone sour (Krutnik, "Living" 62). Their American nightmares drive each protagonist to a lonely, humiliating death.

Groceries

Made and released by Robert Stillman Productions, another small, independent company, *Try and Get Me!* was Endfield's final American film before his forced emigration to escape the blacklist.[1] Adapted by Jo Pagano from his novel *The Condemned*, *Try and Get Me!* (also released under the title *The Sound of Fury*) not only indicts the capitalist system that discards Howard Tyler; like *The Underworld Story*, it also condemns the press for fueling mass hysteria. In this film free enterprise and freedom of the press have become cloaks for the rapacious pursuit of money and power.[2]

The film opens with a blind street preacher barking about the world's evils, urging listeners to "change your directions! . . . Look ye blind that ye may see. . . . I can see a better world," he promises, but warns that "whatsoever a man soweth, that shall he also reap." He is ignored and knocked down by crowds hurtling blindly toward who knows what. If his words clearly apply to Howard Tyler (Frank Lovejoy), a man afflicted with moral blindness who certainly reaps what he sows, they also fit columnist Gil Stanton (Richard Carlson), who learns too late that words can be weapons.

Out of work and increasingly bitter and desperate, Tyler gives his son, Tommy, fifty cents to attend a ballgame, even though the money is needed for food. His pregnant wife, Judy (Kathleen Ryan), voices her frustration at "begging for groceries, begging for doctors. Is that what we came to California for?" The embodiment of the American Dream of westward expansion, self-reinvention, and unlimited possibility, California has become a giant net enclosing their prospects. But a way out presents itself at the bowling alley that night, when Howard meets Jerry Slocum (former Communist Lloyd Bridges), a vain, domineering man with a glib line of patter, who forces a snort on the abstinent Howard and whose leering war anecdotes make Howard feel inferior (Howard never saw combat). Later, Slocum prances shirtless in his room, combing his hair, while boasting that all women are partial to "green"; soon he has Howard stroking his shirt and buttoning his cuff links for him (the homoerotic undercurrent here is unmistakable). But when the "jobs" Jerry had mentioned turn out to be small-time holdups, Howard blanches and Jerry grows surly: "You guys kill me. They kick ya in the teeth and the more they kick ya the better ya like it. Whaddaya lookin' for, handouts?" He throws ten bucks at Tyler and sneers, "Live!" The low angle on Jerry under-lines his dominance over Howard, who meekly yields: after all, he only has to drive the car.

Though Howard stays in the car while Jerry robs a mom-and-pop filling sta-tion / grocery store, we don't. We watch the psychopathic Slocum pistol-whip the attendant and leave the elderly female proprietor in tears. Afterward, Jerry is cocky, Howard ambivalent. But the latter's mixed feelings evaporate after he picks up Tommy and Judy from a neighbor's, where they are watching television. Holding a large bag of groceries, he promises to buy a television set and pretends that his wad of bills is an advance on his salary at the cannery. Unable to partici-pate in the consumer society that proffers brand-new TVs and burnished fruit as proofs of success, Howard, like so many noir protagonists, seeks in crime an av-enue to the glittering prosperity promised by advertisements. Before long he is urging Judy to buy expensive shoes (even while warning Tommy that he might "put somebody's eyes out" with his toy gun). Emasculated by poverty, he briefly feels empowered by the money the stickups bring, but he purchases this bogus manhood at the cost of submitting to Jerry's increasingly wild schemes.

Next we meet the other major characters, attending a barbecue at the well-appointed home of newspaper columnist Gil Stanton. His editor, Hal Clenden-ning (future blacklistee Art Smith), offers Stanton a bonus to write a feature about the raft of recent holdups. "You mean money!" Stanton enthuses. "You know that might make a petty robbery very significant!" Hal reminds him that he has a big following and that his byline will "really sell some papers." Later, in front of the grocery store / filling station that Jerry robbed, Hal and Gil decide to attri-bute the crimes to an Eastern gang: "that always makes good copy," notes Hal. "By the time I'm through," Stanton boasts, "this town will think it's been invaded." But Stanton's guest, Italian professor Vito Simone (Renzo Cesana), wonders if such stories aren't "destructive to public health" and a "distortion of journalistic values." Clendenning answers, "Selling newspapers is . . . the way I make my liv-ing." Simone's lectures, although they serve as the film's conscience, are intru-sively didactic, spelling out themes that the action and visuals make clear enough.[3] For example, as the men speak, the large sign advertising GROCERIES is visible behind them. Groceries were the reason Howard participated in the robbery, and they are Hal's ostensible motive for trumping up violence in his paper. Yet we've already seen that Stanton, with his deluxe barbecue, luxurious home, and bourgeois guests, has no trouble providing for his family; instead of groceries, he feeds his audience sensationalistic stories that fuel his ego.

They also boost that of Slocum, who reads with relish the headline about his robbery ("Hoodlums Expert Gunmen"). One more big score, he assures Howard, and they'll be on "easy street." But this caper—the kidnaping of Donald Miller (Carl Kent), the scion of the town's wealthiest family—is a large step up from the penny-ante stickups Jerry has been executing; Howard has misgivings but quashes them for the promise of a big payoff. The two abduct Miller as he walks to his fancy convertible and force him to drive to a secluded spot. On the drive Jerry enviously comments, "You guys sure treat yourselves all right, don't you?" They tie Miller's hands and gag him, planning to hold him in a barn and demand ransom from his parents. But after they encounter a trysting couple at the allegedly never-visited barn, Jerry panics, binds Miller's feet, and rolls him down a rock-covered hill. Then Jerry brains the poor man with a boulder as Howard screams, "You never said you were gonna kill him!" The scene's blocking—Howard in the shot's foreground as Jerry clubs Miller—makes it appear that Jerry is beating *Howard,* whose grimacing face indicates that he is experiencing the pain of death and whose tightly closed eyes invoke the street preacher's words about moral blindness. Dazed and disheveled, Howard returns home to his sleeping wife, who tells him of her "most wonderful dream." She was in the hospital having her baby, who said, "Daddy." Then she went shopping and bought a dress. Her dream (and Howard's) of domesticity and consumer prosperity has driven him to this sorry plight; but that dream is over, and their nightmare has begun.

If the night-for-night murder sequence is painful to watch, what comes next is even more excruciating. Jerry sets up a double date with his girlfriend, Velma (Adele Jergens), pairing Howard with Velma's friend, a lonely hairdresser named Hazel (Katherine Locke). Velma reflects Jerry's values: she too thinks he is "nature's gift to women" and cares not a whit where his money comes from, so long as he spends it on her. Hazel, a pitiful sad sack, would like nothing better than to settle down with a quiet man like Howard. The men plan to drive to a neighboring town to mail the ransom note, believing that the women will deflect any suspicion about the two strangers. As Howard mails the note, he recalls the murder: its images dissolve over his face, and Jerry's blows pound like his own heart, as musical spikes emphasize his horror. The rest of the evening only deepens Howard's agony: in a nightclub he is made the butt of a comedian's jokes, and this sequence—Howard's nightmare alley—is presented in dizzying canted angles that reflect Howard's disorientation and despair (as well as the drunkenness that has become chronic since his involvement with Jerry). Howard Tyler, it seems, has become a geek. The next morning he returns to Hazel's drab apartment, where he listens to her read the newspaper story about Miller's murder. She believes that "people who do things like this should be . . ." Howard protests that "people do things they don't . . . mean." When she finds Miller's gold tie-clip in Howard's pants (engraved with DM), he blurts out a confession: "I didn't want to take that, Jerry made me. Why did he have to kill him?!" He begins to strangle Hazel, who swears she won't tell. "I've never been in trouble before, I don't know what to do! . . . Oh, Judy," he cries, his hands over his eyes. With Howard temporarily blind, Hazel runs to the police, who await him (along with a horde of gapers) when he finally goes home. Just before he arrives, we cut to Judy and Tommy with a neighbor woman, who complains, "People who can't afford children shouldn't have them." These are the kind of small-minded, self-righteous folks responsible for what is about to happen.

But there are two people delighted with the turn of events: Stanton and Clendenning. The crime has sold a lot of papers. Prof. Simone isn't impressed, however, and warns Stanton that his "direct appeal to the emotionalism of [his] readers . . . is wrong; as a journalist you have great responsibility." Even the sheriff, worried about the possibility of a lynching, asks him to tone it down. Everyone else, however, is proud of him: the mayor congratulates Stanton for his "public service," and Hal announces that they have a big "job ahead of us here, cleaning up this town." No longer just reporting the news, they are creating it; no mere accusers, they have become judges.

Though Stanton is deaf to voices of moderation, he does hear one voice—that of Judy, who comes to his house to plead for his help, standing in a doorway that encloses her in a box even tinier than her husband's cell. At first unmoved, Stanton thaws as she reads Howard's pathetic letter to her. "I'm guilty and I deserve to die," he writes. "And I would die peacefully if I knew you would forget me and forgive me for what I've done to you. You were a good girl, and you deserve something better." He admits his part in the robberies, then writes, "I've been having bad headaches and bad dreams. . . . I'm sorry for everything, sorry for you and Tommy. I'm sorry for Donald Miller and his mother and father." When Judy can't continue, Stanton finishes: "I didn't know Jerry was going to kill him. . . . I'm glad it is all over and I want to die." Unfortunately, producer Robert Stillman wasn't content to let these powerful words stand alone, so Simone enters

to inveigh against hatred and declare that "if a man becomes a criminal, sometimes his environment is defective." Violence is not an individual condition but a
disease caused by "moral and social breakdown. This is the real problem. . . . And
this must be solved by reason, not by emotion, with understanding, not hate."[4]

Stanton now realizes his responsibility, but it's too late; headlines such as
"Brutal Kidnap Murder May Go Unpunished" have already done their work. As
a crowd forms near the jail, we are shown a montage of hands honking car horns
and a throng of furious, shouting faces. The sheriff remarks to Stanton, "Well,
you got your party, all right. How do you like it?" Stanton and his "yellow rag"
have incited a riot, and when the sheriff tries to address the swelling crowd—"In
a democracy there is no place for mob violence!"—a group of men tear down the
loudspeaker. "Are you passin' laws against justice?" one man shouts. These riot-
ers can hear nothing but their own rage, and they vent it by singling out others
who have done the same. Rather than rectify the inequities that have victimized
Howard, or take meaningful political action, they howl for a lynching—which,
the film suggests, is merely the uglier face of the neighborly competition that im-
pels them to best the Joneses by buying a better TV set. Eventually Stanton, jail
bars slashing across his face, apologizes to Tyler, the bars indicating not only that
he is powerless to stem the tide but that he shares Howard's guilt. The mob bowls
over the guards, bursts through the doors and rushes upstairs to the cells, grab-
bing Slocum—who meets their fury with his own—and Howard, who yields to
them as passively as he did to Jerry. Then we cut to Tommy, waking from a nightmare; "Everything's going to be all right," Judy assures him. Not for Howard: he
has been lynched.

The lynching scenes were a major concern of the Breen Office, which insisted
that there be a "voice of morality" present; the sheriff and Simone serve this purpose (Breen to Stillman). Even so, *Try and Get Me!* is as powerful an indictment
of the mob mentality as Fritz Lang's more-famous *Fury*, which appeared in the
mid-1930s, a period much more receptive to progressive message pictures. Indeed, Endfield's film has a broader sweep: like *The Underworld Story*, it attacks
capitalism as well—not just for discarding people like the Tylers but also for
commodifying the news and tainting the freedom of the press. Like other films
of the period, such as Billy Wilder's searing *Ace in the Hole*, *Try and Get Me!*
excoriates the media for inflaming emotions and appealing to people's worst instincts. Clendenning and Stanton use words criminally, never caring who is victimized by what they write: crime is just a commodity to them. Although Howard
Tyler deserves blame for his loss of moral bearings and terrible choices, the film

bravely dissects the social forces responsible as well: the neighbors who deem him a weakling for his inability to feed his family, the justice system that fails him, the economic conditions that render him incapable of resisting Slocum's enticements. Howard is guilty, but his community is also culpable. One of the film's strongest ironies is that the same neighbors who offer no helping hand to the Tylers are able to band together for a collective activity: the murder of one of their kind. Howard may be blind, but they are blind and deaf.

Behind these broad statements lurks another, more specific challenge. *Try and Get Me!* is a protest against the Hollywood blacklist and Communist witch hunt. No, former reds such as Endfield, Bridges, and Smith weren't literally lynched; they were only ostracized, humiliated, and denied their livelihoods. But the parallels are clear enough. *Try and Get Me!* blames not merely the Hollywood reactionaries who encouraged the witch hunt with their smears but also the clamoring masses who believed their sensationalistic stories and, most of all, the studio heads who, like Hal Clendenning, cared more for profits than for people.

The Cost of Living

According to disgruntled cop Webb Garwood (Van Heflin) everybody has an "angle." Talent doesn't matter; what counts are "breaks." He wants money but doesn't want to work for it. "I'd rather be one of those guys who shows up around ten in the morning, after having a big argument with himself over whether he'll drive the station wagon today or the convertible," he tells Susan Gilvray (Evelyn Keyes). Garwood feels he has been denied what is rightfully his: doesn't the American Dream say that everyone has an equal right to a piece of the pie? What Garwood forgets is the cost of living: that actions have consequences and that a right comes with obligations. Hence, according to director Joseph Losey, *The Prowler* (originally titled *The Cost of Living*) is about "false values": the idea that "100,000 bucks, a Cadillac, and a blonde" are the "*sine qua non* of American life . . . and it didn't matter how you got them" (qtd. in Ciment 100). To dramatize these values, he, along with blacklisted screenwriters Hugo Butler and (uncredited) Dalton Trumbo, created Garwood, who, as Reynold Humphries observes, is "the most subtle and far-reaching representation of the relations between masculine self-assurance and class resentment Hollywood has given us" (238). Garwood is a monster; but the film suggests that his appetites are nourished by "a mercenary and materialistic society" (Krutnik, "Living" 62): he differs from others only in degree.

Though the Breen Office objected to the film's "extremely low moral tone, with emphasis on almost animal-like instincts and passions" (they recommended that the leads' attraction be "one of love, rather than one of lust"), the shooting style and mise-en-scène are just as responsible as the script for the film's creeping sense of doom (Breen to Spiegel). *The Prowler* uses many extended takes—according to Losey, designed to create continuity for the actors—to generate a stifling, claustrophobic sense of entrapment that illustrates the feelings of Webb and Susan.[5] Indeed, the motif of enclosure is introduced before the opening titles, as a shadowy man peeps through a window at an unidentified woman. Likewise, when Garwood and his partner, Bud Crocker (John Maxwell), investigate an alleged prowler at the Gilvray home, Garwood goes outside and stares through the window at Susan. He is the prowler, in more ways than one: no mere voyeur, he wants what John Gilvray, a radio DJ, possesses and is always on the prowl for a way to break out of his class trap (another shot in the sequence frames Garwood within a window to capture his sense of enclosure).

Later Garwood wonders what "her angle is," and after Bud informs him that they're "well-heeled," he returns to her home, using the pretext of checking on Susan. The lurking camera seems to spy on them as Garwood takes liberties—rifling her drawers, then asking about her past. Learning that her acting ambitions came to naught, he asks, "Didn't you have enough pull?" He then recounts his own past (they're from nearby towns in Indiana): he won a basketball scholarship, but after being benched as a poor teammate (he was a scorer who never passed the ball), he told off the coach and lost his scholarship. "Just another one of my lousy breaks," he complains. None of this was his fault; it was just bad luck. Now he's "just another dumb cop," a man no better than his unambitious father, who "was too yellow to risk his buck twenty an hour" as an oil-field worker. For Garwood everything is a scam. Consumed with envy and bitterness, he wants "everything free," as Susan observes.

Most of all, he wants Susan, whose husband is rarely home, even though she plays his radio show constantly (to protest the blacklist, Losey had Trumbo serve as Gilvray's voice; Ciment 103). His aural presence is uncanny: during Garwood's third visit, just after he picks the lock on the safe where Gilvray keeps his cigarettes (in the process finding the will that leaves $62,000 to Susan), Gilvray mentions cigarettes on his show. After Garwood overplays his hand during the third visit and Susan slaps him and forces him to leave, he returns (wearing his uniform) to apologize. This ploy works, and when Gilvray plays the sensual tune "Baby," he unwittingly provides the soundtrack for the inception of his wife's

Prowler/policeman Webb Garwood (Van Heflin) wants what he sees in the Gilvray house. *Kobal Collection / Art Resource, NY.*

affair. After the tune finishes, Gilvray signs off with, "The cost of living is going down. . . . I'll be seeing you, Susan."

But not for much longer, for Garwood now has a plan, which is briefly delayed by a dinner with Bud and his wife, where a bored Garwood listens to his partner's tales of fools' gold and a massacre of Indians at a place called Calico, an erstwhile mining village that is now a ghost town. The plan: Garwood asks Susan to accompany him on his two-week vacation in Las Vegas, where he will visit a motor court that he dreams of buying. "Even when you're sleepin' it'd be makin' money for you!" The motel, that quintessential symbol of postmodern America, epitomizes Garwood's rootless insecurity and desire to get something for nothing. Unfortunately, Susan can't accompany him, for her suspicious husband has threatened to kill himself if she leaves him. This obstacle only gives Garwood a better excuse for the next part of his scheme: pretend to dump Susan so she'll grow desperate. He declines to meet her, and when they do meet, he reminds her of their class difference: "You were brought up on Lakeview. . . . I couldn't give you any of that easy lifestyle." He even fakes a conscience: Gilvray would "always be with us," he tells her. "You'd start to hate me." These are all lines in his self-scripted drama, the showstopper of which takes place when Garwood revisits the Gilvray home. Now he truly becomes a prowler: exiting his prowl car, he cuts their screen door and swings the squeaking gate for attention, which prompts a call to the police station. Garwood makes a noise that brings Gilvray outside, carrying a pistol; Garwood kills Gilvray, then grabs his gun and wounds himself in the arm.

At the inquest, Garwood is smooth and credible, full of regret for the terrible accident. He testifies that he has never seen Susan before, and she (using a microphone, as if replacing her husband) corroborates his lie. The verdict? Accidental homicide. After resigning from the police force, Garwood offers Gilvray's brother $700 to pay for funeral expenses (the brother declines; he thinks Susan may be better off alone). Now comes the culminating act in Garwood's drama: win Susan back. At first she rebuffs him, but he soon persuades her with his plausible explanations. Remorsefully, he avers, "I couldn't bring myself to touch a gun again as long as I live." Anyway, "what reason did I have" for killing Gilvray? She had already agreed to go away with him. It was a "freak accident. . . . I'll swear that by the only thing I ever really loved and that's you." Not only does he overcome her misgivings; he even seems to believe his own lies.

They marry, and Garwood uses his victim's bequest to buy the Vegas motor court. He seems to have achieved his dream. But the nature of this dream is revealed as Garwood leaves the motel office that first evening, the "Vacancy" sign burning brightly over his head: his success is as vacant as his values. Instead of a house—the essence of the American dream of domestic tranquility—he dwells in a motel, the architectural embodiment of his soullessness. Is the dream itself empty, or is it only hollow because he has perverted it? Either way, the plan begins to crumble when Susan informs him that she is four months pregnant. What should be joyful tidings spell disaster, for the baby's existence proves the falseness of their testimony and implicates Garwood in Gilvray's murder (in earlier scenes Susan had insinuated that her husband was impotent, so it couldn't be his). Whereas Judy Tyler's pregnancy symbolizes the family's lost potential, Susan's represents the price of Garwood's dream. The frequent shots of Garwood in doorways and the long take as they discuss the pregnancy further imply their entrapment. There are always records of a baby's birth, so where can they go?

Their solution is the same one Americans in trouble have sought for centuries: light out for the Territory, or in this case, for Calico, Bud's ghost town. At first the plan seems to work, as the lovers drive there in Garwood's new Caddy and set up housekeeping in a shack, like any two kids starting out. They dance to "Baby" again (its title now given a double meaning), and Garwood pledges that "our kid's gonna be on the beam the second he gets into the world!" There'll be no lousy breaks for her! But as so often happens in noir, the past catches up with them. The recording of their song also includes the sign-off by the man Garwood murdered: "The cost of living is going down. . . . I'll be seeing you, Susan." No; the cost of their living is about to rise precipitously. As Garwood's luck would have it, Susan goes into labor in the middle of a storm; and he, for once doing the right thing, drives to the nearest town to fetch a doctor, unaware that Bud and his wife plan to surprise them in Calico.

To induce the reluctant doctor to accompany him, Garwood shows him his (no longer valid) badge. The doctor determines that the baby's heartbeat is normal, but Garwood's is not: agitated, he paces around, now staring out the window rather than peering in from the outside. That's not too difficult, since their house doesn't even have a door. Worse, Susan has begun to realize the truth about him and, having seen him take the gun he swore never to touch again, accuses him of having deliberately killed Gilvray. Though he denies it, he has lost his accomplice. After the birth of their baby girl, the doctor drives away before Garwood can stop him, taking with him the baby and Garwood's car keys. Susan has spilled everything to the doctor, and the police are on the way (the doctor recognized Garwood from newspaper stories). Garwood desperately justifies himself: "I'm no worse than anybody else. You work in a store, you knock down on the cash register; a big boss, the income tax. A ward heeler, you sell votes. A lawyer, take bribes. I was a cop, so I used a gun. But whatever I did, I did for you." As the bank robbers in *They Live by Night* would say: they're just thieves like us. The American dream of upward mobility is just an excuse to steal from others before they rob you. "How am I any different from those other guys?" he cries to Susan. "Some do it for a million, some for ten. I did it for sixty-two thousand." Now she knows the whole story: his phony rejection of her, the "accident," the courtroom lies—all a plot to take her money. Finding his spare car key on the floor, Garwood tries to flee, but his passage out of nightmare alley is, ironically, blocked by Bud's approaching car, as if the vestiges of his own better nature are conspiring against him. All alone, with the police in pursuit, Garwood tries to escape by climbing a sand dune that represents his quest for upward mobility. As he reaches the crest (with Susan watching from the window), he is shot down, tumbling to his death in a cloud of dust. He can't escape his unpaid debts.

Webb Garwood is not so different from *Nightmare Alley*'s Stanton Carlisle, whose rise and fall I chronicled at the beginning of this book: both are cynics who exploit others to fulfill their selfish dreams of success. But Carlisle is tormented by guilt over the death of Pete and rendered vulnerable by Lilith; his final abjection and possible rebirth hold out a shred of hope. In contrast, Garwood is unredeemed and perhaps unredeemable. And whereas many of Carlisle's victims (particularly Griswold) are venal strangers who deserve or even welcome their victimization, Garwood's primary victims are those closest to him. The problem is not merely that he lacks a scintilla of empathy or guilt; it is that he has internalized the values of a society that believes self-interest rules and whose history proves that, beneath its noble-sounding principles, its real goals are to conquer and steal from others. In this regard the setting of the final scenes—a former Indian village converted into a mine and then a ghost town—is telling. Calico embodies the history of American exploitation, of stealing land and killing those who once held it, of plundering the earth of its riches, and then abandoning it once it is used up. Garwood is merely another American who pretends the past is irrelevant, that no costs are incurred in such pillage.[6]

Garwood epitomizes the uglier side of this early American Dream, which was, for the native peoples, a nightmare. He also represents its more contemporary vanities: hollowed out by the pursuit of "happiness" at any cost, he embodies the worst aspects of radical individualism. The cash nexus has reduced him to a set of appetites. Money, which has no smell, no feelings, and, as *Body and Soul*'s Charlie Davis reminds us, no memory, has become the measure of all. Unattached and unfeeling, it merely moves from one hand to another; the costs of living never cling to it. Like Garwood, it is void of humanity. Hence, *The Prowler* does not merely condemn a bad apple. Rather, Losey, Butler, and Trumbo declare that the American Dream has become a sham, that the remorseless pursuit of wealth and upward mobility has left in its wake wrecked lives and hollow citizens. The dream of domesticity and home ownership? Just a thin scrim covering a history of theft, violence, and exploitation. The film's emblem of postwar America is not Gilvray's house but the half-built shack where Garwood and Susan set up housekeeping or, better, Garwood's motel—a symbol of the rootless, grasping persons who briefly occupy its rooms.

For these filmmakers—understandably disillusioned by their recent experiences—and, indeed, for most of noir's creators, America's founding principles had been voided or defiled. Individualism, as dramatized in films such as *Dark Passage* and *Hollow Triumph,* had turned people into a set of interchangeable, depthless faces. Upward mobility, as the car films imply, had been blocked by those fiercely guarding their possessions and social standing. Self-reinvention may be possible but only after traumatic experiences obliterate what existed before; otherwise, one mistake dooms you to a life of constant insecurity. Free enterprise masks rapacity, and meaningful collective action is possible (and only briefly) in the underworld. The new technologies and consumer items that promised liberation, security, peace, and luxury instead made us paranoid, hypercompetitive, and insecure.

Yet some vestiges of the Dream remain. A few noir veterans manage either to reintegrate their prewar and postwar identities or start anew, in so doing modeling a means of recovering from the war. These films propose that we must remember trauma, recollect the selves we once were and the values we once held, so that we can either reaffirm or discard them. The portraiture films also moderate *The Prowler*'s gloomy conclusion by implying that the malleability of identity may be liberating insofar as it enables us to evade exploitation. Female filmmakers challenged discrimination by working within and around the studio system to create complex portrayals of the woman's condition and to offer intelligent, sophisticated analyses of marriage and gender roles. A few noir jazz musicians, albeit blackened by associations with antisocial behavior, employed improvisation to engender flexible, hybrid American identities. Leftist filmmakers trenchantly criticized the depredations of capitalism and the perversion of American values, despite being hounded and jailed by self-styled patriots. Perhaps most important, the very existence of the films proved that thoughtful and committed artists were still able to present intellectually, morally, and politically challenging works within a conservative corporate system and that their work was met by audiences willing to watch and listen to them. We should do the same.

INTRODUCTION

1. At that time (1947) the word *geek* bore none of its current associations with computer engineers, their allegedly poor social skills, or their highly developed analytical powers. Yet the word's current connotations—describing a creature at once superhuman and disabled—may derive from this earlier incarnation.

2. Gresham, like so many writers of the period, had joined the Communist Party in the 1930s; he later married poet Joy Davidman (to whom *Nightmare Alley* is dedicated). He underwent psychiatric treatment and later became a devout Christian. None of his other works achieved the success of this, his first novel. See Polito's "Biographical Notes" in *Crime Novels* for further details (980–81). In an irony appropriate to his grim, deterministic tale, Gresham committed suicide in the same hotel where he wrote *Nightmare Alley* (Williams, "Naturalist" 137).

3. Because the film's Stan is an orphan, the movie omits most of the novel's Oedipal conflict, in which young Stan, after witnessing his mother having sex with her lover, is bought off with a toy magic set (Gresham 618–22). His magic acts automatically invoke his filial betrayal, and his guilt over this betrayal and his confused feelings about his parents make him susceptible to Lilith's machinations.

4. In the novel she tells him he has imagined himself as his mother's lover and deliberately takes the mother's place (688). She is said to be "hooked" to him by "an invisible gold wire" (689); in the film her power is illustrated by the weblike barred shadows that surround her in her office.

5. In the novel Grindle had impregnated Dorrie and persuaded her to have an abortion. The girl died of septicemia afterward, and Grindle has been tormented ever since. In 1947 Hollywood it was forbidden even to mention abortion, so the film cleans it up, thereby obviating Grindle's most powerful motive.

6. These scenes in the novel are much more gloomy and expansive, as Stan is driven crazy by violent, paranoid fantasies. Gresham implies that Stan is caught in a classic double bind: all along he has desired to be his nemesis—his mother's lover, Mark Humphries—but once he has become him, he can do nothing but ruin him (771). While on the run, Stan also meets an African American Communist labor organizer, Frederick Douglass Scott, who is on his way to fight Grindle's union-breaking efforts. Scott's presence indicates Gresham's political allegiances and, as Williams

notes, signals a path that Stan "could have taken" ("Naturalist" 129; Gresham 767–76). Stan then kills a policeman whom he confuses with his father (Stan's demons are all associated with gray stubble): this is his "own personal corpse" (781), the alter ego he both fears and inhabits. Finally, Stan shows up at a carnival, and on the novel's last page, he is given the geek job (796).

7. This influence has been analyzed in many critical books on noir. Among many others see Foster Hirsch (53–58), Andrew Spicer (11–16), and Brook, who (not always persuasively) finds in American noir a specific set of German Jewish cultural tropes and patterns. For an erudite reflection on this influence see Elsaesser (420–44), as well as studies of individual directors; among the best of these latter is Gunning's magisterial book on Fritz Lang.

8. Recent illuminating books examining noir's debts to hard-boiled fiction include those of Abbott and Irwin.

9. Critical studies have treated noir using methods ranging from psychoanalysis (Oliver and Trigo; Žižek), narratology (Telotte, *Voices*), gender and race theory (Kaplan; Flory; Krutnik; Wager, *Dangerous*), to philosophy (Conard) and urban planning (Christopher; Dimendberg). New scholarship has unveiled further contexts and concerns: *"Un-American" Hollywood* includes pathbreaking essays about the Hollywood Left; Biesen's *Blackout* helpfully traces the war's material effects on early noir; and Hanson and Grossman have challenged conventional wisdom about women's roles in the films.

10. Dennis Broe notes that the one-year interval following V-J Day was the "greatest strike period in US history" (32).

11. Steve Neale likewise comments that Zeitgeist adherents "find themselves arguing that *noir* registered a dominant ideological mood that was at the same time subversive of dominant values. Such a position is hard either to sustain or to verify" (158).

12. See Osteen, "Face Plates."

CHAPTER ONE: "Someone Else's Nightmare"

1. Negative footage was also used in the dream sequence in an earlier version of the story, the 1939 film *Blind Alley*, directed by Charles Vidor. Both films were adapted from a play by James Warwick.

2. For versions of this statement see, among many others, Borde and Chaumeton (24), Christopher (206), and Oliver and Trigo, who describe noir as "a type of Freudian dream-work marked by condensations and displacements of unconscious desires and fears" (xv).

3. Siegfried Kracauer wrote in 1927 that "the game that film plays with the pieces of disjointed nature is reminiscent of *dreams* in which the fragments of daily life become jumbled" (qtd. in Dimendberg 143).

4. Santos provides a useful survey of the roles of psychiatry and psychiatrists in noir.

5. Ringel cites two midcentury psychoanalysts who explicitly compare psychiatrists to detectives "searching for clues to uncover the mystery" (173).

6. Gabbard and Gabbard note that the work of the psychiatrist in cinema is often "indistinguishable from that of clergymen, caseworkers, school guidance counselors, or even newspaper advice columnists" (xxiii).

7. Ernest Hartmann, for example, argues that dreams' symbolic material is much less important than their dominant emotion, which can be expressed through a variety of scenarios (3–4, 117).

8. Dream symbolism is, for Freud, the language of the unconscious. The dreamer's conscious mind cannot gain access to the unconscious; if he or she could, the unconscious would wither away (Rieff 52).

9. States, reinterpreting Freudian "condensation" in literary terms, argues that metonymy creates most dream imagery in this way (94–123).

10. Comandini was an experienced screenwriter who had been working in Hollywood since the mid-1920s. Among her other credits is the 1934 adaptation of *Jane Eyre* and the 1945 Warner Bros. noir *Danger Signal* ("Adele Comandini").

11. Perhaps it is only an accident that the missing letters, rearranged, spell "act king."

12. If we consider director Ulmer's biography (raised in Vienna, he arrived in the United States in the 1930s and directed a series of well-regarded Yiddish-language films before signing with the Poverty Row company PRC, where he made *Strange Illusion*), we may also find in the film the story of a man struggling to reconcile his Old World past (represented by Muhlbach, with his German name and continental accent) and his emergent American self. For further details about Ulmer's life (as well as some dubious speculation about the "Jewish" characters in the film) see Brook 147–48, 158–59.

13. *The Big Night* is adapted from Stanley Ellin's novel *Dreadful Summit,* for which the passage from *Hamlet* serves as epigraph and in which the crude phallic symbols of gun and cane are even more blatant. Though credited to Ellin, the screenplay was actually written by blacklisted radicals Hugo Butler and Ring Lardner Jr.

14. The film was originally told almost entirely in flashback, but producer Philip Waxman changed it during the editing: see Ciment 116–17.

15. Young Barrymore's relationship with his father was apparently not much different from that of George and his father. Losey spent a great deal of time on and off the set with Barrymore, in effect adopting him during the making of the film. In an irony worthy of noir, after Losey went to England in the wake of his blacklisting, the FBI employed Barrymore to trace and report on Losey (Ciment 116, 118).

16. In this regard his words as he downs a Metaxa—"to the Greeks!"—acquire an additional, creepy significance.

17. The novel's singer, Terry Angelus, is obviously modeled on Billie Holiday, down to the flower in her hair, ubiquitous dog, and nickname, "Ladybird" (Ellin 111–14). In the novel her singing makes George yearn to pull out his, well, gun (112). In both versions, after the show he tries to compliment her but muffs it when he says, "I think you're beautiful too, even if you are a ——" (in the novel he uses the word *nigger*: 114).

18. The novel's conclusion is somewhat different. Frances dies from complications of an abortion that Andy convinced her to undergo, and George's mother is not married to another man but in prison. The novel also carries out Andy's sacrificial role to completion: George shoots Judge after returning to Andy's house, and Andy is killed by a policeman during a climactic struggle with Judge (Ellin 174–75). Flanagan tries to persuade George to let the police believe that Andy killed Judge, but ultimately George decides to emulate his father, who "took what was coming to him," and clears Andy's name by confessing (181).

19. It is possible that *Harry*'s ending was influenced by that of *Woman in the Window,* which premiered a few months before *Harry* was completed.

20. The question of whether Hitchcock is a noir director is a vexed one. Although some of his films display what are considered noir conventions, his work differs in tone and narrative style from most noirs. For thoughtful examinations of Hitchcock's relation to noir see Naremore, "Hitchcock," especially 267–71; and Orr, who adduces as evidence the director's quite different attitudes toward gender (many Hitchcock protagonists are women) and murder, along with the famous Hitchcock transfer-of-guilt motif (156–64).

21. Freedman notes that *Spellbound* marks the first time in American cinema that psychoanalysis is "the means of solving a crime, not a means of committing one" (83). Although Dr. May E. Romm (David O. Selznick's own analyst) is listed as the film's technical adviser, Hitchcock seemed to view the psychiatric elements mostly as a gimmick and once dismissed the picture as "just another man-hunt story wrapped up in pseudo-psychoanalysis" (qtd. in Truffaut 165). Hitchcock later distinguished between "psychological" films and "psychoanalytical" films like *Spellbound,* predicting that the latter were merely a "passing phase" (qtd. in Nugent 21). *Spellbound*'s simplistic depiction of psychoanalysis is but one of its many weaknesses (along with its overwrought score, implausible story, and stilted performance by Gregory Peck, as noted by Hyde 153). Yet it was also among the twenty highest-grossing Hollywood films released between 1945 and 1950 (Chopra-Gant 18). Hence, the film is a telling example of midcentury Americans' fascination with psychiatry and dreams.

22. Freedman later proposes that *Spellbound* holds out the possibility that "psychoanalysis when broadly accepted and thoroughly understood could provide a solution to all problems" (95).

23. As Gabbard and Gabbard observe, she also embodies the problematic notion that women are better off as lovers than as professionals (54).

24. Originally a much longer and more elaborate dream sequence was planned, but it was truncated for reasons of time and money. For information about the production of the sequence see McGilligan, *Alfred Hitchcock* 360–63.

25. As Brill comments, the tale of Ballantine's illness and cure is closer to a fable about "the curse of the evil sorcerer . . . [and] an enchantment . . . overcome by a heroic kiss" than to a realistic story about scientific treatment (259).

26. Brill lists *Rebecca* and *Vertigo* as sharing this theme, but one could also include Hitchcock's *Psycho, I Confess,* and *Marnie,* as well as films noir such as *Murder, My Sweet; The Killers; Out of the Past;* and a score of others, including many I discuss in later chapters.

27. Hitchcock, meanwhile, was engaged in remaking himself as an American director, aided—or was it hindered?—by the notoriously controlling producer David O. Selznick. Hence, we might also read in Ballantine's and Constance's attempts to reinvent themselves a little of Hitchcock's own frustration in learning to cope with American studio heads who insisted on overwriting his dreams with their own.

CHAPTER TWO: Missing Persons

1. Like the dream movies, some switched-identity pictures obliquely allude to the biographies of their directors or performers, many of them émigrés beginning new

lives, sometimes with new names, and carrying an ambivalent attachment to their original homelands and identities.

2. The editing and blocking in this scene have been meticulously analyzed in Porfirio, "*The Killers*."

3. Ian Jarvie correctly describes Jeff's dubious morality (see 177).

4. This brilliantly constructed film contains other such doublings. For instance, Whit hires Jeff twice (first to find Kathie, and then to fetch the incriminating papers from his lawyer, Leonard Eels), and Jeff dupes him both times. Jeff goes on the run twice but escapes neither time.

5. The film's fishing motif is another of its intriguing touches. For example, Jeff's partner's name is Fisher, and the lawyer for whose murder he is framed is named Eels. In the early scenes with Kathie in Acapulco, the lovers are seen on the beach surrounded by a net. Later Jeff swears to Whit that he isn't a "sucker." Whit does his own fishing, trying to catch Jeff by using the deaf kid as bait; later Jeff uses the boy as a decoy to throw off the police. Obviously, as a PI Markham is also a kind of fisherman. He is also being fished out of his other life by Whit and is a fish out of water in Bridgeport. There may also be an allusion here to the myth of the fisher king, with Jeff the exiled monarch who must be sacrificed so that his land becomes fertile once again.

6. Like Julia, Nina Foch was an émigré who reinvented herself. Born in the Netherlands as Nina Consuelo Maud Fock (to Dutch composer Dirk Fock and silent film actress Consuelo Flowerton), she changed her name and lost her Continental accent after moving to the United States, where she studied at the American Academy of Dramatic Arts and signed with Columbia at age nineteen (Brumbaugh).

7. Earlier, Bertha, the maid at Julia's London apartment house, voiced a sharper envy at Julia's class position: "secretary," she scoffs, "sittin' and writin' all day. Call that work!"

8. Coincidentally, Muriel Bolton later cowrote (with Ian McLellan Hunter) the noirish horror picture *The Amazing Mr. X*.

9. One might object that this subversive theme was permitted only because this was a minor film that few people saw and that the studio cared little about. However, Robert Osborne remarks in the Turner Classic Movie channel's afterword that although the film was shot in just ten days on a budget of $175,000, and originally slated to be a B picture, it was so well received in previews that Columbia ended up releasing it as an A film and premiered it at the prestigious RKO theater in Los Angeles. In other words this subtly subversive film was released by a major studio in a major venue.

10. One might also read this 1945 film as an allegory about American involvement in the war. Though forced to take part in the internecine conflicts of old, tired Europe, Americans still resist living out Europe's murderous fantasies and mistakes or imitating its nihilism: we can be free of that past, at least.

11. Benson's first screen credit was for cowriting Alfred Hitchcock's *Shadow of a Doubt*, another story of a clever young woman confronting criminal complicity. Benson also contributed to the scripts for *Little Women*, *Anna and the King of Siam*, and numerous television shows ("Sally Benson"). Turney cowrote *The Man I Love*, the Ida Lupino vehicle treated in chapter 7, and worked on such films as Dorothy Arzner's *The Bride Wore Red*, *Mildred Pierce*, *A Stolen Life*, and *Cry Wolf*. Turney and Barbara Stanwyck worked on three films together (and Turney later wrote for Stanwyck's first television series). Both Benson and Turney, in short, carved out solid

Hollywood careers by lending verisimilitude and strong female characters to so-called women's pictures.

12. Benson's draft (titled *With This Ring* [*I Married a Dead Man*] and dated Jan. 24, 1949) also contains several additional characters and a long scene in Grand Central Terminal. Turney's first pass at the script is dated April 14, 1949; all subsequent versions (dated April 16, 1949; May 5, 1949; and Dec. 16, 1949) contain this prologue and flashback.

13. In the Woolrich novel Helen is a "dreary, hopeless nineteen" (805), but in 1949, when the film was shot, Barbara Stanwyck was well over forty years old. Born Ruby Stevens in 1907, the legendary actress was an expert at remaking herself. Even so, she isn't quite believable as an anxious ingénue: Stanwyck's Helen is herself a bit of a counterfeit.

14. See Osteen, "Face Plates" 130–31.

15. Benson's draft includes a witty effect underlining this doubling. During the train crash "the mirror cracks and seems to fall back, her [Helen's] own reflection going away from here. We HEAR Patrice scream, and then see the mirror fall apart" (Benson 18).

16. Benson's first draft includes a character (not in the novel) named Peggy Marshall, who maliciously plays Hugh's favorite song, Manon's "Un rêve," during a party (see Benson 54). Turney deletes this character and changes the tune. In Benson's first draft the real Patrice had attended art school, so the Harknesses turn the attic into her studio. But Helen can't paint, and revealing her shoddy efforts would destroy her imposture. When the time comes to show her work, however, it has been replaced (Bill's doing) by a work that is "very good, indeed" (Benson draft). The art motif illustrates, perhaps too blatantly, the artificiality of Helen's new self-portrait.

17. His language in the novel is a bit more to the point: "The you I made for myself. . . . You'll *only* be Patrice. I give you that name. Keep it for me, forever" (946–47). In other words he has made her and, by knowing her secret, owns her.

18. In Benson's second draft Mother Harkness makes her confession to the police in person, using the letter as backup (Benson second draft, Feb. 25, 1949).

19. The letter from Breen to Luigi Luraschi, Paramount's director of censorship, requesting the alterations, is dated May 26, 1949: thus the censors must not have read the script dated May 5, 1949 but an earlier one lacking the lines in question. Presumably they were added in anticipation of Breen's objections, which makes their deletion from the film a fascinating example of how studios sidestepped prohibitions when necessary.

20. The studio's initial reader focused on the problematic conclusion: "The entire ending, which tries to be bitter like James M. Cain, is all wrong for the screen. The murder of the villainous Georgesson should be solved, or else it should not remain as a barrier between Patrice and Bill anyway" (Leavitt).

21. Polan comments on the implausibility that Parry's wife's best friend would also know Irene (but that Irene has never met Parry) and observes that these coincidences suggest "the dominance of a logic based not on a coherent narrativity but a dream" (196).

22. But where is the suspense? Even casual movie fans—in 2012 as in 1947—know perfectly well what Humphrey Bogart looks like. As a result we never truly believe in

Parry's "true" face, and the Hollywood star system undermines the film's premise to some degree.

23. This plot twist makes little sense: wouldn't she know the location of the windows in her own apartment? Nor does it seem logical for Parry to visit her there: why would he believe she would now confess to two murders after going to such lengths to cover them up? The falls of Baker and Madge, however, do consummate the many vertical images throughout the film: Parry's original fall from the truck, his climbs up and down Irene's stairs, and the frequent shots of San Francisco's hilly terrain.

24. Henreid certainly read Fuchs's notes: they are annotated in red pencil and tucked into a bound copy of his script of *Hollow Triumph*.

25. Bartok's accent creates a curious set of echoes since Paul Henreid, a Triestine who had immigrated to the United States, doesn't successfully hide his own accent when playing the American Muller. Of course, Henreid was no criminal, but the movie's tale of self-reinvention parallels his own biography.

26. In their generally smart and useful essay V. Penelope Pelizzon and Nancy West write, "If the viewer paid careful attention to the scene of the incision, remembering that Muller's actions are presented in a mirror, she would have realized that Muller, in fact, did mark the left side of his face" (par. 21). They go on to suggest that this is a trick on the audience, who are assumed to be as unobservant as the film's characters and are thus "implicated in the very culture of indifference that the film conveys." But Pelizzon and West are confused by the mirror. Since the camera is facing Muller and the photo as he looks in the mirror, when he marks what looks to be the left side of his face, he is, in fact, marking the right side. The very next shot, in which he's wearing a bandage on the *right* side, clearly shows as much. But this is an easy mistake to make: a viewer automatically reverses a mirror image so that it matches the face looking at it. In earlier drafts of this chapter I too was confused by the mirror image and went so far as to claim that the filmmakers had made a mistake and had *failed to flop the photo*. In other words, I forgot that in a mirror image, what looks to be left (if one stood, as it were, behind the face) reflects one's right side.

About this scene Fuchs writes, "With the picture of Bartok in [the] same position as Muller's face in the mirror, the scar appears in both cases on the right side, and we have no problem. We mustn't get the audience to thinking about this point at all. It must come as news to them when Aubrey [the photo store clerk] tells his boss the scar is on the wrong side." The cigarette "scar" was also Fuchs's idea (29).

27. Just before the murder scene, Muller services the car of Stancyk's thugs in a scene virtually identical to the recognition scene at the Brentwood garage in *The Killers*. But these thugs are less observant than Jim Colfax and fail to recognize Muller as the man they're looking for.

28. Fuchs's notes state that the debts are Bartok's. He continues: "THE IRONY: (a) he has succeeded as Bartok, therefore he must die as Bartok; (b) in trying to do a decent thing, in leaving to start all over, he has undone himself" (39).

29. Fuchs's script notes urge Sekely and Henreid to "WORK LIKE HELL HERE FOR PURE SCHMALZ. Poor Muller, weep for Adonais, for he is dead" (58). But the feeling the scene elicits is closer to sardonic recognition than to mourning because, as I noted earlier, Muller/Bartok's coldness largely defeats our impulse to empathize with him.

CHAPTER THREE: Vet Noir

1. Homer is played by Harold Russell, who actually did lose his hands in the war. Martin Norden argues that the film's portrayal of Homer is "one of the most forthright, sensitive and honest" depictions of physical disability in cinema history (167).

2. This function of disability is common in literary depictions and constitutes one of Ato Quayson's primary types (see 41–42). As I demonstrate below, this tendency holds true in *Act of Violence* as well, where Joe Parkson's limp embodies Frank Enley's moral failing. See Davidson (72–73) for a fuller list of disabled characters in film noir.

3. For the symptoms of PTSD, as described in the fourth edition of the *Diagnostic and Statistical Manual* (the diagnostic handbook used by most clinical psychologists), see Saigh and Bremner 9.

4. Luckhurst describes the flashback as "the central device of cinema's representation of trauma" (179). For an analysis of noir's flashback structure see Telotte, *Voices* 14–17.

5. The films also conform to Mitchell and Snyder's outline of the conventional disability story, which first isolates deviance, explains it, moves it to the center of the narrative, and then normalizes or eliminates it (53–54).

6. As of 1980, thirty-five years after the war, more than a million people had received war-related disabilities benefits from the US government. About fifty-one thousand were categorized as "totally disabled." See Allcountries.org.

7. Director William Wyler, born in Alsace, was, like many noir directors, himself an immigrant.

8. As Waller points out, "The Soldier Comes Home Angry"—sometimes with good reason (95).

9. See Naremore, *More Than Night* 108–10 for an account of this script change and a discussion of Raymond Chandler's original screenplay, in which all three vets are more clearly disabled, and in which Johnny is more blatantly depicted as Buzz's double.

10. As Davidson notes, disability in film noir often points to "anxiety over the stability and definition of gender roles" (59).

11. Chopra-Gant offers a tidy Freudian reading of this conclusion: " 'Dad's' killing of Helen frees Johnny from the encumbrance of his 'delinquent' wife and enables him to pursue a relationship with the altogether more wholesome Joyce" (162). The rushed and gimmicky contrivances used to bring it about, however, make this denouement unconvincing.

12. Brooks's novel, though static and clumsily plotted, thoughtfully examines veterans' alienation. Scott pitched *Crossfire* to the studios as a film attacking anti-Semitism (which he treated as a brand of fascism) rather than as a film about veterans (see "Appendix 5" in Ceplair and Englund 451–54). Friends and associates warned Scott against making this controversial film, which contributed to the crackdown that cost him his career (see Langdon-Teclaw 166–68).

13. To illustrate this inhumanity, Dmytryk employed increasingly shorter lenses, beginning with a 50mm and eventually a 25mm lens, to make Ryan's face appear gradually more demonic, dark, and distorted.

14. In the documentary feature enclosed with the DVD, Dmytryk claims that he shot the scene in this way only to avoid using more than one camera setup, thereby saving money on a tightly budgeted picture.

15. Though the Popular Front agenda of "anti-fascism, anti-racism, and progressive unionism" (Langdon-Teclaw 152) is clear enough in both films, *Cornered* was not chosen by Scott but assigned to him by RKO chief William Dozier.

16. As Krutnik notes, Gerard's "assertive masculine quest becomes an obsessive post-war continuation of the extreme wartime conditions" that had tested him (*Lonely* 134).

17. Original screenwriter John Wexley feared that Dmytryk would whitewash his story, which indicted the Peron government, and thereby soften the film—and he did. According to Ceplair and Englund, the results prove that "screenwriter, director, and producer Communists were far more vulnerable to the dictates of the studio system than to the demands of their ideology" or their party (315). Dmytryk's alleged disgust with Wexley's communism eventually formed part of his "friendly" testimony to HUAC in 1951. See also Navasky 232–37.

18. The film fits the pattern I outline in chapter 4, in which framed narrations describe the narrator's framing for a crime.

19. The premise in Dorothy B. Hughes's source novel is quite different. Its nonveteran protagonist, Sailor, pursues a quest to obtain full payment from his father figure, "The Sen" (Senator Willis Douglass), who had welshed on paying Sailor for his role in a plot to kill the senator's wife and a female informer (see 135–39). A kid from the Chicago streets with an abusive alcoholic father whom he once tried to kill (80), Sailor has made his way up the chain in the senator's criminal organization by serving as a steady, loyal hand. He needs a father yet rebels against male authorities such as Douglass and McIntyre, the Chicago cop who has followed Douglass to this border town. Hughes organizes the novel around three rituals: the killing of Zozobra; a mass including the Procession of Martyrs (142–57); and the town dance. In each ceremony Sailor is offered a rite of passage that could enable him to trust others. The adaptation, by celebrated screenwriters Ben Hecht and Charles Lederer, lightens the mood and renders it more timely by making Gagin a veteran. The film was produced by Joan Harrison, one of only two female producers in Hollywood at the time.

20. Pila's role resembles that of Carol, the female protagonist in *Phantom Lady,* another Harrison-produced noir. In that film Carol assumes an array of active roles to save her employer from being executed for murder.

21. In the source novel, though Sailor is partly humanized by contact with Pancho and Pila (who has a smaller role than in the film), he ultimately fails to redeem himself and ends up shooting both the Sen and McIntyre. Unlike Gagin, Sailor chooses alienation and loneliness over human contact. McIntyre diagnoses Sailor's problem: he has always "blamed the world or something missing in [himself]" (129).

22. Amnesia stories are common in noir even when they don't concern veterans. The lengthy list includes films such as *The Long Wait, The Scarf, Man in the Dark,* and *Shadow on the Wall,* as well as *Street of Chance,* discussed in chapter 2. For a list of other noir films with amnesia plots see Dickos 182–84; for an extensive analysis of noir amnesia see Santos 67–103.

23. Further ironies about memory and knowledge crop up elsewhere in the film: many of Cravat's former acquaintances, including Mel Phillips (Richard Conte),

owner of a nightclub called The Cellar, seem to have amnesia about Cravat; Anzelmo, an ex-Nazi in pursuit of the money, runs a fortune-telling parlor.

24. Both *High Wall* and *Crooked Way* dramatize the stigma attached to cognitively disabled or traumatized veterans, who were often suspected of faking their injuries to gain sympathy and services (see Waller 168).

25. It seems likely that this thematic slant is the work of Cole, a Communist and future member of the Hollywood Ten.

26. This drug was developed during the war, partly as a means to induce truthful confessions from prisoners and partly as a way to weed out malingerers (Luckhurst 58).

27. Bernhardt and his cinematographer, Paul Vogel, frequently employ high angles on Kenet to show him belittled and crushed by the forces surrounding him. Other examples of verticality multiply as the film proceeds: Whitcombe pushes over the stool of Cronner, his building's handyman, when Cronner tries to blackmail him; the push sends Cronner down an elevator shaft to his death.

28. Herbert Marshall, who plays Whitcombe as an able-bodied man, lost a leg during World War I and used a prosthesis to enable him to walk and stand.

29. As a German-born Jew who escaped from Germany in 1933 after being detained by the Gestapo, Bernhardt possessed firsthand experience of such all-powerful institutions. Like many other noir directors, he knew what it meant to be cut off from one's past, having landed in America with almost no understanding of English. Bernhardt's European career and escape are outlined in Brook (167–69).

30. Robert Richards, who scripted the film, was an ex-Communist who was named by his former wife, screenwriter Silvia Richards (Buhle and Wagner, *Radical* 364–65). Richards adapted the script for *Act of Violence* from an original story by WWII veteran Collier Young, who later cofounded Filmakers, Inc., the important independent production company discussed in chapter 7. Zinnemann's later film *High Noon* (1952) is also often read as an allegory of the HUAC era, though he was not a member of the radical Hollywood Left. He also focused on military men in other films of the period: his 1950 film *The Men* deals honestly, if somewhat sentimentally, with the tribulations of physically disabled veterans, and *From Here to Eternity* (1953) superbly depicts the loves and fears of American servicemen on the eve of World War II.

31. Publicity posters for the film treated Parkson's disability as a horror movie trope. A typical one reads: "The killer with the limp is coming your way! He may be lurking behind you at this moment! . . . Listen! Can't you hear that menacing, scraping, shuffle as he approaches? Neither law, nor fear . . . not even a woman's kisses can stop him as he stalks his prey in the most suspenseful screen drama of the season." None of the ads alludes to Parkson's motives, nor to the complicated nature of Enley's guilt (*Act of Violence* posters, Fred Zinnemann Papers, MHLSC).

32. Research suggests that many POWs suffer from PTSD. One study found that, even forty years after the fact, up to 70 percent of former POWs still displayed symptoms. See Schlenger et al. 77.

CHAPTER FOUR: Framed

1. Kent Minturn argues that these painting noirs display a "Romantic notion of the artist as a tortured genius" (282). In addition to the figures in the films I discuss,

one could also cite sculptor Jack Marlow in *Phantom Lady* and Bogart's mad artist, Geoffrey Carroll, in *The Two Mrs. Carrolls,* who obsessively paints his wives as the Angel of Death and then poisons them to revive his moribund muse.

2. For a discussion of how Grable and other "pinup girls" were defined by their body measurements see Renov 184.

3. Leonard Leff points out the homoerotic tinge in the McPherson/Lydecker relationship. For example, when they dine at Waldo and Laura's favorite restaurant, the two men seem to be on a date (7). It is also difficult to miss the innuendos in the opening sequence, when McPherson confronts Lydecker as the latter luxuriates in the bathtub. This subtext is also present in Vera Caspary's source novel, which hints that Lydecker's wooing of Laura is but a set of "gestures" designed to make him appear heterosexual (Caspary, *Laura* 158).

4. Kathryn Kalinak observes that the picture frame "serves to contain the power of her threatening sexuality" (168). Liahna Babener similarly argues that the portrait is "quarantined inside the pictorial space" and usually "sandwiched between men" (95) to signify Laura's domination by males.

5. Royal Brown comments that the theme represents Laura's absence (90); yet it also betokens her continued presence, at least in McPherson's thoughts and senses, as each restatement reinforces "the feeling that he is trying to get it [or her] out of his mind" (Ness 62).

6. Nicholas Spencer asserts that the "prior murder narrative was simply a dream" (137); later in the film McPherson urges Laura to "forget the whole thing like a bad dream." The lyrics Johnny Mercer added to the musical theme make this possibility explicit: "but she's only a dream."

7. In Caspary's novel Diane was having an affair with Laura's fiancé, Shelby Carpenter. The novel's Diane Redfern was born with the name Jennie Swobodo (Caspary, *Laura* 95); thus, this fleshing out of Diane's background adds heft to the doubling motif.

8. Babener concludes that the filmmakers "defeminized" the novel by erasing Laura's voice in order to advance a "misogynist agenda" (86). Caspary herself praised the film but disliked the way it transformed Laura into a "Hollywood version of a cute career girl" (*Secrets* 209). In Jay Dratler's original script, according to Biesen (161) and Kalinak (162–63), Laura was given voice-over narration, which Zanuck urged Preminger to remove. According to Preminger, however, Laura's voice-over was added later, at Zanuck's request, then deleted (Bogdanovich 619). For Preminger's recollections about the production see Bogdanovich (614–21).

9. *The Dark Corner* was also produced by Zanuck at 20th Century–Fox, and was coscripted by Jay Dratler, who cowrote *Laura.*

10. Though allegedly by Raphael, the portrait looks nothing like Raphael's females, instead resembling a touched-up twentieth-century photograph. As Richard Dyer notes, the painting also provides a "grim undertow" to Cathcart's earlier quip that "the enjoyment of art is the only remaining ecstasy that is neither illegal nor immoral" (Dyer, "Postscript" 124).

11. The sculpture most closely resembles Donatello's *Fountain Figure of a Winged Angel* (ca. 1440), though that sculpture is bronze, not marble like the film's piece, and much smaller as well: see *Metropolitan Museum,* "Fountain Figure," www.metmuseum.org/TOHA/hd/dona/ho_1983.356.htm.

12. For versions of this argument see Renov 174–91; Belton 240; and Hanson 1–17.

13. For example, when Christopher wakes in his apartment to find Cornell sitting in a chair near his bed, the camera angles and blocking are nearly identical to those in the 1941 version. Several sequences are absent, however, including a sexually suggestive scene in which Jill saws off Christopher's handcuffs. Crain and Peters also resemble each other more than do Grable and Landis.

14. These shots are virtually identical to the camera movements Preminger uses when McPherson dozes in Laura's apartment.

15. *The Woman in the Window*'s principal photography was completed in June 1944 and *Harry*'s a year later. It is possible that the makers of *Uncle Harry* were imitating *Woman*, but it is more likely that a major motivation for both endings was to satisfy the requirements of the Production Code administrators, who frowned on suicide.

16. In Nunnally Johnson's original script (adapted from a novel by J. H. Wallis), Wanley kills himself. But Lang and producer William Goetz insisted on the dream twist. For more on how the scene was created see McGilligan, *Fritz Lang* (310).

17. As E. Ann Kaplan comments, Legrand is placed within internal frames throughout the film to expose how he is "bounded by, trapped in, bourgeois culture" ("Ideology" 43).

18. Near the beginning of *Woman*, Lang dissolves a clock over Wanley's body to express the same idea.

19. Chris's works were actually painted by John Decker (see McGilligan, *Fritz Lang* 322).

20. This moral, and the fact that Cross ends in a living hell, permitted *Scarlet Street* to pass muster with the Breen Office. It didn't, however, prevent the film from being banned in several cities. For an account of this controversy see Bernstein.

21. Minturn (306) notes that the film alludes to the notorious case of Han van Meegeren, who forged a number of works in the manner of Dutch masters (especially Vermeer) that were sold to the Nazis for large sums. For a fuller account of the Meegeren forgeries see Arnau 242–65.

22. Steele's quasi-expressionist aesthetic ignores the likelihood that the socialist Millet was probably trying to portray the poverty and spiritual desperation of the peasants among whom he was raised.

23. Diane Waldman notes that many postwar American films affirmed an "illusionist" aesthetic and viewed modern art with "hostility and suspicion." Among modernism's alleged offenses were elitism, ugliness, incomprehensibility, and political subversiveness (54, 53).

24. Not only did Dalí write a long analysis of the painting, but he created several variations on it, incorporating its two figures into his 1932 painting *Angelus*, into his *El Ángelus arquitectónico de Millet* (1933)—where the praying peasants become two white stones—and into his *Reminiscencia arqueológica de El Ángelus de Millet* (1935). These multiple versions bear out Schwartz's description of the history of art as "the history of copy rites, of transformations that take place during acts of copying" (248). For images see "Art of Europe": www.artofeurope.com/dali/dal26.htm; and "Meeting Dalí!": http://meetingdali.blogspot.com/2011/06/dalis-obsessions-revealed-in.html.

25. In his analysis of the train wreck scenes Miklitsch similarly describes the aural effects as an "exquisite sonic trope for the psychic dislocations of the postwar world" (78).

26. Rolling up the real Dürer work would be impossible, since it was painted on wood.

27. Although the "Scola copy" is an invention of the filmmakers, Dürer forgeries have long been commonplace. Indeed, in the sixteenth century, according to Arnau, there were far more Dürer forgeries in circulation than genuine Dürer works (119–20). For an analysis and reproduction of *Adoration of the Magi* see *Web Gallery of Art*, "Dürer, Albrecht," www.wga.hu/frames-e.html?/html/d/durer/1/04/2adorat.html.

28. This copy was bequeathed to the Metropolitan Museum of Art; the original is in London's Victoria and Albert Museum. Sometime after 1831 the original of this painting was cut vertically, but the parts were reunited before John Forster bequeathed it to the museum. See *Metropolitan Museum*, "The Painter's Daughter Mary" for further details.

CHAPTER FIVE: Noir's Cars

1. *Double Indemnity* was among the first group of American films screened in France after the war (a collection that also included *The Maltese Falcon* and *Murder, My Sweet*), which prompted critic Nino Frank to coin the term *film noir*.

2. Fotsch observes that insurance company profits expanded immensely as car accidents became common (105), and *Double Indemnity* exploits this trend, deriving its premise from an insurance policy clause. Drivers need insurance, and insurance encourages the desire to "crook the system," as Neff declares: murder and insurance are part of the same game. Further, in the James M. Cain novel on which the film is based, there is an elaborate auto-switching scheme in which Neff (named Huff in the book) attempts to murder Phyllis and pin it on her step-daughter Lola's boyfriend (and Phyllis's lover) Nino Sachetti, by using Sachetti's car as a sign of his identity. See Cain, *Double Indemnity* 87–95.

3. Twin Oaks is one of the innumerable roadside diners in noir films, establishments that, like full service "filling" stations, are now obsolete features of highway culture.

4. Wieder and Hall's *The Great American Convertible* and Vose's *The Convertible* illustrate how the convertible was branded to appeal to a sense of youthful rebellion and was depicted in contemporary advertisements as an emblem of upward mobility.

5. Recall, for example, *Out of the Past*, in which Jeff Markham (now known as Bailey) relates the story of his compromised past to his girlfriend, Ann, during a long drive from Bridgeport to Whit Sterling's home at Lake Tahoe.

6. The used-car dealer in lam films epitomizes the law-abiding thieves who judge others. Selling overvalued or worthless autos, they also indicate the sellers' market that dominated the immediate postwar period (when, because of wartime production curbs, anything on wheels could fetch a price) and prey on the belief in automobility as a path to social mobility. For a discussion of the postwar automobile market see Rae, *American Automobile* 161–77; and Rae, *American Automobile Industry* 99–109.

7. Swede in *The Killers* and Jeff Markham/Bailey in *Out of the Past* also express this desire. Jeff is, however, the only one who achieves it, albeit not for long, as we have seen: when Joe Stefanos drives into Jeff's gas station in his shiny convertible, he pulls Jeff back into his restless past.

8. For details about how this scene was conceived and shot see Lewis's interview in Bogdanovich 675–77.

9. Trumbo worked on the script but received no credit since he was already persona non grata as one of the Hollywood Ten. Shadoian similarly reads the carcasses as "an emblem of the employees at the Armour plant and all sodden adherents to a bourgeois homogeneity" (135).

10. Kitses aptly likens the film's "headlong narrative design" to the loops and rolls of a carnival ride (36).

11. Lackey notes how often the picaro figure appears in American road narratives (8). However, these American vagabonds, at least those who populate film noir, lack the wit and resourcefulness of their continental counterparts.

12. Al's fate bears out David Laderman's point (24) that American naturalist fictions, in which characters are at the mercy of huge implacable forces such as the environment, heredity, or poverty, are also important precursors to noirs such as *Detour* and *They Live by Night*.

13. Andrew Britton's reading of Al as an "obtuse and pusillanimous egotist" (179) whom we should root against misreads Tom Neal's portrayal of Al as a passive (albeit dim) victim of circumstance.

14. Laderman claims that the rain is the narrative catalyst for Al's discovery of Haskell's death (32), but it's more in keeping with the film's automotive theme to see the car as the engine of fate.

15. Osteen, "Big Secret" 84.

CHAPTER SIX: Nocturnes in Black and Blue

1. In the 1940s jazz was used only in incidental scenes, and the jazz was never bebop, though bop had become the dominant style by 1950. According to Butler the association between crime films and jazz began in earnest with the rise of jazz themes for TV series such as *Peter Gunn* and *M Squad* in the late 1950s; these "crime jazz" scores created the impression that earlier noirs employed jazz soundtracks as well (147–53).

2. "*Inaudibility*" is the second quality Gorbman lists in her comprehensive list of film music's properties (73; italics in original).

3. Versions of these arguments appear throughout noir criticism. See, for example, Porfirio, "Dark Jazz" 178; Gorbman 86; Kalinak 120; and McCann 121.

4. Jigger's aims are in line with the Popular Front's goals. The notion that jazz epitomizes democratic cooperation is also offered in several jazz-oriented novels of the period, including Dale Curran's *Piano in the Band,* in which a character declares, "The blues are America, they are all of us, black and white, our reaction to a world made too complex for us, a world in which we are subjects of great forces we can't face and fight directly" (16). Later in that novel, an interracial jam session is held in the Communist Party's meeting hall under a portrait of Lenin (120). Near the end, pianist/protagonist George Baker proposes that "we organize [musicians] into a co-

operative and we play our own music. . . . We find a small public for that real music, we plug at it, make that public grow" (208). Ideas about jazz as a democratic force also appear in the writings of the Albert Murray/Stanley Crouch school of contemporary jazz criticism.

5. Richard Whorf was Jewish, and, as Vincent Brook suggests, "jazz and noir [also] intersect with Jewishness in the person, and name, of Jigger Pine" (202). Nicky, played by Elia Kazan, also fills the stereotypical role of the young Jewish intellectual. The two, then, are located in a racial gray area. Krin Gabbard remarks on the conflicting representations of African Americans here: although black players' abilities are portrayed as primitive, Leo's solos were actually played by African American trumpeter Snooky Young (112).

6. As Brook comments, "What better moniker than 'Jigger' to specify a Jewish black wannabe?" (202).

7. One exception occurs in *Appointment with Danger*, a run-of-the-mill pseudodocumentary from 1951, which features a score by Victor Young. Bebop comes up during a conversation between undercover postal inspector Al Goddard (Alan Ladd) and gangster Earl Bettiger's girlfriend, Dodie (Jan Sterling), who asks Goddard, "You like bop?" He answers, "Bop? Is that where everybody plays a different tune at the same time?" She replies, "You just haven't heard enough of it. Have you heard Joe Louie's 'Oh Me, Oh My?' . . . What he can do with a horn! He belts it and melts it and rides it all over the ceiling!" In the next scene she listens, transfixed, to a record that sounds less like bop than like raucous big band swing. "Get this," she says. "Flatted fifth." Goddard protests, "Look, I wouldn't know a flatted fifth if they gave one away with every purchase." The dialogue (by Richard Breen and Warren Duff) displays some knowledge of modern jazz (e.g., that the use of the flatted fifth was a bebop harmonic innovation). But it also depicts bop as a symptom of Dodie's promiscuity and disregard for convention.

8. For an excellent account and analysis of the bebop revolution see DeVeaux.

9. Butler calls the solo "masturbatory" (62), but since "Jeannie" is pretending to enjoy it and urging Cliff to his exertions, it's at least mutual masturbation, if not simulated intercourse.

10. In the source novel Woolrich refers to the musicians' "possessed, demonic" faces and describes the room as a "Dante-esque Inferno," where the sounds and abundant reefers bring "terror into her soul" (144).

11. As McCann astutely notes, the musicians' blousy sleeves adumbrate Steve's arm cast (124), thereby implying jazz's role in fostering his sexual obsession.

12. These two Siodmak films employ the same song, "I'll Remember April," to signify nostalgia and lost love. In *Phantom Lady* it becomes the main musical theme after the phantom lady plays it on the jukebox during the night of the murder. In *Criss Cross* Anna picks out the song's melody on the piano, giving voice to Steve's yearning and to her own apparent regret for losing him and taking up with Slim Dundee.

13. I discuss how this fear is manifest particularly in *D. O. A.* in "The Big Secret" (84).

14. Cantor points out that director Ulmer, an aficionado of classical music, probably would have disapproved of Al's playing jazz (150).

15. A perfect example of this stereotype appears in Ida Lupino's first directorial effort, 1949's *Not Wanted*, in which jazz pianist Steve Ryan (Leo Penn) impregnates

the naive Sally Kelton (Sally Forrest), then abandons her. He has to "travel light," he insists, and even if such selfish restlessness may be "a sickness," he can't help it. I discuss this film and Lupino's other directorial and authorial work in chapter 7.

16. Joe's mother provides some of the film's best moments. In one scene Joe asks her, "How would you feel if I married a murderess?" She replies, "I wouldn't mind, as long as she was a nice girl." The screenplay, by hard-boiled novelist Jonathan Latimer (with help from Harrison), contains plenty of snappy dialogue: when Frances, in costume on a movie set, wearies of Joe's accusations, she dismisses him with "Hop on your scooter, sonny boy, and blow! I've got to emote."

17. The musical sequences in the film are quite believable: Duryea appears to play the piano in several scenes, and June Vincent was in fact a big band singer. The songs—solid midcentury pop—were written for the film by Edgar Fairchild and Jack Brooks.

18. The protagonist is not a musician in either the earlier film or in the source text.

19. The story makes little sense, but it testifies, like the films discussed in the first chapter, to the pervasive influence, and mistrust, of Freudian psychology in midcentury Hollywood. While perusing Belknap's books, Bressard thumbs a copy of Freud's *Studies in Hysteria.*

20. Although their music is definitely of the moldy fig variety, this first interracial jazz group to appear in noir represents a progressive vision. The fact that nobody even comments on the musicians' race may say less about the state of race relations than about Louis Armstrong's singular ability to cross racial boundaries.

21. The implausibility of Armstrong and company agreeing to work with such a novice (not to mention the unlikelihood of the novice's turning them down) is hard to swallow, but we are to understand that Stan is a kid who doesn't yet know what really matters.

22. These scenes feature other musical interludes, including a lively performance of "La Bota" and Vic Damone's lugubrious rendition of "Don't Blame Me," which, despite his exaggerated emoting and flaring nostrils, effectively expresses Stan's feelings for Jane.

23. Stan is doubled with little Artie Dell, the bratty son of one of Jane's friends: on a ride with Jane and Stan, Artie causes a wreck by stomping on the gas pedal; Stan later pulls the same trick to escape from Sonny's muscle men.

24. *Odds* is often cited as the last noir of the classic period. The film was produced by Belafonte's own company, HarBel Productions, and its screenplay credited to African American novelist John O. Killens, though it was actually written by the blacklisted radical Abraham Polonsky. In William McGivern's source novel Ingram is not a musician but a professional gambler.

25. Belafonte insisted on presenting Ingram as a flawed character and hoped the film would "change the way America was doing business" (Buhle and Wagner, *Dangerous* 184–85).

26. Wise's previous film, *I Want to Live!,* also featured a dynamic jazz score by Johnny Mandel, as well as remarkable performances by an interracial bebop combo including Art Farmer and Gerry Mulligan.

27. About *I Want to Live!* protagonist Barbara Graham—a convicted killer who cultivates a taste for avant-garde jazz—Wise wrote, "Human beings . . . don't come in

clearly definable shades of black and white. They come in grays, and often the shades of gray are all but indiscernible" (qtd. in Butler 119). Polonsky wanted to use a simpler ending, but Belafonte sided with Wise in advocating for the explosion; see Server, Polonsky interview (91); and Buhle and Wagner, *Dangerous* 184.

28. Though the source novel's premise is the same as the film's, half of its action occurs after the failed robbery, as Ingram and Slater hole up in a farmhouse. They eventually achieve a rapprochement after Ingram refuses to abandon the wounded Slater, which enables Slater to perceive Ingram (whom he calls "Sambo") as a human being—indeed, as a "buddy"—and incorporate him into the schema of male homosocial relations he discovered during the war.

29. Butler points out that the major influence on this new jazz scoring was Stan Kenton; Mancini and Rogers, for example, used many Kenton musicians on their soundtracks (106).

30. Stanfield argues that American films of this period frequently "represented urban decay through the trope of the burlesque dancer and stripper" (5).

31. For all its virtues James Naremore's terrific short book on the film barely mentions the music.

32. Katz and Hamilton's score was rejected in favor of Bernstein's (Butler 136). Martin Milner's guitar work was dubbed by John Pisano.

33. McCann writes that *Sweet Smell* presents jazz as a "model of hip interracial affinity at odds with a demagogic, and masculinist, popular culture" of Hunsecker and Falco (129). Gabbard likewise observes that the film "associates the music with idealism and a refusal to compromise with the mediocrities represented by Sidney, J. J., and most of the film's other characters. It places Steve very much on the right side of the art vs. commerce binarism," and thus stands as "one of the most flattering portraits" of a jazz musician ever seen in American film (128–29).

34. Lupino was in ill health through much of the troubled shoot, which may have given her performance the world-weary edge it needed (see Donati 124). Her singing was dubbed by Peg La Centra.

35. Adrienne McLean offers a list that includes Lizabeth Scott in *Dark City, I Walk Alone, The Racket,* and *Dead Reckoning;* Lauren Bacall in *To Have and Have Not* and *The Big Sleep;* and Ava Gardner in *The Killers* (13). I would add Nancy Guild in *Somewhere in the Night,* Lupino in *Private Hell 36,* and Ellen Drew (though she doesn't sing on camera) in *The Crooked Way.* Rita Hayworth also memorably asks us to "Put the Blame on Mame" in *Gilda* and delivers sultry melodies in *The Lady from Shanghai* and *Affair in Trinidad.* For further analyses of the role of torch singers and blues women in noir see Miklitsch (192–241).

36. Pagano also wrote the screenplay for *Try and Get Me* (discussed in this book's conclusion) and the film's source novel, *The Condemned.*

37. The film lacks flashback narration and the violence typical of noir. However, its nightclub scenes and multiple betrayals justify Gabbard's description of it as a "*film noir* with musical characters" (269).

38. San isn't the only troubled male in this film. Almost every male character is damaged (Sally's husband, Roy, suffers from war-induced PTSD; neighbor Johnny has a disabled hand), weak (Joey is an ephebe trying to prove himself to his boss), or despicable (Nicky).

39. This song was so well-known, having been a hit in several different versions, that many filmgoers at the time would have "heard" its lyrics even during instrumental versions.

40. In addition to being a dynamic actress, accomplished screenwriter, and the only female director in Hollywood at the time, Lupino was a composer and capable pianist. But she had a singing voice that one contemporary likened to a "nutmeg grinder" (qtd. in Donati 141–42). We hear the grinder again in *Private Hell 36* (a film she cowrote for her company, Filmakers); her character, Lily Marlowe, seems to be a reincarnation of the *Road House* character.

CHAPTER SEVEN: Femmes Vital

1. Cowie similarly writes that noirs "afforded women roles which are active, adventurous and driven by sexual desire" (135), and she lists a few of the female-authored films I discuss in this chapter (136). For a list of female noir protagonists and writers see Martin 222–25.

2. According to D'Ann Campbell, between 1940 and 1947 women held more than half of all clerical jobs. Clerical work was more secure, more traditionally feminine, and less physically demanding than factory work; it also encouraged relationships with educated coworkers. In short, clerical work was "classy" (108).

3. Molly Haskell distills the "woman's film" into four types: the sacrificial story, the tale of affliction, the romance of choice between lovers, and the narrative of female competition (163–64). Doane offers somewhat different categories in *The Desire to Desire* (36): the medical case study, the maternal melodrama, the love story, and the Gothic.

4. Helen Hanson notes, however, that noir deals with "the investigation of the female, the female Gothic with the investigation of the male" (42).

5. Martin lists thirty-three noirs on which women worked as producers, writers, or directors and which also highlighted central female characters (223–24). She lists twenty-seven more involving women writers but not featuring female protagonists.

6. For more background about the negotiations between Breen and the studio see Biesen 141–42.

7. According to the IMDb entry on *Mildred Pierce,* seven other writers also worked on the film, including three additional women: Margaret Gruen, Louise Randall Pierson, and Margaret Buell Wilder.

8. In Cain's novel Mildred's first business is wholesaling her home-baked pies, which become a pungent symbol of her effort to bring the kitchen into the business world: Cain, *Mildred Pierce,* 74–78, 99–100.

9. The film's buildings represent Mildred's shifting identities: the modest Pierce home shows her initial petit bourgeois status; Monty's cabin manifests her buried sexual desire; the restaurant embodies her social mobility; the Beragon estate represents her class aspirations.

10. See also Krutnik, *Lonely* 62. Grossman points out that the Warner Bros. promotional materials recast the film's "representation of female struggle and agency as malevolent" (57).

11. The films are *Phantom Lady, Nocturne, Ride the Pink Horse,* and *The Strange Affair of Uncle Harry.*

12. Hanson writes that Carol's investigation enables her to "ascertain the suitability of the hero as marriage partner" (26), but it's hard to see how she ascertains anything about Henderson, who remains in jail, unchanged and unable to help himself, until the conclusion.

13. Another of the other five was Anita Loos. By 1944 no woman was on the list.

14. According to Ford the actors "discussed all possible sexual permutations . . . including a homosexual attachment" between the male characters. Ford also recalls that the actors didn't know how the film would turn out: "Sometimes we would all be on the set in the morning and Virginia would come in with the script and hand it to us" (qtd. in Martin 215). For a more extensive discussion of the homosexual elements in the film see Dyer, "Resistance" 117–22. For background about the negotiations between the filmmakers and the Production Code Administration see Stokes 30–35.

15. Doane remarks of this scene that Mundson is the "stability against which Gilda is measured. He is predictable and does not deceive the eye" (*Femmes* 106). But Mundson is the one who changes position in the scene and thereby alters the triangle, and his opacity resists penetration by the viewer's eye.

16. The song was written specifically for the film by Doris Fisher and Allan Roberts (Stokes 35–36). Doane asserts that Gilda's striptease offers a metaphor for the entire narrative, which peels away "layers of Gilda's disguises in order to reveal the 'good' woman underneath" (*Femmes* 107). I would add that Farrell is just as much in disguise as she is; her striptease also unveils his nature.

17. Doane, for example, writes that the "image of volatile sexuality attached to Gilda is too convincing" for the rushed ending to undo (*Femmes* 108). Andrew Spicer (103) claims that this ending was added at Van Upp's insistence, but in support he quotes only Martin, who is merely speculating (214–15). Stokes also makes this claim but provides no evidence (29).

18. Walker had previously worked on several B pictures for Poverty Row studios PRC and Republic. One of her early scripts (1943) was for a film called *Danger! Women at Work,* about three gals who try to run a trucking company, a slight comedy that reflects the postwar concern about women in the workforce. Three of her Republic pictures were crime dramas; one of them, *End of the Road,* is a noirish story about a man falsely accused (a crime writer helps to free him: "Gertrude Walker"). Walker reused the wrong-man device in her original story for *Railroaded!* (adapted by John C. Higgins and directed by Anthony Mann), a frame-up tale in which beauty operator Clara Calhoun (Jane Randolph) falsely testifies about a robbery of her establishment organized by her boyfriend, Duke Martin (John Ireland). The sister of the framed man, Rosie Ryan (Sheila Ryan), becomes (like Carol in *Phantom Lady*) an amateur sleuth, meanwhile juggling the attentions of Martin and Detective Mickey Ferguson (Hugh Beaumont). Clara's moral crisis and Rosie's determination provide much of the film's interest. Walker's last film work was the screenplay and story for a 1951 Republic picture called *Insurance Investigator. The Damned Don't Cry,* adapted from her story "Case History," is the best film made from Walker's writing.

19. The scene in which Ethel is interviewed by an employment agency closely resembles two scenes in Cain's *Mildred Pierce:* both women want higher-class jobs than their qualifications allow; both turn down jobs as housemaids. It seems likely that Wald, who produced both films, borrowed the scene from Cain's novel. See Cain, *Mildred Pierce* 43–50.

20. The slapping scene drew the attention of the censors, who insisted that the beating be softened and shortened (*"The Damned Don't Cry"* PCA file).

21. Frings also authored the original story for *Hold Back the Dawn* and the screenplay for the Gothic *Guest in the House* (1944) before moving to Paramount. Her most celebrated cinematic work was the screen adaptation of William Inge's play *Come Back, Little Sheba.* After retiring from movie work, she wrote for television and then returned to theater. Her adaptation of Thomas Wolfe's *Look Homeward, Angel* enjoyed a successful Broadway run in 1958–59 and won her the 1958 Pulitzer Prize for Drama ("Ketti Frings").

22. Frings's other noir, *Dark City,* also depicts complicity. In it Dan Haley (Charlton Heston) is complicit in the suicide of a tourist named Arthur Winant because he fails to stop his associates from cheating Winant in a card game.

23. The trial scenes were drastically shortened in the course of script revisions. Frings's first draft (dated Nov. 18, 1948) does not depict Cleve and Thelma discussing her testimony, as in the finished film; this material was introduced in the version dated Jan. 4, 1949. *File on Thelma Jordon* script files.

24. This gambit went through various versions. In the first drafts Thelma cuts the car's lights to cause the crash. Apparently feeling that wasn't sufficient, in the draft of Feb. 7, 1949, Frings has Thelma both cut the lights *and* burn Tony with the lighter! The lines about the chameleon appear in the first draft, dated Nov. 18, 1948 (Frings, *File on Thelma Jordon* script files).

25. Yet ads for the film presented Thelma as a femme fatale with lines such as "Nothing stops Thelma Jordon. . . . She'll lie . . . kill . . . or kiss her way out of anything" (Paramount press sheets). Successive screenplay drafts show Frings softening Thelma's character. For example, in the first two drafts Thelma herself suggests that Cleve hire Willis. In the "final white" version (Feb. 7, 1949), Cleve comes up with the plan (*File on Thelma Jordon* script files).

26. The novel lacks this flashback, as do earlier drafts of the screenplay by Barre Lyndon and Jonathan Latimer. Lyndon's initial version (dated Jan. 6, 1947) and Latimer's draft (Jan. 15, 1947) begin, like the source novel, with the exam. Lyndon's second draft (July 25, 1947) starts at the moment of Wilma's near-rape. Lyndon's first draft lacks the necessary hook—why is this woman acting so strangely?—and his second iteration risks undermining viewers' sympathy for Wilma before the story even starts. Frings's first draft (Feb. 18, 1948, under the title "Strange Deception") cannily places the flashback where it stands in the film and thus thrusts the audience immediately into a dramatic situation.

27. In the epigraph to the source novel, *Be Still, My Love,* author June Truesdell writes that Wilma "is the victim of CONDITIONED REFLEXES just as surely as the test animals in her own laboratory" (5).

28. The near-rape scene, shot on May 28, 1948, was the final scene filmed, according to Hal Wallis's script notes. As one might expect, the scene was a bone of contention between the studio and the Breen Office. Stephen Jackson, a PCA administrator, wrote to Wallis in February of 1948 that the film could not show any struggle preceding the near-rape; another letter of March 8 reiterates the complaint. After assurances from the studio the PCA approved the film in April. In May, though, Jackson wrote angrily to Wallis, protesting that he and director William Dieterle had refused to let the PCA representative on set as the scene was shot. In none of the screenplay drafts,

however, is there any indication that Wilma complies with the young man's advances. In Truesdell's novel she doesn't resist but seems to grow passive as Bill (named Frank) kisses her: "She rested there, her lips slightly parted, her heart lost in the surging sound of his pulse" (25).

29. *Cyclothymia* is an older psychiatric term for what is now usually called a bipolar disorder. The term does not exist in the source novel, which instead uses the term *parathyroic* (Truesdell 112, 165–66). "Cyclothymia" and its variations were added in early script drafts by Lyndon and the first writer hired, Allen Rivkin (*Be Still* 108). Frings contributed the idea of showing Dorgan reading Bill's exam (*Strange Deception* 70).

30. The two men rudely speak about her, in her presence, as if she weren't there: "What do you do with her when she's like this, Warren?" Dorgan asks. "Flowers, candy, a mink coat?" Dorgan's attitude hints at the sexist assumptions female professionals faced at the time: a moody dame can surely be pacified with gifts.

31. The boxing scenes, along with some clever ideas for "trick shots," originated with Frings (*Strange Deception*).

32. In the novel Wilma doesn't hesitate to agree. Truesdell's Tuttle, unlike the film's, hates her job, loathes her students, and refers to her colleagues as "pigs" (135).

33. Truesdell's novel is much harsher in this respect, repeatedly suggesting that all academics are stuffy and boring and that Wilma willfully deludes herself. Frings's screenplay tones down the novel's anti-intellectualism.

34. For *The Accused*, Frings earned $2,000 per week, whereas male writers Barre Lyndon, Allen Rivkin, and Jonathan Latimer earned $1,500, $1,500, and $1,250 per week, respectively. No doubt partly in recognition of her work on *The Accused*, after completing the first draft of *Thelma Jordon* Frings renegotiated her contract to receive $2,250 per week to complete that script (see Wallis, Contract with Ketti Frings, Dec. 21, 1948).

35. As Pam Cook notes, Ann is repeatedly filmed "as if she is in prison" (for example, from behind her railed bedstead: 62).

36. As Ronnie Scheib astutely observes, "it is his naming of the desired, feared, and repressed sexual relationship" with Bruce that "triggers the shutting off of his voice, and exaggerates and displaces the already multiply-displaced sexuality" (60).

37. R. Barton Palmer aptly points out that the doctor, an "archly patriarchal figure who sees women as prisoners of their own nature," views Louise as an enigma who can be explained only by "discourses . . . articulated by men" (157, 158).

38. Richards also scripted the Fritz Lang film *Secret beyond the Door*, a Gothic-noir hybrid about female entrapment in marriage. She underwent Freudian therapy in the mid-1940s and credited it with saving her life (Francke 52–53). A former Communist, she was subpoenaed by HUAC in 1953; worried about her two children (she was separated from husband Robert Richards) and pressured by the men in her life, including writing partner Richard Collins and lawyer Martin Gang, she cooperated with the committee. "My decisions about HUAC were passive—those of a woman," she later admitted (qtd. in Navasky 266). Richards retired from film work after 1952 (aside from scripting Lang's *Rancho Notorious*) and became a nursery school teacher. See Navasky 264–68, who, like Buhle and Wagner, misspells her first name as "Sylvia"; her film title credits spell it "Silvia."

39. This ending was encouraged by Breen, who recommended to Jack Warner a conclusion in which Louise was found "incurably insane" (Breen to Warner, August 26, 1946).

40. The PCA files demonstrate how difficult it was to squeeze in any tough material. The censors objected to any reference to "dope addiction" and to the suggestion that some of the inmates might be prostitutes. They also insisted that the film indict not the system but only "corrupt" officials (Breen to Warner, June 10, 1949, 1–2). The most absurd objection—one that delayed the granting of the film's certificate of approval—involved the implication that inmates might actually take showers in the nude and that other inmates might see them that way! See letter from Breen to Warner July 22, 1949; see also the memo from Jack Vizzard (a Breen staffer) to Warner.

41. Kellogg and cowriter Bernard Schoenfeld received an Oscar nomination for the screenplay. Kellogg had previously written the original stories for *White Heat* and the Anthony Mann/John Alton film *T-Men*.

42. Ophuls, the original choice, was debilitated by an attack of shingles, so Berry was hired. But when Berry fell behind schedule, he was fired and Ophuls rehired. Production manager Robert Aldrich estimated that between a third and a half of the finished film is Berry's work (Eyles 24–25). Laurents had previously scripted Hitchcock's *Rope* and later forged a distinguished theatrical career that included the librettos for *West Side Story* and *Gypsy*.

43. Enterprise was co-owned by Charles Einfeld, David L. Loew, and A. Pam Blumenthal. The studio produced nine features between 1947 and 1949, including *Body and Soul* and *Force of Evil,* but the box-office failure of its would-be blockbuster, *Arch of Triumph,* doomed it (Eyles 20–21).

44. Originally cast as Leonora, Ginger Rogers wouldn't approve a script, so the younger and more credible Bel Geddes took her place. Smith Ohlrig was allegedly based on Howard Hughes, who insisted on seeing the rushes every evening but never demanded changes (Eyles 23–24). *Caught*'s Smith is likely a latent homosexual: his relationship with his valet, Franzi, indicates his proclivities about as clearly as a Hollywood film of the period could do so. The character differs considerably from the one in Libbie Block's novel, where he is a passive boy-man who cares little about money and really wants to collect art and is dominated by his older brother Earnest, who asks for Maud's hand in marriage by appealing to her mother.

45. In her brilliant reading of this scene Doane remarks that Leonora's laugh "breaks the mirror relation between Ohlrig and his image," and notes the reversal of Leonora's spectatorial role (*Desire* 159, 162).

46. These scenes depart widely from the novel, in which Maud's child does not die and in which she is portrayed as a loving mother. A mildly satirical coming-of-age story, *Wild Calendar* depicts Maud marrying and divorcing Ohlrig, getting a humble job, then wedding hotel employee Sonny Quinada, who, unlike the film's do-gooder doctor, is narrow-minded and rather unpleasant. The novel's title implies that women must pass through adolescence, young adulthood, courtship, marriage, and motherhood in the proper order. If these stages occur in the "wrong" order, the woman will be stunted or regress. *Wild Calendar* does contain a blunted critique of marriage: at one point Maud wonders if "marriage is a cage" (Block 310), and she seems happiest, though she doesn't seem to realize it, when single.

47. Enterprise was in serious financial trouble by 1948 and folded before *Caught* was released in early 1949. Though the film was distributed by MGM, the studio had little interest in promoting it, and *Caught* did poorly at the box office.

48. Coscripted by future blacklistee Paul Jarrico, *Not Wanted* was credited to Elmer Clifton, but he had a heart attack at the outset of the shoot, and Lupino took over. An earlier version of the script, entitled *Bad Company,* was considered by Enterprise before it went to Lupino. For more on the film's production history see Donati 148–53.

49. Lupino and company conducted lengthy negotiations with the PCA to get the story approved; for details see Waldman, "Not Wanted" 21–31. Quite grateful to the censors for working with her, Lupino was outraged when an interview she had granted to Virginia McPherson of UPI was used to mock the film in an article entitled "A Degenerate Article about a Degenerate Industry," when it appeared in the *Ashland (WI) Daily Press* in February of 1949. Lupino wired Breen, expressing her shock and assuring him that the "key note" of her remarks to McPherson had been gratitude toward the code administrators (Lupino telegram). Breen wrote to the *Daily Press*'s editor defending the film.

50. Wald, who had written the original story and coauthored the screenplay (with Albert Maltz) for *The Naked City,* also cowrote *Outrage* and *Not Wanted.*

51. The mise-en-scènes of the two settings underline these differences: high-key lighting and a lavish apartment in San Francisco; low-key lighting and repeated shots of doors and enclosures in LA (Seiter 108).

52. This situation gains additional resonance when one realizes that cowriter Young had been married to the ambitious, glamorous, and highly successful Lupino.

53. This sequence contains a couple of inside jokes: when the driver announces that they'll see their "favorite stars of stage and screen," the next shot is of Ida Lupino. And one of the homes they gawk at is hailed as the residence of the world-renowned star of *The Miracle on 34th St.,* Edmund Gwenn—the actor playing Jordan in the film we're watching!

54. Scheib writes that Eve represents Graham's "former driving, future-oriented ambition," whereas Phyllis embodies the "take-it-as-it-comes intimacy that tempts him in middle age" (64). This reading, however, makes bigamy seem innocuous and Graham psychologically sound.

55. Seiter writes that the film insists on marriage as a "social arrangement" (112), but that interpretation ignores the central importance of childbearing and -rearing to the story—the Grahams' desire to adopt and Harry's care of his baby in his other marriage.

CHAPTER EIGHT: Left-Handed Endeavor

1. For a helpful account of the Popular Front's rise and fall see Ceplair and Englund 83–199.

2. See Ceplair and Englund 268; Navasky xiii; and the Dassin interview in Mc-Gilligan and Buhle 209.

3. The roster includes *A Walk in the Sun* and *Edge of Darkness* (both directed by the radical Lewis Milestone and scripted by Rossen); *A Guy Named Joe, Tender*

Comrade, and *Thirty Seconds over Tokyo* (scripted by Trumbo); *Cornered* and *Cross-fire* (directed by Edward Dmytryk, produced by Adrian Scott); *Destination Tokyo, This Gun for Hire,* and *Pride of the Marines* (scripted by Albert Maltz; the last-named film starred John Garfield); *Action in the North Atlantic* and *Sahara* (written by John Howard Lawson); *Objective: Burma* (scripted by Lester Cole); and *The Master Race* (written and directed by Herbert Biberman). Except for Milestone, Garfield, and Rossen, these artists were all members of the indicted Hollywood Ten.

4. Lawson and Irving Pichel contributed many articles; Polonsky wrote for *HQ* as well. See Buhle and Wagner 291–300.

5. For a summary of Hollywood labor struggles in the 1940s see May 180–95; for a more expansive account see Ceplair and Englund 209–53.

6. The journal that Trumbo edited, the *Screen Writer,* unwittingly helped to bring on the reaction by publishing James M. Cain's proposal to found an American Authors Authority, which would oversee credits and copyrights for screenwriters. His idea—which aimed to protect the intellectual property of writers and was therefore thoroughly capitalist in spirit—was quickly and viciously attacked as "communistic." See Tim Palmer (65–66) and the Dassin interview in McGilligan and Buhle (211).

7. Lawson, Dmytryk, Cole, Trumbo, Maltz, Biberman, and Scott, along with writers Samuel Ornitz, Alvah Bessie, and Ring Lardner Jr.—the so-called Hollywood Ten—all went to prison. For a brief list of the Ten's credits before the hearings see Navasky (80–81). Bertolt Brecht, who also testified, left the United States and never served jail time. The others subpoenaed were Milestone, Rossen, and director Pichel; actor Larry Parks; and writers Richard Collins, Gordon Kahn, Howard Koch, and Waldo Salt.

8. The best and most thorough account of the hearings remains that of Ceplair and Englund (254–98).

9. The full statement is printed in Appendix 6 of Ceplair and Englund (455).

10. The red scare was not, of course, confined to Hollywood. Broe notes that more than 20 percent of the workforce in the early 1950s was subjected to loyalty oaths; workers risked investigation or loss of employment if they failed to sign (84).

11. Earl Browder was the general secretary of the CPUSA in the 1930s, and Henry Wallace, who was President Franklin Roosevelt's vice president during the war, ran for president as a Socialist in 1948.

12. Kemp asserts that noir offers "far too many . . . examples of left-wing slant to be credibly attributed to a handful of individuals" (268), adducing as his test case *Where Danger Lives,* a product of the reactionary Howard Hughes's era at RKO. Although Kemp seems to conflate all social criticism with "leftism," he nonetheless makes a persuasive case that noir as a whole critiques the "cash nexus," condemns the "wealth-based class system," and dramatizes how rampant individualism shatters communities (Kemp 269).

13. It is not an accident that ten of the sixteen films on Hirsch's list were independent productions. Nor is it a surprise that among their makers, eleven directors and nine writers were either blacklisted or deemed politically suspect by HUAC (J. Hirsch 91). Hirsch also declares that "after 1951, the blacklist rendered the social critique of films gris not only inconceivable, but impossible" (91).

14. Hirsch writes that the 1930s gangster films presented a "symptomatic" critique, while the later films offer a "systematic implicit critique" (85). By *symptomatic* he means that the critique must be extracted by critics; by *implicit* he means that the critique is deliberate. But these terms seem misleading (*implicit* actually means "explicit") and rely on too much speculation about the earlier filmmakers' intentions; hence I have substituted different terms.

15. In his interview in *Tender Comrades*, Dassin calls it a "really dumb picture" (207).

16. The original script, by Malvin Wald and Albert Maltz, swooped through the working and impoverished classes of New York City, pointedly contrasting street sweepers and homeless people with upper-class citizens. Dassin and producer Mark Hellinger, a former investigative journalist who had also produced *The Killers* and *Brute Force* for Universal, aimed to imitate the documentary aesthetic they admired in Italian neorealism (see Prime 145–47). Their decision to shoot on the streets of New York was as radical as the content, which, Dassin feared, would be challenged by the studio heads, particularly after Maltz was subpoenaed by HUAC. And it was.

17. When the script was first submitted to the censors (as *Hard Bargain*) on November 1, 1948, the Breen Office objected to the implication that Rica is a prostitute (Breen to Jason S. Joy). This letter specifies several other objections to the sexual suggestiveness in the scenes between Conte and Cortesa. The producers agreed to reshoot the scenes to eliminate suggested nudity and sex. A letter to Joy from Robert Bassler of the PCA (Feb. 24, 1949) notes that Rica would be given a job as a fortune teller. The film was approved on June 20, 1949. Despite these alterations, *Variety* enthused about its "torrid sex" and "no-holds barred love sequences" (Rev., Sept. 7, 1949). Its reviewer was quite aware that Rica is a prostitute.

18. In his review Bosley Crowther, no Communist, recognized the leftist implications of the story, writing, "you will never be able to eat an apple or tomato again without calling up visions of trickery, mayhem, vandalism and violent death."

19. In the interview accompanying the DVD Dassin relates how Zanuck shot the ending while he was away and, earlier, had forced him to add the Polly character, whom Dassin calls "useless." But Dassin himself had lobbied for the casting of Cortesa instead of Shelley Winters, whom Zanuck wanted for the role. Bezzerides comments: "I had [to deal with] the producer's chickenshit changes, the director's girlfriend, and Zanuck's ideas" about the beginning and ending, all of which, he believes, weakened the final product (qtd. in Server, "Thieves' Market" 120).

20. Their evaluation is hardly to be trusted, since among the other films singled out as "communist" was the hugely popular and adamantly liberal *Best Years of Our Lives*.

21. The first version of the story is a "treatment"—a 132-page prose narrative— called *Love-Lies-Bleeding*, by Jack Patrick. Patrick's story is much less concerned with class than is Rossen's finished script.

22. Broe asserts that the stairway represents the passage from one class to another (67), but it more likely stands for the class hierarchy itself, and Milestone uses verticality throughout the film to represent class relations.

23. Neve argues that the film presents political life largely as a "front, thinly disguising the determining material forces" ("Red" 191), a reading that suggests a vulgar

Marxist perspective. But this interpretation fails to acknowledge the characters' mixed emotions about wealth, class, and each other.

24. Davis's name is spelled two different ways in the film. On the brush he gives to Peg it is spelled "Charlie," but in many of the boxing posters it is spelled "Charley." I've chosen the former since, presumably, Davis would know how to spell his own name. Roberts was given his name—the same name as the coproducer—to avoid the possibility that his name was that of a real crook (Eyles 16). Actor Lloyd Gough's name was then spelled "Goff," but I have used the spelling by which he was best known. Gough, too, was blacklisted and unable to work in Hollywood from 1952 until 1964.

25. Garfield, whom Andersen calls the "first axiom" of "film gris" (258), was among the first "Method" actors to become a Hollywood star. Born Jacob Julius Garfinkle in New York's Lower East Side in 1913, Garfield was a committed leftist who emerged from New York's Group Theatre and often played roles that evoked his own early years as a slum kid who fought his way to the top (Andersen 258).

26. Polonsky allegedly came up with the story during a short walk from Paramount to Enterprise and "made a present" of it to Enterprise co-owner Charles Einfeld (Polonsky, qtd. in McGilligan and Buhle 485). The original concept for *Body and Soul* was based on the life of boxer Barney Ross; when Ross was arrested on a drug charge, Einfeld wanted to cancel the picture, but Rossen insisted on carrying it through (Eyles 16); see Eyles for an informative history of Enterprise's brief moment in the sun.

27. Robert Wise's *The Set-Up* also portrays a boxer directed to take a dive, but its protagonist, aging pug Stoker Thompson (Robert Ryan), isn't in on the fix. Though admirable in his uncompromising devotion to his dream, Stoker is more pathetic than heroic: he believes he is just a fight away from a title shot, but it's clear that he is really one fight away from brain damage or death. This strikingly directed fable is set in a place called Paradise City, near a club called Dreamland, and depicts its boxers as innocents pursuing delusions of success, unaware that they are pawns in a game of profit-taking. Even more than *Body and Soul*, *The Set-Up* shows how the boxers enact their fans' appetites for violence, fame, and success. In the end Stoker wins his fight but is beaten so severely afterward that, luckily for him, he will never fight again. *Champion* seemed so similar to *The Set-Up* that RKO sued its producers (Stanfield, "Monarch" 79); see Stanfield's "Monarch" for a fine survey of the postwar boxing movie.

28. Originally the film was to be titled *Tiger, Tiger, Burning Bright* (Eyles 16).

29. Watching this scene, it is difficult not to recall that Garfield and Lee both died after being stigmatized and hounded by red-baiters. Here, alas, art adumbrates life.

30. Rossen and Polonsky disagreed about the ending. Rossen wanted to conclude with Charlie being shot by Roberts's thugs and falling into a barrel of trash but finally accepted Polonsky's more positive ending, which jibes more smoothly with the film's fable-like tone. For further details see Neve, "Red" 194–95, and "Abraham Polonsky" 486.

31. For other versions of this argument see Polonsky, quoted in May 226 ("gangsterism is capitalism or the other way around"); Mason 74; Andersen 259.

32. Munby notes that Leo's "perception of himself . . . as hopelessly anachronistic in the face of new forms of 'organization' is shared by a whole host of protagonists in

the postwar gangster-syndicate film" (130), such as those in *The Gangster, I Walk Alone,* and *New York Confidential.* The syndicate film constitutes a significant subgenre of 1950s crime films; unlike red noir, however, most of these films are exposés or pro–law enforcement vehicles.

33. There may be an allusion here to *The Communist Manifesto*'s comparison of modern bourgeois society to a "sorcerer" (Marx and Engels 478).

34. Polonsky observes, "I don't ask myself 'Now what are the social issues I have to realize here?' There's a Marxian world view behind my films, not because I plan it that way. That's what I am" (qtd. in Kemp 268). Marx's analysis of the four forms of alienation appears in the *Economic and Philosophic Manuscripts of 1844.* See Tucker 72–77.

35. The agents overheard and transcribed a conversation between Polonsky and Wolfert in which the two acknowledged that the phone was probably tapped. Polonsky sardonically reminded Wolfert, "You know, we're not living in a police state. . . . We're living in a free democracy." See Buhle and Wagner, *Dangerous Citizen* (235–38) for a transcript of this conversation.

36. Polonsky hated David Raksin's music for this scene. The piece, "Regeneration," rises to a triumphant major-chord conclusion, seeming incompatible with the degradation and remorse pictured ("Abraham Polonsky" 489).

37. Stuart Kaminsky notes that the heist film derives from stories of "communal quests requiring cooperation of men with special powers" (qtd. in Telotte, "Fatal Capers" 164). For helpful analyses of the heist picture see Telotte, "Fatal Capers"; and Mason 97–105.

38. Huston's film shares the distinction as the first true heist film with the B picture *Armored Car Robbery,* directed by Richard Fleischer: both films were released on the same day, June 8, 1950. The two films constitute the dexter and sinister arms of the subgenre. Whereas *Asphalt* explores the lives and motives of its humble criminals, Fleischer's film presents a police detective (played by Charles McGraw) as its protagonist and paints its criminals, especially leader Dave Purvis (William Talman), as psychopaths and selfish weasels.

39. Tropes of gaming and gambling appear in almost every heist picture, regardless of its politics. For example, Stanley Kubrick's *The Killing* depicts a race-track robbery; *Kansas City Confidential* (Phil Karlson) uses four playing cards as identifying marks and depicts many card games; *5 against the House* (also directed by Karlson) concerns a casino heist; Johnny Ingram, in *Odds against Tomorrow,* is a compulsive gambler. These tropes not only reflect the idea that the gangs are playing a game but also indicate the risks involved in their left-handed endeavors.

40. The name of the hotel thus predicts and sardonically comments on Dix's final pilgrimage back to Kentucky. As Mason suggests, the gang—consisting of two Italian Americans and a WASP southerner, and headed by two men with German names—constitutes a miniature American melting pot (138).

41. May asserts that the gang members display a "communal spirit" that contrasts favorably with the corruption of officials such as Ditrich (243). But he goes too far in claiming that they embody "family values": although they do come together, their solidarity is fragile and ephemeral.

42. Joshua Hirsch outlines three strategies by which red noirs deconstruct divisions between crime and legitimate society. If *Force of Evil* uses what he calls

"simile"—juxtaposing criminals and noncriminals to show their similarities—*Asphalt Jungle* relies more on "antiphrasis"—reversing values to depict criminals as honorable and the "legal" world as dishonorable (85).

43. Hayden, who plays the rock-solid Dix, ironically became one of the first "friendly" witnesses in the second round of HUAC hearings, not long after *Asphalt Jungle* was released. Tormented by guilt for naming names, he spent his later years apologizing and condemning the blacklist. See Ceplair and Englund 364, 391; and Navasky 129–30, where Hayden speaks of his self-contempt after testifying. In the latter, Hayden tersely summarizes the predicament of all the witnesses: "Cooperate and I'm a stool pigeon. Shut my mouth and I'm a pariah" (130).

44. In another of the blacklist era's grotesque ironies Marc Lawrence, who plays Cobby, became a "friendly" witness during the second round of HUAC hearings. Lawrence told Lee Server that testifying was "like a stab in the back. You're still breathing, but you . . . can't get the thing out of your back" (Server, "Marc Lawrence" 53).

45. Henry Blankfort, *Underworld*'s coscreenwriter, was the cousin of fellow radical writer Michael Blankfort, who named him before HUAC. Afterward, Henry Blankfort left the movie business (Buhle and Wagner, *Radical* 365–66).

46. Bowing to pressure from distributors, the filmmakers cast a white actress, Mary Anderson, as Molly (Neve, *Film* 178). Close scrutiny of key scenes reveals that all words referring to Molly's race were overdubbed in postproduction (the actors' lips form other words). The MPA censor board reports that the word *nigger* was removed from the film for screenings in Massachusetts, Ohio, and Pennsylvania. The Breen office had earlier recommended that the filmmakers remove the word: see letter from Breen to Forrest Judd of Allied Artists.

47. As Buhle and Wagner observe, the liberals leading the defense committee "look a lot like the real-life Civil Rights Congress—as many in the noir audience would have recognized—at that moment frantically pursued by the FBI, baited by [HUAC] and finally destroyed after several dramatic campaigns for southern African-American defendants" (*Radical* 344).

48. Similar media lynchings were occurring at that moment in Hollywood, led by right-wing columnists such as Westbrook Pegler and George Sokolsky of the *Hollywood Reporter* (Humphries 235).

49. This critical stance probably explains certain newspaper reviewers' antipathy for the film. See, for example, Bosley Crowther's review in the *New York Times* of Sept. 27, 1950.

50. The film's ultimate title was a last-minute decision: the picture was first submitted to the censors for approval under the title *The Whip*, and later versions were entitled *The Whipped*; even its first reviews (e.g., by the *Hollywood Reporter* and *Variety* of March 1950), call it by that name. It was finally submitted for certification in May 1950 under its current title (PCA File, *The Underworld Story*).

CONCLUSION

1. Endfield didn't want to cooperate with HUAC (doing so seemed to him "seedy") or to plead the Fifth, so he immigrated to England and rebuilt his career there (Neve, *Film* 180). His recollection, in 1989, is clear-eyed about how the Hollywood Left was

deluded by Stalinism and communism. But the witch hunt, Endfield claims, was mostly just publicity-mongering. He concludes that in the end "it's hard to say who was more wrong," the witch hunters or the Communist apologists (qtd. in Neve, *Film* 181).

2. Naremore writes that the film is such a "thoroughgoing indictment of capitalism and liberal complacency that it transcends the ameliorative limits of the social-problem picture" (*More Than Night* 127): that is, the problems do not merely stem from corruption but inhere in the institutions themselves.

3. Against Endfield's wishes Stillman insisted on including these preachy scenes (Neve, *Film* 179).

4. Although these words sound like bland liberal pieties, to include them, the filmmakers had to ignore the Breen Office's warnings that the movie should include no "philosophizing" that "might seem to relieve your murderers of the blame for their crimes and put it on society generally" (Breen to Robert Stillman).

5. To produce the fine performances in this film, Losey rehearsed his actors for almost two weeks, then shot the film in a spare nineteen days (Ciment 99).

6. Even Garwood's car testifies to this history: the Cadillac automobile was named for the French explorer Antoine Laumet de La Mothe, sieur de Cadillac, who founded the city of Detroit. Cadillac embodied both the Dream and the fraud: not a nobleman, as he claimed, he actually emigrated to America to escape debtors, then reinvented himself as a dandy and aristocrat (ehow.com).

FILMOGRAPHY

Asterisks indicate blacklistees.

The Accused. Dir. William Dieterle. Scr. Ketti Frings. Paramount, 1949.
Act of Violence. Dir. Fred Zinnemann. Perf. Van Heflin and Robert Ryan. Scr. Robert L. Richards. MGM, 1949.
Anatomy of a Murder. Dir. Otto Preminger. Music by Duke Ellington. Columbia, 1959.
Appointment with Danger. Dir. Lewis Allen. Paramount, 1951.
Armored Car Robbery. Dir. Richard Fleischer. RKO, 1950.
The Asphalt Jungle. Dir. John Huston. MGM, 1950.
The Best Years of Our Lives. Dir. William Wyler. Perf. Dana Andrews, Fredric March, and Harold Russell. MGM, 1946.
The Bigamist. Dir. Ida Lupino. Scr. Collier Young. Filmakers, 1953.
The Big Combo. Dir. Joseph H. Lewis. Music by David Raksin. Allied Artists, 1955.
The Big Night. Dir. Joseph Losey.* Scr. Hugo Butler,* Dalton Trumbo* [uncredited], and Joseph Losey. United Artists, 1951.
Black Angel. Dir. Roy Neill. Universal, 1946.
The Blue Dahlia. Dir. George Marshall. Scr. Raymond Chandler. Paramount, 1946.
The Blue Gardenia. Dir. Fritz Lang. Story by Vera Caspary. Warner Bros., 1953.
Blues in the Night. Dir. Anatole Litvak. Warner Bros., 1941.
Body and Soul. Dir. Robert Rossen.* Scr. Abraham Polonsky.* Perf. John Garfield.* Enterprise/United Artists, 1947.
Brute Force. Dir. Jules Dassin.* Prod. Mark Hellinger. Scr. Richard Brooks. Universal, 1947.
Caged. Dir. John Cromwell. Scr. Virginia Kellogg and Bernard C. Schoenfeld. Perf. Eleanor Parker. Warner Bros, 1950.
Caught. Dir. Max Ophuls. From the novel *Wild Calendar,* by Libbie Block. Enterprise/MGM, 1949.
Champion. Dir. Mark Robson. United Artists, 1949.
The Chase. Dir. Arthur Ripley. United Artists, 1946.
Cornered. Dir. Edward Dmytryk.* Scr. John Paxton. Story by John Wexley.* Prod. Adrian Scott.* RKO, 1945.
Crack-Up. Dir. Irving Reis. Scr. John Paxton, Ben Bengal,* and Ray Spencer. RKO, 1946.

Criss Cross. Dir. Robert Siodmak. Scr. Daniel Fuchs. Universal, 1949.

The Crooked Way. Dir. Robert Florey. United Artists, 1949.

Crossfire. Dir. Edward Dmytryk.* Prod. Adrian Scott.* RKO, 1947.

"*Crossfire:* Hate Is like a Gun." DVD featurette with *Crossfire.* Turner Entertainment, 2005. DVD.

The Damned Don't Cry. Dir. Vincent Sherman. Perf. Joan Crawford. Story by Gertrude Walker. Warner Bros., 1950.

Dark City. Dir. William Dieterle. Scr. John Meredyth Lucas and Larry Marcus; adapted by Ketti Frings. Paramount, 1950.

The Dark Corner. Dir. Henry Hathaway. Scr. Jay Dratler and Bernard Schoenfeld. 20th Century–Fox, 1946.

Dark Passage. Dir. Delmer Daves. Perf. Humphrey Bogart, Lauren Bacall, and Agnes Moorehead. Warner Bros., 1947.

The Dark Past. Dir. Rudolph Maté. Perf. Lee J. Cobb and William Holden. Scr. Philip MacDonald, Michael Blankfort,* and Albert Duffy. Columbia, 1948.

Dark Waters. Dir. André De Toth. Scr. Joan Harrison and Marian Cockrell. Benedict Bogeaus/United Artists, 1944.

Dead Reckoning. Dir. John Cromwell. Perf. Humphrey Bogart, Lizabeth Scott. Columbia, 1947.

Desperate. Dir. Anthony Mann. RKO, 1947.

Detour. Dir. Edgar G. Ulmer. Perf. Tom Neal and Ann Savage. PRC, 1945.

The Devil Thumbs a Ride. Dir. Felix Feist. RKO, 1947.

D. O. A. Dir. Rudolph Maté. United Artists, 1950.

Double Indemnity. Dir. Billy Wilder. Paramount, 1944.

The File on Thelma Jordon. Dir. Robert Siodmak. Scr. Ketti Frings. Paramount, 1950.

5 against the House. Dir. Phil Karlson. Columbia, 1955.

Force of Evil. Dir. Abraham Polonsky.* Perf. John Garfield* and Thomas Gomez. Enterprise/MGM, 1948.

From Here to Eternity. Dir. Fred Zinnemann. Columbia, 1953.

Fury. Dir. Fritz Lang. MGM, 1936.

The Gangster. Dir. Gordon Wiles. Allied Artists, 1947.

Gilda. Dir. Charles Vidor. Prod. Virginia Van Upp. Perf. Rita Hayworth, Glenn Ford, and George Macready. Columbia, 1946.

Gun Crazy. Dir. Joseph H. Lewis. Scr. MacKinlay Kantor, Millard Kaufman, and Dalton Trumbo.* United Artists, 1949.

High Wall. Dir. Curtis Bernhardt. Scr. Sydney Boehm and Lester Cole.* MGM, 1947.

The Hitch-Hiker. Dir. Ida Lupino. Perf. Edmond O'Brien, Frank Lovejoy, and William Talman. RKO, 1953.

Hollow Triumph. Dir. Steve Sekely. Scr. Daniel Fuchs. Perf. Paul Henreid and Joan Bennett. Eagle-Lion, 1948.

I Wake Up Screaming. Dir. Bruce Humberstone. Perf. Victor Mature, Betty Grable, and Laird Cregar. 20th Century–Fox, 1942.

I Walk Alone. Dir. Byron Haskin. Paramount, 1948.

I Want to Live! Dir. Robert Wise. United Artists, 1958.

"Jules Dassin Interview." *Thieves' Highway.* Criterion Collection, 2005. DVD.

Kansas City Confidential. Dir. Phil Karlson. United Artists, 1952.

The Killers. Dir. Robert Siodmak. Universal, 1946.

The Killing. Dir. Stanley Kubrick. United Artists, 1956.

Kiss Me Deadly. Dir. Robert Aldrich. Scr. A. I. Bezzerides. United Artists, 1955.

La chienne. Dir. Jean Renoir. Braunberger-Richebé, 1931.

Laura. Dir. Otto Preminger. Scr. Jay Dratler, Samuel Hoffenstein, and Betty Reinhardt. Music by David Raksin. Perf. Gene Tierney, Clifton Webb, and Dana Andrews. 20th Century–Fox, 1944.

Little Caesar. Dir. Mervyn LeRoy. First National, 1931.

The Maltese Falcon. Dir. John Huston. Warner Bros., 1941.

The Man I Love. Dir. Raoul Walsh. Perf. Ida Lupino. Scr. Catherine Turney. Warner Bros., 1947.

The Man with the Golden Arm. Dir. Otto Preminger. United Artists, 1955.

The Men. Dir. Fred Zinnemann. United Artists, 1950.

Mildred Pierce. Dir. Michael Curtiz. Scr. Ranald MacDougall and Catherine Turney (uncredited). Perf. Joan Crawford. Warner Bros., 1945.

Murder, My Sweet. Dir. Edward Dmytryk.* RKO, 1944.

My Name Is Julia Ross. Dir. Joseph H. Lewis. Scr. Muriel Roy Bolton. Columbia, 1945.

The Naked City. Dir. Jules Dassin.* Prod. Mark Hellinger. Scr. Albert Maltz* and Malvin Wald. Universal, 1948.

New York Confidential. Dir. Russell Rouse. Warner Bros., 1955.

The Night Holds Terror. Dir. Andrew Stone. Columbia, 1955.

Nightmare. Dir. Maxwell Shane. United Artists, 1956.

Nightmare Alley. Dir. Edmund Goulding. Perf. Tyrone Power. 20th Century–Fox, 1947.

Nocturne. Dir. Edwin L. Marin. Prod. Joan Harrison. Perf. George Raft. RKO, 1946.

No Man of Her Own. Dir. Mitchell Leisen. Scr. Sally Benson and Catherine Turney, from the novel *I Married a Dead Man,* by Cornell Woolrich. Paramount, 1950.

Notorious. Dir. Alfred Hitchcock. RKO, 1946.

Not Wanted. Dir. Ida Lupino. Scr. Paul Jarrico* and Ida Lupino. Emerald/RKO, 1949.

Odds against Tomorrow. Dir. Robert Wise. Scr. John O. Killens [Abraham Polonsky*]. United Artists, 1959.

Out of the Past. Dir. Jacques Tourneur. Perf. Robert Mitchum, Jane Greer, and Kirk Douglas. RKO, 1947.

Outrage. Dir. Ida Lupino. Scr. Collier Young, Malvin Wald, and Ida Lupino. Filmakers/RKO, 1950.

Phantom Lady. Dir. Robert Siodmak. Prod. Joan Harrison. Perf. Franchot Tone and Ella Raines. Universal, 1944.

Possessed. Dir. Curtis Bernhardt. Perf. Joan Crawford. Scr. Silvia Richards* and Ranald MacDougall. Warner Bros., 1947.

The Postman Always Rings Twice. Dir. Tay Garnett. Perf. John Garfield* and Lana Turner. MGM, 1946.

Private Hell 36. Dir. Don Siegel. Scr. Ida Lupino and Collier Young. Filmakers, 1954.

The Prowler. Dir. Joseph Losey.* Scr. Hugo Butler* and Dalton Trumbo.* Horizon/United Artists, 1951.

The Public Enemy. Dir. William A. Wellman. Warner Bros., 1931.

Railroaded! Dir. Anthony Mann. Scr. John C. Higgins. Story by Gertrude Walker. PRC, 1947.

Ride the Pink Horse. Dir. Robert Montgomery. Prod. Joan Harrison. From the novel by Dorothy B. Hughes. Universal, 1947.

Road House. Dir. Jean Negulesco. Perf. Ida Lupino, Cornel Wilde, Richard Widmark. 20th Century–Fox, 1948.

Scarface. Dir. Howard Hawks. United Artists, 1932.

Scarlet Street. Dir. Fritz Lang. Scr. Dudley Nichols. Perf. Edward G. Robinson, Joan Bennett, and Dan Duryea. Diana Productions/Universal, 1945.

The Set-Up. Dir. Robert Wise. RKO, 1949.

Shockproof. Dir. Douglas Sirk. Columbia, 1949.

Somewhere in the Night. Dir. Joseph L. Mankiewicz. 20th Century–Fox, 1946.

Spellbound. Dir. Alfred Hitchcock. Perf. Ingrid Bergman and Gregory Peck. Selznick, 1945.

The Strange Affair of Uncle Harry. Dir. Robert Siodmak. Prod. Joan Harrison. Universal, 1945.

Strange Illusion. Dir. Edgar G. Ulmer. PRC, 1945.

The Strange Love of Martha Ivers. Dir. Lewis Milestone. Scr. Robert Rossen.* Paramount, 1946.

Street of Chance. Dir. Jack Hively. Paramount, 1942.

The Strip. Dir. Leslie Kardos. Perf. Mickey Rooney. MGM, 1951.

Sweet Smell of Success. Dir. Alexander Mackendrick. Perf. Burt Lancaster, Tony Curtis, and Martin Milner. United Artists, 1957.

They Live by Night. Dir. Nicholas Ray. Perf. Cathy O'Donnell, Farley Granger, and Howard Da Silva.* RKO, 1948.

Thieves' Highway. Dir. Jules Dassin.* Scr. A. I. Bezzerides. 20th Century–Fox, 1949.

Touch of Evil. Dir. Orson Welles. Universal-International, 1958.

Try and Get Me! Dir. Cyril Endfield.* Scr. Jo Pagano. Robert Stillman Productions/ United Artists, 1950.

The Two Mrs. Carrolls. Dir. Peter Godfrey. Warner Bros., 1947.

The Underworld Story. Dir. Cyril Endfield.* Perf. Dan Duryea. Scr. Craig Rice, Cyril Endfield and Henry Blankfort.* Filmcraft/United Artists, 1950.

Vicki. Dir. Harry Horner. Perf. Jean Peters, Jeanne Crain, Elliott Reid, and Richard Boone. 20th Century–Fox, 1953.

Walk a Crooked Mile. Dir. Gordon Douglas. Columbia, 1948.

White Heat. Dir. Raoul Walsh. Perf. James Cagney and Edmond O'Brien. Warner Bros., 1949.

The Woman in the Window. Dir. Fritz Lang. Perf. Edward G. Robinson, Joan Bennett, and Dan Duryea. International Pictures, 1944.

You Only Live Once. Dir. Fritz Lang. Perf. Henry Fonda and Sylvia Sidney. United Artists, 1937.

WORKS CITED

The abbreviation MHLSC indicates Margaret Herrick Library Special Collections, Los Angeles.

Abbott, Megan E. *The Street Was Mine: White Masculinity in Hard-Boiled Fiction and Film Noir.* New York: Palgrave Macmillan, 2002. Print.

"Abraham Polonsky." Interview by Paul Buhle and Dave Wagner. McGilligan and Buhle 481–94.

The Accused script notes. Hal Wallis Papers. MHLSC.

Act of Violence posters. Fred Zinnemann Papers. MHLSC.

"Adele Comandini." *Internet Movie Database.* Web. Dec. 20, 2011.

Allcountries.org. *U.S. Census 2000.* "11. National Defense and Veterans Affairs." Sec. 593, "Disabled Veterans Receiving Compensation." Web. Dec. 26, 2011.

Als, Hilton. "This Woman's Work." *New Yorker* March 28, 2011: 108–11. Print.

Andersen, Thom. "Afterword." Krutnik, Neale, Neve, and Stanfield 264–75.

———. "Red Hollywood." Krutnik, Neale, Neve, and Stanfield 225–63.

Anderson, Edward. *Thieves Like Us.* 1937. Polito 214–377.

Arnau, Frank. *Three Thousand Years of Deception in Art and Antiques.* Trans. J. Maxwell Brownjohn. London: Cape, 1961. Print.

Arnheim, Rudolf. "On Duplication." Dutton, *The Forger's Art* 232–45.

"Art of Europe." Web. May 14, 2012. www.artofeurope.com/dali/dal26.htm.

Babener, Liahna. "De-feminizing *Laura:* Novel to Film." *It's a Print! Detective Fiction from Page to Screen.* Ed. William Reynolds and Elizabeth A. Trembley. Bowling Green, OH: Bowling Green St. U Popular P, 1994. 83–102. Print.

Balkun, Mary McAleer. *American Counterfeit: Authenticity and Identity in American Literature and Culture.* Tuscaloosa: U of Alabama P, 2006. Print.

Basinger, Jeanine. *A Woman's View: How Hollywood Spoke to Women, 1930–1960.* London: Chatto and Windus, 1993. Print.

Bassler, Robert. Letter to Jason S. Joy. Feb. 24, 1949. TS. PCA file, *Thieves' Highway.* MHLSC.

Belton, John. *American Cinema/American Culture.* New York: McGraw-Hill, 1994. Print.

Benson, Sally. *With This Ring [I Married a Dead Man].* Jan. 24, 1949. TS. *No Man of Her Own* script files. MHLSC.

———. *With This Ring [I Married a Dead Man]*. Feb. 25, 1949. TS. *No Man of Her Own* script files. MHLSC.

Bernstein, Matthew. "A Tale of Three Cities: The Banning of *Scarlet Street*." *Cinema Journal* 35.1 (1995): 27–52. Print.

Beverly, William. *On the Lam: Narratives of Flight in J. Edgar Hoover's America*. Jackson: UP of Mississippi, 2004. Print.

Biesen, Sheri Chinen. *Blackout: World War II and the Origins of Film Noir*. Baltimore: Johns Hopkins UP, 2005. Print.

Billman, Larry. *Betty Grable: A Bio-bibliography*. Westport, CT: Greenwood, 1993. Print.

Blackwelder, Julia Kirk. *Now Hiring: The Feminization of Work in the United States, 1900–1995*. College Station: Texas A&M UP, 1997. Print.

Block, Libbie. *Wild Calendar*. Cleveland: World Publishing, 1947. Print.

Bloom, Harold, ed. *Sigmund Freud's "The Interpretation of Dreams."* New York: Chelsea House, 1987. Print.

Bogdanovich, Peter. *Who the Devil Made It*. New York: Knopf, 1997. Print.

Borde, Raymond, and Etienne Chaumeton. "Towards a Definition of *Film Noir*." Silver and Ursini, *Film Noir Reader* 17–25.

Brandell, Jerrold R., ed. *Celluloid Couches, Cinematic Clients: Psychoanalysis and Psychotherapy in the Movies*. Albany: SUNY P, 2004. Print.

———. "Eighty Years of Dream Sequences: A Cinematic Journey Down Freud's 'Royal Road.'" *American Imago* 61.1 (2004): 59–76. Print.

———. "Introduction." Brandell, *Celluloid Couches* 1–18.

Breen, Joseph. Letter to Forrest Judd. July 27, 1949. TS. PCA file, *The Underworld Story*. MHLSC.

———. Letter to Jack Warner. August 26, 1946. TS. PCA file, *Possessed*. MHLSC.

———. Letter to Jack Warner. June 10, 1949. TS. PCA file, *Caged*. MHLSC.

———. Letter to Jack Warner. July 22, 1949. TS. PCA file, *Caged*. MHLSC.

———. Letter to Jason S. Joy. Nov. 5, 1948. TS. PCA file, *Thieves' Highway*. MHLSC.

———. Letter to Luigi Luraschi. May 26, 1949. TS. PCA file, *No Man of Her Own*. MHLSC.

———. Letter to Robert Stillman. May 3, 1950. TS. PCA File, *Try and Get Me!* MHLSC.

———. Letter to Sam Spiegel. Nov. 2, 1949. TS. PCA File, *The Prowler*. MHLSC.

Brill, Lesley. *The Hitchcock Romance: Love and Irony in Hitchcock's Films*. Princeton, NJ: Princeton UP, 1988. Print.

Britton, Andrew. "*Detour*." Cameron 174–83.

Broe, Dennis. *Film Noir, American Workers, and Postwar Hollywood*. Gainesville: UP of Florida, 2009. Print.

Brook, Vincent. *Driven to Darkness: German Émigré Directors and the Rise of Film Noir*. New Brunswick, NJ: Rutgers UP, 2009. Print.

Brooks, Richard. *The Brick Foxhole*. New York: Harper, 1945. Print.

Brown, Royal. *Overtones and Undertones: Reading Film Music*. Berkeley: U of California P, 1994. Print.

Brumbaugh, Gary. "Mini-Biography: Nina Foch." *Internet Movie Database*. Web. Dec. 21, 2011.

Buhle, Paul, and Dave Wagner. *Radical Hollywood: The Untold Story behind America's Favorite Movies*. New York: New P, 2002. Print.

———. *A Very Dangerous Citizen: Abraham Lincoln Polonsky and the Hollywood Left.*
Berkeley: U of California P, 2001. Print.

Butler, David. *Jazz Noir: Listening to Music from "Phantom Lady" to "The Last Seduction."* Westport, CT: Praeger, 2002. Print.

Cain, James M. *Double Indemnity.* 1936. New York: Vintage, 1992. Print.

———. *Mildred Pierce.* 1941. New York: Vintage, 1989. Print.

———. *The Postman Always Rings Twice.* 1934. Polito 1–95.

Cameron, Ian, ed. *The Book of Film Noir.* New York: Continuum, 1993. Print.

Campbell, D'Ann. *Women at War with America: Private Lives in a Patriotic Era.*
Cambridge, MA: Harvard UP, 1984. Print.

Cantor, Paul A. "Film Noir and the Frankfurt School: America as Wasteland in Edgar Ulmer's *Detour.*" Conard 139–61.

Caruth, Cathy. "Introduction to Psychoanalysis, Trauma and Culture I." *American Imago* 48.1 (1991): 1–12. Print.

Caspary, Vera. *Laura.* 1942. Rpt. with an Afterword by A. B. Emrys. New York: Feminist P at the City U of New York, 2005. Print.

———. *The Secrets of Grown-Ups.* New York: McGraw-Hill, 1979. Print.

"Catherine Turney." *Internet Movie Database.* Web. Dec. 21, 2011.

Ceplair, Larry, and Steven Englund. *The Inquisition in Hollywood: Politics in the Film Community, 1930–1960.* Berkeley: U of California P, 1983. Print.

Chopra-Gant, Mike. *Hollywood Genres and Postwar America: Masculinity, Family and Nation in Popular Movies and Film Noir.* New York: I. B. Tauris, 2006. Print.

Christopher, Nicholas. *Somewhere in the Night: Film Noir and the American City.*
New York: Free P, 1997. Print.

Ciment, Michel, ed. *Conversations with Losey.* London: Methuen, 1985. Print.

Conard, Mark T., ed. *The Philosophy of Film Noir.* Lexington: UP of Kentucky, 2006.
Print.

Cook, Pam. "*Outrage* (1950)." Kuhn 57–72.

Copjec, Joan, ed. *Shades of Noir.* London: Verso, 1993. Print.

Cowie, Elizabeth. "*Film Noir* and Women." Copjec 121–65.

Crowther, Bosley. Review of *The Underworld Story. New York Times* Sept. 27, 1950.
PCA file, *The Underworld Story.* MHLSC.

———. Review of *Thieves' Highway. New York Times* Sept. 24, 1949. PCA file, *Thieves' Highway.* MHLSC.

Cullen, Jim. *The American Dream: A Short History of an Idea That Shaped a Nation.*
New York: Oxford UP, 2003. Print.

Curran, Dale. *Piano in the Band.* New York: Reynal and Hitchcock, 1940. Print.

"*The Damned Don't Cry.*" PCA file, MHLSC.

Davidson, Michael. "Phantom Limbs: Film Noir and the Disabled Body." *GLQ* 9.1–2 (2003): 57–77. Print.

de Bolla, Peter. "The Stain of the Signature." *Fiction and Economy.* Ed. Susan Bruce and Valeria Wagner. Houndmills: Palgrave MacMillan, 2007. 63–81. Print.

DeLillo, Don. *Americana.* 1971. Rev. ed. New York: Viking, 1989. Print.

DeVeaux, Scott. *The Birth of Bebop: A Social and Musical History.* Berkeley: U of California P, 1997. Print.

Dickos, Andrew. *Street with No Name: A History of the Classic American Film Noir.*
Lexington: UP of Kentucky, 2002. Print.

Dimendberg, Edward. *Film Noir and the Spaces of Modernity.* Cambridge, MA: Harvard UP, 2004. Print.

Dixon, Wheeler Winston, ed. *American Cinema of the 1940s: Themes and Variations.* New Brunswick, NJ: Rutgers UP, 2006. Print.

———. "Movies and Postwar Recovery." Dixon 162–81.

Doane, Mary Ann. *The Desire to Desire: The Woman's Film of the 1940s.* Bloomington: Indiana UP, 1987. Print.

———. *Femmes Fatale: Feminism, Film Theory, Psychoanalysis.* New York: Routledge, 1991. Print.

Donati, William. *Ida Lupino: A Biography.* Lexington: UP of Kentucky, 1996. Print.

Dutton, Denis. "Art Hoaxes." *Encyclopedia of Hoaxes.* Ed. Gordon Stein. Detroit: Gale Research, 1993. Web. July 10, 2008. http://denisdutton.com/art_hoaxes.htm.

———. "Artistic Crimes." Dutton, *The Forger's Art* 172–87.

———, ed. *The Forger's Art: Forgery and the Philosophy of Art.* Berkeley: U of California P, 1983. Print.

Dyer, Richard. "Postscript: Queers and Women in Film Noir." Kaplan, *Women in Film Noir* 123–29.

———. "Resistance through Charisma: Rita Hayworth and *Gilda.*" Kaplan, *Women in Film Noir* 115–22.

ehow.com. "Where Did the Name Cadillac Come From?" Web. June 23, 2011. www.ehow.com/about_5313197_did-name-cadillac-come.html.

Ellin, Stanley. *Dreadful Summit.* New York: Simon and Schuster, 1948. Print.

Ellison, Ralph. *Shadow and Act.* New York: Vintage, 1964. Print.

Elsaesser, Thomas. *Weimar Cinema and After: Germany's Historical Imaginary.* London: Routledge, 2001. Print.

Emerson, Ralph Waldo. "Self-Reliance." *Essays: First and Second Series.* New York: Vintage/Library of America, 1990. 27–52. Print.

Erickson, Glenn. "The Restoration of *Kiss Me Deadly.*" *Film Noir of the Week: Friday, July 13, 2007.* Web. August 20, 2011. www.noiroftheweek.com/2007/07/restoration-of-kiss-me-deadly-1955.html.

Eyles, Allen. "Films of ENTERPRISE: A Studio History." *Focus on Film* 35 (April 1980): 13–27. Print.

Field, Patrick. "No Particular Place to Go." Wollen and Kerr 59–64.

Fisher, Steve. *I Wake Up Screaming.* 1941. Rev. ed. 1960. New York: Vintage/Black Lizard, 1991. Print.

Flinn, Caryl. *Strains of Utopia: Gender, Nostalgia, and Hollywood Film Music.* Princeton, NJ: Princeton UP, 1992. Print.

Flory, Dan. *Philosophy, Black Film, Film Noir.* University Park: Pennsylvania St. UP, 2008. Print.

Fotsch, Paul Mason. "*Film Noir* and Automotive Isolation in Los Angeles." *Cultural Studies* ↔ *Critical Methodologies* 5.1 (2005): 103–25. Print.

Foucault, Michel. *Discipline and Punish: The Birth of the Prison.* Trans. Alan Sheridan. New York: Pantheon, 1978. Print.

Francke, Lizzie. *Script Girls: Women Screenwriters in Hollywood.* London: BFI, 1994. Print.

Frank, Arthur W. *The Wounded Storyteller: Body, Illness, and Ethics.* Chicago: U of Chicago P, 1995. Print.

Franklin, Benjamin. *The Autobiography.* New York: Vintage/Library of America, 1989. Print.

Freedman, Jonathan. "From *Spellbound* to *Vertigo:* Alfred Hitchcock and Therapeutic Culture in America." *Hitchcock's America.* Ed. Jonathan Freedman and Richard Millington. New York: Oxford UP, 1999. 77–98. Print.

Freud, Sigmund. *Civilization and Its Discontents.* 1930. Trans. James Strachey, with a biographical introduction by Peter Gay. New York: Norton, 1989. Print.

———. *The Interpretation of Dreams.* 1900. Ed. and trans. James Strachey. New York: Avon, 1972. Print.

Frings, Ketti. *The Accused.* Sept. 21, 1948. TS. *The Accused* script files. MHLSC.

———. *The File on Thelma Jordon.* Nov. 18, 1948. TS. *The File on Thelma Jordon* script files. MHLSC.

———. *The File on Thelma Jordon.* Jan. 4, 1949. TS. *The File on Thelma Jordon* script files. MHLSC.

———. *The File on Thelma Jordon.* Feb. 7, 1949. TS. *The File on Thelma Jordon* script files. MHLSC.

———. *Strange Deception.* Feb. 18, 1948. TS. *The Accused* script files. MHLSC.

Fuchs, Daniel. Untitled Notes on *Hollow Triumph.* TS. Dec. 26, 1947. Paul Henreid Papers. MHLSC.

Gabbard, Krin. *Jammin' at the Margins: Jazz and the American Cinema.* Chicago: U of Chicago P, 1996. Print.

Gabbard, Krin, and Glen O. Gabbard, *Psychiatry and the Cinema.* 2nd ed. Chicago: U of Chicago P, 1999. Print.

Gay, Peter. *Freud: A Life for Our Times.* London: Dent, 1988. Print.

"Gertrude Walker." *Internet Movie Database.* Web. Dec. 29, 2011.

Giddens, Anthony. *The Consequences of Modernity.* Stanford, CA: Stanford UP, 1990. Print.

Gioia, Ted. *The History of Jazz.* New York: Oxford UP, 1997. Print.

Gorbman, Claudia. *Unheard Melodies: Narrative Film Music.* Bloomington: Indiana UP, 1987. Print.

Gray, J. Glenn. *The Warriors: Reflections on Men in Battle.* New York: Harper and Row, 1970. Print.

Gresham, William Lindsay. *Nightmare Alley.* 1946. Polito 516–796.

Grossman, Julie. *Rethinking the Femme Fatale in Film Noir: Ready for Her Close-up.* New York: Palgrave Macmillan, 2009. Print.

Gunning, Tom. *The Films of Fritz Lang: Allegories of Vision and Modernity.* London: BFI, 2000. Print.

Hammett, Dashiell. *The Maltese Falcon.* 1930. *Complete Novels.* Ed. Steven Marcus. New York: Library of America, 1999. 387–585. Print.

Hanson, Helen. *Hollywood Heroines: Women in Film Noir and the Female Gothic Film.* London: I. B. Tauris, 2007. Print.

Harris, Oliver. "Film Noir Fascination: Outside History, but Historically So." *Cinema Journal* 43.1 (2003): 3–24. Print.

Hartmann, Ernest. *Dreams and Nightmares: The New Theory on the Origin and Meaning of Dreams.* New York: Plenum, 1998. Print.

Haskell, Molly. *From Reverence to Rape: The Treatment of Women in the Movies.* New York: Holt, Rinehart and Winston, 1974. Print.

Hastie, Amelie. *The Bigamist*. London: BFI/Palgrave Macmillan, 2009. Print.

Hillis, Ken. "Film Noir and the American Dream: The Dark Side of Enlightenment." *Velvet Light Trap* 55.1 (2005): 3–18. Print.

Hirsch, Foster. *The Dark Side of the Screen: Film Noir*. New York: Da Capo, 1983. Print.

Hirsch, Joshua. "Film Gris Reconsidered." *Journal of Popular Film and Television* 34.2 (2006): 82–93. Print.

Hughes, Dorothy B. *Ride the Pink Horse*. 1946. New York: Canongate, 2002. Print.

Hughes, Langston. "Harlem [2]." *Montage of a Dream Deferred*. 1951. *The Collected Poems of Langston Hughes*. Ed. Arnold Rampersad. New York: Vintage, 1994. 426. Print.

Humphries, Reynold. "The Politics of Crime and the Crime of Politics: Postwar Noir, the Liberal Consensus and the Hollywood Left." Silver and Ursini, *Film Noir Reader 4* 227–45.

Hyde, Thomas. "The Moral Universe of Hitchcock's *Spellbound*." *A Hitchcock Reader*. Ed. Marshall Deutelbaum and Leland Poague. Ames: Iowa St. UP, 1986. 153–61. Print.

Irwin, John T. *Unless the Threat of Death Is behind Them: Hard-Boiled Fiction and Film Noir*. Baltimore: Johns Hopkins UP, 2006. Print.

Jackson, Stephen. Letter to Hal Wallis. Feb. 9, 1948. TS. PCA file, *The Accused*. MHLSC.

———. Letter to Hal Wallis. March 8, 1948. TS. PCA file, *The Accused*. MHLSC.

———. Memo to Hal Wallis. May 18, 1948. TS. PCA file, *The Accused*. MHLSC.

Jacobowitz, Florence. "The Man's Melodrama: *The Woman in the Window* and *Scarlet Street*." Cameron 152–64.

Jameson, Fredric. "Seriality in Modern Literature." *Bucknell Review* 18.1 (1970): 63–80. Print.

Jarvie, Ian. "Knowledge, Morality, and Tragedy in *The Killers* and *Out of the Past*." Conard 163–85.

"Jean-Francois Millet." *Wikipedia*. Web. July 13, 2008. http://en.wikipedia.org/wiki/Jean-Fran%C3%A7ois_Millet.

"Jules Dassin." Interview by Patrick McGilligan. McGilligan and Buhle 199–224.

Kalinak, Kathryn. *Settling the Score: Music and the Classical Hollywood Film*. Madison: U of Wisconsin P, 1992. Print.

Kaplan, E. Ann. "Ideology and Cinematic Practice in Lang's *Scarlet Street* and Renoir's *La chienne*." *Wide Angle* 5.3 (1983): 32–43. Print.

———., ed. *Women in Film Noir*. Rev ed. London: BFI, 1998. Print.

Kemp, Philip. "Nightmare Factory: HUAC and the Politics of Noir." *Sight and Sound* 55.4 (1986): 266–70. Print.

"Ketti Frings." *Internet Movie Database*. Web. Dec. 30, 2011.

Kitses, Jim. *Gun Crazy*. London: BFI, 1996. Print.

Krutnik, Frank. *In a Lonely Street: Film Noir, Genre, Masculinity*. London: Routledge, 1991. Print.

———. "'A Living Part of the Class Struggle': Diego Rivera's *The Flower Carrier* and the Hollywood Left." Krutnik, Neale, Neve, and Stanfield 51–78.

Krutnik, Frank, Steve Neale, Brian Neve, and Peter Stanfield, eds. *"Un-American" Hollywood: Politics and Film in the Blacklist Era*. New Brunswick, NJ: Rutgers UP, 2007. Print.

Kuhn, Annette, ed. *Queen of the 'B's: Ida Lupino behind the Camera*. Trowbridge, UK: Flicks, 1995. Print.

Lackey, Kris. *RoadFrames: The American Highway Narrative*. Lincoln: U of Nebraska P, 1997. Print.

Laderman, David. *Driving Visions: Exploring the Road Movie*. Austin: U of Texas P, 2002. Print.

Langdon-Teclaw, Jennifer. "The Progressive Producer in the Studio System: Adrian Scott at RKO, 1943–1947." Krutnik, Neale, Neve, and Stanfield 152–68.

Latimer, Jonathan. *Be Still, My Love*. TS. Jan. 15, 1947. *The Accused* script files. MHLSC.

Lears, Jackson. *Fables of Abundance: A Cultural History of Advertising in America*. New York: Basic Books, 1994. Print.

———. [T. J. Jackson Lears]. "From Salvation to Self-Realization: Advertising and the Therapeutic Roots of the Consumer Culture, 1880–1930." *The Culture of Consumption: Critical Essays in American History, 1880–1980*. Ed. Richard Wightman Fox and T. J. Jackson Lears. New York: Pantheon, 1983. 3–38. Print.

Leavitt, Doris. "Summary: *I Married a Dead Man*." Oct. 29, 1948. TS. *No Man of Her Own* script files. MHLSC.

Lebeau, Vicky. *Psychoanalysis and Cinema: The Play of Shadows*. London: Wallflower, 2001.

Leff, Leonard. "Becoming Clifton Webb: A Queer Star in Mid-century Hollywood." *Cinema Journal* 47.3 (2008): 3–28. Print.

Levine, Lawrence W. "Jazz and American Culture." *The Jazz Cadence of American Culture*. Ed. Robert G. O'Meally. New York: Columbia UP, 1998. 431–47. Print.

Lott, Eric. "The Whiteness of Film Noir." *American Literary History* 9.3 (1997): 542–66. Print.

Luckhurst, Roger. *The Trauma Question*. London: Routledge, 2008. Print.

Lupino, Ida. "Eleanor and Anna Roosevelt Broadcast." TS of radio program. KECA. Feb. 18, 1949. PCA file, *Not Wanted*. MHLSC.

———. Telegram to Joseph Breen. Feb. 9, 1949. TS. PCA file, *Not Wanted*. MHLSC.

Lyndon, Barre. *Be Still, My Love*. Jan. 6, 1947. TS. *The Accused* script files. MHLSC.

———. *Be Still, My Love*. July 25, 1947. TS. *The Accused* script files. MHLSC.

Maltby, Richard. "The Politics of the Maladjusted Text." Cameron 39–49.

Martin, Angela. "'Gilda Didn't Do Any of Those Things You've Been Losing Sleep Over': The Central Women of 40s Films Noirs." Kaplan, *Women in Film Noir* 202–28.

Marx, Karl. *Capital*. Vol. 1. Trans. Samuel Moore and Edward Aveling. Ed. Friedrich Engels. Tucker 294–438.

Marx, Karl, and Friedrich Engels. *Manifesto of the Communist Party*. Ed. Friedrich Engels. Tucker 469–500.

Mason, Fran. *American Gangster Cinema: From "Little Caesar" to "Pulp Fiction."* London: Palgrave Macmillan, 2002. Print.

Maxfield, James. *The Fatal Woman: Sources of Male Anxiety in American Film Noir, 1941–1991*. Madison: Fairleigh Dickinson UP, 1996. Print.

May, Lary. *The Big Tomorrow: Hollywood and the Politics of the American Way*. Chicago: U of Chicago P, 2000. Print.

McCann, Sean. "Dark Passages: Jazz and Civil Liberty in the Postwar Crime Film." Krutnik, Neale, Neve, and Stanfield 113–29.

McClary, Susan. *Feminine Endings: Music, Gender, and Sexuality.* Minnesota: U of Minnesota P, 1991. Print.

McGee, Tom. *Betty Grable: The Girl with the Million-Dollar Legs.* Lanham, MD: Vestal, 1995. Print.

McGilligan, Patrick. *Alfred Hitchcock: A Life in Darkness and Light.* New York: Reganbooks, 2003. Print.

———. *Fritz Lang: The Nature of the Beast.* New York: St. Martin's, 1997. Print.

McGilligan, Patrick, and Paul Buhle. *Tender Comrades: A Backstory of the Hollywood Blacklist.* New York: St. Martin's, 1997. Print.

McGivern, William P. *Odds against Tomorrow.* 1957. London: Xanadu, 1991. Print.

McLean, Adrienne L. "'It's Only That I Do What I Love and Love What I Do': *Film Noir* and the Musical Woman." *Cinema Journal* 33.1 (1993): 3–16. Print.

"Meeting Dali!" Web. May 14, 2012. http://meetingdali.blogspot.com/2011/06/dalis-obsessions-revealed-in.html.

Metropolitan Museum of Art. "The Painter's Daughter Mary (1750–1826). Copy after Thomas Gainsborough. (English, mid-19th century)." Web. May 8, 2012. www.metmuseum.org/Collections/search-the-collections/110000883.

———. Timeline of Art History: Works of Art. "Fountain Figure of a Winged Infant." Web. July 22, 2008. www.metmuseum.org/TOAH/hd/dona/ho_1983.356.htm.

Meyer, Leonard B. "Forgery and the Anthropology of Art." Dutton, *The Forger's Art* 77–92.

Meyerowitz, Joanne. "Beyond the Feminine Mystique: A Reassessment of Postwar Mass Culture, 1946–1958." *Not June Cleaver: Women and Gender in Postwar America, 1945–1960.* Ed. Joanne Meyerowitz. Philadelphia: Temple UP, 1994. 229–62. Print.

Mijolla, Alain de. "Freud and the Psychoanalytic Situation on Screen." *Endless Night: Cinema and Psychoanalysis, Parallel Histories.* Ed. Janet Bergstrom. Berkeley: U of California P, 1999. 188–99. Print.

Miklitsch, Robert. *Siren City: Sound and Source Music in Classic American Noir.* New Brunswick, NJ: Rutgers UP, 2011. Print.

"Mildred Pierce." *Internet Movie Database.* Web. Dec. 30, 2011.

Mills, Katie. *The Road Story and the Rebel: Moving through Film, Fiction and Television.* Carbondale: Southern Illinois UP, 2006. Print.

Minturn, Kent. "*Peinture Noire:* Abstract Expressionism and *Film Noir.*" Silver and Ursini, *Film Noir Reader 2* 270–309.

Mitchell, David T. "Narrative Prosthesis and the Materiality of Metaphor." *Disability Studies: Enabling the Humanities.* Ed. Sharon L. Snyder, Brenda Jo Brueggeman, and Rosemarie Garland-Thomson. New York: MLA, 2002. 15–30. Print.

Mitchell, David T., and Sharon L. Snyder. *Narrative Prosthesis: Disability and the Dependencies of Discourse.* Ann Arbor: U of Michigan P, 2001. Print.

Morris, Christopher D. *The Hanging Figure: On Suspense in the Films of Alfred Hitchcock.* Westport, CT: Praeger, 2002. Print.

Mottram, Eric. "Blood on the Nash Ambassador: Cars in American Films." Wollen and Kerr 95–114.

Munby, Jonathan. *Public Enemies, Public Heroes: Screening the Gangster from "Little Caesar" to "Touch of Evil."* Chicago: U of Chicago P, 1999. Print.

Murray, Albert. "Improvisation and the Creative Process." *The Jazz Cadence of American Culture*. Ed. Robert G. O'Meally. New York: Columbia UP, 1998. 111–13. Print.

Nadelson, Theodore. *Trained to Kill: Soldiers at War*. Baltimore: Johns Hopkins UP, 2005.

Naremore, James. "Hitchcock at the Margins of Noir." *Alfred Hitchcock: Centenary Essays*. Ed. Richard Allen and S. Ishii-Gonzales. London: BFI, 1999. 262–77. Print.

———. *More Than Night: Film Noir in Its Contexts*. Berkeley: U of California P, 1998. Print.

———. *Sweet Smell of Success*. London: BFI/Palgrave Macmillan, 2010. Print.

Navasky, Victor S. *Naming Names*. New York: Viking, 1980. Print.

Neale, Steve. *Genre and Hollywood*. London: Routledge, 2000. Print.

Ness, Richard R. "A Lotta Night Music: The Sound of *Film Noir*." *Cinema Journal* 47.2 (2008): 52–73. Print.

Neve, Brian. *Film and Politics in America: A Social Tradition*. London: Routledge, 1992. Print.

———. "Red Hollywood in Transition: The Case of Robert Rossen." Krutnik, Neale, Neve, and Stanfield 184–97. Print.

Norden, Martin F. *The Cinema of Isolation: A History of Physical Disability in the Movies*. New Brunswick, NJ: Rutgers UP, 1994. Print.

Nugent, Frank S. "Mr. Hitchcock Discovers Love." 1946. *Alfred Hitchcock Interviews*. Ed. Sidney Gottlieb. Jackson: UP of Mississippi, 2003. 17–22. Print.

Oliver, Kelly, and Benigno Trigo. *Noir Anxiety*. Minneapolis: U of Minnesota P, 2003. Print.

Orr, John. *Hitchcock and 20th Century Cinema*. London: Wallflower, 2005. Print.

Osteen, Mark. "The Big Secret: *Film Noir* and Nuclear Fear." *Journal of Popular Film and Television* 22.2 (1994): 79–90. Print.

———. "Face Plates: *T-Men* and the Problem of *Noir* Counterfeiting." *Quarterly Review of Film and Video* 24.2 (2007): 125–42. Print.

Pagano, Jo. *The Condemned*. New York: Prentice-Hall, 1947. Print.

Palmer, R. Barton. *Hollywood's Dark Cinema: The American Film Noir*. New York: Twayne, 1994. Print.

Palmer, Tim. "Side of the Angels: Dalton Trumbo, the Hollywood Trade Press, and the Blacklist." *Cinema Journal* 44.4 (2005): 57–74.

Paramount press sheets. MHLSC.

Parker, Francine. "Discovering Ida Lupino." *Action* 2.3 (1967): 19. Print.

Pastos, Speros. *Pin-Up: The Tragedy of Betty Grable*. New York: Berkley, 1987. Print.

Patrick, Jack. *Love-Lies-Bleeding*. TS. N.d. *The Strange Love of Martha Ivers* script files. MHLSC.

Pelizzon, V. Penelope, and Nancy West. "'A Perfect Double Down to the Last Detail': Photography and the Identity of Film Noir." *Post Script* 22.3 (2003). Web. July 4, 2010.

Polan, Dana. *Power and Paranoia: History, Narrative, and the American Cinema, 1940–1950*. New York: Columbia UP, 1986. Print.

Polito, Robert, ed. *Crime Novels: American Noir of the 1930s and 40s*. New York: Library of America, 1997. Print.

Pomerance, Murray. *An Eye for Hitchcock*. New Brunswick, NJ: Rutgers UP, 2004. Print.

Porfirio, Robert. "Dark Jazz: Music in the *Film Noir*." Silver and Ursini, *Film Noir Reader 2* 176–87.

———. "*The Killers*: Expressiveness of Sound and Image in *Film Noir*." Silver and Ursini, *Film Noir Reader* 177–87.

———. "No Way Out: Existential Motifs in the *Film Noir*." Silver and Ursini, *Film Noir Reader* 77–93.

Prime, Rebecca. "Cloaked in Compromise: Jules Dassin's 'Naked City.'" Krutnik, Neale, Neve, and Stanfield 142–51.

Quart, Barbara Koenig. *Women Directors: The Emergence of a New Cinema*. New York: Praeger, 1988. Print.

Quayson, Ato. *Aesthetic Nervousness: Disability and the Crisis of Representation*. New York: Columbia UP, 2007. Print.

Rae, John B. *The American Automobile: A Brief History*. Chicago: U of Chicago P, 1965. Print.

———. *The American Automobile Industry*. New York: Twayne, 1984. Print.

Reid, David, and Jayne L. Walker. "Strange Pursuit: Cornell Woolrich and the Abandoned City of the Forties." Copjec 57–96.

Renov, Michael. *Hollywood's Wartime Women: Representation and Ideology*. Ann Arbor, MI: UMI Research P, 1988. Print.

Rieff, Philip. "The Tactics of Interpretation." Bloom 51–57.

Ringel, Shoshana. "Talk Therapy: The Representation of Insight in the Cinema." Brandell, *Celluloid Couches* 169–90.

Rivkin, Allen. *Be Still, My Love*. TS. Dec. 9, 1946. *The Accused* script files. MHLSC.

———. Letter to Hal Wallis. Oct. 14, 1946. TS. Hal Wallis Papers. MHLSC.

Rothberg, Michael. *Traumatic Realism: The Demands of Holocaust Representation*. Minneapolis: U of Minnesota P, 2000. Print.

Ruthven, K. K. *Faking Literature*. Cambridge, UK: Cambridge UP, 2001. Print.

Sagoff, Mark. "The Aesthetic Status of Forgeries." Dutton, *The Forger's Art* 131–53.

Saigh, Philip A., and J. Douglas Bremner. "The History of Posttraumatic Stress Disorder." Saigh and Bremner 1–17.

Saigh, Philip A., and J. Douglas Bremner, eds. *Posttraumatic Stress Disorder: A Comprehensive Text*. Boston: Allyn and Bacon, 1999. Print.

"Sally Benson." *Internet Movie Database*. Web. Dec. 21, 2011.

Santos, Marlisa. *The Dark Mirror: Psychiatry and Film Noir*. Lanham, MD: Lexington, 2010. Print.

Scheib, Ronnie. "Ida Lupino: Auteuress." *Film Comment* 16.1 (1980): 54–64. Print.

Schlenger, William E., et al. "Combat-Related Posttraumatic Stress Disorder: Prevalence, Risk Factors, and Comorbidity." Saigh and Bremner, *Posttraumatic Stress Disorder* 69–91.

Schrader, Paul. "Notes on *Film Noir*." Silver and Ursini, *Film Noir Reader* 53–64.

Schwartz, Hillel. *The Culture of the Copy: Striking Likenesses, Unreasonable Facsimiles*. New York: Zone, 1996. Print.

Seiter, Ellen. "*The Bigamist* (1953)." Kuhn 103–17.

Server, Lee. "If You Don't Get Killed It's a Lucky Day: A Conversation with Abraham Polonsky." Server, Gorman, and Greenberg 87–92.

———. "Marc Lawrence: The Last Gangster." Server, Gorman, and Greenberg 47–54.

———. "The Thieves' Market: A. I. Bezzerides in Hollywood." Server, Gorman, and Greenberg 115–22.

Server, Lee, Ed Gorman, and Martin H. Greenberg, eds. *The Big Book of Noir.* New York: Carroll and Graf, 1998. Print.

Shadoian, Jack. *Dreams and Dead Ends: The American Gangster Film.* 2nd ed. New York: Oxford UP, 2003. Print.

Shakespeare, William. *Hamlet, Prince of Denmark. The Annotated Shakespeare.* Ed. A. L. Rowse. New York: Greenwich, 1984. Print.

Shell, Marc. *Money, Language, and Thought: Literary and Philosophic Economies from the Medieval to the Modern Era.* Berkeley: U of California P, 1982. Print.

Silver, Alain. "*Kiss Me Deadly:* Evidence of a Style." Silver and Ursini, *Film Noir Reader* 209–35.

———. "*Uncle Harry.*" Silver and Ward 297–98.

Silver, Alain, and Linda Brookover. "What Is This Thing Called *Noir?*" Silver and Ursini, *Film Noir Reader* 261–73.

Silver, Alain, and James Ursini, eds. *Film Noir Reader.* New York: Limelight, 1996. Print.

———. *Film Noir Reader 2.* New York: Limelight, 1999. Print.

———. *Film Noir Reader 4: The Crucial Films and Themes.* Pompton Plains, NJ: Limelight, 2004. Print.

Silver, Alain, and Elizabeth Ward, eds. *Film Noir: An Encyclopedic Reference to the American Style.* 3rd ed. Woodstock, NY: Overlook, 1992. Print.

Simmel, Georg. *The Sociology of Georg Simmel.* Ed. and trans. Kurt H. Wolff. Glencoe, IL: Free P, 1950. Print.

Smith, Robert. "Mann in the Dark: The *Films Noir* of Anthony Mann." Silver and Ursini, *Film Noir Reader* 189–201.

Sparshott, Francis. "The Disappointed Art Lover." Dutton, *The Forger's Art* 246–63.

Spencer, Nicholas. "1944: Movies and the Renegotiation of Genre." Dixon 117–39.

Spicer, Andrew. *Film Noir.* Harlow, UK: Longman, 2001. Print.

Stanfield, Peter. *Body and Soul: Jazz and Blues in American Film, 1927–63.* Urbana: U of Illinois P, 2005. Print.

———. "A Monarch for the Millions: Jewish Filmmakers, Social Commentary, and the Postwar Cycle of Boxing Films." Krutnik, Neale, Neve, and Stanfield 79–96.

States, Bert O. *The Rhetoric of Dreams.* Ithaca, NY: Cornell UP, 1988. Print.

Stokes, Melvyn. *Gilda.* London: BFI/Palgrave Macmillan, 2010. Print.

Straw, Will. "Documentary Realism and the Postwar Left." Krutnik, Neale, Neve, and Stanfield 130–41.

Telotte, J. P. "Fatal Capers: Strategy and Enigma in Film *Noir.*" *Journal of Popular Film and Television* 23.4 (1996): 163–69. Print.

———. *Voices in the Dark: The Narrative Patterns of Film Noir.* Urbana: U of Illinois P, 1989. Print.

Rev. of *Thieves' Highway. Variety* Sept. 7, 1949. PCA file, *Thieves' Highway.* MHLSC.

Thomas, Deborah. "Psychoanalysis and Film Noir." Cameron 71–87.

Thwaites, Tony. *Joycean Temporalities: Debts, Promises, and Countersignatures.* Gainesville: UP of Florida, 2001. Print.

Tierney, Gene, with Mickey Herskowitz. *Self-Portrait.* New York: Wyden, 1978. Print.

Truesdell, Joan. *Be Still, My Love.* London: Boardman, n.d. [1947]. Print.

Truffaut, Francois, with Helen Scott. *Hitchcock.* New York: Simon and Schuster, 1983. Print.

Tucker, Robert C., ed. *The Marx-Engels Reader.* 2nd ed. New York: Norton, 1978. Print.

Turney, Catherine. *I Married a Dead Man.* May 5, 1949. TS. *No Man of Her Own* script files. MHLSC.

——. *The Lie.* Dec. 16, 1949. TS. *No Man of Her Own* script files. MHLSC.

——. *With This Ring [I Married a Dead Man].* April 16, 1949. TS. *No Man of Her Own* script files. MHLSC.

United States. Dept. of Commerce. *United States Census of Population: 1950.* "Special Reports: Population Mobility—States and State Economic Areas." Vol. 4. Tables 1–6. 4B 13–29. Washington: United States Government Printing Office, 1950. Print.

Vizzard, Jack. Memo to Jack Warner. Oct. 14, 1949. TS. PCA file, *Caged.* MHLSC.

Vose, Ken. *The Convertible: An Illustrated History of a Dream Machine.* San Francisco: Chronicle, 1999. Print.

Wager, Jans B. *Dangerous Dames: Women and Representation in the Weimar Street Film and Film Noir.* Athens: Ohio UP, 1999. Print.

——. "Jazz and Cocktails: Reassessing the White and Black Mix in Film Noir." *Literature/Film Quarterly* 35.3 (2007): 222–28. Print.

Waldman, Diane. "The Childish, the Insane, and the Ugly: The Representation of Modern Art in Popular Films and Fiction of the Forties." *Wide Angle* 5.2 (1982): 52–65. Print.

——. "Not Wanted (1949)." Kuhn 13–19.

Walker, Michael. "*Film Noir:* Introduction." Cameron 8–38.

Waller, Willard. *The Veteran Comes Back.* New York: Dryden P, 1944. Print.

Wallis, Hal. Contract with Barre Lyndon. Jan. 30, 1947. TS. Hal Wallis Papers. MHLSC.

——. Contract with Jonathan Latimer. Jan. 6, 1947. TS. Hal Wallis Papers. MHLSC.

——. Contract with Ketti Frings. Feb. 18, 1948. TS. Hal Wallis Papers. MHLSC.

——. Contract with Ketti Frings. Dec. 21, 1948. TS. Hal Wallis Papers. MHLSC.

Walsh, Andrea S. *Women's Film and Female Experience, 1940–1950.* New York: Praeger, 1984. Print.

Web Gallery of Art. "Dürer, Albrecht." Web. July 27, 2008. www.wga.hu/frames-e.html?/html/d/durer/1/04/2adorat.html.

Welsch, Tricia. "Sound Strategies: Lang's Rearticulation of Renoir." *Cinema Journal* 39.3 (2000): 51–65. Print.

Wieder, Robert, and George Hall. *The Great American Convertible: An Affectionate Guide.* New York: Doubleday, 1977. Print.

Williams, Tony. "*The Big Night* (1951): A Naturalist *Bildungsroman.*" Silver and Ursini, *Film Noir Reader 4* 95–107.

——. "The Naturalist Horizons of *Nightmare Alley* (1947)." *Excavatio* 22.1-2 (2007): 121–37. Print.

——. "*Phantom Lady,* Cornell Woolrich, and the Masochistic Aesthetic." Silver and Ursini, *Film Noir Reader* 129–43.

Wollen, Peter, and Joe Kerr, eds. *Autopia: Cars and Culture.* London: Reaktion, 2002. Print.

Wollheim, Richard. "Dreams." Bloom 77–87.

Woolrich, Cornell [as William Irish]. *I Married a Dead Man.* Polito 797–973.

———. *Phantom Lady.* 1942. New York: Pocket, 1944. Print.

Žižek, Slavoj. *Looking Awry: An Introduction to Jacques Lacan through Popular Culture.* Cambridge, MA: MIT P, 1991. Print.

INDEX

Page numbers in italics refer to photographs.

Accused, The, 199, 201–3, 282–83nn23–34

Ace in the Hole, 254

Act of Violence, 97, 100–104, 187, 272nn30–31; amnesia in, 78–79, 100, 104; function of disability in, 101, 270n2; and informing, 100, 101, 104

advertisements, 5, 135, 251, 275n4

African Americans, 11–12, 178; Hollywood representation of, 155, 277n5; and jazz, 16, 155, 156–57, 172–73, 178, 245, 290n46; rarely featured in film, 154, 158

agency, 126, 208; and American Dream, 3, 20–21, 143–44; automobiles and, 134; as noir theme, 20–21, 46; psychiatric stripping of, 98, 205; women and, 197, 199, 280n10

Aldrich, Robert, 150, 284n42

Algren, Nelson, 174

alienation, 48, 76, 97, 289n34; and individualism, 69, 249; as noir theme, 14, 77–78, 92

Alton, John, 70, 95, 96, 176

American Dream, 4, 5, 12, 47, 75, 142, 198; agency at core of, 3, 20–21, 143–44; automobiles and, 134, 152; as chimera and sham, 64, 249, 260; and criminality, 4, 199, 226; and domesticity, 99–100, 101, 258, 260; in hitchhiking films, 135, 144; and individualism, 4, 135; jazz and, 156, 170, 179; *No Man of Her Own* depiction of, 62, 64; in portraiture films, 107–8, 126; *The Prowler* depiction of, 221, 249–50, 255, 260; pursuit of as nightmare, 10, 199; pursuit of happiness and, 2, 17; red noir films on, 221, 226, 234, 242–43; and self-reinvention, 45, 79, 105, 115, 250; *Try and Get Me!* depiction of, 249–50; of upward mobility, 10, 63, 231, 259

amnesia, 15, 271n22; in dream films, 37–40; in identity films, 47, 49–50, 59; in vet noir films, 77, 78–79, 88, 92, 93–96, 97, 99, 100, 104

Anatomy of a Murder, 174

Andersen, Thom, 225, 288n25

Anderson, Edward, 136

Andrews, Dana, 81, 109, *111*

Angelus (Millet), 127–28, 274n22

antifascism, 12, 221, 285–86n3

anxiety, 13, 14, 161, 270n10; automobiles and, 152; postwar, 12, 13, 78, 97

Appointment with Danger, 277n7

Arlen, Harold, 156

Armored Car Robbery, 289n38

Armstrong, Louis, 158, 170, 172, 278nn21–22

art forgery, 4, 16, 274n21, 275n27; and authorship, 122; in *La chienne,* 120–21; in *Crack-Up,* 106–7, 127–30; in *Laura,* 110, 112; and originality, 107, 127–28, 129–30, 131; in *Scarlet Street,* 122–25

Ashley, Edward, 163, 165

Asphalt Jungle, The, 220–21, 239–44, 289n38, 289–90nn40–43; as heist film, 239, 240, 289n38

atomic bomb, 12, 151, 161

authenticity, 4–5, 107, 179, 220–21

authorship: cinematic, 17, 106, 119, 185, 215–16, 218; and forgery, 122; and identity, 120, 124

automobiles, 16, 132–53, 275n2; and American Dream, 134, 152; as amoral space, 16, 133, 135, 137, 148, 150, 152, 199; and autonomy, 134, 143, 151; and commodification, 133, 134, 135, 142, 150; criminals and, 135, 136, 146, 148, 149; as domestic space, 133, 135, 136–37, 139, 148; and freedom, 16, 132, 135, 136, 148; and guns, 140–41, 145, 147; and identity, 133, 134, 135, 137; loss of, 135, 145; and masculinity, 147; and mobility, 16, 139, 142, 143, 144; in postwar period, 133–34, 135, 152; and risk, 135, 145, 147; and roadside restaurants, 143, 275n3; and sexuality, 135, 137, 140; and sovereignty, 143, 145; as Trojan horse, 16, 135, 148, 149, 151; used, 139, 142–43, 275n6. *See also* convertibles; hitchhikers; hitchhiking films; lam films

automobility, 133, 135, 147, 152; and criminality, 136; and mobility, 16, 134, 142, 261

autonomy, 99, 148, 181, 183; automobiles and, 134, 143, 151

Babener, Liahna, 111, 112, 273n4, 273n8
Bacall, Lauren, 65, 68
Balkun, Mary McAleer, 5
Barnes, George, 234
Barrymore, John, Jr., 28, 265n15
Basinger, Jeanine, 191
Baudry, Jean-Louis, 21
Beaumont, Hugh, 83, 281
bebop, 158, 276n1, 277n7
Belafonte, Harry, 172, 173, 278nn24–25
Bel Geddes, Barbara, 211, 284n44
Belton, John, 4, 93
Bennett, Bruce, 179, 189
Bennett, Joan, 70, 106, 117, 121–22
Benson, Sally, 48, 188, 267–68n11; and *No Man of Her Own*, 61, 64, 268n12, 268nn15–16, 268n18
Bernhardt, Curtis, 97, 100, 205, 272n27, 272n29
Bernstein, Elmer, 176–77, 279n32
Berry, John, 211, 284n42
Bessie, Alvah, 286n7
Be Still, My Love (Truesdell), 202, 203, 282nn26–27, 283nn32–33

Best Years of Our Lives, The, 13, 77, 81–82, 270n1, 287n20
betrayal, 53, 88, 170, 239; and blacklist era, 221, 240–41; and secrets, 229, 237
Beverly, William, 135
Bezzerides, A. I., 227
Biberman, Herbert, 285–866n3, 286n7
Biesen, Sheri Chinen, 112, 189, 273n8
Bigamist, The, 147, 215, 216–18, 285nn51–55
Big Combo, The, 77, 174–76
Big Heat, The, 187
Big Night, The, 28–30, 44, 265nn13–18
Black Angel, 165–67, 278n17
blacklist, 17–18, 221, 228, 240, 247, 286n13; fight against, 244–45; onset of, 223–24; red noir films on, 245–47, 255; studio heads and, 223, 247; testifying and informing during, 223, 290nn43–44; use of "fronts" during, 223, 224, 255. *See also* red scare and witch hunt
blackness, 184; jazz and, 16, 154, 155, 160, 161, 166, 178, 180
Black Path of Fear, The (Woolrich), 31
Blankfort, Henry, 290n45
Blind Alley, 264n1
Block, Libbie, 211, 284n46
Blue Dahlia, The, 78, 82–84, 270nn9–11
Blue Gardenia, The, 168–70
Blues in the Night, 156–58, 277nn5–6
blues music, 156–58, 160, 167, 177, 179, 182
blues philosophy, 173
"Body and Soul" (song), 181, 233
Body and Soul, 5, 220, 231–34, 249, 288nn24–30
Boehm, Sydney, 97
Bogart, Humphrey, 65, 67, 68, 88, 268–69n22; and Hollywood Ten, 222–23
Bolton, Muriel Roy, 58, 188, 267n8
Bond, Anson, 214
Boone, Richard, 115
boxing, 231–33, 288n27
Brackett, Leigh, 188
Brandell, Jerrold, 42
Brecht, Bertolt, 286n7
Bredell, Woody, 51
Breen, Joseph, 254, 256, 284n40, 285n49
Breen, Richard, 277n7
Breen Office. *See* censors

Brick Foxhole, The (Brooks), 84, 270n12
Bridges, Lloyd, 250, 255
Brill, Lesley, 43, 266n26
Britton, Andrew, 276n13
Brodie, Steve, 54, *85*, 139
Broe, Dennis, 139, 225, 230, 264n10, 286n10, 287n22
Brook, Vincent, 264n7, 277nn5–6
Brooks, Richard, 84, 270n12
Browder, Earl, 224, 286n11
Brown, Royal, 273n5
Brute Force, 225–26, 287n15
Buhle, Paul, 220, 224, 290n45, 290n47
Butler, David, 154, 158, 159, 276n1, 277n9, 279n29
Butler, Hugo, 255, 265n13

Caged, 207–10, 284nn40–41
Cagney, James, 148
Cain, James M., 11, 133, 188, 286n6
Campbell, D'Ann, 280n2
Cantor, Paul, 142, 277n14
capitalism, 4, 240, 261; and crime, 17, 220, 228, 234–35, 240–41, 249; *Force of Evil* on, 234–37, 249; Marx and Engels on, 227, 235–36; *Strange Love of Martha Ivers* on, 189, 231; *Try and Get Me!* on, 250, 291n2
Carnovsky, Morris, 88, 227
Carroll, Madeleine, 192
Caruth, Cathy, 79
Caspary, Vera, 112, 273n3, 273n7
Cassavetes, John, 147
cathartic cure, 22, 25, 42
Caught, 5, 211–14, 284–85nn44–47
censors, 137, 188; and *The Accused*, 282–83n28; and *The Bigamist*, 218; and *Caged*, 284n40; and *Damned Don't Cry*, 282n20; and *Gilda*, 199; and *No Man of Her Own*, 64, 268n19; and *Not Wanted*, 285n49; and *The Prowler*, 256; and *Scarlet Street* and, 274n20; and *Thieves' Highway*, 287n17; and *Try and Get Me!*, 254, 291n4; and *The Underworld Story*, 290n46, 290n50
Ceplair, Larry, 222, 224, 271n17
Chamberlain, Howland, 29, 237
Chandler, Raymond, 11, 270n9
Chase, The, 31–34, 44, 45

chien andalou, Un, 40
chienne, La, 106, 116, 119–22, 126, 274n17
children, 187–88, 189, 253
Chopra-Gant, Mike, 13, 78, 270n11
Christopher, Nicholas, 22
class, 226, 241, 255; mobility between, 2, 58, 62; *Naked City* on, 226, 287n16; *The Strange Love of Martha Ivers* on, 220, 228, 230, 287n22
Cobb, Lee J., 19, 227
Cochran, Steve, 31, 198
Cockrell, Marian, 192
Coffee, Lenore J., 188
Cohn, Harry, 192, 215
Cold War, 78, 79, 97, 100, 144
Cole, Lester, 97, 285–86n3; and Hollywood Ten, 272n25, 286n7
Collins, Ray, 127
Collins, Richard, 283n38, 286n7
Comandini, Adele, 25, 265n10
Committee for the First Amendment, 222–23, 244
commodification, 228–29, 232, 234, 246; of art and artist, 109, 120, 123; automobiles and, 133, 134, 135, 142, 150; of women, 170, 190, 193, 199, 211
Communists and communism, 12, 176–77n4, 286n11; Hollywood Left and, 221, 271n17, 290–91n1
community, 3, 48, 69, 215–16
complicity, 199, 200–201, 204
Condemned, The (Pagano), 250
condensation, 14, 22, 24–25, 43, 264n2, 265n9
Conference of Studio Unions, 222
conformity, 3, 16, 18, 240
Conrad, William, 232
consumer goods, 2, 5, 6, 10, 261
consumerism, 6, 12, 249, 251
Conte, Richard, 169, 175, 227, 271–72n23
conversion narratives, 20, 23, 47
convertibility, 134, 138–39, 140, 152
convertibles, 142, 143, 144, 145, 147, 151, 201; and convertibility, 16, 134, 138–39; as means of empowerment, 147–48; as sign of mobility, 144, 275n4
Cook, Elisha, Jr., 159
Cook, Pam, 204

Cooper, George, 85

Cooper, Maxine, 150

Corey, Jeff, 226

Corey, Wendell, 199, 201

Cornered, 78, 86–87, 271nn15–17, 285–86n3

Cortesa, Valentina, 227

counterfeiting, 16, 62

Cover Girl, 192

Cowie, Elizabeth, 280n1

Cowl, Jane, 63

Crack-Up, 106–7, 127–31, 274–75nn21–27

Craig, James, 170

Crain, Jeanne, 115

Crawford, Joan, 189, 197, 205

Cregar, Laird, 108, 115

crime and criminality, 17, 24, 25, 130, 242–43; and American Dream, 4, 199, 226; automobiles and, 135, 136, 146, 148, 149; capitalism and, 17, 220, 228, 234–35, 240–41, 249; as left-handed form of human endeavor, 17, 220, 243; noncriminals and, 289–90n42; organized, 220, 234–35, 240–41, 289nn41–42; and upward mobility, 63, 220–21, 259

crime jazz, 174, 279n29

Criss Cross, 160, 277nn11–12

Cromwell, John, 208

Cronyn, Hume, 225

Crooked Way, The, 78, 95–97

Crossfire, 84–86, 270–71nn12–14; HUAC and, 86

Crowther, Bosley, 287n18

Cullen, Jim, 2, 3, 47

Cummings, Robert, 31, 202

Cummins, Peggy, 140, *141*

Curran, Dale, 276–77n4

Dalí, Salvador, 40, 127–28, 274n24

Dall, John, 140, *141*

Damarest, William, 170

Damned Don't Cry, The, 197–99, 281–82nn19–20

Damone, Vic, 278n22

D'Andrea, Tom, 66

Danger! Women at Work, 281n18

Dark Corner, The, 106, 113–15, 273nn9–11

Dark Passage, 48, 65–69, 268–69nn22–23

Dark Past, The, 19, 24–25, 45

Dark Waters, 192

Da Silva, Howard, 83, 138, 245

Dassin, Jules: and *Brute Force*, 225, 226; and Hollywood Left, 17, 220, 221; and *Naked City*, 226, 287n16; and *Thieves' Highway*, 227, 228, 287n19; and witch hunt, 224, 228, 234

Daves, Delmer, 65

Davidson, Michael, 77

Dead Reckoning, 88–90

de Bolla, Peter, 124

Decker, John, 274n19

Declaration of Independence, 2, 209

Dekker, Albert, 51, 150

DeLillo, Don, 5

democracy, 12, 220

Desperate, 139–40, 276n7

Detour, 142–44, 161–62, 276nn12–14

Deutsch, Helen, 137

Devil Thumbs a Ride, The, 144

Diana Productions, 14, 121–22

Dieterle, William, 282n28

Dietrichson, Phyllis, 185

Dimendberg, Edward, 132, 175

disability, 15, 77, 78, 93, 270n2, 270n5; cognitive, 77, 78, 80; and gender roles, 270n10; and jazz, 154, 168; and masculinity, 78, 83; moral, 77, 101

disabled veterans, 15–16, 77–79, 93, 105, 170, 214; and amnesia, 77, 78–79, 88, 92–97, 99, 100, 104; statistics on, 80, 270n6; stigma attached to, 272n24; and trauma, 78, 79, 80, 87, 88, 93, 97–98, 100. *See also* veterans

Diskant, George, 139

displacement, 14, 22, 25, 33, 264n2

Dmytryk, Edward: and *Cornered*, 86, 271n17, 285–86n3; and *Crossfire*, 84, 270–71nn13–14, 285–86n3; and HUAC, 223, 286n7

D.O.A., 160–61, 171

Doane, Mary Ann, 193, 213, 281nn15–17, 284n45

domesticity, 148, 179; and American Dream, 99–100, 101, 258, 260; automobiles and, 133, 135, 136–37, 139, 140, 148; heterosexual, 78, 86; women and, 186, 188, 190

Donatello, 114, 273n11

Double Indemnity, 13, 132, 133, 188, 275nn1–2

doubles, 49, 54, 55, 88, 93, 113, 116

Douglas, Kirk, 54, 228

Downs, Cathy, 113, *114*

Dowson, Ernest, 111–12

Dozier, William, 271n15

Dratler, Jay, 273nn8–9

Dreadful Summit (Ellin), 265n13, 265n15, 265n17–18

dreams, 15, 22, 23, 107; and cinema, 21, 264n3; and emotion, 23, 44–45, 265n7; Freudian theory on, 20, 22–23, 24, 265n8; and guilt, 19, 26, 33, 36, 44–45; and identity, 20, 21; in jazz films, 162; and memory, 25, 41–42; as message from beyond, 26, 44; oedipal, 24, 25–26, 28; and reality, 33; and self-reinvention, 20, 21, 37, 47; as someone else's, 19–20, 23, 33, 36–37, 40; trauma in, 26, 42–43, 44; and uncon-scious, 24, 28, 265n8; as warning, 33–34, 36–37, 44

dream sequences, 15, 20–21, 264n1; in *The Chase*, 32–34; in *The Dark Past*, 19, 24–25; in *Laura*, 110, 273n6; in *Nightmare Alley*, 15; in *Possessed*, 206; in *Spellbound*, 40–43, 266n24; in *The Strange Affair of Uncle Harry*, 34, 36–37, 44, 45; in *Strange Illusion*, 25–26, 44; in *Stranger on the Third Floor*, 21; in *Try and Get Me!*, 252; in *The Woman in the Window*, 118, 274n16

Duff, Warren, 277n7

Dunne, Philip, 222–23

Dürer, Albrecht, 129, 275nn26–27

Duryea, Dan, 106, 118, 166, 245

Dyer, Richard, 273n10

Einfeld, Charles, 288n26

Ellin, Stanley, 265n13

Ellington, Duke, 174

Ellison, Ralph, 173

Emerald Productions, 214, 215

Emerson, Ralph Waldo, 2–3

émigrés. *See* immigrants

Endfield, Cyril, 17, 220, 250; and witch hunt, 224, 245, 250, 255, 290–91n1

End of the Road, 281n18

Engels, Frederick, 230, 235, 237

Englund, Steven, 222, 224, 271n17

Enterprise Studios, 14, 284n43; and *Body and Soul*, 231, 234, 288n26; and *Caught*, 211, 214, 285n47

expressionism, 82, 129

Federal Bureau of Investigation (FBI), 238, 289n35, 290n47

feminism, 185, 210, 215

femme fatales, 17, 185, 193, 196, 282n25

femme noir, 187, 188–91, 218, 219; *The Accused*, 199, 201–3, 282–83nn23–34; *The Bigamist*, 147, 215, 216–18, 285nn51–55; *Caged*, 207–10, 284nn40–41; *Caught*, 5, 211–14, 284–85nn44–47; *The Damned Don't Cry*, 197–99, 281–82nn19–20; *Dark Waters*, 192; *Gilda*, 192–97, 281nn14–17; *Mildred Pierce*, 188–91, 216, 280nn7–10; *Not Wanted*, 214; *Outrage*, 203–4, 283nn35–36; *Phantom Lady*, 159, 171, 192, 271n20, 272–73n1, 277nn9–12, 281n12; *Possessed*, 205–7, 283–84nn37–39

File on Thelma Jordon, The, 199–201

Filmakers, Inc., 211, 215–16, 218

film gris, 225, 286n13, 288n25

film industry, 2, 13, 21, 23, 223; émigré directors in, 11, 20, 264n7, 266–67n1; female filmmak-ers and, 17, 58, 180, 185, 187–88, 191–92, 214, 218–19, 261; film noir and, 13–14; gender views of, 112, 185, 193; HUAC and, 86, 101, 221, 222–23, 224, 240, 283n38; independent production companies in, 14, 211, 250, 284n43, 286n13; and melodrama, 14, 23, 187, 189, 216; screenwriters and, 188, 215, 224, 286n6; view of jazz by, 17, 155. *See also* blacklist; censors

film noir origins and definition, 11–12, 14, 132, 264n9, 275n1

Fisher, Doris, 281n16

Fisher, Steve, 15

fishing, 55, 56, 267n5

flashbacks, 270n4; in dream films, 39, 265n14; in femme noir films, 201, 205–7, 216, 282n26; in identity films, 51, 61; in jazz films, 162, 166; musical themes associated with, 161–62; in portraiture films, 106, 107, 109, 127; as prototypical noir device, 51, 79–80, 106; in vet noir films, 80, 82, 83

Fleischer, Richard, 289n38
Fletcher, Lucille, 188
Flinn, Caryl, 161, 162
Foch, Nina, 19, 58, 267n6
Fontaine, Joan, 216, 218
Force of Evil, 234–39, 288–89nn32–36; on capitalism and crime, 220, 234–37, 249
Ford, Glenn, 193, 281n14
Forrest, Sally, 170, 214, 277–78n15
Fotsch, Paul, 132, 275n2
Fouchardière, Georges de la, 116
fracturing, 6, 53–54, 129, 131
frame narratives, 106, 109, 112, 127
framing, 106, 107, 118, 125; in *La chienne*, 120, 274n17; in *The Dark Corner*, 113, 114; in *I Wake Up Screaming*, 108, 109; in *Laura*, 110, 112
Francke, Lizzie, 187
Frank, Arthur, 80
Frank, Nino, 275n1
Franklin, Benjamin, 2
Freedman, Jonathan, 37, 266nn21–22
freedom and liberty, 4, 5, 10, 21, 75; American Dream and, 12, 100; automobiles and, 16, 132, 135, 136, 148; as ideal, 2, 249
Freudianism, 278n19; on dreams, 20, 22–23, 24, 265n8
Frings, Ketti, 188, 199, 203, 282nn21–24
From Here to Eternity, 272n30
Fuchs, Daniel, 70, 71, 75, 76, 269n26, 269nn28–29
Fuller, Samuel, 137
Fury, 254

Gabbard, Glen O., 263–64n6, 266n23
Gabbard, Krin, 263–64n6, 266n23; on jazz films, 170, 171, 277n5, 279n33
Galatea/Pygmalion myth, 106, 110
gangster films, 4, 17, 25, 225, 287n14
Gardner, Ava, 51, 52
Garfield, John, 133, 220, 231, 234, 285–86n3; biographical information on, 231, 288n25; and witch hunt, 224, 288n29
Garmes, Lee, 211
Garnett, Tay, 133
Gay, Peter, 23

geek, 163, 253, 263n1; in *Nightmare Alley*, 1, 6, 9, 10
gender roles, 54, 125, 170, 270n10; female filmmakers on, 191–92, 214, 217, 261; femme noir films on, 199, 208, 214, 217; jazz and, 154, 163; postwar anxieties about, 17, 115, 185. *See also* women
Gershwin, George and Ira, 156
Giddens, Anthony, 150
Gilda, 192–97, 281nn14–17
Gioia, Ted, 163
Goetz, William, 274
Gomez, Thomas, 91, 235
Goodman, Benny, 156
Gorbman, Claudia, 154, 161
Gothic, 187, 192, 280n4
Gough, Lloyd, 231, 288n24
Goulding, Edmund, 1
Grable, Betty, 108, 109
Graebner, William, 13
Granger, Farley, 137, *138*
Gray, J. Glenn, 101–2
Green, Johnny, 233
Greene, Eve, 188
Greene, Mort, 163
Greer, Jane, 54, *57*
Gresham, William Lindsay, 8, 263n2
Griffith, E. H., 192
Grossman, Julie, 185, 192
guilt, 24, 25, 26, 168, 260; America and, 76, 105; dreams and, 19, 26, 33, 36, 44–45; *Spellbound* depiction of, 38, 39, 43
Gun Crazy, 5, 136, 140–42, 187, 276nn9–10
Gunning, Tom, 125, 136

Hall, George, 275n4
Hamlet, 25, 26, 28, 265n13
Hammett, Dashiell, 11, 46, 47
Hampton, Lionel, 156
Hannah, Dorothy, 188
Hanson, Helen, 280n4, 281n12
hard-boiled fiction, 11, 15, 115, 192, 264n8
Harline, Leigh, 163
Harris, Oliver, 116, 119
Harrison, Joan, 34, 36, 37, 159, 163, 271n19; as producer, 191–92, 280n11

Hartmann, Ernest, 44, 265n7
Haskell, Molly, 280n3
Hastie, Amelie, 215, 217
Hathaway, Henry, 113
Hayden, Sterling, 220, 223, 290n43
Hays Office, 36
Hayward, Lillie, 188
Hayworth, Rita, 112, 185, 192–93, *196*
Hecht, Ben, 271n19
Heflin, Van, 100, *102*, 205, 228, 255, *257*
heist films, 239, 240, 243, 289nn37–39
Hellinger, Mark, 287n16
Henreid, Paul, 69, 70, 71, *72*, 75, 76, 269n24;
    biographical information on, 269n25
Higgins, John C., 281n18
High Wall, 78, 97–100, 272nn24–30
Hillis, Ken, 3, 134
Hirsch, Foster, 19, 46–47
Hirsch, Joshua, 225, 287n14, 289–90n42
Hitchcock, Alfred, 42, 191, 266nn26–27; and
    film noir, 266n20; and *Spellbound,* 37, 38, 40,
    42, 266n21
The Hitch-Hiker, 145–47
hitchhikers, 133, 144, 148, 150; challenge to
    ownership by, 134–35; and lawlessness, 147
hitchhiking films: *Detour,* 142–44, 161, 162,
    276nn12–14; *The Devil Thumbs a Ride,* 144;
    The Hitch-Hiker, 145–47; *The Night Holds
    Terror,* 147–48
Hively, Jack, 49
Holiday, Billie, 156
Hollow Triumph, 48, 69–76, 120, 249,
    269nn25–29
Hollywood Left, 12–13, 17–18, 100, 220–48, 261,
    286n12; and communism, 221, 290–91n1; and
    film noir, 224–25, 286n12. *See also* blacklist
Hollywood Quarterly, 221–22, 286n4
Hollywood Ten, 222–23, 285–86n3, 286n7
Holmes, Taylor, 103, 208
homosexuality, 33, 83, 165, 284n44; in *Gilda,*
    193, 281n14; in *Laura,* 109, 273n3
homosociality, 33, 88, 89, 279n28
Hopper, Edward, 234
Horizon Pictures, 14
House Un-American Activities Committee
    (HUAC), 97, 104, 247; and Hollywood, 86,
101, 221, 222–23, 224, 240, 283n38; naming
    names for, 223, 290n43
Howe, James Wong, 231
Hughes, C. J. Pennethorne, 21
Hughes, Dorothy B., 271n19
Hughes, Howard, 284n44, 286n12
Hughes, Langston, 173–74
Humphries, Reynold, 241, 255
Huston, John, 46; and *The Asphalt Jungle,* 220,
    241–42, 244; and Committee for the First
    Amendment, 222–23, 244
Huston, Virginia, 55, 164
Hyde, Thomas, 43

"I Can't Believe That You're in Love with Me,"
    162–63
identity, 4, 16, 30; American, 15, 79, 184;
    authorship and, 120, 124; automobiles and,
    133, 134, 135, 137; consumer goods and, 5, 10;
    dreams and, 20, 21; as fluid and malleable, 47,
    92, 107, 115, 261; forged, 115, 125; Franklin and
    Emerson on, 2, 3; *Nightmare Alley* on, 10, 15;
    in portraiture films, 106, 107, 115, 120, 122, 127,
    131, 261, 280n9; in postwar period, 4, 5, 97; in
    switched-identity films, 39, 42, 48, 50; in vet
    noir films, 77, 78, 82, 89, 96, 97; women and,
    58–59, 60, 198, 210; writing as certification of,
    39, 63
I Married a Dead Man (Woolrich), 61, 62, 64,
    268n13, 268n17
immigrants, 4, 37, 76, 93; returning vets feeling
    like, 81, 82, 93; and switched-identity films,
    48, 266–67n1
individualism, 76; and alienation, 69, 249; and
    American Dream, 4, 135; and community, 3;
    Dark Passage on, 69, 261; *Hollow Triumph*
    on, 249, 261; ideology of, 2, 48; noir critique
    of, 4, 15, 107, 221, 260, 261
informers, 149, 226; in *Act of Violence,* 100, 101,
    104; during blacklist era, 223, 290nn43–44; in
    Force of Evil, 237, 239
Ingster, Boris, 21
innocence: and evil, 140; lost, 92, 97, 170, 243
International Alliance of Theatrical Stage
    Employees (IATSE), 222
isolation, 48, 77–78, 92; automobiles and, 133, 134

I Wake Up Screaming, 106, 107–9, 115
I Want to Live, 174, 278–79nn26–27

Jaffe, Sam, 202, 240
Jameson, Fredric, 5–6
Jarrico, Paul, 285n48
jazz, 154–84; and American Dream, 170, 174; big-band, 175; and blackness, 16, 154, 155, 160, 161, 166, 178, 180; crime jazz, 174, 279n29; and cultural anxieties, 154, 161, 176; in *Detour,* 161, 162; and disability, 154, 168; improvisation in, 155, 162, 173, 180, 182; New Orleans–style, 158–59, 167; noir association with, 16, 154; and postwar world, 12, 154, 155, 158, 163; as quintessentially American, 155, 184; as rebellion, 161; respectability and legitimacy of, 172, 179; and sexuality, 16, 154–55, 159, 160–61, 165, 175, 176, 277n9, 277n11; as symbol of otherness, 154–55; tolerance and idealism in, 16–17, 170, 279n33; unsavory connotations of, 17, 155, 159, 171, 174, 175, 176, 178; and violence, 154, 155, 161, 168
jazz films, 162, 168, 249; *The Big Combo,* 77, 174–76; *Black Angel,* 165–67, 278n17; *The Blue Gardenia,* 168–70; *Blues in the Night,* 156–58, 277nn5–6; *Criss Cross,* 160, 277nn11–12; *Dead on Arrival,* 160–61, 171; *The Man I Love,* 179–81, 188, 279–80nn34–39; *Nightmare,* 167–68, 278n19; *Nocturne,* 163–65, 191, 278n16; *Odds against Tomorrow,* 172–74, 278–79nn24–28, 289n39; *Phantom Lady,* 159, 171, 192, 271n20, 272–73n1, 277nn9–12, 281n12; *Road House,* 181–84; *The Strip,* 170–72, 178, 278nn20–23; *Sweet Smell of Success,* 176–78, 279nn31–33
jazz musicians, 163, 168, 178, 179; as childlike and weak, 157, 170, 183; as effeminate, 155, 163, 277–78n15; female singers, 16–17, 179–80, 183–84; as idealistic, 179, 279n33; and interracialism, 16, 177, 278n20, 279n33; and mental disturbance, 16, 155, 163, 277–78n15; whites as, 16, 155
Jews, 155, 277n5
Johnson, Nunnally, 274n16
Johnston, Eric, 222
Jolson, Al, 156
justice, 29, 30, 254

Kahn, Gordon, 286n7
Kalinak, Kathryn, 154, 155, 273n4, 273n8
Kaminsky, Stuart, 289nn37–38
Kaplan, E. Ann, 274n17
Karlson, Phil, 289n39
Kazan, Elia, 223, 277n5
Kellogg, Virginia, 188, 207, 210, 284n41
Kemp, Philip, 11, 224–25, 286n12
Kenton, Stan, 279n29
Killens, John O., 278n24
Killers, The, 48, 50–54, 266n26
Kiss Me Deadly, 5, 150–52, 158
Kitses, Jim, 141, 276n10
Koch, Howard, 286n7
Kracauer, Siegfried, 264n3
Krutnik, Frank, 11, 24, 78, 271n16, 285–86n3
Kubrick, Stanley, 289n39
Kuhn, Annette, 215

Lackey, Kris, 134, 276n11
Laderman, David, 276n12, 276n14
lam films, 135–42, 275n6; *Gun Crazy,* 5, 136, 140–42, 187, 276nn9–10; *Shockproof,* 137; *They Live by Night,* 136–39, 158
Lancaster, Burt, 50, 52, 160, 177, 225
Lang, Fritz, 123, 136, 168, 254; and *La chienne,* 121–22, 123, 125; and *Scarlet Street,* 106, 116; and *Women in the Window,* 36, 106, 116, 119, 274n16
Lardner, Ring, Jr., 265n13, 286n7
Latimer, Jonathan, 278n16, 283n34
Laura, 106, 109–12, 273nn3–8; musical theme play in, 110, 273n5
Laurents, Arthur, 211, 284n42
Lawrence, Marc, 240, 290n44
Lawson, John Howard, 224, 285–86nn3–4, 286n7
Lears, Jackson, 4–5
Lebeau, Vicky, 21
Lederer, Charles, 271n19
Lee, Canada, 224, 232, 288n29
Leff, Leonard, 273n3
leftist filmmakers. *See* Hollywood Left
Leigh, Janet, 100, *102*
Leisen, Mitchell, 61
Levine, Lawrence, 156

Lewis, John, 172
Lewis, Joseph H., 140, 174
Little Caesar, 4
Look Homeward, Angel, 282n21
Loos, Anita, 281n13
Lorre, Peter, 31, 34, 166
Los Angeles, 71, 132–33, 150, 171
Losey, Joseph, 17, 28, 220, 249–50; and blacklist, 224, 256, 265n15; and *The Prowler,* 255, 256, 260, 291n5
Lott, Eric, 155
Lovejoy, Frank, *146,* 250
loyalty oaths, 223, 286n10
Luckhurst, Roger, 79, 270n4
Lupino, Ida, 17, 214–15, 218, 280n40; as actress, 179, 180, 181, 182, *183,* 214, 279n34; and *The Bigamist,* 211, 215, 218, 285n53; and *The Hitch-Hiker,* 145; and *Not Wanted,* 214, 215, 277–78n15, 285nn48–49; and *Outrage,* 203, 204, 215
lynching, 254

MacDougall, Ranald, 189
machines, 150, 153, 243
Macready, George, 58, 193
Maltby, Richard, 12, 14
Maltese Falcon, The, 46–47, 54, 90, 275n1
Maltese Falcon, The (Hammett), 46, 47
Maltz, Albert, 188, 285–86n3, 286n7, 287n16
Mancini, Henry, 174, 279n29
Man I Love, The, 179–81, 188, 279–80nn34–39
Mankiewicz, Joseph L., 92
Mann, Anthony, 139, 281n18
Man with the Golden Arm, The, 174
Marin, Edwin L., 163
marriage, 17, 86, 197, 203, 205, 211; *The Bigamist* on, 211, 216–18, 285n55; career women and, 196; *Caught* on, 211–14, 284n46; changing ideas of, 186–87, 217–18; as economic arrangement, 211; female filmmakers on, 191, 214, 261; and female sexuality, 193, 195, 203, 217; as form of abduction, 59, 60; *Gilda* on, 193, 195; *My Name Is Julia Ross* on, 58, 59, 60; *No Man of Her Own* on, 63, 64–65; as proper women's role, 186, 191
Marshall, Herbert, 99, 130, 245, 272n27

Martin, Angela, 280n5
Marx, Karl, 227, 230, 233, 235, 237, 283n34
masculinity, 15, 88–89, 197, 214, 255; automobiles and, 147; in *The Bigamist,* 216, 217; in *The Big Night,* 28, 29, 30, 45; and disability, 78, 83; hitchhiking and, 145; veterans' redefining of, 78, 79
Mason, Fran, 289n40
Mason, James, 212, *213*
masquerade, 54, 62, 73–74, 194, 195
Massey, Raymond, 118, 205
Maté, Rudolph, 19, 160
Maxfield, James, 58
May, Lary, 220, 225, 289n41
Mayo, Virginia, 82, 149
McCann, Sean, 277n11, 279n33
McClary, Susan, 163
McGilligan, Patrick, 122, 220
McGivern, William, 278n24, 279n28
McLean, Adrienne, 180, 279n35
Medford, Harold, 197
media, 221, 248; *The Asphalt Jungle* on, 243–44; and red scare, 224, 245, 290n48; *Try and Get Me!* on, 250, 254; *The Underworld Story* on, 221, 245–46, 249
Meegeren, Han van, 274n21
melodrama, 14, 23, 187, 189, 216
memory, 39, 80, 87, 162, 260; and dreams, 25, 41–42; and forgetting, 79; loss of, 49–50, 93, 96, 98, 104; and music, 163, 169; postwar America's crisis of, 104, 105; reliability of, 106–7; and trauma, 22, 23, 104. *See also* amnesia
Men, The, 272n30
Mercer, Johnny, 156, 273n6
Meredyth, Bess, 188
metonymy, 22, 24–25, 41, 43, 265n9
Meyer, Leonard, 128
Meyerowitz, Joanne, 186
Mijolla, Alain de, 22
Miklitsch, Robert, 275n25
Mildred Pierce, 188–91, 216, 280nn7–10
Milestone, Lewis, 228, 285–86n3, 286n7, 287n22
Millet, Jean-Francois, 127–28, 274n22
Mills, Katie, 134
Minturn, Kent, 272–73n1, 274n21

mirrors, 62, 96, 116, 117, 119, 125

mise-en-scène, 31, 189, 234, 256, 285n51

mistaken identity. *See* switched-identity films

Mitchell, David T., 77, 78, 270n5

Mitchum, Robert, 54, 85

mobility, 3, 15, 47, 140; automobiles and, 134, 137, 142, 143, 144; class, 2, 58, 62; and identity, 20; social, 3, 4, 12, 16, 141, 189. *See also* upward mobility

modernist art, 127, 274n23

modernity, 3, 4–5, 14, 150–51

Moffat, Kathie, 185

money, 62, 170–71, 260

Monroe, Marilyn, 241

Moorehead, Agnes, 66, 208

More Than Night (Naremore), 14

motherhood, 17, 149, 186, 187–88, 191, 214

Motion Picture Alliance for the Preservation of American Ideals (MPAPAI), 222, 228, 287n20

Motion Picture Association of America, 222

Munby, Jonathan, 236, 288–89n32

Murder, My Sweet, 77, 266n26, 275n1

Murray, Albert, 173

music: in *The Big Combo*, 174–75; in *Black Angel*, 166, 278n17; blues, 156–58, 160, 167, 177, 179, 182; crime jazz scoring, 174, 279n29; and flashbacks, 161–62; inaudibility of, 154, 276n2; and memory, 163, 169; in *Nightmare*, 167; in *Nocturne*, 163–64; swing, 156, 158, 174, 178, 277n7. *See also* jazz

My Name Is Julia Ross, 48, 58–60, 267nn6–9

Nadelson, Theodore, 88, 99, 101

Naked City, 226–27, 287n16

Naremore, James, 13, 14, 224, 291n2

Navasky, Victor, 223, 224

Neale, Steve, 12, 187, 264n11

negative footage, 19, 264n1

Nelson, Ralph, 196

Ness, Richard, 110

Neve, Bria, 287–88n23

Nichols, Dudley, 122

Night Holds Terror, The, 147–48

Nightmare, 167–68, 278n19

Nightmare Alley, 1, 6–10, 249, 263–64nn2–6; on identity and mobility, 11, 15

nightmares. *See* dreams

Night Shift (Wolff), 180

Nocturne, 163–65, 191, 278n16

No Man of Her Own, 48, 60–65, 267–68nn11–20; and censors, 64, 268n19; source novel for, 61, 62, 64, 268n13, 268n17

Norden, Martin, 270n1

Notorious, 13

Not Wanted, 214, 277–78n15, 285nn48–49

objectivity, 16, 107

O'Brien, Edmond, 50, *146*, 149, 160, 216

Odds against Tomorrow, 172–74, 278–79nn24–28, 289n39

O'Donnell, Cathy, 81, 138, *138*

oedipal complex, 24, 25–26, 27, 28, 263n3

Oliver, Kelly, 14, 264n2

Ophuls, Max, 211, 284n42

organized crime, 220, 234–35, 240–41, 289–90nn41–42

originality, 106, 107, 127; and forgery, 107, 127–28, 129–30, 131

Ornitz, Samuel, 286n7

Orr, John, 3

Osborne, Robert, 267n9

outlaw road movies, 135

Out of the Past, 5, 48, 54–58, 77, 266n26, 267nn4–5

Outrage, 203–4, 283nn35–36

Pagano, Jo, 180, 250, 279n36

Painter's Daughters, The, 130, 275n28

Palmer, R. Barton, 207, 283n37

Parker, Eleanor, 207, *209*

Parker, Francine, 215

Parks, Larry, 286n7

Parsonnet, Marion, 193

past, 20, 37, 48, 105, 259; and future, 94; and present, 5

patriarchy, 17, 204, 205

Patrick, Jack, 287n21

Paxton, John, 84, 86

Peck, Gregory, 37, 266n21

Pegler, Westbrook, 290n48

Pelizzon, V. Penelope, 72, 73, 74, 269n26

Perry, Eleanor, 188

Petrified Forest, The, 25

Pevney, Joseph, 164, 227, 231

Phantom Lady, 159, 171, 192, 271n20, 272–73n1, 277nn9–12, 281n12

photography, 9, 82, 139; and cinema, 73, 76

Piano in the Band (Curran), 276–77n4

picaro figure, 143, 276n11

Pichel, Irving, 286n4, 286n7

Planer, Franz, 31

Polan, Dana, 65, 69, 268n21

Polonsky, Abraham, 17, 220, 289n34; blacklisting and wiretapping of, 224, 238, 289n35; and *Body and Soul,* 231, 234, 288n26, 288n30; and *Force of Evil,* 234, 238, 289nn35–36; and *Odds Against Tomorrow,* 278n24, 278–79n27

Popular Front, 87, 221, 271n15, 276–77n4

Porfirio, Robert, 159, 160

portraiture films, 4, 16, 106, 131, 261, 272–73n1; *La chienne,* 106, 116, 119–22, 126, 274n17; *The Dark Corner,* 106, 113–15, 273nn9–11; *I Wake Up Screaming,* 106, 107–9, 115; *Laura,* 106, 109–12, 273nn3–8; *Scarlet Street,* 106, 116, 122–26, 274nn19–20; *Vicki,* 115–16, 274n13; *The Woman in the Window,* 36, 106, 116–19, 266n19, 274nn14–18

Possessed, 205–7, 283–84nn37–39

Postman Always Rings Twice, The, 133

posttraumatic stress disorder (PTSD), 33, 170, 272n32, 279n38; in vet noir films, 79, 82, 85–86, 88, 89, 90, 98

postwar period, 20, 82, 135, 217–18; anxieties of, 12, 13, 78, 97; and automobiles, 133–34, 152; and identity, 4, 5, 97; and jazz, 12, 154, 155, 158, 163; and memory, 104, 105; paranoid atmosphere of, 97, 221, 226

Preminger, Otto, 110, 174, 273n8, 274n14

press. *See* media

Prime, Rebecca, 226

prison, 75, 136, 207–10, 211

Prowler, The, 239–40, 255–60, 291nn5–6; American Dream in, 221, 249–50

psychiatrists and psychiatry, 6, 11, 22, 23, 202, 211; and patients' agency, 98, 205

psychoanalysis, 2, 5, 73–74; and detective work, 22, 39, 264n5; in dream films, 21, 22, 24, 25, 37, 38, 41, 42, 266n25, 266nn21–22; in femme

noir films, 206–7, 284n39; in *Nightmare Alley,* 8, 9, 10

Public Enemy, The, 4

pursuit of happiness, 1, 3, 5, 48, 76, 107, 260; and American Dream, 2, 17; and consumerism, 6, 249

Quart, Barbara Koenig, 215

Raft, George, 164, 165

Railroaded!, 281n18

Raines, Ella, 34, 159, 192

Rainey, Ma, 180

Raksin, David, 110, 174, 289n36

rape, 201, 202–4, 282–83n28

Raphael, 273n10

Ray, Nicholas, 137

Reagan, Ronald, 222

realism, 80, 225, 231

reality, 33; and representation, 107, 108, 131

redemption, 20, 47, 211; returning veterans and, 95, 96, 97, 99

"red noir," 224–25, 247, 249; *Body and Soul,* 5, 220, 231–34, 249, 288nn24–30; *Brute Force,* 225–26, 287n15; *Force of Evil,* 220, 234–39, 249, 288–89nn32–36; *Naked City,* 226–27, 287n16; *The Prowler,* 221, 239–40, 249–50, 255–60, 291nn5–6; *The Strange Love of Martha Ivers,* 220, 228–31, 287–88nn20–23; *Thieves' Highway,* 220, 227–28, 287nn17–19; *Try and Get Me!,* 221, 239–40, 250–55, 291nn2–4; *The Underworld Story,* 221, 245–47, 249, 290n46, 290nn49–50

red scare and witch hunt, 11, 100, 222, 240, 286n10; fight against, 222–23, 244–45, 255; mass media and, 224, 245, 290n48; paranoid atmosphere during, 12, 97, 221, 226. *See also* blacklist

reenactment, 79, 80, 162; in vet noir films, 88, 99, 102, 103–4

Reis, Irving, 129

religion, 5, 8, 10

Renoir, Jean, 106, 119, 120

Renov, Michael, 186

representation, 16, 106–7, 124; and reality, 107, 108, 131

Reville, Alma, 191
Richards, Robert, 97, 101, 272n30
Richards, Silvia, 188, 205, 210, 272n30, 283n37;
    and HUAC, 223
Ride the Pink Horse, 77, 88, 90–92, 191,
    271nn19–21
Ringel, Shoshana, 264n5
Ripley, Arthur, 31
Rivkin, Allen, 283n29, 283n34
Road House, 181–84
Roberts, Allan, 281n16
Roberts, Bob, 231
Roberts, Marguerite, 188
Roberts Production, 231
Robert Stillman Productions, 250
Robinson, Edward G., 106, 116, *117,* 132, 167
Rogers, Shorty, 174, 279n29
Romm, May E., 266n21
Rooney, Mickey, 170, 171
Ross, Barney, 288n26
Rossen, Robert, 17, 156, 220, 228, 231, 285n3,
    288n30; and HUAC, 223, 286n7
Rothberg, Michael, 80
Rudolph, Eleanor, 163
Rugolo, Pete, 174
Russell, Harold, 270n1
Ruthven, K. K., 120
Ryan, Robert, 84, *85,* 100, 172, 211, *213,* 288n27

Sagoff, Mark, 128
Salt, Waldo, 286n7
Santos, Marlisa, 43, 49–50, 59, 72, 93, 94
Scarface, 4
Scarlet Street, 106, 116, 122–26, 274nn19–20
Scheib, Ronnie, 204, 283n36, 285n54
Schoenfeld, Bernard, 284n41
Schwartz, Hillel, 124, 130
Scott, Adrian, 84, 86, 271n15, 285–86n3, 286n7
Scott, Lizabeth, 89, 229
Screen Actors Guild, 222
Screen Writer, 286n6
screenwriters: and blacklist, 222, 223, 224, 255;
    and control over product, 215, 224, 286n6;
    women as, 58, 180, 187, 188, 192, 214
secrets, 228–29, 230–31
Seiter, Ellen, 216, 285n55

Sekely, Steve, 70, 75
self-division, 53–54, 65–66
self-reflexivity, 67, 106, 116
self-reinvention, 3, 5, 37, 48, 69, 123, 249; after
    trauma, 80, 261; and American Dream, 45,
    79, 105, 115, 250; and dreams, 20, 21, 37, 47;
    Emerson and Franklin on, 2–3, 47, 92; noir
    critique of, 2, 4, 15–16, 20, 47, 76; in *Out of the
    Past,* 54–55, 58; portraiture films on, 15, 107,
    112, 113, 131; in *Spellbound,* 38, 39, 42, 43; vet
    noir films on, 79, 91–92, 95, 97, 101, 105, 142
Selznick, David O., 266n27
Set-Up, The, 231, 288n27
sexuality: *The Accused* on, 199, 201; automobiles
    and, 135, 137, 140; female, 169, 197, 199, 201,
    203, 214, 217; *Gilda* on, 193, 194, 195, 197; jazz
    and, 16, 154–55, 159, 160–61, 165, 175, 176,
    277n9, 277n11; marriage and, 193, 195, 203,
    217; *Outrage* on, 204, 283n36
Shadoian, Jack, 4, 51, 150, 276n9
Shane, Maxwell, 167
Shaw, Artie, 156
Shell, Marc, 62
She Wouldn't Say, 196
Shockproof, 136, 137
Simmel, Georg, 228–29, 240–41, 243
singers, 16–17, 94, 96, 164, 179, 279n35; in *The
    Man I Love,* 179–80; in *Road House,* 182–83
Siodmak, Robert, 34, 37, 50, 159, 160, 200
Sirk, Douglas, 137
Smith, Art, 91, 225, 232, 251, 255
Smith, Bessie, 180
Snyder, Sharon L., 77, 78, 270n5
social mobility. *See* mobility
social realism, 225, 231
sodium pentothal, 98, 130, 272n26
Sokolsky, George, 290n48
Somewhere in the Night, 78, 79, 92, 93–95, 97,
    271–72n23
sovereignty, 211, 217; automobiles and, 143, 145
Soviet Union, 12, 104
Sparshott, Francis, 124
Spellbound, 37–44, 63, 266nn23–27; dream
    sequence in, 40–43, 266n24; patronization of
    women in, 45, 203; psychoanalysis in, 37, 38,
    41, 42, 266nn21–22, 266n25

Spencer, Nicholas, 13, 273n6

Spicer, Andrew, 281n17

Stanfield, Peter, 156, 179

Stanwyck, Barbara, 60, 132, 189, 199, 268n13

States, Bert, 22, 41, 265n9

Stillman, Robert, 253, 290–91n3

Stone, Andrew, 147

Strange Affair of Uncle Harry, The, 5, 34–37, 191, 266n19, 274n15; dream sequence in, 34, 36–37, 44, 45

Strange Illusion, 25–28, 27, 44, 45

Strange Love of Martha Ivers, The, 228–31, 287–88nn20–23; on class oppression and hierarchy, 220, 228, 230, 287n22

Stranger on the Third Floor, 21

Straw, Will, 12

Street of Chance, 48–50, 271n22

strikes, 12, 222, 264n10

Strip, The, 170–72, 178, 278nn20–23

subjectivity, 3, 16, 107, 163

suicide, 29, 50, 60, 165, 168

surveillance, 42, 65, 148, 204; red scare and, 97, 100, 245

Susman, Warren, 11

Sweet Smell of Success, 176–78, 279nn31–33

swing music, 156, 158, 174, 178, 277n7

switched-identity films, 15, 47, 48, 49, 76, 107, 142, 266–67n1; *Dark Passage,* 48, 65–69, 268–69nn22–23; *Hollow Triumph,* 48, 69–76, 120, 249, 269nn25–29; *The Killers,* 48, 50–54, 266n26; *My Name Is Julia Ross,* 48, 58–60, 267nn6–9; *No Man of Her Own,* 48, 60–65, 267–68nn11–20; *Out of the Past,* 5, 48, 54–58, 77, 266n26, 267nn4–5; *Street of Chance,* 48–50, 271n22

syndicate films, 288–89n32

Talman, William, 145, *146,* 289n38

technology, 2, 100, 147, 150, 153

Telotte, J. P., 65–66, 69, 240

therapeutic ethos, 2, 5, 6, 22–23, 249, *See also* psychoanalysis

therapy, 5, 22, 157, 206–7, 284n39

They Live by Night, 136–39, 158

Thieves' Highway, 220, 227–28, 287nn17–19

Thieves' Market (Bezzerides), 227

Tierney, Gene, 109, 112

Together Again, 196

Toland, Gregg, 82

Tourneur, Jacques, 54

trauma, 26, 44, 78, 79, 97–98, 100; in dreams, 26, 42–43, 44; and flashbacks, 80; and memory, 87, 98, 261; and reenactments, 88, 102; and reinvention, 93. *See also* posttraumatic stress disorder (PTSD)

Trigo, Benigno, 14, 264n2

Trojan horses, 16, 135, 148, 149, 151

Truesdell, June, 202, 203, 282nn26–27, 283nn32–33

Trumbo, Dalton, 17, 220, 285–86n3, 286n6; blacklisting of, 223, 244; and *Gun Crazy,* 141, 276n9; and Hollywood Ten, 221, 276n9, 286n7; and *The Prowler,* 221, 255, 256

truth, 77, 98, 119, 130, 272n26

Try and Get Me!, 221, 239–40, 250–55, 291nn2–4; and censors, 254, 291n4

Tucker's People (Wolfert), 234

Turney, Catherine, 188–89, 267–68n11; and *The Man I Love,* 61, 180, 268n12, 268n16; and *No Man of Her Own,* 58, 61, 64

Two Mrs. Carrolls, The, 272–73n1

Ulmer, Edgar G., 25, 142, 265n12, 277n14

Underworld Story, The, 221, 245–47, 249, 290nn49–50; and censors, 290n46, 290n50

United States v. Paramount, 14, 223

upward mobility, 2, 4, 5, 11, 60, 144, 249; and American Dream, 10, 63, 231, 259; automobility and, 142, 261; convertibles as emblem of, 275n4; crime and, 63, 220–21, 259; jazz and, 155, 171

Van Upp, Virginia, 191, 192–93, 196–97, 215

Vaughan, Benjamin, 2

verticality, 55, 272n27, 287n22

Veteran Comes Back, The (Waller), 80–81

veterans: emotional bonds of, 78, 82; readjustment by, 80–86; reintegration of, 80, 105. *See also* disabled veterans

vet noir, 77–105, 107, 168, 270n5; on American Dream, 93, 97, 100; amnesia in, 77, 78–79, 88, 92, 93–96, 97, 99, 100, 104; flashbacks in, 80,

vet noir *(continued)*
82, 83; identity in, 77, 78, 82, 89, 96, 97;
optimism in, 249, 261; PTSD in, 79, 82,
85–86, 88, 89, 90, 98; on reenactment, 88, 99,
102, 103–4; restitution and revenge in, 86–92;
on self-reinvention, 79, 91–92, 95, 97, 101, 105,
142; violence in, 103, 105
vet noir films: *Act of Violence,* 78–79, 97,
100–104, 187, 272nn30–31; *Best Years of Our
Lives,* 13, 77, 81–82, 270n1, 287n20; *The Blue
Dahlia,* 78, 82–84, 270nn9–11; *Cornered,* 78,
86–87, 271nn15–17, 285–86n3; *The Crooked
Way,* 78, 95–97; *Crossfire,* 84–86, 270–
71nn12–14; *Dead Reckoning,* 88–90; *Ride the
Pink Horse,* 77, 88, 90–92, 191, 271nn19–21;
Somewhere in the Night, 78, 79, 92, 93–95, 97,
271–72n23
Vicki, 115–16, 274n13
Vidor, Charles, 194, 264n1
violence, 11, 28, 53, 58, 84, 85; jazz and, 154, 155,
161, 165, 168; vet noir films and, 103, 105
vision motif, 27, 29
Vogel, Paul, 272n27

Wagner, Dave, 224, 233, 290n47
Wald, Jerry, 188, 197, 207, 281n19
Wald, Malvin, 215, 285n50, 287n16
Waldman, Diane, 274n23
Waldorf Statement, 223
Walker, Gertrude, 188, 197, 281n18
Wallace, Henry, 224, 286n11
Waller, Willard, 80–81, 270n8
Wallis, Hal, 199
Walsh, Raoul, 179, 180
Wanger, Walter, 121–22
Warner Bros., 188, 207, 280n10
Warwick, James, 264n1
Waxman, Philip, 265n14
Webb, Clifton, 109, *114*
Weidman, Jerome, 197
West, Nancy, 72, 73, 74, 269n26
Wexley, John, 271n17
White Heat, 148–49, 187
Whorf, Richard, 156, 277n5

Wieder, Robert, 275n4
Wild Calendar (Block), 211, 284n46
Wilde, Cornel, 137, 175, 182, *183*
Wilder, Billy, 13, 49, 132, 254
Williams, Tony, 6, 29
Wilson, Teddy, 156
Wise, Robert, 172, 278–79nn26–27, 288n27
Wolfert, Ira, 234
Wolff, Maritta, 180
Wollheim, Richard, 23
Woman in the Window, The, 36, 106, 116–19,
266n19, 274nn14–18
"woman's film," 187, 280n3
women, 17, 89, 103, 112, 165, 185, 199, 217, 280n1;
and agency, 197, 199, 280n10; attribution of
evil to, 83–84, 195; career, 196, 216; commodification of, 170, 199; and domesticity, 186, 188,
190; and identity, 58–59, 115; and marriage,
59, 60, 186–87, 191, 193, 195, 196, 203, 217; and
money, 62, 193; and motherhood, 17, 149, 186,
187–88, 191, 214; as nightclub singers, 179–80,
279n35; as prisoners, 207–10; and sexuality,
169, 197, 199, 201, 203, 214, 217; working, 11, 17,
186, 189–91, 280n2. *See also* femme noir;
gender roles
women filmmakers, 17, 185, 218–19, 261; as
producers, 191–92; as screenwriters, 58, 180,
187, 188, 192, 214
women's portraits. *See* portraiture films
Woolrich, Cornell, 11, 49, 159, 165, 277n10; *The
Black Path of Fear,* 31; *I Married a Dead Man,*
61, 62, 64, 268n13, 268n17
World War II, 4, 5, 11, 20, 267n10
writing, 39, 63
Wyler, William, 77, 222–23, 270n7

Young, Collier: and Lupino, 214, 215, 218,
285n52; screenplays by, 145, 211, 272n30
You Only Live Once, 136

Zanuck, Darryl F., 9, 109, 228, 273nn8–9
Zeitgeist theory, 12, 264n11
Zinnemann, Fred, 97, 102, 103, 272n30
Žižek, Slavoj, 118–19